Dear Roy & Muriel,

Because I know that you both have a deep and abiding faith in God I would like to share this little book with you.

Each morning as you read a page I pray that the message it contains will make each day of 1985 a little happier for you.

Thanks for being such good friends.

Love always
Helen Freeman

THE
MOMENT
TO
DECIDE

THE
MOMENT
TO
DECIDE

JAN S. DOWARD

This book is published in collaboration with the Youth Department as an enrichment of the Morning Watch devotional plan.

REVIEW AND HERALD PUBLISHING ASSOCIATION

Washington, DC 20039-0555
Hagerstown, MD 21740

All *SDA Bible Dictionary* references are paged from the revised edition, 1979.
Texts credited to N.E.B. are from *The New English Bible*. © The Delegates of the
Oxford University Press and the Syndics of the Cambridge University Press 1961, 1970.
Reprinted by permission.
Texts credited to N.I.V. are from *The Holy Bible: New International Version*.
Copyright © 1978 by the New York International Bible Society. Used by permission of
Zondervan Bible Publishers.
Texts credited to Phillips are from J. B. Phillips: *The New Testament in Modern
English*, Revised Edition. © J. B. Phillips 1958, 1960, 1972. Used by permission of
Macmillan Publishing Co., Inc.
The Scripture quotations marked R.S.V. in this publication are from the Revised
Standard Version of the Bible, copyrighted 1946, 1952 © 1971, 1973.
Bible texts credited to T.E.V. are from the *Good News Bible*—Old Testament:
Copyright © American Bible Society 1976; New Testament: Copyright © American Bible
Society 1966, 1971, 1976.

Library of Congress Cataloging in Publication Data

Doward, Jan S.
  The moment to decide.

  1. Devotional calendars—Seventh-day Adventists.
I. Title.
BV4811.D63   1984   242'.2   84-3258

ISBN 0-8280-0234-7

PRINTED IN U.S.A.

DEDICATED

especially to my dear wife, Loneva. Through the long months of writing, "Lonnie" has furnished the right balance of encouragement and inspiration to keep me on course.

Jan S. Doward

I was born October 19, 1925, in Seattle, Washington. My mother liked the first name of the famous Polish pianist Jan Paderewski, and for a second name she chose Stanford University. Thus the Jan Stanford!

I grew up in the north end of Seattle before it became so citified. The book *Puget Sound Boy* (R&H, 1973) captures a little of my boyhood in that delightful countryside with its woods and winding trails. Toward the end of my high school training but before I had a chance to graduate, I was drafted into the U.S. Army in February, 1944.

I entered the service as a conscientious objector. The decision arose from my own convictions, for I had not yet heard of Seventh-day Adventists or 1A0. On my own I had to battle it out with the military. At first they sent me for training with the field artillery, but later the government authorities sent me to the medical department. While on a troop ship en route to combat, I heard the Adventist message from Floyd Cromwell. It took fifty-six days of zigzagging all over the Pacific and laying over in the islands before we reached Okinawa. I got there the first part of July, 1945, just at the tail end of the battle but saw enough action for a battle star. A Baptist chaplain baptized me at Ishikawa beach on the Pacific side of the island. He refused to perform the service unless I became a member of his church first. It was the shortest membership they ever had!

When I returned from the armed services, I attended Walla Walla College, where I received a B.A. degree in history. I had hoped to be sent to Japan as a missionary, but the call was never forwarded to me (a strange series of events kept me working full time for the North American natives instead). I was teacher/principal of grade schools and junior academies for a decade, then I went on to teach for still another seven years, finally finishing my teaching career at Columbia Academy in 1970. There I taught Bible and history and also began the first secondary film production class in the denomination. (I did some graduate studies in film production and communications at Boston University in 1963-1964 but later received an M.A. degree from Andrews University in church history. I used film for my thesis production.)

From Columbia Academy I was called to become an assistant youth director at the General Conference. For ten years I wrote material and produced films for the Youth Department.

I have been engaged in writing and film production on my own for the past few years. So many ideas need expression, and there was so little time during off-hours to produce, that I broke away from full-time employment to share with others in a much wider way.

Besides writing and doing still photography, I currently produce short films for TV and sell them through an agency in New York City to such markets as cable television and the armed services.

I wrote the book *The Moment to Decide* because I have felt for years that the Bible characters speak to each of us about life's choices. From their decisions—good and bad—we can gain insight into daily living.

It all started as a Week of Prayer series for senior youth, and I have finally expanded the material into a book on the choices of various Bible characters. Nothing has been fictionalized, but all has been carefully researched with the hope that the reader will probe further into the study of God's Word to make personal decisions for time and eternity.

"Once to every man and nation comes the moment to decide,
In the strife of Truth with Falsehood, for the good or evil side."
—From "The Present Crisis"
by James Russell Lowell.

FREEDOM OF CHOICE

For I know the thoughts that I think toward you, saith the Lord, thoughts of peace, and not of evil, to give you an expected end. Jer. 29:11.

God spoke these words through the prophet Jeremiah at a time when the long stretch of the seventy years of captivity seemed overwhelming. False prophets had predicted a speedy release from the Babylonian bondage, yet God reminded His people that it would go the full term. A whole decade had slipped by when Jeremiah recorded these words, and another six remained. Yet God wanted so much to let the Israelites know that His thoughts toward them were of peace. In spite of their captivity, all things would eventually come out well for them in the end.[1]

As we begin this new year we are jolted by the reminder that we are still earthbound within the bondage of a cruel satanic control of this planet. God has not told those living in the last days how many years they would have to wait. God has given an open-ended prediction, yet the ultimate release will come. Jesus will appear in the flaming eastern sky!

In the midst of a world of tension, God's thoughts toward us are of peace. And those thoughts spring from a love that allows both angels and men the freedom of choice. God risked much misunderstanding in allowing this freedom. His character would be maligned. Yet He knew that the only way for genuine voluntary obedience was through granting this freedom of choice. Neither angels nor men could develop in any other way. Intelligent beings created in His image were worthy of such a privilege.

This year's devotional study focuses on the men, women, boys, and girls of Scripture who made choices that shaped their lives for or against God. These were real people with a real humanity, and basically, human nature has not changed since those ancient days.

Against the background of these decisions should be placed the warm glow of God's loving thoughts of peace and His longing for humanity to choose to give Him the affection He deserves.

---

[1] *The SDA Bible Commentary,* vol. 4, p. 459.

THE FIRST ENEMY AGENT

**And when the woman saw that the tree was good for food,
. . . she took of the fruit thereof, and did eat. Gen. 3:6.**

The first temptation wasn't labeled. It came wrapped in an unobtrusive package of aid to the newlyweds. Eve stopped long enough to listen to a ventriloquist version of the lie that by disobedience she and her husband could enter into a higher, more exalted knowledge than they had ever experienced. God had shortchanged them, the voice insisted. Satan projected his own perverted concepts through the mouth of a beautiful creature, and Eve listened instead of running.

A casual reading makes it sound as if Satan read her mind, repeating to Eve her very thoughts. But the devil cannot read minds. He is a keen observer, though, and listens carefully. Unconsciously Eve muttered to herself.

"Eve had wandered near the forbidden tree, and her curiosity was aroused to know how death could be concealed in the fruit of this fair tree. She was surprised to hear her queries taken up and repeated by a strange voice. . . . Eve was not aware that she had revealed her thoughts by conversing to herself aloud." [1]

The enemy got Eve's attention by flattering her about her beauty and suggesting the possibility of her entering a higher state. Satan stated the truth of God's words by the tongue-in-cheek, raised-eyebrow method, conveying doubt. Eve took the bait.

The enemy had her when she took the fruit he had plucked. The rest was easy. She ate. And immediately the pulse-pounding excitement of transgression went into effect.

With face flushed and hands full, Eve ran back to Adam, panting out her nerve-tingling experience. Satan didn't need to be on hand for this part; she had become his agent.

Eve's choice didn't happen by accident. She felt too smart to worry about staying by Adam's side. She was too sure of herself to be concerned about lingering near the forbidden tree and too daring to be concerned about distrusting God.

[1] *Review and Herald*, Feb. 24, 1874.

CONNED INTO CORRUPTION

And the man said, The woman whom thou gavest to be with me, she gave me of the tree, and I did eat. Gen. 3:12.

When Eve came running with her hands full of the forbidden fruit, Adam knew immediately what had happened. Her eyes told the whole story. They danced with unnatural excitement as she poured out her tale of transgression. And she would die; he knew that. He had never seen death, but he knew it meant separation.

So why did Adam eat? Was he hungry? Hardly. He had a whole garden full of delicious fruit. Appetite may have been the vehicle, but Adam was not famished. Nor could it be that he hankered for some new taste sensation. Adam's choice sprang from emotion. He allowed reason to be shoved aside by feeling, and whenever that happens disaster results.

It is said that Adam was not deceived. That is true only in the sense that he did not succumb to the enemy's bait. Satan knew better than to hope for success that way. But by working through Eve he could gain access to the mind and override Adam's reason. Adam deceived himself. He conned himself into believing that God could not supply another woman as lovely as Eve. In his deep feeling for her he forgot his operation. He forgot that the same God who had anesthetized him the first time could supply another Eve and heal any emotional scars, as well.

Whenever we allow our emotions to deceive us blame follows. It acts like clockwork. How often after some infatuation, some emotional binge that turns away from obedience, does a person feel that he is really better off! Then the bubble bursts, and blame follows.

Adam first accused Eve, and then he blamed God. Out of his affection for Eve he had snatched the fruit and eaten it, but when God asked him about it he said, "It's the woman's fault . . . the woman *You* gave me!" That should tell us something about the power of sin and the damning betrayal of the emotional choice.

THAT MYSTERIOUS CHOICE

Not as Cain, who was of that wicked one, and slew his brother. And wherefore slew he him? Because his own works were evil, and his brother's righteous. 1 John 3:12.

Aside from the mention of his birth and his awful deed of killing his brother, there isn't a hint in Scripture regarding Cain's childhood and youth. He certainly did not have all those contemporary worldly influences to contaminate his character that we must resist. There were no street gangs, no suburban neighborhood bad company to veer his attention from God. He didn't listen to blaring rock on the radio or gaze glassy-eyed at the steady bombardment of distorted life on TV. Nor was there any junk food or heavy concentration of sugar to alter body chemistry and make it more difficult to grasp spiritual things. No drugs, booze, or tobacco—absolutely nothing we can finger as the culprit to influence his life. Yet he chose to serve self instead of his Maker.

"Sin is an intruder, for whose presence no reason can be given. It is mysterious, unaccountable; to excuse it is to defend it." [1]

In the case of Cain, it is a recycling of the pride-filled thoughts that originated with Satan. "He permitted his mind to run in the same channel that led to Satan's fall—indulging the desire for self-exaltation and questioning the divine justice and authority." [2]

Cain felt, as so many feel today, that it would show some sort of weakness to follow exactly God's plan of redemption. People, like Cain, want to do things their own way. Choosing the course of self-dependence is quite "natural." So Cain brought his fruit. "After all," he reasoned, "it's good fruit—nothing wrong with it. I grew it and picked it with my own hands. God will just have to accept what I'm bringing." So he brought his fruity gift, but the essential part, which demonstrated a need for a Saviour, was left out. His killing of Abel was only an outworking of an inner hate in his refusing to accept God's method of salvation.

---

[1] *The Great Controversy*, p. 493.
[2] *Patriarchs and Prophets*, p. 71.

THE FOLLOWERS OF REBELLION

Woe unto them! for they have gone in the way of Cain. Jude 11.

Eve's first baby elated her because she felt sure God had provided the world's Redeemer. What a shattering disappointment! Not only did this baby become the first murderer but also the father of that long line of rebellious sinners who were determined to remain loyal to Satan.

Cain knew he should have died for his bloody deed, but God in His mercy spared him the death penalty. Yet Cain felt no gratitude, remorse, or repentance. He stayed stubbornly to his evil course, choosing to serve self.

Cain headed east of Eden and founded a city named after his eldest son. For fifteen centuries this line of hardened sinners clung to Satan's deceptions in misrepresenting the character and purposes of God. They were intellectual and physical giants, but they produced gigantic sinners until God in His mercy cut short the antediluvian race.

In dealing with Cain and his descendants, God demonstrated to the universe the true nature of rebellion and what would happen if He permitted sinners to live forever. The longer men lived, the more evil became their course. The inhabitants of the unfallen worlds then could see clearly the result of Satan's type of government. The choice these descendants of Cain made in their rebellion graphically illustrates how entrenched they became in their hostility toward God. And in His own comprehensive wisdom God was showing through it all that He intended not only to put down rebellion but eventually to open to all the very inner workings and nature of the devilish scheme Satan had devised for his form of government.

As the end approaches, those two long lines of the loyal and the disloyal will become more distinct. Today you are deciding which line you will follow.

ABEL, THE STALWART BELIEVER

By faith Abel offered unto God a more excellent sacrifice than Cain, by which he obtained witness that he was righteous. Heb. 11:4.

Undoubtedly from their earliest childhood both Cain and Abel heard the story of how their parents had failed the simplest test of loyalty God could devise. When Adam took them back to the shining gate and they saw the angel flashing beams of light like a mighty sword to guard the entrance to the garden, the boys probably asked a lot of questions. And Adam, faithful to his trust as a father, explained not only the story of the fall but also how God had provided a plan to rescue humanity.

Abel's choice to love and serve God still shines as a marvelous example of someone who caught the depths of God's love in his youth. It was no quick decision, no hasty choice, but a steady conviction settling over him as he grew up that here was a God who cared so much that He did not abandon the human race and leave them isolated to be the easy prey of a vicious enemy. When he was old enough to offer his own lamb for a sacrifice, he did so with deepest reverence. He brought the very best of his own flock and understood the profound significance in what God required as an act of faith.

Deep down it bothered Cain to ask his younger brother for a lamb. It would be so much easier if they both thought the same way. Cain kept pressing Abel to join in his feelings of rebellion. Sinners bent on their own evil course are most persistent proselytizers. And when God answered by fire and consumed Abel's offering, it was too much for Cain.

Cain's private little talk with his brother after that was nothing more than an angry effort to bring Abel into line. Abel's refusal to follow Cain demonstrates the depths of his faith. He was willing to become a martyr rather than to buckle under the demands of a self-worshiper.

14

THE MAN WITHOUT A FUNERAL

By faith Enoch was translated that he should not see death; and was not found, because God had translated him: for before his translation he had this testimony, that he pleased God. Heb. 11:5.

There once dwelt on this planet a people who outlived and outperformed anyone known today. The antediluvians have no comparison. We are like children with Tinkertoys compared with their abilities. They would shatter Olympic records, wipe out mental achievements, and abolish all records of development.

Since Adam lived nine centuries, many learned firsthand the history of the two trees in the garden. It was tough for skeptics in those days. Nobody could deny the existence of Eden. There it stood, just in sight, its entrance barred by angels.

But despite all this, there was the nasty problem of sin. Its cancerous growth had spread everywhere. The physical and mental giants produced gigantic sinners. They plunged into iniquity beyond the realm of our understanding.

In the midst of this scene lived a man whose rational choice to head in another direction was rewarded accordingly.

When sin seems more attractive than righteousness, when peer pressure and sinful performance hold more charms than integrity and purity, it is time to turn aside long enough to see the possibilities of something better. We need very much to understand the full impact of Enoch's choice.

Then one day Enoch was gone. He never celebrated his 366th birthday, nor was he present at his funeral. He was translated without dying. And it wasn't any secret rapture. "In the presence of the righteous and the wicked, Enoch was removed from them. Those who loved him thought that God might have left him in some of his places of retirement; but after seeking him diligently, and being unable to find him, reported that he was not, for God took him." [1]

---

[1] *Spiritual Gifts,* vol. 3, p. 57.

WHY NOAH
COULD STAND UP TO RIDICULE

But Noah found grace in the eyes of the Lord. Gen. 6:8.

Before he ever received any Heaven-sent instruction about building that massive three-decked houseboat, Noah believed and trusted his God.

When the moment came for God's last appeal to humanity He didn't put the ark building contract out for local bids or ask for volunteers. He had already selected His builder, and if ever there was a man who could deliver a protracted saw-and-hammer sermon, it was Noah.

The Bible says, "By faith Noah, being warned of God of things not seen as yet, moved with fear, prepared an ark to the saving of his house." [1] Noah simply reverenced his God. That word *fear* in the verse means a godly fear. And once anyone understands who the great God of the universe is, no amount of words little men can say means one thing. Noah couldn't care less about all the noise.

And it did come, you know. Nobody could build a houseboat 515 feet long, 86 feet wide, and 52 feet high on dry ground without causing some commotion. It might not have caused any stir in some well-known flood plain, but there had never been a flood before, because it had never rained. So Noah drew crowds. They came from curiosity, but once there, they had great fun. They spent their probationary time ridiculing the preacher-carpenter. Ellen White writes, "They caricatured him and criticized him. They laughed at him for his peculiar earnestness and intense feeling in regard to the judgments which he declared God would surely fulfill. They talked of science and of the laws controlling nature. Then they held a carnival over the words of Noah, calling him a crazy fanatic." [2]

Did you catch that? "A carnival over the words of Noah." It was great sport teasing and taunting. Come one, come all! Entertainment for the whole family! But Noah never flinched. The sounds reaching his ears didn't register any hurt because he had made a firm decision to respond to the trustworthiness of his God.

---

[1] Heb. 11:7.
[2] *The SDA Bible Commentary,* Ellen G. White Comments, on Gen. 6:12, 13, p. 1090.

RECYCLING THE DAYS OF NOAH

But as the days of Noe were, so shall also the coming of the Son of man be. Matt. 24:37.

Obviously the majority did not side with Noah's preaching or his project. But just where would you have stood?

There were those who felt a deep conviction that Noah was right, but they couldn't stand the peer pressure. In time these became the boldest scoffers around.

As the years passed and God's ark that Noah was building began to take shape, the crowds became even more defiant. The weather forecast remained always the same—very pleasant, with no rain or storms in sight. Just a nice, even sunshine filtered through that lovely water canopy above the earth. It was very reassuring. Noah's message seemed absolutely absurd.

And then one day the sky became dark with birds flying in orderly fashion right toward the ark. Animals from the forests and fields made their way up the gangplank as if guided by some unseen hand. What could be happening?

Charles T. Everson, a popular preacher of many years past, used to surmise a classic explanation from one of the so-called scientists of Noah's day: "Oh, this phenomenon is easily explained! It is just like this: This is an innate propulsion of the animal kingdom animated by the supreme activity of the subconscious mind and superinduced by posterior spheres of cerebral afterglow; sensitizing every scintilla of the corporeality of the brute creation, thus effecting a translocation of their materialistic concepts to more salubrious environments." [1]

But when the black depths of the rising floodwaters reached beyond the highest peaks, that sort of explanation certainly would sound like so much philosophical flapdoodle.

Yet our text for today forcefully reminds us that our generation must make a similar choice. We shall either listen to the smooth words of men or respond to God's last warning message!

---

[1] *Bible Lectures* (Mountain View, Calif.: Pacific Press Pub. Assn., 1929), pp. 180, 181.

WHEN A SAINT STUMBLES

And Noah . . . drank of the wine, and was drunken. Gen. 9:20, 21.

It is always embarrassing when great and good men stumble. Noah is no exception. The Biblical account of his drunkenness protrudes from the pages of God's Word like an ugly sore. It jars. All the nice efforts to explain that perhaps this godly man may not have noticed the difference between sweet and fermented wine simply vaporize under scrutiny. He knew what those intemperate antediluvians had done before the Flood. We wish somehow that Noah had kept looking at rainbows and had died peacefully in his sleep.

But the Bible faithfully records the positive and the negative. It never leaves "gaps in the tape." It tells the truth. Today if someone in the Christian community were writing a biography of Noah, he might think it prudent to leave this part out. It might not pass the book committee anyway.

Noah did more than momentarily turn in his temperance button. He chose to keep imbibing because of that diabolical trap of presumption. "As Satan assails men with this (presumption), he obtains the victory nine times out of ten." [1] Satan has a very good batting average, doesn't he? Christians know full well how loving and gracious God is, so Satan lures them to satisfy their carnal natures by indulging in whatever passions and pleasures come naturally, trusting that God will forgive.

The great tragedy in such cases is that the enemy and his host sneer at Heaven about the impossibility of obedience. When we misrepresent God, the evil forces rush forward with taunting.

While any stumbling saint can find forgiveness with God, there will never remain any desire for recycling the presumptuous act. The very sin can serve as a terrible reminder. When Satan returns with the same temptation, he will find the real worshiper of God very conscious of the great controversy. God's faithful people will choose to have no part in bringing disrepute on God's name.

---

[1] *Testimonies*, vol. 4, p. 44.

THE TOWER BUILDERS

So the Lord scattered them abroad from thence upon the face of all the earth: and they left off to build the city. Therefore is the name of it called Babel. Gen. 11:8, 9.

Among the many changes after the Flood was the fact that it would now rain. The climatic conditions were permanently altered. In God's loving selection, He chose to use the beautiful, natural phenomenon of the reflection and refraction of the sun's rays through raindrops as a symbol of His promise never again to destroy the earth by water. Those who were in tune with their Maker could look up with assurance at the bright rainbow arched against the sky and trust His promise that the rain would bring a blessing instead of universal destruction.

But as the earth once again began to be repopulated, a major segment of society did not accept rainbows as a sign for believing. Apostasy once again caused separation, not only from God but from their own kindred. Irritated by the God-lovers, the disbelievers moved from the mountains to the plains. They had decided to build a city and a tower. God intended for humanity to scatter throughout the earth, but these people were determined to form a tightknit community that would eventually form a universal empire. It was a gigantic plan of rebellion with Satan as its invisible leader.

The whole project was designed as a pride-filled endeavor to turn the minds of future generations away from the Creator. They chose to disbelieve, and that choice was the foundation of their folly.

Heaven settled the matter by confounding their language. By scattering, the disbelievers fulfilled God's original design and had an opportunity for reflection and repentance. Modern "tower builders" who reject God's Word for their self-seeking, confused theories would do well to consider this lesson from the ancient past.

WHEN GOD CALLED FOR A MOVING DAY

By faith Abraham, when he was called to go out into a place which he should after receive for an inheritance, obeyed; and he went out, not knowing whither he went. Heb. 11:8.

It's hard to imagine moving without knowing where you are going or what you will do when you get there. We who are sheltered by the modern conveniences of contracts and insurance policies can read a passage like this without catching its full impact.

Abraham had a comfortable home and enough wealth to stay in Ur of the Chaldees and later in Haran. But God called him to leave the idolatry of the moon worshipers and the influences that might hinder him from becoming the father of the faithful.

So without a travel brochure or any detailed description of the far-off place God was sending him to, Abraham waved goodbye to all he had known and loved and started off. He hadn't the slightest idea what the new country would be like, whether the land was fertile or if the soil condition was good. It was a faithful choice, following God's leading.

And when he arrived in the so-called Land of Promise, Abraham found something that must have stirred his deepest emotions. The audio-visual effects of the Canaanite worship were devastating. The screams of the human sacrifices, the grossly immoral ceremonies, could not help but make him shudder. Why had he exchanged the surroundings of one form of idolatry for those of another? He could have doubted God, but he didn't. His Friend had a reason. Here Abraham would stand alone, without the tug of relatives or friends.

He could have doubted again when famine struck and he was forced to leave Canaan for Egypt. But he never winced. Clinging tenaciously to God's promise, he remained undaunted.

Real faith does not buckle under adversity, but it endures trials, knowing that God is still in the shadows. Such a witness will remain as a testimony for others as did Abraham's altars.

LYING OR TRUSTING

O keep my soul, and deliver me: let me not be ashamed; for I put my trust in thee. Let integrity and uprightness preserve me; for I wait on thee. Ps. 25:20, 21.

God had called Abraham to represent His character. As the father of the faithful, he was to show the world and an onlooking universe an example of genuine trust. But when Abraham moved to Egypt because of the famine in Canaan, he simply did not measure up to that high calling. He lied. Not a big lie by human adjustable standards, but certainly a shade off the truth.

He told Pharaoh that Sarah was his sister. She was the daughter of his father but not of his mother. However, Abraham stated this in such a way as to convey the idea that he was not married to her. Abraham figured this was really not a falsehood. "But this concealment of the real relation between them was deception. No deviation from strict integrity can meet God's approval." [1] And because of his lack of faith, the ruler snatched Sarah from him and placed her in his harem. Even though she was about the retirement age of 65 when they had left Haran, Sarah had retained enough of her youthful beauty to cause the Egyptian monarch to desire her for a wife. This half-truth scheme nearly backfired on Abraham. If God hadn't stepped in, he would have lost Sarah for good. [2]

But Abraham didn't learn from that experience. He repeated the performance when he came to Abimelech of Gerar. Again he tried to pass off Sarah as his sister—with almost disastrous results. Again God stepped in and warned Abimelech in a dream that he was as good as dead if he touched Sarah.

God in His great mercy was trying to lead Abraham to a higher level of faith in which he could trust Him in spite of the seemingly impossible situation.

Since Satan is the father of lies, God cannot accept any deviation from truth by His children. That is why He has provided a sure way of escape for those who trust Him completely, no matter how difficult the situation.

[1] *Patriarchs and Prophets*, p. 130.
[2] *SDA Bible Dictionary* (revised edition), p. 980.

THE END OF A BUSINESSMAN'S DREAM

Then Lot chose him all the plain of Jordan. . . . And [he] pitched his tent toward Sodom. Gen. 13:11, 12.

It is always tragic when people choose to "pitch their tents" toward Sodom. A decision like this invariably springs from a selfishness that blinds the mind to the enormity of sin. Any such decision is doomed to failure. Too late Lot would learn of the terrible effect of those burning words of Genesis 13:13: "But the men of Sodom were wicked and sinners before the Lord exceedingly."

But before we cast blame on Lot for choosing the valley and letting his uncle take the uplands, we must remember that he made a natural choice. Sodom was a businessman's dream, a place for profit and pleasure. The continual commerce of the desert caravans enriched the marketplaces with all sorts of sensory delights. There was little thought of any real labor. The whole year seemed one round of festivities, probably ranging from the Date Palm Parade to the Olive Grove Beauty Contest.

In addition to the wealth and luxury, however, something was terribly wrong in Sodom. It was impossible to hide the sickening crime rate, the twisted sex, and the awful violence. Sodom was like some beautifully upholstered sewer. It was no place for a worshiper of God to live. But Lot felt secure. He would have family worship. His children would be trained in the way of the Lord, he thought.

After frequent trading trips into Sodom, Lot became convinced that he should move nearer the market. The family may have urged him along. It was silly to live so far out in the country and have to spend all that time traveling back and forth.

So Lot pitched his tent closer and closer, until one day he sold it and began house-hunting in Sodom. By the time the angels arrived, he was living right in the city that had become a byword for wickedness. The quick-cash, time-off imbalance had done its work. It was the end of this businessman's dream.

A SALT MONUMENT TO SELFISHNESS
Remember Lot's wife. Luke 17:32.

Jesus spoke those words in the setting of an end-time prophecy—a warning not to repeat the tragic attitudes and behavior patterns that turned Mrs. Lot into sodium chloride.

Biblical history furnishes us with little information about this woman. Her name isn't even mentioned. But we can glean enough to realize that she was a "selfish, irreligious woman, and her influence was exerted to separate her husband from Abraham. But for her, Lot would not have remained in Sodom, deprived of the counsel of the wise, God-fearing patriarch." [1]

From the beginning when the decision was made to move to the valley, a sort of collective insanity pervaded the family. While Lot dreamed of worldly possessions, his wife undoubtedly thought of the wonderful shopping bargains in Sodom. There would be so many "advantages" for the children too. After all, she didn't want the youngsters to grow up as uncouth bumpkins from the hills. They could listen to the Sodomite Symphony and take in all the class and culture of those bustling crossroad cities of the plain.

Mrs. Lot was the type who could see no real benefit from anything spiritual. Her life was wrapped up in the accumulation of things and the whirl of social life.

When the final night came, she sat stunned. It was unreal. To think of leaving her fine home and all her friends and relatives was beyond her. She could not run, so she sat. When morning came and the seconds ticked off the final countdown, she did not appreciate the angels' last warning. Too long had she forgotten God's goodness and love, and now with everything on the line it seemed too much to leave. Ungrateful for deliverance, she rebelled against God for tearing her away from all that she really loved.

Presumptuously she turned back. Her ungrateful forgetfulness of God was why Jesus warned us to remember.

---

[1] *Patriarchs and Prophets*, p. 174.

CORRUPTED BY BAD COMPANY

**Do not be deceived: "Bad company ruins good morals." 1
Cor. 15:33, R.S.V.**

Tucked away in the last part of Genesis 19 is a nasty little story
that we shouldn't overlook simply because of the ugly account of
incest. Considering contemporary times, we need to carefully
scrutinize it. How could such a thing happen? How could two girls
who grew up in an outwardly God-fearing home slip so low as to
think that conceiving children by their own father was right?

Sin has an uncanny ability to distort. And when distortion
becomes fixed, a fantastic phenomenon of justifying the very evil
that is destroying from within results.

Lot's daughters were caught up in the parental sweep of
moving to Sodom. After every trip into the city they undoubtedly
tingled with excitement. Long before they actually lived down
there we can imagine how thrilled they were with all the sights and
sounds of Sodom. Every exposure to the place brought them to
tiptoe. Just watching the three-horse chariot races and seeing the
nightlife of the place was enough to turn them on. The little Jordan
Valley Junior Academy didn't hold nearly the attraction of the
Twin-City High School with its super sports events, dances, and
hoopla.

Misguided by their home religion, they soon began to adjust
their concepts to fit the class and culture they desired. Every
occasion of partying and contact with their Sodomite friends only
bolstered the false notion that this was real living.

Lot undoubtedly had a lovely family at first. But the story
unraveled into a tragic tale that brought only misery and
unhappiness, all because of a misguided choice.

"The sinful conduct of his daughters was the result of the evil
associations of that vile place. Its moral corruption had become so
interwoven with their character that they could not distinguish
between good and evil. Lot's only posterity, the Moabites and
Ammonites, were vile, idolatrous tribes, rebels against God and
bitter enemies of His people." [1]

---

[1] *Patriarchs and Prophets,* pp. 167, 168.

THE WAITING WE NEED TO LEARN

Wait on the Lord: be of good courage, and he shall strengthen thine heart: wait, I say, on the Lord. Ps. 27:14.

If there is one thing Christians have a difficult time understanding, it is the silence of God. Claiming the promises of His Word seems to demand an immediate and forthright answer from Heaven. But how often they hear no voice, no evidence that God is within the shadows! Waiting on the Lord seems such an uncomfortable exercise.

After a decade of waiting for the Lord's promise to be fulfilled, Abraham and Sarah decided it was long enough. Like the little girl who wanted to "help God bloom the rose" and opened the petals, only to watch them wither and drop off, this aging couple realized the fruits of their impatience at a time when they could least afford to have such a disturbance in their household. Worse still, their tragic choice of having Abraham marry Hagar is still with us today. The descendants of both Sarah and Hagar, the Jews and the Arabs, keep alive the tensions in the Middle East. What a far-reaching effect of that one impatient choice!

But it did seem plausible. It always does. "Maybe God is waiting for us to do *something*" is the natural response to fulfillment. The element of truth in that is stretched to mean taking things in our own hands, as did Abraham and Sarah.

Humanity always has ways of juggling customs and traditions to fit its own convenience. But Heaven still looks upon plurality of wives as sin and certain destruction to peace in any home.[1]

Ishmael was not the son of promise. Sarah would have to wait until she was nearly 90, twenty-five years from the time of the initial promise, to bear Isaac, the son God had planned.[2]

But why does God wait so long? What is it that we should understand from His silence after He has promised? His tests of delay come not only for the individual's sake but to demonstrate to a disbelieving and angry foe that we do trust enough to wait for God. When we fail, Satan triumphs!

---

[1] *SDA Bible Dictionary*, p. 980; *Patriarchs and Prophets*, p. 145.
[2] *SDA Bible Dictionary*, p. 980.

COMFORT FOR A HARD DECISION
Thou God seest me. Gen. 16:13.

It all started with Hagar's pregnancy. Sarah's faith had buckled under the burden of advancing age, so she suggested to Abraham that perhaps the promised son could be had through her handmaiden. But the moment this Egyptian servant became aware that she was with child by Abraham, she slipped into a very haughty attitude. Suddenly she had vaulted into the privilege of wife status, and it went to her head. Added to this was her unwillingness to allow her child to be passed off as Sarah's son.

It is difficult for us to grasp the profound feelings Hagar had because we are so conscious of birth control and population problems. But in those days barrenness carried a real stigma and dishonor. That is why she tossed her head and lifted her chin to the sky. She was to be the mother of Abraham's child!

But all her proud actions and smart-mouthed talk brought down the wrath of Sarah, who is not to be excused for her verbal abuse of Hagar. We must remember, however, that Sarah was only following her native Mesopotamian laws by humiliating a haughty slave-concubine. Sarah got so tense about the matter that Hagar finally fled south across the desert.[1]

She had almost reached the Egyptian border when an angel in human form met her at a well-known spring near Shur. He commanded Hagar to return and submit to Sarah. That would be hard. But with the encouragement that God would also give her a great nation, she did return. We know she decided to return in the face of known difficulties because she trusted God.

Hagar had expected to die after actually seeing God's messenger, and called Him "the God of seeing." Her expression of faith should encourage us in times of great stress when we must make a difficult choice. It should remind us that God never allows us to get out of His sight, but He cares and comforts us as He did this Egyptian woman so long ago.

---

[1] *The SDA Bible Commentary*, vol. 1, p. 318.

THE SUPREME FAITH OF GOD'S FRIEND

And the scripture was fulfilled which saith, Abraham believed God, and it was imputed unto him for righteousness: and he was called the Friend of God. James 2:23.

After Isaac's birth Abraham settled down to enjoy his twilight years in peace and tranquillity. It had been seventeen years since he had heard any direct words from God, but he knew and loved his God with all his heart. He didn't need to hear God calling directly to sustain his faith.

But then God called again, and this time the words, thundering from heaven, pierced his heart like a sharp jab and cut it to the quick: "Take now thy son, thine only son Isaac, . . . and offer him . . . for a burnt offering." [1]

Stunned and shocked, Abraham waited for further word. It didn't come. Only the sound of the wind against the tent could be heard. He went out to look up at the stars and waited, knowing that God had promised his seed would be as numerous as those twinkling gems against the dark velvet of night. But there was only the awful silence and the pounding of his old heart.

Satan, of course, was on hand to make some of his own suggestions. Maybe Abraham hadn't heard correctly. After all, would God ask someone to carry out a heathen custom and transgress the divine law that forbids killing? Maybe senility had set in, and the voice was a figment of his imagination.

But Abraham recognized God's voice. He would need more strength than ever before, but he would follow his Friend's divine command. Obedience for him meant overriding his emotions. So in silence he suffered alone, claiming the promises that he had heard from his Friend so many years before.

Abraham expected that God would raise his boy to life, but we must remember that he had never even heard of a resurrection. It had not happened in the history of the world up to that time. No wonder, then, he was called "the Friend of God"!

---

[1] Gen. 22:2.

OBEDIENCE IS A BEAUTIFUL THING

Now faith is the substance of things hoped for, the evidence of things not seen. Heb. 11:1.

His name meant "he laughs," yet during that stark moment on Mount Moriah there wasn't a hint of joy. The shocking truth that he, Isaac, the son of promise, was to be sacrificed must have triggered a whole series of emotional charges that ranged from amazement to terror, submission, and finally to faith and trust.

The story of Abraham's towering faith in willingly offering his son overshadows Isaac's own faith. But Isaac was a partner in this ordeal. His willingness to lay down his life gallantly testified to a trust that had awakened within his own soul.

Isaac's tired old father was no match for his youthful strength. If he had so chosen, he could have brushed Abraham aside and fled down the mountain. "But Isaac had been trained from childhood to ready, trusting obedience, and as the purpose of God was opened before him, he yielded a willing submission." [1]

Isaac's obedient choice did not happen by accident. Somewhere in his twenty years of life he had learned that love and obedience are interlocked. True obedience does not mean blindly following orders. The obedience Isaac displayed is always born out of the most profound love. This kind of obedience does not seek to squirm free from self-expression, but only checks love's requirements.

If it is true that Abraham learned a valuable insight into the meaning of redemption, then what could be said for Isaac, who typified Christ?

So on that day atop Mount Moriah two men—one old and one young—learned a great truth. Sin comes with a terribly high price tag. To reach humanity both the Father and the Son suffered. The love that prompted the heavenly Father to give His only Son that we might have eternal life was balanced by the Son's own willing response. "Though he were a Son, yet learned he obedience by the things which he suffered." [2]

---

[1] *Patriarchs and Prophets*, p. 152.
[2] Heb. 5:8.

IF GOD IS LEADING, WHY HESITATE?

And they called Rebekah, and said unto her, Wilt thou go with this man? And she said, I will go. Gen. 24:58.

She was vivacious, energetic, courteous, kind, and so beautiful. The Bible says, "The damsel was very fair to look upon."[1] Her charm swept the old man off his feet. It was a stunning meeting. Eliezer, Abraham's trusted servant, had just completed a five-hundred-mile trip with his caravan to find a wife for his master's 40-year-old son. In swift answer to the first recorded prayer in the Bible, Rebekah suddenly appeared! She fulfilled Eliezer's request not only by offering him a drink of water but by offering to water his ten camels, as well. And since a thirsty camel can easily drink 30 gallons (32 liters), Rebekah may have hand poured 300 gallons (317 liters) of water!

This satisfied Eliezer. He wanted to waste no time. Talk about snappy! He would have liked nothing better than to have turned right around the next day and have headed for home with this charming girl.

The story unfolds rapidly. Eliezer refused to eat until he had explained his mission to Rebekah's menfolk. The family wanted Eliezer to stay at least ten days, but he wanted to be on his way.

Swept up in the excitement of Rebekah's fulfilling Eliezer's prayer, the men seemed to forget one thing—Rebekah's consent. Even though women were not permitted to sit in on male conversations, undoubtedly Rebekah had been conveniently eavesdropping through the tent wall. When they called her at last, she answered unhesitatingly with those three thrilling words, "I will go."

Why would she make such a prompt choice? Without even so much as a passport picture or letter she was willing to leave because she saw God's hand in the matter. "She believed, from what had taken place, that God had selected her to be Isaac's wife."[2]

Far too many people strain "providential leadings" to fit their own desires. But not in Rebekah's case. Carefully scrutinized, the pieces fell into place, definitely indicating that God was truly guiding. Rebekah's faith was rewarded for her prompt choice.

---

[1] Gen. 24:16.
[2] *Patriarchs and Prophets*, p. 173.

THE CURSE OF THE SCHEMING CHOICE
Upon me be thy curse, my son. Gen. 27:13.

Isaac and Rebekah remained childless for nineteen years, but in their twentieth year together, Rebekah gave birth to twin boys, Esau and Jacob. Instead of the children drawing them together, they caused the parents to drift apart. Because of selfish stubbornness and manipulative scheming these two lovers felt so estranged that at last they glared at each other across a chasm of distrust.

Playing favorites is never safe, and both Isaac and Rebekah pushed favoritism to the hilt. Isaac clung stubbornly to Esau, while Rebekah longed to see Jacob receive the promised blessing.

Like so many who panic in the clutch, Rebekah failed to sense God's overruling providence and miracle-working power. It seemed, as it always does, that either you act now or the game is lost.

Jacob was 77 at the time and ought to have known better than to try playacting while his mother did the cooking. He did complain that he would be cursed if he were caught, but Rebekah replied, "Upon me be thy curse, my son."

Rebekah paid the penalty that all must suffer who try to build on a lie. Sin is never so terrible as when it seems to succeed. She and her son pulled off the little trick with the blind old father, but in doing so she lost her beloved Jacob for good. She also lost all real connection between herself and her husband; the final ties were severed. And she lost Esau, who could never trust his mother again. She lost her peace of mind, and guilt tortured her until she finally came to the Lord with tears of bitter repentance.

But the darkest curse of all was that she sent her favorite son into the world with a twisted concept—the distorted conviction that sin can be made to pay. What a tragedy that a once-beautiful girl, who otherwise could have left us with a track of light leading to God, ended her womanhood in a curse because of her scheming choice!

THE BLIND MOUTH

And Isaac loved Esau, because he did eat of his venison. Gen. 25:28.

This is a surprising and most disappointing commentary on a patriarch who should have stood tall in leadership. Instead, his blind partiality for his firstborn son, Esau, was based in part on the fact that he loved his venison. His olfactory nerves just tingled when the savory meat was prepared, and his tastebuds created sensations that short-circuited all reason. Vicariously he could participate in Esau's derring-do and enjoy his meat at the same time. It was very pleasant.

No matter how much Rebekah reasoned with him and pointed out that Heaven had disqualified Esau on the basis of his own materialistic bent, Isaac refused to accept Jacob as the inheritor of the birthright. Again and again she presented the subject. If we consider this man's peaceful habit patterns, he may not have argued back at all, but simply nodded to her that he understood and then stubbornly clung to his own favorite, Esau. It was an impossible situation because Isaac kept recycling his thoughts through the medium of his appetite until finally he became fossilized in his stubborn choice.

We finally get a picture of this prematurely old man losing his eyesight and waiting, not for any deep spiritual insights, but for more venison. He slumped down into what we could easily call a "blind mouth." His stubbornness in showing such partiality created division, jealousy, misery, and galling bitterness.

Is it any wonder that Scripture says, "Stubbornness is as iniquity and idolatry"?[1] Isaac would never have thought of worshiping some idol. He believed and taught otherwise. Yet he daily skidded closer to the brink of a type of idolatry that could plunge him over the abyss of eternal disaster without his even knowing what had happened. "Isaac was in danger of incurring the divine displeasure."[2] Today are we in any danger of allowing our appetite to interfere with our reason?

---

[1] 1 Sam. 15:23.
[2] *Patriarchs and Prophets*, p. 180.

BE CAREFUL WHAT YOU WANT

Looking diligently lest any man fail of the grace of God; . . . lest there be any fornicator, or profane person, as Esau, who for one morsel of meat sold his birthright. Heb. 12:15, 16.

Esau was obviously a robust, athletic, adventure-loving free spirit—a fine animal. Undoubtedly he was a likable sort with a flashing smile and dark, dancing eyes that spoke of thrills and danger. But he was profane. That is what the Bible writer calls him. Profane. He was not interested in, nor did he appreciate, sacred things. Spiritual matters bored him. What a man could feel, taste, hear, and see immediately were more important than abstract ideas such as prayer or a future life. The here-and-now meant everything to Esau, just as God had predicted it would.

Esau had natural traits that, rightly developed, could have sent him into the ranks of God's great leaders. Instead he chose to serve himself and the present. His was a consistent pattern of decisions to satisfy the constant clamorings of his carnal nature, until at last his character was fixed.

That is why he could stumble into the tent that day and pant out his desire for a bowl of his favorite red-lentil stew seasoned with garlic and onions. He bartered his birthright, which included not only being spiritual leader but receiving a double portion of his father's estate, as well.[1]

When he finally cried over losing the birthright, it wasn't the spiritual portion he missed, but the property that mattered most to him. He wept not because he had sinned, but that he had lost his inheritance for good. He reminds us of the weeping criminal behind bars who is sorry—sorry he got caught. Esau's tears reflected only the twisted mind of a man locked into the tragic failure of his own decisions. It was no arbitrary act on God's part. God's foreknowledge never means foreordaining. Esau went to his grave a profane person, the product of that old saying "Be careful what you want because you'll get it." He got it.

---

[1] *SDA Bible Dictionary*, p. 153.

THE NIGHT OF CONVERSION

And he dreamed, and behold a ladder set up on the earth, and the top of it reached to heaven: and behold the angels of God ascending and descending on it. Gen. 28:12.

Jacob had the outward traits that seemingly had an advantage over the more worldly minded Esau. Jacob was the type who could win the award for "most likely to succeed." He certainly endeared himself to Rebekah. His mild manners and gentle ways made him Mamma's boy for sure. He showed her such deep devotion and attention—and more than that, he was spiritually minded. Truly, with his near obsession for obtaining the spiritual birthright, he was a natural for winning her heart and the hearts of those who judge by outward appearances. But Jacob was an unconverted man. He might have placed a high regard for the eternal over temporal things and even have worshiped God, but he did not see the need of a Saviour. Not then. "Jacob had not an experimental knowledge of the God whom he revered. His heart had not been renewed by divine grace." [1]

That can mean only one thing. Jacob knew about God, he loved to talk about Him, he responded to spiritual things, but he retained the concept that he could do something to earn his right to stand before Him. And that is very dangerous. It leads to false actions that outwardly achieve some sort of performance record but miserably fail to do anything about cleansing the heart.

But when Jacob had to flee for his life because of an infuriated brother, he felt secure no longer. The second night out he was totally drained.[2] Lonely beyond words and far from home, he curled up with a rock for a pillow. And then God spoke. He gave him a dream. It was such a powerful experience that Jacob awoke and called the place Bethel—"the house of God." [3]

"That night, Jacob, the petted son of his mother, experienced the new birth, and became a child of God." [4]

What in that dream made the difference in his decision? It was the picture of the Saviour, who was the ladder extending from earth to heaven, bridging the gulf that sin had made.

[1] *Patriarchs and Prophets*, p. 178.
[2] *The SDA Bible Commentary*, vol. 1, p. 381.
[3] *Ibid.*, p. 383.
[4] *Sons and Daughters of God*, p. 127.

AGREEING WITH YOUR ADVERSARY
The Lord watch between me and thee, when we are absent one from another. Gen. 31:49.

These words sound pleasant to us today. We like the sweet benediction of peace they seem to convey. But we often forget that the Mizpah, or "watchtower" as it is called, was spoken by the scheming, conniving, crafty idolator Laban, who wanted to make absolutely sure that his son-in-law, Jacob, wouldn't return and do him harm. Laban uttered these words at the end of a most tense situation.

While Laban was away sheepshearing, Jacob decided it was time to pack up and head for home. He had been cheated and lied to for twenty years and had had enough. He would have left long before if it had not been for the thorny worry of meeting Esau, his angry brother. But now the situation in Mesopotamia had deteriorated so badly that he had to get his flocks and herds and family moving toward the mountains of Gilead. Unfortunately he could travel only about ten miles a day. He had put about 275 miles between himself and the home of his grasping father-in-law before Laban caught up with him.[1]

Laban's main worry was that someone had absconded with his family idol. According to the laws of his land, the holder of the household god could be guaranteed the title to the father's properties. Always thinking of life in terms of cash on the old barrelhead, Laban had to retrieve that image. He never did. Rachel lied and kept sitting on it.[2]

What followed was a heated reminder by Jacob of the whole sordid history of how Laban had treated him. Laban couldn't deny the charges, and in the end he decided it was the better part of wisdom to depart in peace. Especially since he had been warned in a dream not to hurt Jacob in any way.

Thus the heap of stones. Thus the Mizpah. So long as Jacob was not in Haran, Laban would consent to God's care over Jacob and his family. To his credit—and a lesson for us—Jacob chose to agree quickly with his adversary and leave in peace.

---

[1] *The SDA Bible Commentary*, vol. 1, p. 400.
[2] *SDA Bible Dictionary*, p. 1108.

PERSISTENCE IN PRAYER

For thus saith the Lord; We have heard a voice of trembling, of fear, and not of peace. . . . Alas! for that day is great, so that none is like it: it is even the time of Jacob's trouble; but he shall be saved out of it. Jer. 30:5-7.

Its modern name means "the blue river," but when Jacob reached the Jabbok his mind was not on any beauty of this desert stream. His brother, Esau, and four hundred of his men were riding hard toward him. It didn't look good. All the friendly gestures and gifts he had sent ahead had been spurned. Sending his family across the Jabbok ford, he remained behind to pray. Defenseless, his only safety now rested with God.[1]

Alone amid lurking beasts of prey and marauding criminals in a wild and desolate land, Jacob prayed as he had never prayed before. Suddenly at midnight a hand reached out and grabbed him with a viselike grip. Jacob naturally responded by wrestling with this unknown antagonist. There in the darkness he fought for his very existence—or so it seemed.

As they wrestled, the mysterious assailant reached out and with just a finger touched Jacob's thigh. Immediately he was crippled. Now he knew whom he had been fighting! It was Christ Himself—the Angel of the Covenant!

Right then and there Jacob decided not to let go until the Lord gave him the assurance of acceptance. He persisted in his prayer for a blessing. If he hadn't repented beforehand, this would have been sheer presumption, but now God could answer his prayer. Jacob had finally learned how vain it was to trust in his own methods and schemes. Now he realized he must place absolute trust in the Saviour, then the blessing could be given.

This strange incident holds special meaning for those living in the last days. Like Esau, the wicked will seek to destroy those who trust fully in God. Then genuine Christians will fully understand persistance in prayer in order to receive Heaven's blessing for deliverance.

---

[1] *SDA Bible Dictionary*, p. 542.

THE SECRET OF DINAH'S DOWNFALL

For what fellowship hath righteousness with unrighteousness? 2 Cor. 6:14.

The story of Dinah is a shocker. Outside the mention of her birth and her inclusion in the list of family members finally going to Egypt, she passes unnoticed into history except for the record of her seduction and the awful aftermath of that terrible event.

The stage was set when her father, Jacob, bought a piece of property near the town of Shechem, nestled neatly in the middle of the pass between Mount Gerizim and Mount Ebal. What seemed such a pleasant location for the large family turned into a nightmare of violence and bloodshed because Jacob's teen-age daughter, Dinah, did not share his principles about not mingling with the heathen.[1]

It is one thing from a sense of compassion in seeking to turn their minds toward God, to associate with those who do not love the Lord. It is quite another to be driven by curiosity to know the customs and ways of the world. The unguarded intimacy invariably spells trouble. "He who seeks pleasure among those that fear not God is placing himself on Satan's ground and inviting his temptations."[2]

Dinah was only about 15 at the time.[3] Genesis 34:1 simply says that she "went out to see the daughters of the land," but that in itself is a very revealing statement.

The secret of Dinah's downfall and disgrace hinges entirely on her foolish notion that she could cope independently with the forces of evil. Dinah definitely felt sure of herself, so she sauntered downtown alone. Undoubtedly she felt that she was a big girl now, quite capable of handling any situation, thank you. But she paid a very high price for her independent spirit and soon discovered how low Canaanite morals were. The scars of that day's damage remained and affected her whole future, for she was listed as apparently still unmarried, an independent member of Jacob's family, when they moved to Egypt years later.[4]

---

[1] *SDA Bible Dictionary*, pp. 1017, 1018.
[2] *Patriarchs and Prophets*, p. 204.
[3] *The SDA Bible Commentary*, vol. 1, p. 412.
[4] *Ibid.*, p. 469.

WRONG VALUES PRODUCE
WRONG CHOICES

And Jacob said to Simeon and Levi, Ye have troubled me to make me to stink among the inhabitants of the land. Gen. 34:30.

When Simeon and Levi heard of the seduction of their sister Dinah, they were rightfully angry, but their anger misguided them into an action of deception and cruel revenge.

Hamor, the father of the young man who had raped Dinah, requested Jacob's consent to a marriage. He made no apology for his son's conduct. He merely demanded that Jacob give Dinah to his son. No one seemed concerned about asking Dinah's consent. The request simply reflected the low moral standards of the Canaanites. Perhaps Hamor thought this union would begin a long history of intermarriage between his people and Jacob's family.

Simeon and Levi temporarily masked their real fury. They pretended that intermingling would be possible only if all the men of Shechem would be circumcised. Hamor presented this proposition to the town council, and it was accepted.

Simeon and Levi waited until the third day, when the men were sore and helpless, then stealthily crept into the city and massacred the entire male population. They took Dinah home and left Shechem in ruins. Their gruesome act left the sad spectacle of a city of widows and orphans.

Jacob was stunned. He reminded his sons of the fearful results of that day's damage. The other Canaanites could band together now and destroy his whole family. But Simeon and Levi defended their awful actions. "Should he deal with our sister as with an harlot?" [1] they asked.

Their drastic decision was prompted by the false concept that the family name was more important than God's reputation. They were more concerned with the shame than with any sin committed against God. And whenever people place family pride above God, wrong actions invariably follow. But putting God's character first always points toward right actions.

---

[1] Gen. 34:31.

BURYING IDOLS

Put away the strange gods that are among you, and be clean. Gen. 35:2.

The words of our text for today were spoken by Jacob after Simeon's and Levi's terrible deed of massacring the males of Shechem. By divine revelation Jacob had been instructed to pull up stakes and head about twenty miles south to Bethel, not only to pitch camp there but to build an altar for worshiping the true God. But without first clearing the camp of the defilement of idolatry, Jacob could not conceive of returning to that sacred spot where so many years before he had pledged allegiance to the Lord.[1]

Jacob wasn't blind. He knew his wives and servants harbored idols. And now with the spoils of Shechem there were plenty of distractions around. Rachel had secretly stashed her father's little figurine away when they had left Mesopotamia. These ugly little nude goddesses of fertility with accentuated sex features were common and most certainly a bad influence on the whole camp. Jacob might have tolerated them before, but now such idols must go.[2]

We are not told how everyone reacted to his plea. His deeply moving account of how God had led him must not have fallen on deaf ears, because they did come forward not only with the idols they had privately tucked away but with their jewelry, as well. Off came the earrings. Whatever thing that was worn that could be a stumbling block to true worship they got rid of. The outward cleansing of the body was to symbolize the inner purification of the heart. Whether the family moved from fear of discovery or out of genuine desire to change before God, nothing is said. But they did take off their ornaments and toss aside their idols, "and Jacob hid them under the oak which was by Shechem."[3]

Whenever a decision such as this is made, the best way to continued worship is to bury all idols out of sight. But people sometimes, as it were, go back to the oak of Shechem and begin digging them up. Once the distractions to worship are buried, we should leave them there.

[1] *The SDA Bible Commentary,* vol. 1, pp. 416, 417.
[2] *SDA Bible Dictionary,* p. 1108.
[3] Gen. 35:4.

JOSEPH'S BRIGHT CHOICE

Thou wilt keep him in perfect peace, whose mind is stayed on thee: because he trusteth in thee. Isa. 26:3.

There is hardly a Bible narrative more poignant than that relating the moment when Joseph was dragged from the dry pit and sold as a slave to the passing Ishmaelites. To be rejected and mistreated by his own brothers was bad enough, but to face the prospects of future slavery was more fearful than death. And as the caravan headed south we can only imagine the shuddering thoughts that crowded into the mind of this 17-year-old. Looking off to the east, he could see the distant hills of home, and it was too much. "For a time Joseph gave himself up to uncontrolled grief and terror." [1]

The details of the trip to Egypt are not recorded, but somewhere along that tedious route Joseph had to make a choice. Either he would allow himself to head down the dark canyon of self-pity and end up in the gloomy cul-de-sac of depression, paranoia, or personality quirks or he could dry his eyes and turn to his father's God. Fortunately his childhood lessons of love and reverence for the God of Jacob came forward, and in his bright choice he became a man. He might be tempted and tried at every turn, but by focusing his attention on the God of heaven he could surmount any trial. And in this decision he would realize the truth about real self-worth, achievement, and peace with God and man.

But in making such a decision there could be no hiding of his devotions. If after Potiphar had bought him at the slave block he had tried to conceal his principles in order to gain his favor, he would have slipped and fallen. But Joseph had pledged allegiance to the God of his fathers and made absolutely no effort to hide that fact. By looking heavenward instead of outward or inward, he became immune to the sights and sounds of the vice around him.

More than this, his unswerving forthrightness enabled him to find favor wherever he worked. He was prosperous in everything he attempted, not because of some direct miracle, but because God added His blessing to the quick-witted energy and industry of this dedicated young man.

---

[1] *Patriarchs and Prophets*, p. 213.

A QUESTION FOR REAL FAITH

How then can I do this great wickedness, and sin against God? Gen. 39:9.

Even though Potiphar treated him almost like a son, Joseph was still a slave in a strange land. And in that status he demonstrated that faith is not some abstract theological term, but an active choice in deciding to represent God's character regardless of the circumstances. Joseph kept his mind stayed on God's goodness and greatness, which did much to block out the sights and sounds of vice and corruption about him. But the devil has a way of using human agents to reach out after those with such a high degree of selectivity.[1]

Mrs. Potiphar wasn't exactly subtle in her approach. It is written that she "cast her eyes upon Joseph; and she said, Lie with me." [2] And this wasn't some onetime thing. She kept up her adulterous drive day after day. Even if she were much older than Joseph and about as attractive as a stovepipe, the seductive temptation was very real. Not necessarily because of any overpowering sexual urges, but because as a slave Joseph faced a very grim choice.

Then one day it happened. She caught him alone, and this time it wasn't any whispered allurement. She grabbed his garment and clung tightly. Right then and there was the final moment to decide. His future hung in the balance.

Joseph didn't dare risk using physical force to free himself. Instead of wrestling, he spun out of his outer garment and fled, leaving Mrs. Potiphar with a piece of his clothing and the question that he had asked her before. How could he do this great wickedness and sin against God?

Even with the so-called evidence, Potiphar didn't really believe his wife. If he had, Joseph would have been put to death for attempted rape. But Potiphar felt he had to maintain his own reputation, so he had Joseph thrown in jail. And that fact alone is a mighty testimony of just how far Joseph was willing to go with his faith.[3]

---

[1] *Patriarchs and Prophets*, p. 217.
[2] Gen. 39:7.
[3] *Ibid.*, p. 218.

PASSING THE FINAL TEST OF LOVE

We know that we have passed from death unto life, because we love the brethren. 1 John 3:14.

Before his conversion, the life of Judah was little more than an ugly blotter smeared with dark deeds ranging from permissive sexual behavior to terrible cruelty. He gave little evidence of being the future leader of the most important tribe in Israel and the progenitor of Christ. Yet, sometime within the two decades that Joseph had been in Egypt, Judah had made the choice to follow the Lord and allow Him to transform him into a true representative of the Most High.[1]

Judah passed the final test of love that day when he stood before Joseph and pleaded eloquently for the life of his younger brother Benjamin, who was apparently doomed to a life of slavery. Judah would willingly go into slavery himself rather than see Benjamin subjected to such torture.

Joseph knew that Judah wasn't playacting. He wasn't giving some memorized speech. Joseph had put much pressure on his brothers to see whether they had changed.

Joseph was totally disguised to his brothers. He was much older now and cleanshaven, while they wore the typical semitic beards. Dressed in his royal regalia and using the Egyptian language gave him a chance to find out whether those who had been so mean and cruel to him when he was only 17 had been transformed. So when he listened that day to Judah's noble offer, is it any wonder that it touched every fiber and tender nerve ending of his emotions? He didn't leave the room as before, but burst into tears. He knew that love had finally conquered.

Judah did not change by himself. There is no way to love like that without first yielding to the painful promptings of the Holy Spirit. But God never leaves us with simply a troubled conscience and conviction. He converts, then re-creates us in His own image if we are willing. The case of Judah should encourage all of us to make a similar choice.

---

[1] *The SDA Bible Commentary*, vol. 1, p. 452.

UNSTABLE AS WATER

Reuben, thou art my firstborn, my might, and the beginning of my strength, the excellency of dignity, and the excellency of power: unstable as water, thou shalt not excel. Gen. 49:3, 4.

What starts out as a hopeful picture of what Jacob deeply longed to see in his firstborn son turned into a bleak forecast. Because Reuben had committed incest at Edar so many years before, he became unworthy of the birthright blessing.

We are not told Reuben's first reaction as he listened to his father, Jacob, give this deathbed pronouncement. Perhaps he accepted it for what it was, an inspired commentary on his life.

But what was it about Reuben that made him this way? What kind of decisions had he made that caused him to be unstable as water? We see him in action when the other brothers wanted to kill Joseph. Instead of standing up as the eldest son and emphatically saying No, he suggested that they put Joseph in a pit, thinking he would just walk away and then release him later on. He didn't want to be placed under any pressure. He may have been worthy of some recommendation for suggesting no murder, but it would have been far better for him to be brave enough to stand up for what was truly right at that moment.

Reuben had absolutely no fixed principles. He was swayed by those nearest him. He went along with his brothers in the terrible deception of telling their father that Joseph had been killed by a wild beast. He could be molded. He was the type who had to have strong influence for good around to make it. Otherwise his moral power collapsed.

The problem lies in the fact that people like Reuben are influenced by the last person they talk to, because they have no real connection with Heaven. They playact their way through life and tend to trust to their own strength. "They are like Reuben, unstable as water, having no inward rectitude, and like Reuben they will never excel. What you need is to see your dependence upon God, and to have a resolute heart." [1]

---

[1] *The SDA Bible Commentary*, Ellen G. White Comments, on Gen. 49:3, 4, p. 1098.

ON BEING LIKE CHRIST

Love your enemies, bless them that curse you, do good to them that hate you, and pray for them which despitefully use you, and persecute you; that ye may be the children of your Father which is in heaven. Matt. 5:44, 45.

After seventeen very happy and tranquil years of living amid all the love and devotion possible, Jacob at age 147 very quietly and peacefully passed away.[1] But right after the funeral, his sons felt very uneasy. Trepidation seized them. Could it be that Joseph was only waiting until dear old dad died before taking revenge on them for their cruelty so long ago? Maybe he had covered up his real feelings until Jacob was gone, but now things might be different. Certainly with Joseph second in command in all Egypt, he was in a position to do just that! And the more they talked among themselves, the more they quivered over the possibilities. Memory, stimulated by a very alert conscience, recalled that tragic scene when Joseph had pleaded for his life and called on them one by one to help him. But none had had the courage to defend him. The years had not erased the vivid picture of his looking back pitifully and crying and calling to them as the slave traders departed.

It was too much to bear. They had to find out what he intended to do now but didn't dare approach Joseph themselves. Quite possibly their messenger was Benjamin. Since he was Joseph's full brother, he might have an in with the great leader. "We pray thee, forgive the trespass of the servants of the God of thy father."[2]

Did you ever notice the next three words? "And Joseph wept." It was too much for him. He broke down because his dear brothers never knew the depths of his feelings toward them. Long before this he had made the choice to forgive them. It hurt him to think that even for an instant they should hold such a misconception of his love. How much like Christ! Joseph's patience and meekness under the cruelest injustice were much like Jesus' when He faced the abuse of wicked men and forgave them in spite of their actions.

---

[1] *SDA Bible Dictionary*, p. 545.
[2] Gen. 50:17.

CHOOSING CIVIL DISOBEDIENCE

By faith Moses, when he was born, was hid three months of his parents, because they saw he was a proper child; and they were not afraid of the king's commandment. Heb. 11:23.

After the bright days of Joseph had passed, suddenly the pro-Hebrew regime vanished from the Egyptian scene.

The harsh heel of the new government policies ground down the hapless Hebrews. The fertile pasturelands of Goshen were not a pleasant place to be living right then. They were packed with Hebrew slaves who were herded to forced labor construction sites to build the great edifices for the Egyptian royalty. The new autocratic Pharaoh turned a clever piece of political expediency to avoid any possibility of revolt by enforcing stricter and stricter measures.

But worse than this was his birth-control decree. All baby boys were to be killed and the girls saved. It would be just a matter of time before the Hebrew population would be totally under control. We can only imagine the raw terror that must have swept through the Hebrew ranks when they heard the latest government news bulletin. The impact must have sent a shudder through the hearts of every pregnant woman.

But one slave couple were not afraid of the king's commandment. That is what it says in our verse for today. "They were not afraid." Amram and Jochebed made up their minds that they would trust the God of heaven and defy the king's diabolical order. Their daughter Miriam was safe, and little 3-year-old Aaron had slipped under the wire of the new rule. When their infant son, Moses, was born, they were determined to choose civil disobedience. This brave couple simply would not comply and drown their baby boy in the Nile.[1]

A crisis of this magnitude can be met without fear only if the conditions for a firm commitment to fear God in reverential worship have been met first. Then we too can meet any situation as Amram and Jochebed did.

---

[1] *The SDA Bible Commentary*, vol. 1, p. 501.

JOCHEBED'S CHOICE

A woman that feareth the Lord, she shall be praised. Prov. 31:30.

When Jochebed learned the happy news that she would actually get paid for taking care of her own child, she made a choice for time and eternity. She decided right there and then that if Moses would ultimately be taken from her, she would put more time, more effort, into his training for God than she had in training her other two children.

We are given only a wee bit of Biblical information about this woman, and she quickly fades from view. Yet what a tremendous impact on Hebrew history came from her son whom she trained so well!

Just what was it that Jochebed put into the young mind of Moses before he left for the Egyptian court? "She showed him the folly and sin of idolatry, and early taught him to bow down and pray to the living God, who alone could hear him and help him in every emergency." [1]

Within a dozen years Jochebed had to pack into his life everything she was ever going to say or do. There would be no rerun of this experience. There never is for parents, but for Jochebed the decision to give Moses a solid grip on the Creator had a real sense of urgency. She prayed while she worked to provide a consistent pattern of showing Moses the truth about God and His power to save.

When at last Moses had to leave his familiar mud hut in Goshen for the Egyptian palace, it may have been a tearful farewell. But Jochebed could rest assured that she had done her best. No matter what happened to Moses from that time forth, he could never escape the influence and training of his godly mother. She may have been a slave in exile, but Jochebed had put first things first.

What a legacy, not only for Moses, who became the great leader of Israel, but for all mothers who are inspired to make a similar choice! Jochebed showed the high value God Himself places upon the work of the mother. In her hands, perhaps more than anyone else's, is molded much of the destiny of the child. And as our text says, "she shall be praised" when she has worked in the fear of the Lord.

---

[1] *Patriarchs and Prophets*, p. 244.

THE GIRL WITH THE RIGHT ATTITUDE

Even a child is known by his doings, whether his work be pure, and whether it be right. Prov. 20:11.

Her Hebrew name was adapted from an Egyptian word that meant "the beloved one." [1] And when we watch her skillful action and prudent timing at the Nile as she approached the Egyptian princess concerning her baby brother, we realize how perfectly the name fits. Without Miriam's clever tact the story of Moses and the whole of Hebrew history would never have been written. She is an important link in the account. What a responsibility rested on this 12-year-old girl! [2]

Obviously Miriam had been instructed beforehand on what to say. Jochebed had made the arrangements, but it was Miriam's choice to carry it out in her own way and at the right time.

Miriam was not the type to grumble about obeying. We don't hear her complaining, "Oh, why do I have to watch over my kid brother? I don't want to go down to that dirty old river! Why do I always have to do chores like this?" Many children her age would have made it utterly impossible to formulate such a scheme, because of their recalcitrant attitude.

But Miriam had early decided that obedience was a beautiful thing and that her own joy was wrapped up in becoming a part of the thrilling action of saving her baby brother.

Miriam waited. We don't know how long, but she stayed put down there among the papyrus. She observed everybody coming and going. Her legs may have been cramped, her muscles tired, but the thrill of being there and timing her behavior made it worthwhile.

Suddenly she heard voices! Pharaoh's daughter and her maidens were coming to the river to bathe. Miriam's keen eyes picked up the compassion and tender looks of the princess as the lid of that little ark was lifted and Moses cried. How quickly she slipped into her role! "Shall I go and call a Hebrew nurse for you?" Perfect! Years later she could still rejoice over her part.

---

[1] *SDA Bible Dictionary*, p. 745.
[2] *The SDA Bible Commentary*, vol. 1, pp. 501, 890.

THAT DAILY DECISION

By faith Moses, when he was come to years, refused to be called the son of Pharaoh's daughter; choosing rather to suffer affliction with the people of God, than to enjoy the pleasures of sin for a season. Heb. 11:24, 25.

One of the most outstanding choices ever recorded in Scripture is found in today's text. The transition from living in a mud hut and associating with garlic-reeking, clay-digging, straw-gathering slaves to dwelling in the dazzling splendor of the Egyptian palace and the sophistication of court life was stunning.

Moses stood at the crossroads. Either he would continue worshiping the true God and would identify with His people or he would renounce everything and become an Egyptian. It was a weighty decision for a 12-year-old lad. But Jochebed's instructions and prayers paid off.

Moses lived at the nerve center of the most powerful and highly civilized nation on earth. For the next twenty-eight years he had to back up his original decision daily. It was not a onetime thing. There were plenty of pressures beyond that, pressures that built daily!

"By the laws of Egypt all who occupied the throne of the Pharaohs must become members of the priestly caste; and Moses, as the heir apparent, was to be initiated into the mysteries of the national religion." [1] Imagine being forced to take courses like Idolatry I, Superstition II, and Religion of Ra! Instead of going along with the school program, nodding on cue because it was more convenient, Moses refused to buckle. Not by any threats or inducements of reward could the priests and philosophers turn him away from worshiping the true God. "His firmness in this respect was tolerated, because he was the king's adopted grandson, and was a universal favorite with the most influential in the kingdom." [2]

Because he was favored, he was presented with even more pressures. He was a winner and was consistently applauded. This is heady stuff and capable of causing ruin. But Moses made that daily decision to identify with God and His people.

[1] *Patriarchs and Prophets*, p. 245.
[2] *Spiritual Gifts*, vol. 3, p. 184.

MOSES' MISTAKE

And it came to pass in those days, when Moses was grown, that he went out unto his brethren, . . . and he spied an Egyptian smiting an Hebrew. . . . And he looked this way and that way, and when he saw there was no man, he slew the Egyptian, and hid him in the sand. Ex. 2:11, 12.

Moses had seen taskmasters beating his people before, but now the time for revolt seemed ripe. After all, he was 40 years old and in what seemed to be his prime of life. He had all the degrees from the University of Egypt and was certainly qualified, as far as he was concerned.

Moses had observed his people being nearly crushed by grinding cruelty, and secretly he felt that if he was ever to act and step into his appointed role as their deliverer, certainly the time had come. That is why, with fire in his eyes, he strode over to the taskmaster that day. The taskmaster kept right on beating the hapless Hebrew. He undoubtedly figured the Egyptian ruler approaching him approved of such action. But Moses killed him when he was sure there were no witnesses.

Of course, the freed slave ran back to the mud huts of Goshen and broadcast the news. Like wildfire it spread through the whole slave section of the country. Moses received the shock of his life the next day when he tried to break up a heated Hebrew argument that had slipped into the fisticuffs stage. "Who made thee a prince and a judge over us?" was a question that stung him.[1] His own people were not ready for deliverance, not the way he had planned it anyway. Everything backfired. Soon he was forced to flee the country, because there was an all-points bulletin out on him.

Why did Moses murder the Egyptian in the first place? Before we condemn him, remember that we all tend to take accumulated data and carefully sorted facts that appeal to us and bend them to fit what we like to call "providential." In reality we are taking affairs into our own hands, just as Moses did. Moses' method would never have ascribed the glory to God.

---

[1] Ex. 2:14.

PHARAOH'S HARDENED HEART

And the Lord said unto Moses, When thou goest to return into Egypt, see that thou do all those wonders before Pharaoh, which I have put in thine hand: but I will harden his heart, that he shall not let the people go. Ex. 4:21.

For some people this is a very difficult text. It seems to just ooze predestination. Actually there are ten such statements that refer to hardening Pharaoh's heart. And from a superficial reading it does appear that Pharaoh had no choice in the matter. He seemed doomed to play his tough role and go down an unconverted man. But in the light of the issues at stake in the great controversy over God's character, this sort of reasoning would only support Satan's lies. God simply is not the arbitrary and severe person that the enemy pictures Him to be. He respects and honors each person's choice in his or her eternal destiny. The same sun may shine on a pound of butter and a pound of clay. One melts and the other hardens. It is only in this sense that God hardened Pharaoh's heart.[1]

Moses provided Pharaoh with one striking evidence after another that God rules the universe. But each time a miracle was performed Pharaoh became more determined to resist. And that resistance hardened him until he had to stand there in frozen shock and look down on the dead face of his firstborn.

Pharaoh's pride-filled heart set the stage for him to proceed from one form of determined rebellion to another, regardless of how awesome God's demonstrated power.[2]

What can we learn from this Egyptian king's experience? How can we profit from knowing that he hardened his own heart against the Lord? "Those who are quieting a guilty conscience with the thought that they can change a course of evil when they choose, that they can trifle with the invitations of mercy, and yet be again and again impressed, take this course at their peril. . . . The experience, the education, the discipline of a life of sinful indulgence, has so thoroughly molded the character that they cannot then receive the image of Jesus."[3]

---

[1] *The SDA Bible Commentary,* vol. 1, p. 516.
[2] *Ibid.,* p. 519.
[3] *Patriarchs and Prophets,* p. 269.

THE MIXED MULTITUDE
And a mixed multitude went up also with them. Ex. 12:38.

The night of the Passover was exciting enough, but when the great Exodus finally got under way there was a lot of dust and commotion in Goshen. Whole families were on the move. Those who were not ready stuck their heads out the doors to see what was going on, and then the urge hit them. Everybody from senior citizens to little children seemed headed for the Promised Land.

"In this multitude were not only those who were actuated by faith in the God of Israel, but also a far greater number who desired only to escape from the plagues, or who followed in the wake of the moving multitudes merely from excitement and curiosity. This class were ever a hindrance and a snare to Israel." [1]

Nobody is quite sure of the identity of these non-Israelites, except we do know that some at least had intermarried with the Hebrews. [2] One thing is sure, though, from the foregoing statement: They were not all moved by right motives. They made a choice to go with God's people simply on the basis of "Let's get out of here before we get hurt!" "Everybody's going," or "What's going on?" And a decision that is prompted by fear, emotion, or curiosity alone is doomed to dissatisfaction sooner or later.

Whenever we read of the children of Israel murmuring, it is almost certain to have started with this mixed multitude. Disillusionment set in. There were no more plagues for the fearful to cringe about, so they anticipated trouble, whether it be no water, no food, or no leader in the immediate vicinity. The excitement-hungry found the steady grind of the daily trek and hard duties a little too much, and the curiosity seekers found nothing so curious anymore when each day meant a tedious hike across the desert.

So the mixed multitude became exceedingly impatient. They were leaders in the apostasy at Sinai, suggesting a golden calf for worship. Right along with the leeks, onions, garlic, and meat, they missed having a god that would smile benignly on their carnality. Could any of us become a part of the mixed multitude?

[1] *Patriarchs and Prophets*, p. 281.
[2] *The SDA Bible Commentary*, vol. 1, pp. 556, 557.

WHY MOSES CHOSE TO TAKE ADVICE

And Moses' father in law said unto him, The thing that thou doest is not good. . . . So Moses hearkened to the voice of his father in law, and did all that he had said. Ex. 18:17-24.

There is hardly any work quite so exhausting as counseling people about their problems. And certainly the children of Israel had plenty of problems. Having just left the rigid rules of Egypt, where so much of their lives had been preplanned and controlled, they now found themselves forced to make their own decisions. So they turned to Moses for counsel.

And he sat down from dawn to dusk listening, advising, and explaining. Imagine the potential for nervous exhaustion with more than 2 million people on the roster! [1]

Jethro, Moses' father-in-law, who had come to visit camp, shook his wise old head. "What is this thing you're doing?" he asked. And Moses explained how much the people needed someone to guide them in the way of the Lord. That was all fine, but Jethro told him quite frankly that it would never work. Not with a one-man all-day session as he had just witnessed. "You'll surely wear out!" he warned. And then Jethro unfolded a sharp administrative scheme that would utilize the devout men in camp on a chain of command that began with "rulers of thousands" and went down to "rulers of tens." [2] Moses would then be freed from the small-claims-court procedures to handle the weightier matters. It was a brilliant idea, and Moses quickly followed through with the plan.

This says something about Moses as a person. Many simply cannot take advice. They steel themselves against anyone who would dare to suggest they might not have their act together. Pride takes over, and they instantly take the hands-on-hips stance with that arrogant question "Do you know who I am?"

Moses chose to take advice because he had been in close contact with God. Meekness and humility follow those who have pressed in close to the Lord and have learned of Him.

---

[1] *The SDA Bible Commentary*, vol. 1, p. 556.
[2] Ex. 18:21.

MANNA-GATHERING DOUBTERS

And it came to pass, that there went out some of the people on the seventh day for to gather, and they found none. And the Lord said unto Moses, How long refuse ye to keep my commandments and my laws? Ex. 16:27, 28.

As hard as slavery had been in Egypt, there had been a certain sordid security to the arrangement. The children of Israel may have paid rent with pieces of their lives, but at least they had food and shelter. As they pressed deeper and deeper into the Sinai desert many became nervous. Nobody had died of starvation yet. Nobody was even really hungry. But the very idea that it might happen caused profound apprehension.

Doubts have a way of feeding on every particle and fragment of information available until at last there is seemingly no way out, around, or through the impasse. That is what happened to the Hebrews out there in the wilderness. They worried, and worry gave way to doubt, and doubt brought them to stark fear.

And then early one morning the ground was covered with a small white round thing like hoar frost. The people chattered excitedly among themselves asking, "Manna?" or "What is it?" [1] Moses introduced them to the angels' food, the bread the angels brought each predawn. They ate manna, or what-is-it bread, for forty years. [2]

But there had to be a little instruction at first. And that is where the doubters edged forward. They could not seem to surmount that built-in squirrelly instinct. They went beyond the allotted two dry quarts (1.8 dry liters) per person and tried to stash it away for the future. But lo and behold, it bred worms and stank. [3] God was trying to take them from degradation to trust. Then on Friday it was time to store up for the Sabbath, and sure enough, some of them chose to disbelieve the double-portion miracle and went out to gather manna on the Sabbath. Their scrounging for breakfast failed, and that was when God asked how long they would continue to distrust Him who ever cares for His children.

---

[1] Ex. 16:15, margin.
[2] *Patriarchs and Prophets*, p. 297.
[3] *The SDA Bible Commentary*, vol. 1, pp. 577, 580.

FLABBY LEADERSHIP

They made a calf in Horeb, and worshipped the molten image. Thus they changed their glory into the similitude of an ox that eateth grass. They forgat God their saviour. Ps. 106:19-21.

It was a moment when firm leadership was desperately needed, but he wasn't up to it. Aaron listened to the clamoring crowd and mildly remonstrated with them, but his tone and manner only fanned their unreasoning frenzy. They wanted a visible god!

Aaron thought it might turn off the people to request their jewelry; it didn't. They ripped off their earrings and piled them high so that he could build them a golden calf.

And once Aaron had melted the metal down and formed the kind of god they had seen in Egypt, the people shouted long and loud, "These be thy gods, O Israel, which have brought thee up out of the land of Egypt." [1] "And Aaron basely permitted this insult to Jehovah. He did more. Seeing with what satisfaction the golden god was received, he built an altar before it, and made proclamation, 'Tomorrow is a feast to the Lord.' " [2]

That was all they needed. It is all people today need. Get someone in a leadership capacity with a flaccid character to provide a blessing or testimonial at whatever secular event desired, and the crowds will sing his praises.

What makes such an act so bad is that it is so often done with the calm assurance that all is well. The people really liked Aaron. They noticed the difference between him and Moses, who later stalked into camp and in righteous indignation smashed the tablets of stone and knocked down their golden calf. Aaron would not have acted like that. They admired his gentleness and patience. Moses was too negative. But God does not look at it that way. The so-called patience and calm assurance in wrongdoing is nothing more than ego. Voice culture and good acting add the dimension people love. But we must always remember that "of all the sins that God will punish, none are more grievous in His sight than those that encourage others to do evil." [3]

[1] Ex. 32:8.
[2] *Patriarchs and Prophets*, p. 317.
[3] *Ibid.*, p. 323.

ETERNAL LIFE ON THE LINE

Yet now, if thou wilt forgive their sin—; and if not, blot me, I pray thee, out of thy book which thou hast written. Ex. 32:32.

This passage of Scripture is broken by a sob. Moses, realizing the terrible enormity of the Israelites' sin in worshiping the golden calf, actually put his own eternal life on the line for their sakes. The Lord had lifted Moses to the heights of that rarified atmosphere of heavenly love. He had brought out the best in this man who typifies the Good Shepherd. There is no way God could accept atonement from Moses; only One could do that. But Moses did show how great was his love for the people. It is one thing to offer to die physically for someone else. It is quite another to be willing to be blotted from the book of life forever!

It is written that Moses had made the choice to stand with the people of God because "he had respect unto the recompense of the reward." [1] That may sound like a selfish reason for standing with God's people—hoping for the reward. But here that is swept away as we see his noblest choice in action.

But how could anyone love people who were so obstreperously bent on turning to their own evil ways? Just how do you become motivated to love those who are determined to be mean-mouthed and rebellious? Loving is not liking. We may be totally disgusted and turned off by what people say and do, but that does not deter real love. Moses had not lapsed into some dreamy-eyed, sentimental statement about his feelings. He had just stalked into camp, smashed the tables of stone, ripped down the golden calf, ground it to powder, and made the people drink the very water where the flecks of gold dust had settled. He could be stern and forceful, yet he could also offer hope and love. He was in balance. Real love is not sentimentality. It does not pamper and coddle, but it does put itself on the line.

Moses had right motives because he had a right trust. And watching him automatically turns your eyes toward the Lord.

[1] Heb. 11:26.

DISASTER AT THE WORSHIP SERVICE

There is a way which seemeth right unto a man; but the end thereof are the ways of death. Prov. 14:12.

Moses' nephews Nadab and Abihu had just spent a week in study and meditation for their new priesthood positions.[1] Prior to this they had hiked partway up Sinai with their father, Aaron, and the seventy elders and had seen firsthand the glory of the Lord. The brand-new tabernacle was now completed, and it was time for them to step into their sacred role as representatives of the people. Next to Moses and Aaron, they held the highest positions in Israel.

But the high honor, the special privileges, they enjoyed were not met by any corresponding depth of dedication. Throughout their childhood and youth they had always had a sloppy way of thinking about obedience. It seemed to them that if they did things nearly right, that should be acceptable. "Who cares?" was their attitude.

That was why they made such untidy preparations for the worship service that afternoon. And who cared if they took a little sip of alcohol? They wouldn't get drunk—just enough to relax a bit before the service began. Self-control was never a part of their habit patterns anyway, so they made a final, fatal choice that moment before the worship began. Instead of taking the fire for their censers off the altar—the one that had been started by a bolt from heaven—they casually sauntered over and took coals from the common fire from their hearth. After all, they figured, fire is fire. What difference does it make? [2]

But obedience does make a difference to the Lord! While the people were bowed in worship, rejoicing over God's blessing in accepting their new tabernacle, fire shot out from the Lord and struck Nadab and Abihu dead. The people were stunned. What had happened? It wasn't long before they found out. God cannot accept carelessness and rounded-corner thinking, especially in leadership.

In this age of casualness and tacky worship behavior, isn't it time we remembered Nadab and Abihu?

[1] *The SDA Bible Commentary*, vol. 1, p. 748; *Patriarchs and Prophets*, p. 359.
[2] *The SDA Bible Commentary*, vol. 1, pp. 748, 749; *Patriarchs and Prophets*, pp. 359-362.

THE FATE OF THE UNDISCIPLINED

The rod and reproof give wisdom: but a child left to himself bringeth his mother to shame. Prov. 29:15.

Our text for today doesn't exclude the father. Both parents are put to shame and suffer agony at the fate of a spoiled child.

In the case of Aaron, he was required to suffer in silent anguish when his two sons Nadab and Abihu were struck down. God spoke through Moses that Aaron must not show the slightest signs of grief. He must not seem to sanction disobedience or to show the slightest sympathy for sin. And although Aaron proceeded to carry on his high-priestly functions, his heart was wrenched with a profound sorrow. He knew his own negligence as a father had set the stage for his boys' cremation that afternoon.

Aaron had never taught his sons self-control. His own flaccid character could not cope with firm discipline. He had allowed Nadab and Abihu to follow their own inclinations. They never knew what No meant. They could make a fuss, and father would fold. When Aaron attempted to discipline and make things final, the boys knew very well that he meant it was semifinal. They soon learned that by stamping their feet and crying loudly enough, they could make father give in.

Aaron never chose to correct them because he had the mistaken notion that a little laying on of the hands might be misunderstood. He decided, like so many parents, that permissiveness is equated with love and that a spanking might somehow stunt the development of a child's personality or something. Aaron never understood how much he was setting up his boys for a false concept of obedience.

Little brats become big brats. Although Aaron witnessed the sudden destruction of his sons, many parents are forced to watch in abject horror as their children follow a protracted process of destruction, owing to self-centered habits. Because of their own false sympathy they live to see the fate of the undisciplined.

MIRIAM'S MURMURING

For where envying and strife is, there is confusion and every evil work. James 3:16.

When the children of Israel reached the wilderness campsite of Hazeroth, about 37 miles (60 kilometers) northeast of Mount Sinai, they were forced to halt because Miriam had suddenly contracted that dreadful disease, leprosy.[1] The entire camp waited a week before the divine judgment that had plagued her was removed and she was restored to health. It was more than a little embarrassing; it was downright humbling. Miriam's pride was brought down to the dust by this experience, as God intended it should be.

The seeds of envy tend to be miniscule, but now fast they grow! With Miriam, jealousy began to sprout when she learned that her brother Moses had married Zipporah. Miriam's family and national pride was wounded because he had not chosen a Hebrew woman.[2] Zipporah was a very timid, gentle person, but it made no difference to Miriam. She cared not that Zipporah was an affectionate wife. All Miriam could see was that this swarthy Midianite was not a Hebrew. And it didn't matter that the Midianites were related to the Israelites, either. She was stung by the whole thing.

Jealousy ever seeks fresh soil for its evil roots to find nourishment. Miriam's envious feelings found new ground in Jethro's visit and his suggestion to Moses of a better organizational structure. Needing a sympathizer, Miriam sought her brother Aaron, who shared her feelings. They felt that Jethro's influence might exceed theirs. When the seventy elders were appointed, Miriam and Aaron were not consulted, and that excited their jealousy even more.[3] But using Zipporah's slightly darker complexion and national background as an excuse, she registered her complaint in that direction rather than admitting the real reason.

"Envy is one of the most satanic traits that can exist in the human heart, and it is one of the most baleful in its effects." [4] Miriam had made a disturbing choice, and God demonstrated dramatically how He felt about the matter.

---

[1] *SDA Bible Dictionary*, p. 465.
[2] *Patriarchs and Prophets*, p. 383.
[3] *Ibid.*, pp. 382, 383.
[4] *Ibid.*, p. 385.

THE DAMAGE OF THE EVIL REPORT

And they brought up an evil report of the land which they had searched unto the children of Israel. Num. 13:32.

For forty days the Israelites waited expectantly at Kadesh-Barnea for the return of the spies. The whole congregation was on tiptoe. Into the camp suddenly walked those twelve men carrying all the fruity visual aids from the Promised Land. Against the bleak, rocky background of the surrounding wasteland, the effect must have been fantastic. The people went wild with excitement.

But mounting above the din of the cheering crowd came the steady pile-driving beat of the discouraging note. The spies agreed that it was truly a land flowing with the proverbial "milk and honey," but ten of them decided it was too much to risk taking. "Nevertheless," they warned, "the people be strong that dwell in the land." [1] That word *nevertheless* turned the tide. The ten weak-kneed spies filled in the graphic negative details. Those tales of fortifications, of walled cities, and of giants roaming the land did the trick.

The people did not want to believe "If only the two men had brought the evil report, and all the ten had encouraged them to possess the land in the name of the Lord, they would still have taken the advice of the two in preference to the ten, because of their wicked unbelief." [2]

And that night the whole congregation had a cry session. Have you ever heard more than 2 million people bawling? It must have been some sound effects! The next day they were determined to go back to Egypt. And had not God intervened, the insane mob would have killed the two faithful spies.

From that point on the Biblical narrative is a tragic tale. Except for a few brief recorded outbreaks of rebellion, the Israelites dropped from sight as they wandered in the wilderness, all because of their unbelieving choice.

[1] Num. 13:28.
[2] *Patriarchs and Prophets*, p. 390.

OPEN PIT FOR REBELLION

And the earth opened her mouth, and swallowed them up, and their houses, and all the men that appertained unto Korah, and all their goods. They, and all that appertained to them, went down alive into the pit. Num. 16:32, 33.

Although he was a cousin to Moses, the relationship wasn't that meaningful to Korah.[1] What did amount to something, as far as he was concerned, was status. He had been assigned the ministry of music for the sanctuary, but what he really wanted was the priesthood.[2] Why shouldn't he and his family have rights to this? And so jealousy took root.

But jealousy seldom operates alone. It needs a sympathizing ear. Living on the south side of the encampment, near Korah were Dathan and Abiram. They too had a grudge. Since they were descendants of Reuben, the eldest son of Jacob, they claimed they had rights to the civil authority of Israel.

With such strong feelings it was natural that these three should get their heads together in a well-laid plot to overthrow the established leadership of Moses and Aaron. Soon their whispering skills paid off, and they had 250 princes with them in nodding approval. It was like a mini-great controversy.

Korah made it appear that the children of Israel had been wronged.[3] And for those who are at fault nothing sounds sweeter than words of sympathy and praise. So Korah poured it on. "We would long ago have entered Canaan if it weren't for Moses and Aaron," he claimed. It was their mismanagement that had led the Israelites back into the wilderness. If only Korah were leader, things would be different.

When Moses finally heard of the plot, he turned the matter over to the Lord. And God required a showdown in twenty-four hours. That gave time for reflection and repentance, but these men still stubbornly chose to insist on their self-styled rights. There was nothing more God could do, so they went down alive into the pit.

Today we live in a climate of the Korah-type attitude. What will our choice be? To stand firm for God, or our own selfishness?

---

[1] *Patriarchs and Prophets*, p. 395.
[2] *The SDA Bible Commentary*, vol. 1, p. 875.
[3] *Patriarchs and Prophets*, pp. 396, 397.

THE WATERS OF STRIFE

They angered him also at the waters of strife, so that it went ill with Moses for their sakes. Ps. 106:32.

At the end of their forty years of wilderness wandering, the children of Israel were once again near Kadesh, not far from the hills of Canaan. Suddenly the waters that had gushed out near camp during their journey dried up. This ought to have told them something. They were now about to enter the Promised Land. But instead of rejoicing and accepting the little test God placed before them to see if they could actually walk by faith for a moment, the same old turbulent spirit arose, and they began griping about the lack of water. Without the slightest reflection on past providential care, they took up the old hue and cry again. "Would God that we had died when our brethren died before the Lord!" [1]

They were actually saying that they wished they had been destroyed in the rebellion of Korah rather than to face what they saw as sure death from thirst. It was a miserable murmuring. This second generation of Hebrews hadn't seemed to learn a thing in all their wanderings.

"Here now, ye rebels," Moses cried. "Must we fetch you water out of this rock?" [2] And with that he took his rod and struck the rock twice.

The waters gushed out in miraculous form, but Moses' irritated feeling wiped out the full effect. "By his rash act Moses took away the force of the lesson that God purposed to teach. The rock, being a symbol of Christ, had been once smitten, as Christ was to be once offered. The second time it was needful only to speak to the rock, as we have only to ask for blessings in the name of Jesus." [3]

Worse, Moses' quick, angry choice confirmed the old charge that he and Aaron performed miracles by themselves. "Must we fetch you water?" supported that claim. For that brief moment Moses forgot how God can help us in times of severe stress. No matter how unexpected the temptation, our God can deliver.

[1] Num. 20:3.
[2] Verse 10.
[3] *Patriarchs and Prophets*, p. 418.

THE BRONZE SNAKE

And as Moses lifted up the serpent in the wilderness, even so must the Son of man be lifted up:.that whosoever believeth in him should not perish, but have eternal life. John 3:14, 15.

When the Israelites took time out for murmuring at Kadesh they missed the golden opportunity of making a beeline to Canaan. Their hesitation cost them a denial of passage through Edom, and they were forced to take a long southerly detour through a dreary sandy wasteland.[1] The hot hike with their backs to the Promised Land triggered a new phase of complaint. This time they added the notion that they loathed "this light bread," the manna.[2]

Every day of their wandering, God had given them shade by day and a pillar of fire at night. He had seen to it that there wasn't a feeble person among them. Their clothes hadn't worn out, and their feet didn't swell. Their bread and water were sure. And even the poisonous snakes and scorpions of the desert hadn't bothered them. But now, since they didn't appreciate His loving care, God removed His protective hand, and suddenly the camp was under a snake attack!

The snakes had been there all along, of course, but now they seemed to come from every quarter. It was enough to give everyone screaming fits. Most folk do a quickstep dance to the nearest exit at the sight of a coiled, hissing snake. And to have these serpents crawling into tents and over blankets was enough to make the Hebrews forget about any other complaints.

That is why they turned to the only man who had a real connection with God. Moses prayed, and God answered with directions to make a bronze serpent and lift it high on a pole. There was life in a look *if* they believed in the symbol of the Saviour who was to become sin for humanity.

The fatal poison in their bloodstream was like sin, and the only remedy was through faith. Some chose to believe and were immediately cured. But others died. It seemed absurd to them to find relief in looking at some bronze serpent on a pole. They refused to accept the divine provision, and they perished.

[1] *The SDA Bible Commentary*, vol. 1, p. 894.
[2] Num. 21:5.

PROPHECY OF THE APOSTATE PROPHET

I shall see him, but not now; I shall behold him, but not nigh: there shall come a Star out of Jacob, and a Sceptre shall rise out of Israel. Num. 24:17.

This beautiful, elevating Messianic prophecy was uttered by none other than Balaam, the apostate prophet. We have no books by Balaam, but we do have these and other sublime words spoken while he was under the complete control of God's Spirit.

We first find Balaam living in Mesopotamia when Balak's messengers pleaded with him to come down and curse the people of God. Balaam's eyes sparkled at the thought of the riches and honor Balak offered. He acted as though he wanted to know the will of the Lord in the matter, even though his heart hankered for those promised rewards.

"There are thousands at the present day who are pursuing a similar course. They would have no difficulty in understanding their duty if it were in harmony with their inclinations. It is plainly set before them in the Bible or is clearly indicated by circumstances and reason. But because these evidences are contrary to their desires and inclinations they frequently set them aside and presume to go to God to learn their duty. With great apparent conscientiousness they pray long and earnestly for light. But God will not be trifled with." [1]

So double-minded Balaam determined to go, and en route he had the famous dialog with his donkey. The poor beast with more than twenty-twenty vision had halted at the sight of the menacing angel and was beaten by the perverted prophet. Yet Balaam was so blinded by his own selfishness that the discussion with his beast didn't seem abnormal.

We next see him teamed up with Balak in a seven-altar sacrificial ceremony. Three times Balak set up the props, and each time Balaam uttered only blessings. Unfortunately Balaam chose to cling to his covetousness and double-minded ways rather than turning to the Redeemer whom he had predicted would come.

---

[1] *Patriarchs and Prophets*, pp. 440, 441.

THE COURAGE OF THEIR CONVICTIONS

And the Lord spake unto Moses, saying, The daughters of Zelophehad speak right. Num. 27:6, 7.

It was an age when sons took obvious status priority. So it is refreshing to read of the five daughters of Zelophehad, who boldly pressed forward to lay claim to what they considered their rightful inheritance. Mahlah, Noah, Hoglah, Milcah, and Tirzah left such an impact on Moses that he mentioned their names several times, and Joshua even included the list in his book. Considering the times and the predominance of an all-male landscape, these five young ladies certainly must have left an indelible mark on the minds of the leaders.

While the Israelites were still on the steppes of Moab awaiting orders to cross Jordan, Moses gave the command for a male headcount from each tribe as a determining basis for dividing up the Promised Land.[1] The last census had been taken thirty-eight years earlier, and now it meant property division—who was going to get what piece of real estate. And that was when the five daughters of Zelophehad went into action. Since no females were on the census list and their dad had no sons, it seemed only fair that they should get a piece of the upcoming inheritance.

The presentation of their cause was made in front of the door of the tabernacle with Moses, Eleazar the high priest, the princes, and the whole congregation. It was a most interesting moment.

Moses had absolutely no reference point. It was unprecedented in the history of Israel. He immediately took it to the Lord, and back came the answer: "The daughters of Zelophehad speak right: thou shalt surely give them a possession."[2]

We should never equate passivity with meekness. God expects us to possess boldness in laying claim to those causes based on fairness and equality. The choice these five daughters made in presenting their claim through God's appointed channels received Heaven's blessing. This should encourage us when we have to stand up for our own convictions.

[1] *The SDA Bible Commentary*, vol. 1, p. 917.
[2] Num. 27:7.

TMTD-3

WHY MOSES NEVER COMPLAINED

The eternal God is thy refuge, and underneath are the everlasting arms. Deut. 33:27.

One of the most touching requests in Scripture is when Moses pleaded with God to be allowed to go over Jordan and see the Promised Land before he died. After having shepherded the children of Israel through all those long years of wandering, he yearned to see the country he had talked about so much. The promise of that goodly land created a longing that spilled over into a pathetic petition that could bring tears to anyone's eyes if he would place himself in the situation. "I pray thee, let me go over, and see the good land that is beyond Jordan." [1]

Yet God said No. Moses was to die and never cross Jordan into the Promised Land.

Many consider this a rather harsh treatment for only that one mistake at Meribah. (Surely, they figure, God should have allowed this old man, who had done so much for so long in leading Israel, to see the goodly land before he died.)

But Moses didn't think so. When God said, "Speak no more unto me of this matter," that was enough. [2] Some have the notion that God responds like a human being and might have been talked out of His stand if Moses had kept pleading. But God changes not. We dare not shape God into our own image. Whereas we might allow Moses to slip under the wire and wink at his departure from right because we would like to pad the mistake with the years of service, God does not think that way.

And Moses knew that. He chose not to complain. Even though he longed to see the Promised Land, God could not allow him passage over Jordan. The Lord had forgiven him for his sin at Meribah, but Moses knew how much harm preferential treatment would do to the people. God's impartial justice is as strong as His mercy. That is why Moses uttered no complaint. Included in some of his last words are those of our text for today, because he understood God's position of fairness. But the Lord went beyond even Moses' expectations and resurrected him—the first among men!

---

[1] Deut. 3:25.
[2] Verse 26.

ADOPTED INTO THE FAMILY OF GOD

For the Lord your God, he is God in heaven above, and in earth beneath. Joshua 2:11.

These words were spoken by a heathen prostitute living in a wall-side apartment in Jericho. Rahab the harlot, though steeped in heathenism and engaged in one of humanity's oldest professions, had early caught the significance of God's miraculous leading of His people. She knew about the great Red Sea deliverance and the latest news of how the Hebrews had wiped out the tough Amorite kings Sihon and Og. The advancing Israelites, as they made their dry-riverbed crossing of the Jordan at flood season, had sent shivers through the whole populace of her hometown. She had done a lot of thinking long before the spies knocked on her door.

The two spies Joshua sent out on a secret mission tried to slip into Jericho during the evening foot-traffic rush hour from the surrounding fields. For the best added cover they had headed directly for the place where strangers often mingled. Now, some folk have sought to show that Rahab was only an innkeeper, but careful Biblical research proves otherwise.[1] Regardless of the intended cover, the spies were spotted. Their whole scheme fell apart because Jericho was in such a state of emergency that every stranger looked suspicious.

Rahab admitted having seen the men, but in a series of lies turned the authorities away on a wild-goose chase.[2] God accepts people just as they are, wherever they are. As the light and truth of God's power to protect and save developed, her infant faith grew into a deeper experience.

Although her former reputation stayed with her in name, it actually stands as proof of God's ability to transform. That scarlet cord dangling from the window apartment in Jericho is a reminder of her choice to become adopted into the family of God. Rahab finally appears in the faith hall of fame, for it is written, "By faith the harlot Rahab perished not."[3]

---

[1] *The SDA Bible Commentary*, vol. 2, p. 182.
[2] *Ibid.*, p. 183.
[3] Heb. 11:31.

THE FATAL CHOICE

And the Lord said unto Joshua, Get thee up; wherefore liest thou thus upon thy face? Israel hath sinned, . . . for they have even taken of the accursed thing. Joshua 7:10, 11.

The seemingly invincible forces of Israel were stunned. The men from Ai had chased the Hebrews in an embarrassing rout that left thirty-six Israelites dead. What had gone wrong? How could God's people suffer such an ignominious defeat after they had so swiftly smashed the superior forces of Bashan on or near the Golan Heights, wiped out the heathen east of Jordan, and recently cleaned up on the fortress city of Jericho? What made it so embarrassing was that Ai was such a little burg.

But the voice of God thundered. It was a time for prompt action, not repining. There was sin in the camp. The whole nation was accountable for the crime of theft. In defiance of the most direct command, someone had stolen goods out of Jericho.

Secretly Achan had snatched a costly royal Shinar mantle from the spoils, plus silver and a wedge of gold. His covetousness, which had gradually taken a grip on him, held him firmly at the time the Israelites were mopping up Jericho. Achan had chosen to accept his covetous tendencies rather than turn to the Lord in full obedience. And worse, he kept choosing this evil trait even when the Lord provided time for repentance.

Lots were cast. And down the line in a most impressive ceremony came the call—first the tribe, then the family, then the household. Achan just stood there, deciding to remain silent to the very last. Finally the finger of God selected him, and then, and only then, did he admit his crime.

But an admission like this in the face of indisputable facts is no confession. Achan, like so many others caught in the clutches of crime, would never have confessed if he had thought he could get away with it. And even then he referred to the stolen property as "a goodly Babylonish garment." [1]

----
[1] Joshua 7:21.

DECEIVED BY VISUAL AIDS

And the men . . . asked not counsel at the mouth of the Lord. Joshua 9:14.

With the destruction of both Jericho and Ai, the Gibeonites living in the four hill cities to the west knew they were next. But instead of accepting the Lord's provision for all Canaanites if they would renounce their idolatry and connect themselves with Israel, they resorted to stratagem.[1]

It was a strange delegation that quietly edged into the camp at Gilgal. Their beasts of burden were loaded with old sacks and patched wineskins. The ambassadors themselves wore worn-out sandals and old clothes. The Gibeonites had selected the very best visual aids and their top actors for the occasion.

"We've come from a far country," they explained, "and we'd like to make a treaty with you."

God had specifically warned Israel about making any sort of treaty with the Canaanites. That is why Joshua and his high-ranking officers had a nagging doubt. "How do we know you don't lie among us?" they asked.

This was the Gibeonites' cue. With award-winning gestures and convincing appeal they showed Joshua and his men the moldy bread that was supposed to have been taken hot out of the oven when they left. Then they gave a rundown of their wardrobe, which was seemingly proof positive that they had traveled from some distant country on the far borders at Canaan.

Joshua and his princes felt that they did not need to bother the Lord when their own eyes were apparently so trustworthy.

Three days later Israel discovered the ruse. The Gibeonites lived right in the midst of them! But the treaty had been made, and there was no backing down from the oath.

We could avoid many pitfalls in life if only we would trust in the Lord instead of leaning on our own understanding, as Joshua and his men did. "In all thy ways acknowledge him, and he shall direct thy paths."[2]

---

[1] *Patriarchs and Prophets*, pp. 505-507.
[2] Prov. 3:6.

JOSHUA'S FINEST HOUR

Then spake Joshua to the Lord . . . , and he said in the sight of Israel, Sun, stand thou still upon Gibeon; and thou, Moon, in the valley of Ajalon. Joshua 10:12.

When the word spread throughout the surrounding Canaanite communities that Gibeon had made a treaty with Israel, the other heathen nations were totally dismayed. Five Amorite kings banded together to take revenge on Gibeon for forming a league with the invading Israelites. There was no way the Gibeonites could withstand such an onslaught. They quickly dispatched a runner to Gilgal to urge Joshua and his forces to hasten to the hill country and fight for them.

Joshua made an all-night forced march and arrived just as the five kings and their superior armies were preparing for a siege.[1] The Lord had promised Joshua that He would fight for His people, and true to His word, He rained down great hailstones, killing more of the enemy than were killed by the Israelite soldiers.

But time was not on Joshua's side. He looked at the enemy scattering in headlong retreat toward their rocky strongholds. From the summit of the pass at Beth-horon he could see the sun over Gibeon to the east and the pale moon barely visible over the valley of Ajalon to the west.[2] The enemy must not have time to regroup. It was imperative to strike when they were totally disorganized. The precise moment had come for his famous prayer.

And God heard. The sun did not set for "about a whole day."[3]

Joshua failed to ask God about the battle with Ai. He forgot to seek the Lord regarding the Gibeonites. But this time he chose to turn to the Lord instead of relying on himself. And that decision made all the difference.

"Those who achieve the greatest results are those who rely most implicitly upon the Almighty Arm. The man who commanded, 'Sun, stand still upon Gibeon; and thou, Moon, in the valley of Ajalon,' is the man who for hours lay prostrate upon the earth in prayer in the camp at Gilgal. The men of prayer are the men of power."[4]

---

[1] *Patriarchs and Prophets*, p. 508.
[2] *The SDA Bible Commentary*, vol. 2, p. 226.
[3] Joshua 10:13.
[4] *Patriarchs and Prophets*, p. 509.

THE COURAGEOUS CHOICE

Now, lo, I am this day fourscore and five years old. As yet I am as strong this day as I was in the day that Moses sent me. . . . Now therefore give me this mountain. Joshua 14:10-12.

Just before Joshua began distributing the Promised Land among the various tribes there came a most poignant moment in the history of Israel. An 85-year-old man edged his way forward to lay claim to a piece of real estate. He had reached a time in life when many would be content to sit in a rocker and reminisce about past winters, but that was not for Caleb. He and Joshua were now the oldest members in the camp, and Caleb wanted Hebron. "Give me this mountain" rings with an exultant courage based on faith in the God of heaven.

And why Hebron, of all places? Caleb knew something about that place. It was the very seat of the dreaded Anakim giants who had caused such quaking among the doubting spies so many years before. Caleb wasn't speaking of the city of Hebron alone, but of the surrounding country where the giants were now hiding in considerable force in the caves and rocky hillsides.[1]

Caleb's choice was not based on the fact that he was as strong as he had ever been. It was not just that he had lived a healthful life and could still be a warrior. It was, as he put it to Joshua, because "I wholly followed the Lord my God."[2] He took God at His word. Caleb held no reservations. He didn't wait to play it safe, but he trusted in the might of the Lord. When God said He would send His fear before the Israelites to drive out the enemy, Caleb believed every word of it. And that is why he lost himself in a great cause. He had a sense of mission for his Master. And he not only took Hebron but kept right on fighting. He did not settle down to enjoy his inheritance.

Often when we are faced with seemingly insurmountable odds and the temptations from the enemy face us like giants, it would be wise to remember this old warrior's request and say with him, "Give me this mountain!"

[1] *The SDA Bible Commentary,* vol. 2, p. 248.
[2] Joshua 14:8.

THE ANSWER TO THE COWARDLY TRIBES

And Joshua spake unto the house of Joseph, . . . Thou shalt drive out the Canaanites, though they have iron chariots, and though they be strong. Joshua 17:17, 18.

During the division of Palestine the tribes of Joseph, Ephraim, and the half tribe of Manasseh living on the west bank of Jordan came to Joshua with a request for more land. Since they were of such superior numbers, they demanded a double portion of property.[1] They already owned the richest land around, including the fifty-mile (eighty-kilometer) coastal plain of Sharon, but they wanted more. They had an exalted opinion of themselves and felt that because Joshua belonged to the tribe of Ephraim he would certainly give them some preference.

Joshua never stooped to argue their numerical greatness, but he remained inflexible. "If you are such a great people," he told them, "and God has blessed you, He will continue to help you conquer the land. You are certainly able to take care of yourselves."

"The hill country isn't enough for us," they complained. "Besides, all the Canaanites that dwell in the valley have chariots of iron."

Ah! So that was it! What they really were admitting was that they lacked faith and courage to meet the challenge of driving out the enemy. They wanted the real estate already conquered. Their complaint of not having enough property was based on a choice not to fight for it.

Frequently we may slip into that cowardly choice of wanting to avoid conflict with our sins. We feel that it is impossible to overcome them, so, like the tribes of Joseph, we try to ease our conscience by adjusting our lives to accommodate them.

Ephraim never did drive out the enemy but allowed them to live in their midst as long as they paid tribute. But it didn't work. In the end the close proximity to idolatry destroyed from within. As it was later written, "Ephraim is joined to idols: let him alone."[2]

---

[1] *Patriarchs and Prophets*, p. 513.
[2] Hosea 4:17.

A MISUNDERSTANDING OVER ED

And the children of Reuben and the children of Gad called the altar Ed: for it shall be a witness between us that the Lord is God. Joshua 22:34.

After the distribution of the land of the various tribes, Joshua summoned the tribes of Reuben, Gad, and the half tribe of Manasseh. For six or seven years these tribes had fought faithfully beside their brethren for the promised property.[1] Now it was time to go home across the Jordan, and Joshua gave his final blessing as they departed.

It may have been while en route home that the idea struck them that it might be a good idea to erect a great altar just like the one that had been set up in Shiloh. In time their children might be looked upon as strangers because the tabernacle was so far from the east bank of Jordan, and this would be a reminder that they too belonged to Israel. Unfortunately they did not inform the other tribes of what they were doing when they built this altar called Ed, which means "witness," near where the children of Israel had made their miraculous Jordan crossing.

Soon rumors went the rounds, and the strange tidings drifting back suggested apostasy. What were these two-and-one-half tribes up to anyway? The death penalty was to be enforced for anyone who built an altar of sacrifice other than the authorized one.

Top-ranking leaders from the other tribes converged at Shiloh. There was a lot of heated anger and excitement. The hotheads among them wanted to go to war immediately against the two-and-one-half tribes living on the east side of Jordan.[2] Fortunately the more levelheaded ones prevailed, and finally, with Phinehas as leader, they sent a delegation over to see what was happening.

To their credit the two-and-one-half tribes chose not to answer in kind, even in the face of false accusations. Civil war was averted because they knew that their own motives were right and they could afford to be calm and considerate.

[1] *The SDA Bible Commentary*, vol. 2, p. 286.
[2] *Patriarchs and Prophets*, p. 518.

THE OLD LEADER'S FINAL APPEAL

**Choose you this day whom ye will serve; . . . but as for me
and my house, we will serve the Lord. Joshua 24:15.**

Those words were spoken by an old warrior who stood before
the heads of the Israelite tribes and their representatives that day at
Shechem. Joshua, who wanted to give the leaders a final appeal
before he died, deliberately chose Shechem because it held so
many sacred memories. God's covenant with Abraham and Jacob,
and the nation of Israel itself when they took their solemn vows
years before, was wrapped up in this place.

But Joshua knew something. He wasn't the kind of leader who
is interested only in cosmetics, in glossing over the real situation.
He was a realist to the core. He knew that some of the people were
secretly worshiping idols. There was still plenty of mopping up to
do to clear the region of the heathen, but the armies had been
disbanded, and people were settling down. And that situation
induced some to turn to those heathen rites, which would most
certainly be their downfall.

Joshua urged the leaders to consider if they honestly wanted to
become like the surrounding heathen with their degrading
religious services of perverted sex and sacrificing of children. He
stung the whole assembly that day with bold words about the
contrasting conditions in those nations who had been wiped out by
the advancing armies of God's people. He reminded the leaders
that God Himself had sent hornets ahead and not one of those
wicked nations had been able to withstand the forces of Heaven.
So he wanted them all to make a choice that day—a choice
between the gods of the heathen and the Lord of heaven. The
decision was theirs. But as for him and his household, the choice
was final. They would serve the Lord.

If ever a leader presented the distinct lines of what a living faith
in Christ means, it was Joshua.

THE GENERATION THAT KNEW NOT

And there arose another generation after them, which knew not the Lord, nor yet the works which he had done for Israel. Judges 2:10.

So long as Joshua and the elders that outlived the great leader were alive, the people of Israel served the Lord. But then the religion of the new generation began to unravel. Our text indicates that they "knew not the Lord." That doesn't mean they had poor memories or a lack of historians to remind them of God's leading in the past. It simply points to the tragic fact that this new generation did not choose to have an experimental religion. Instead the people desired the self-indulgent life of settling down with the enemy. Somehow they never realized the truth that coexistence with idolatry would come with a very high price tag. They would pay again and again until ultimately they would find themselves in abject slavery to the very people they had originally come to subdue.

But they had received plenty of warnings. At the very outset of Judges 2 the angel of the Lord appeared on the scene, reminding the people how God had led them from Egypt to the Promised Land. Instead of enjoying the fruits of a peaceful experience in the region God had chosen, the messenger reminded them that the enemy in their midst would be "thorns in your sides," and the gods of the heathen would be a "snare unto you."

The people wept when they heard this. They wept in shame at the truth of what had already transpired.[1] And while it is one thing to weep and feel sorry for past mistakes, it is quite another to dry the eyes and go forward in true repentance, refusing to return to the old ways. Apparently the people wept more for failures than in deep repentance.

We would do well to remember just what it was the generation following Joshua and the elders forgot. To refuse to build a life around the full knowledge of God's providential guidance of the past is to pave the way for future spiritual failure.

[1] *The SDA Bible Commentary*, vol. 2, pp. 316, 317.

TWO CHOICES AND A DUET

Then sang Deborah and Barak . . . , saying, Praise ye the Lord for the avenging of Israel, when the people willingly offered themselves. Judges 5:1, 2.

Somewhere on the road between Ramah and Bethel grew a special palm tree where Deborah the prophetess sat and judged the people who came to her for counsel.[1] She is the only judge mentioned as possessing the prophetic gift, and divine inspiration certainly was needed at the time.[2] For twenty years the strong Canaanite forces along the northern border had oppressed Israel, but now God had given the command for deliverance.[3]

So Deborah sent for Barak, who lived about ninety miles (145 kilometers) to the north in Kedesh.[4] Barak had been selected by Heaven to meet the forces of Sisera at Mount Tabor. Deborah made it plain that God would deliver Israel down there on the plains by the Kishon River.

Now, it is one thing to give nodding approval of the prophetic gift, but it is quite another to believe in it to the point of placing your whole reputation and future on inspiration. But Barak did just that. He chose to recruit the ten thousand men as directed, and he led them into battle on one condition: " 'If you will go with me, I will go,' " he told Deborah. " 'But if you will not go with me, I will not go.' "[5] He knew of her morale-boosting abilities and the power of her presence.

Deborah had to make a choice too. She could have hemmed and hawed about her position and her need to stay there under the palm tree. But she trusted implicitly the voice from heaven.

The combination of those two choices in mutual desire to deliver Israel prodded the people of the Lord into action. As our text says, "The people willingly offered themselves."

Barak means "lightning,"[6] and it is written that Deborah was "the wife of Lapidoth," which means "torches" or "flashes."[7] The combination of bold, fiery leadership produced the results. Sisera was utterly defeated and killed, while fleeing for his life. No wonder these two could sing their duet of victory for God.

[1] *The SDA Bible Commentary*, vol. 2, p. 330.
[2] *Ibid.*
[3] *Ibid.*, p. 329.
[4] *Ibid.*, map opposite p. 385.
[5] Judges 4:8, R.S.V.
[6] *SDA Bible Dictionary*, p. 120.
[7] *The SDA Bible Commentary*, vol. 2, p. 330.

GOD'S CHOICE OF MEN

And the Lord said unto Gideon, By the three hundred men that lapped will I save you, and deliver the Midianites into thine hand. Judges 7:7.

For seven years the wild, nomadic Midianite hordes swept through the land, plundering like a devouring plague. The Israelites had forsaken their God, and He had left them to their fate of oppression from this fierce desert people. But the time was ripe for deliverance.

When God called Gideon to lead an attack on these marauding forces it was all this humble man could do to visualize how he could be a general. Thus the double fleece check before engaging in such a dangerous venture.

Recruiting an army in those days did not include draft cards, but the blowing of a trumpet. And when the final head count was made, Gideon had 32,000 men. But about four miles to the north of the Hill Moreh, the Midianites spread out 135,000 strong.[1] That was why Gideon hesitated in making the usual prebattle proclamation. All those who had just gotten married, built a new house and hadn't dedicated it, or planted a vineyard and hadn't eaten the grapes could go home.[2] More than this, the law stated that anybody who was fearful of combat could pack up and leave too. Gideon's army looked puny enough without making that sort of announcement!

Then God spoke. "You have too many men." With a sick feeling, Gideon watched as more than two thirds of his army headed for home.

Again God spoke. "The people are yet too many; bring them down unto the water, and I will try them for thee there."[3]

It looked like an immediate advance against the Midianites, but nearly ten thousand men got casually down on their knees to drink from the stream, while only three hundred scooped up water in their hands while keeping an eye on the enemy.

"By the simplest means character is often tested. Those who in time of peril were intent upon supplying their own wants were not the men to be trusted in an emergency."[4]

---

[1] *The SDA Bible Commentary*, vol. 2, p. 347.
[2] *Patriarchs and Prophets*, pp. 548, 549.
[3] Judges 7:4.
[4] *Ibid.*, p. 549.

AN ANSWER TO ARROGANCE

A soft answer turneth away wrath: but grievous words stir up anger. Prov. 15:1.

The tribe of Ephraim was the most populous and important tribe in the northern sector of Palestine. And it went to their heads. They became increasingly arrogant and jealous for their ranking position. It had started when Joshua was leader. Since he was an Ephraimite and they were such a large tribe, the notion stuck that somehow nothing should be done without their first being consulted.

When Gideon gave the call to arms, the Ephraimites remained behind. Only when the victory against the Midianites was sure did they rally to his call to cut off the enemy as they fled across the Jordan. Instead of rejoicing in the victory over a common enemy, they met Gideon with a mean-spirited reproach. They wanted credit for the victory and were ticked off that Gideon should even go into battle without first consulting them. " 'Why didn't you call us when you went to fight the Midianites?' " they complained.[1]

The natural response to their haughty attitude and sense of superiority would have been to tell them how stupid their senseless jealousy looked in light of what happened. It would have been quite easy to meet them with a fiery rebuttal. And right there Gideon had to make a decision. His choice of a soft answer to arrogance is rarely seen, but it is most certainly worth repeating when similar situations arise.

" 'What I was able to do is nothing compared with what you have done. Even the little that you men of Ephraim did is worth more than what my whole clan has done. After all, through the power of God you killed the two Midianite chiefs, Oreb and Zeeb. What have I done to compare with that?' "[2]

The Ephraimites did achieve a victory by their secondary efforts at the Jordan, but it is noteworthy to watch Gideon under stress very diplomatically turning aside their blatant envy and wrath by not even mentioning his own achievements. His self-control has left us with a quality lesson in courtesy to appease anger.

[1] Judges 8:1, T.E.V.
[2] Verses 2, 3, T.E.V.

SNARE OF THE GOLDEN EPHOD

And Gideon made an ephod. . . : and all Israel went thither a whoring after it: which thing became a snare unto Gideon, and to his house. Judges 8:27.

Gideon's nobility of character shone brilliantly when he refused to let the people crown him king after the destruction of the Midianites. The Israelites looked to him as their leader and wanted him and his son to rule over them. But Gideon turned down the offer, saying, "The Lord shall rule over you." [1]

But then something tragic happened. Gideon called for the people to bring the most valuable of the booty they had taken. And the people gladly gave. Spreading a garment on the ground, they threw down those golden ornaments, which came to about 42 pounds 10 ounces (19.3 kilograms) in all. [2] From this he fashioned a golden ephod, an imitation of the breastplate worn by the high priest.

How could this brave and noble man set such a bad example? What could make him choose to construct such an object in the first place. Satan suggested several things to Gideon that might explain his thinking.

When the angel appeared to him, he commanded Gideon to offer a sacrifice on the rock. Gideon felt sure that he had been appointed a priest by that act. He did not consult the Lord about this, but proceeded according to his feelings. Further, he may have been resentful toward the Ephraimites for their arrogant behavior and may not have wanted to go to Shiloh, where the tabernacle was located, to worship. [3]

The problem was, Gideon never asked the Lord about any of his plans, but went ahead on his own. The results were tragic. The very man who had chopped down idols and delivered Israel led them back into idolatry.

Gideon's story is a warning to all of us. No matter how good our intentions, every act influences others, especially if we hold positions of leadership. Our only safety lies in humbly seeking the Lord as Gideon did prior to his spiritually fatal mistake.

[1] Judges 8:23.
[2] *The SDA Bible Commentary*, vol. 2, p. 354.
[3] *Ibid.*, p. 355.

THE DANGER OF RASH WORDS

Be not rash with thy mouth, and let not thine heart be hasty to utter any thing before God: for God is in heaven, and thou upon earth: therefore let thy words be few. Eccl. 5:2.

It would be difficult to find a more dramatic demonstration of rash words than the vow uttered by Jephthah just prior to his combat with the Ammonites. The Spirit of God had come over him as he passed through Gilead and Manasseh to recruit troops, but the presence of the Spirit of God does not overrule freedom of choice. And His blessing does not guarantee infallibility.[1] So under the emotional stress of the moment as he was about to enter upon his dangerous mission, Jephthah blurted out a rash vow:

"If God will deliver the children of Ammon into my hands, then whoever comes to meet me through the doors of my house when I return in peace shall surely be the Lord's, and I will offer it up as a burnt offering."

As so many who make pledges in times of danger, Jephthah fell into the trap of uttering words that he had not thought through. It was a snap choice uttered at the wrong time. No Hebrew was obligated to fulfill a vow if it meant performing a wrong act.[2] One wonders what would have happened if it had been a dog that trotted out of his house?

But it wasn't a dog. When he returned victorious from battle, out danced his one-and-only child. His daughter was so glad to see him that she cavorted with her timbrel toward him, joyous at the great victory and the return of her daddy. Jephthah blanched. Stunned by her presence, he tore his clothes in mourning.

Did he offer her as a burnt offering? We have no way of knowing for sure what happened. It is simply one of those puzzling passages of Scripture that provides us with no definite conclusion.

We must leave the story veiled in mystery—the way it comes to us. Yet out of this tragic account still stands the lesson of the rash vow. We should avoid uttering hasty words at all costs.

---

[1] *The SDA Bible Commentary*, vol. 2, p. 376.
[2] *Patriarchs and Prophets*, p. 506.

HAUGHTY ONCE TOO OFTEN
Pride goeth before destruction, and an haughty spirit before a fall. Prov. 16:18.

The Ephraimites had a habit of remaining very passive toward enemy oppression or attack, but when others took the initiative and won a victory for Israel they elbowed their way forward and arrogantly demanded recognition. Gideon met this envious foolishness with conciliatory words. When the Ephraimites accosted Jephthah they were even meaner. This time they came splashing across the Jordan fords into Gilead and mouthed haughty words that ultimately led to their undoing.

Confronting Jephthah, they shouted, " 'Why did you cross the border to fight the Ammonites without calling us to go with you? We'll burn the house down over your head!'

"But Jephthah told them, 'My people and I had a serious quarrel with the Ammonites. I did call you, but you would not rescue me from them. When I saw that you were not going to, I risked my life and crossed the border to fight them, and the Lord gave me victory over them. So why are you coming up to fight me now?' " [1]

Good question. They had allowed their pride to drive them into a decision to start a war. In spite of Jephthah's reasonable answer, they began taunting their relatives by saying that the tribes on the east bank of the Jordan were fugitives, the worst of scum, the very dregs of society.

It was enough. Through signal fires and trumpet calls, Jephthah rallied his army again and took control of the fords.[2] Suddenly the Ephraimites found out what being a fugitive was all about. They stampeded for the river in desperate flight.[3]

Because of all the traffic across the fords, the only way to identify the Ephraimites was to have them pronounce the word *Shibboleth,* meaning "a bunch of twigs." [4] Any word with that beginning sound would have worked. The Ephraimites' dialect did not include the necessary sounds. They said Sibboleth instead, and so forty-two thousand of them perished. It was a humiliating defeat for such haughtiness.

[1] Judges 12:1-3, T.E.V.
[2] *The SDA Bible Commentary,* vol. 2, p. 379.
[3] *Ibid.,* p. 380.
[4] *SDA Bible Dictionary,* p. 1026.

THE DEMANDS OF INFATUATION

Then his father and his mother said unto him, Is there never a woman among the daughters of thy brethren, or among all my people, that thou goest to take a wife of the uncircumcised Philistines? And Samson said unto his father, Get her for me; for she pleaseth me well. Judges 14:3.

Here we have a classic case of youthful stubbornness in rebelling against the authority of God and all the careful early parental preparation, training, and counsel. Samson wanted his own way. He found infatuation with this young Philistine woman far more pleasing to his tastes than anything he had experienced in the local church.

Manoah and his wife must have felt the pangs all parents with high spiritual values feel when their child rebels against what they have done to guide him toward God.[1] Twice the Angel of the Lord—Christ Himself—had appeared to them, explaining in most emphatic terms the need for temperance and the effect of prenatal influence. Faithfully they had accepted their responsibility and had carried out the divine instructions as best they knew.

But somewhere along the way Samson made a decision to serve himself instead. "Had Samson obeyed the divine commands as faithfully as his parents had done, his would have been a nobler and happier destiny. But association with idolaters corrupted him."[2] Even the constant repeating of the marvelous story of the Angel ascending in the flame after meeting with Manoah and his wife didn't faze Samson. It was all very marvelous, but "Get her for me." Miracles and spiritual matters meant little to him because of the emotional tug of infatuation.

The persistence of this sad choice did not die with Samson. Time has worn smooth the hackneyed argument that those not of the faith somehow are far more attractive. And once that choice is made, Satan sees to it that emotions run faster than reason. "To all who seek first to honor Him, God has promised wisdom; but there is no promise to those who are bent upon self-pleasing."[3]

---

[1] *The SDA Bible Commentary*, vol. 2, pp. 383, 384.
[2] *Patriarchs and Prophets*, p. 562.
[3] *Ibid.*, p. 563.

SAMSON'S LAST CHOICE

And Samson called unto the Lord, and said, O Lord God, remember me, I pray thee, and strengthen me, I pray thee, only this once. Judges 16:28.

The story of Samson is one of wine, women, and song. And the tunes for those songs invariably had heavy overtones of sensuality and lewdness. He simply did not choose to bring his clamoring wild passions under control.

The banner headlines of his wrenching the Gaza city gate from its place and carrying it and the posts and bars to the top of the hill en route to Hebron were startling indeed. The problem was, such news items also carried the behind-the-scene report that he had gone to Gaza to visit a harlot! So Samson would have been very much of an embarrassment to us. We would not have enjoyed hearing about all of his extracurricular activities.

Once he married outside the faith, he was led to a tragic ending. His mistress down in the Valley of Sorek finally did him in. Delilah was a flirt. That's what her name means—*"flirt."* [1] She was a charmer. He couldn't take it. That was why her consistent whining finally got to him. It wasn't the haircut but a final disregard for God that weakened Samson.

Then Samson embarked on another trip to Gaza, this time for painful Philistine eye surgery that left him blind. But somewhere in the dreary days of darkness as he sweat doing excruciating menial labor, Samson saw deep into his own soul. That was when he cried out in profound repentance.

When the day arrived for the grand festival in honor of Dagon, the fish god, Samson's heart was obviously with the Lord. [2] The combination of his own repentance, exaltation of the heathen god by the Philistines, and his blindness turned Samson's last choice into a prayer that brought the house down. It was a stunning defeat for the Philistines, yet imagine what could have been the end of Samson's career had he chosen to turn to God earlier!

---

[1] *SDA Bible Dictionary,* p. 281.
[2] *The SDA Bible Commentary,* vol. 2, p. 399.

NAOMI'S MAGNANIMOUS CHOICE

And Naomi said unto her two daughters in law, . . . The Lord deal kindly with you, as ye have dealt with the dead, and with me. Ruth 1:8.

Those words were spoken by a woman who knew suffering. They are noble words, uttered from a heart touched by the tenderness of profound love. Naomi chose to put self aside and urged her daughters-in-law to return to their homeland rather than press her legitimate, customary claims upon them. But to understand the full impact of what she was saying, we must go back a decade.

The famine-choked region of Judah had driven Elimelech, his wife, Naomi, and their two sickly sons from their home in Bethlehem to the high tableland east of the Dead Sea in Moab. There amid the abundant supply of water, the rich soil, and semitropical vegetation, this little family had hoped to start again. It wouldn't be easy living in a foreign land, but at least the Moabites spoke a similar language.[1]

Then tragedy struck. Elimelech died, leaving Naomi with her sons Mahlon, or "sickness," and Chilion, or "wasting." [2] After the death of their father, the boys married Moabite girls, hoping that sons would be born to perpetuate their father's name.[3] Besides this, they obviously thought of their widowed mother, who would need help in her old age. But within a short time both boys died, leaving three widows sorrowing together.

When Naomi heard that the famine was over in her homeland, she naturally started her trek north and westward. Orpah and Ruth, in true oriental custom, followed her. But as they neared the borders of Moab, Naomi realized the tremendous sacrifice these Moabite girls were making. So three times she urged them to return and find husbands for themselves.

We must not misunderstand Naomi's urging. Of course she wanted them to stay beside her. Ruth and Orpah meant much to her. But Naomi, the ideal mother-in-law, exemplifies the truth about the God in heaven. She wanted the girls free to make their own choice.

---

[1] *The SDA Bible Commentary*, vol. 2, p. 429.
[2] *SDA Bible Dictionary*, pp. 697, 203.
[3] *The SDA Bible Commentary*, vol. 2, p. 430.

THE EFFECTIVE WITNESS

And Ruth said, Intreat me not to leave thee, or to return from following after thee: for whither thou goest, I will go; and where thou lodgest, I will lodge: thy people shall be my people, and thy God my God. Ruth 1:16.

It would be difficult to find a more sublime affirmation of love and trust. Ruth stammered out these words as tears streamed down her face and as she clung to her mother-in-law.

Naomi had urged her Moabite daughters-in-law to return home. She had kissed them, and they had cried together there on the borders of Moab. Finally Orpah decided that she ought to return home. She loved Naomi dearly, but the tug of her homeland was greater.

Now Ruth stood alone. With Orpah gone, it was more difficult to decide. Yet, Ruth was different. She saw something that held her like a great lodestone. The sweet influence of Naomi's life was far greater than any pull of relatives, friends, or home country. Ruth had seen the true God reflected in the life of her mother-in-law, and that effective witness helped her make the final choice. Even if it meant living in a strange land, Ruth knew she would feel most comfortable with Naomi and her God.

The story of Ruth's subsequent marriage to Boaz makes fascinating reading. The unique blend of ancient customs and providential guidance furnishes clues as to how God manages to lead when we submit to Him.

Boaz, undoubtedly a middle-aged man, married this young Moabitess with no prejudice in his heart. His own father had married Rahab, the harlot, and he had grown up in a home that displayed the power of God's winning ways.[1]

The book of Ruth closes with a most interesting genealogy. Ruth and Boaz had a son named Obed, who became the father of Jesse, the father of David—in direct line of the progenitors of Jesus. And it all came to pass because a mother in Israel showed such a pronounced likeness to a gracious heavenly Father that Ruth the Moabitess could not resist His love.

---

[1] *The SDA Bible Commentary,* vol. 2, pp. 434, 435.

THE RETURN OF A PRECIOUS GIFT

For this child I prayed; and the Lord hath given me my petition which I asked of him: therefore also I have lent him to the Lord. 1 Sam. 1:27, 28.

Hannah found herself on the receiving end of a persistent harassment especially designed to bring her to a premature grave. She was happily married to Elkanah, a very wealthy and influential Levite who loved the Lord. But as year after year passed and she remained childless, the situation changed. It was important in those days to perpetuate the father's name, so according to the customs of the times Elkanah married a second wife.

Enter Peninnah. The Scriptures simply report, "and Peninnah had children, but Hannah had no children," [1] which says it all. "Peninnah, the new wife, was jealous and narrow-minded, and she bore herself with pride and insolence." [2] "Satan employed her as his agent to harass, and if possible exasperate and destroy, one of God's faithful children." [3] Hannah's hopes were crushed and her life made perfectly miserable as Peninnah ridiculed her at every turn.

Finally, during one of the annual feasts when Elkanah had given Hannah a double portion of food to indicate that his affection for her was as strong as if she had a son, Hannah refused to eat. How could she enjoy a meal when Peninnah was at it again with her jealousy-ridden taunts? Elkanah tried his best to comfort Hannah, but nothing worked.

And that was when she prayed. With tears welling up in her eyes she poured out her heart longing for a baby boy. The old priest Eli saw her lips moving and assumed that she was drunk. His sharp rebuke startled Hannah. With quivering lips she explained that she had been praying. Eli, deeply touched by this, pronounced a blessing instead.

A year later Hannah held a baby son in her arms. From anguish of spirit, God had allowed her to triumph, and she followed through with her vow to give back to the Lord this precious gift—Samuel—as long as he lived.

---

[1] 1 Sam. 1:2.
[2] *Patriarchs and Prophets*, p. 569.
[3] *The SDA Bible Commentary*, Ellen G. White Comments, on 1 Sam. 1:8, p. 1008.

VOICE IN THE NIGHT

And Samuel grew, and the Lord was with him, and did let none of his words fall to the ground. 1 Sam. 3:19.

It is hard to think of Samuel without thinking of dedication. From the moment of his birth, his mother, Hannah, dedicated him to the Lord. And at a very early age Samuel himself chose to follow through with that dedication.

It wasn't easy. Once his mother placed him in Eli's charge he was exposed to a lot more than the religious surroundings of the sanctuary. The high priest's sons, Hophni and Phinehas, were the very embodiment of evil and hypocrisy. Their consistent thievery and desire to satisfy their sexual cravings when the women came to worship made the religious ceremonies stink. Samuel couldn't ask his parents about the matter; they came up only once a year. Undoubtedly Samuel felt reluctant to discuss things with Eli. So there was only one Source—God. In God's own time He would answer the puzzling question of why there was such a marked difference between His principles and the gross misconduct of spiritual leadership.

Then one night God called. Samuel was sound asleep when he heard his name. He thought Eli had called, and twice he jumped out of bed and ran to the old man's side. The last time, Eli sensed that it was the Lord and gave Samuel the exact words to say when the voice came again: "Speak, Lord; for thy servant heareth." [1]

Samuel crawled back into his own little bed, but it is doubtful that he slept. Tucking the covers up tightly under his chin, he probably peered into the darkness and waited breathlessly for God to call again.

"Samuel! Samuel!"

Samuel was so excited that he forgot to say Lord. But God understood, and the startling message He gave, of how He was about to end the evil, thrust the boy into the role of prophet. "When but twelve years old, the son of Hannah received his special commission from the Most High." [2] It was the final stamp of approval from the God of heaven on a youngster who chose to follow his Maker.

---

[1] 1 Sam. 3:9.
[2] *The SDA Bible Commentary,* Ellen G. White Comments, on 1 Sam. 3:4, p. 1010.

GOOD MAN, POOR FATHER

And the Lord said to Samuel, Behold, I will do a thing in Israel, at which both the ears of every one that heareth it shall tingle. In that day I will perform against Eli. . . . I will judge his house . . . because his sons made themselves vile, and he restrained them not. 1 Sam. 3:11-13.

When God spoke to Samuel that night, His words were not words of sweet peace and tranquillity. The first revelation Samuel received as a prophet came as a divine rebuke against the house of Eli because of an overindulgent father.

Although he was priest and judge of Israel, Eli had chosen the path of least resistance in dealing with his sons. Hophni and Phinehas had always been able to mold their dad to suit their own stubborn desires. They did what they pleased. And because they did, they never learned to respect him as a parent, or God as divine ruler. They grew up totally undisciplined, becoming a curse not only to Eli but to all Israel.

"Many are now making a similar mistake. They think they know a better way of training their children than that which God has given in His word. They foster wrong tendencies in them, urging as an excuse, 'They are too young to be punished. Wait till they become older, and can be reasoned with.' Thus wrong habits are left to strengthen until they become second nature."[1]

When Eli finally did get around to saying anything to his sons it was a flabby rebuke. Telling them "naughty, naughty" when the obvious stench of their immoral conduct with the women who came to worship was so strong that it couldn't be ignored anymore was too little too late. Hophni and Phinehas ignored the old man and went on their indulgent way.

Eli's great sin was in passing over lightly the crimes of his rebellious sons, who occupied a sacred office. "He should first have attempted to restrain evil by mild measures; but if these did not avail, he should have subdued the wrong by the severest means."[2] It was a faulty choice.

---

[1] *Patriarchs and Prophets*, pp. 578, 579.
[2] *Ibid.*, p. 578.

THE SONS OF BELIAL

Now the sons of Eli were sons of Belial; they knew not the Lord. 1 Sam. 2:12.

Hophni and Phinehas were by blood relationship the sons of Eli, but by selfish choice they were the sons of Belial, which literally means "sons without worth." [1] Moses had described those who urged their fellow Israelites to bow down to other gods as "children of Belial," and centuries later the apostle Paul used Belial as a proper name for Satan. [2] So as these boys grew up and consistently made decisions to serve their own carnal cravings, they became essentially "sons of Satan." And while it is true that Eli played his part in not restraining them early in life, it was their choice in the end to continue their headstrong direction.

With each warning God gave to turn them from their evil course there was a more determined resistance to restraint. God's forbearance only hardened their hearts further. The problem was, their influence as priests infected all Israel like a dread disease. That is why God allowed a chain of circumstances to arise that would punish sin with sin.

When the Philistines attacked Israel and about four thousand of God's people lost their lives, the Israelites asked why the Lord had smitten them before the Philistines. Looking to the ark of the covenant as some sort of magical charm, they decided to take it into battle against the enemy. Without sensing any regret for their own sins, Hophni and Phinehas escorted the sacred ark of God into battle amid great rejoicing among the Hebrews.

This act sealed their doom. The Philistines rallied to fight more fiercely than ever before, and caused the Israelites, who had entered the battle without prayer or the blessing of God, to beat a precipitous retreat. Not only were thirty thousand men, including Hophni and Phinehas, killed that day but also the ark of God was taken by the hated Philistines.

Both young men paid the price for their stubborn, selfish choices.

---

[1] *The SDA Bible Commentary,* vol. 2, p. 462.
[2] *Ibid.*

REVIVAL AND SEVERE TEST

The children of Israel did put away Baalim and Ashtaroth, and served the Lord. 1 Sam. 7:4.

Ground down for forty years by Philistine bondage, the children of Israel seemed to lose all sense of God's power to lead them. Even after the sacred ark had been miraculously returned to them, it took God's people another twenty years to figure out that God had not deserted them, but that they had turned their backs on Him.[1]

During that time they were essentially in double bondage, not only to the heathen Philistines but also to their gods, as well. Somehow both the male and female deities held a special attraction for the Israelites. Baal supposedly cared for the vegetation and their livestock. And Ashtoreth, the goddess of fertility, encouraged the lowest forms of worship possible.[2] This goddess of sexual love was represented by a nude woman with grossly accentuated sex features, and it was during the act of worshiping this deity that the use of temple prostitutes and wild sex orgies took place.[3]

Is it any wonder that Samuel finally called for a revival?

But that very gathering stirred up suspicions among the Philistines, who considered this assembly a declaration of independence. The Israelites were totally unprepared for war, and when the news reached them that the enemy forces were on the march, they turned to Samuel to lead them to the Lord. "Cease not to cry unto the Lord our God for us," they pleaded.[4]

It was a severe test, not only for Samuel, who had to wait for the Lord while watching the marshaling enemy army out of the corner of his eye, but to the people themselves, who might panic.

But their choice to serve God was heartfelt and deep, and He could then protect them. This time He sent a thunderstorm that totally discomfited the enemy. And once they were routed, Samuel erected a stone monument called Ebenezer, saying, "Hitherto hath the Lord helped us."[5] We too should have memories of our revival victories.

---

[1] *The SDA Bible Commentary*, vol. 2, pp. 480, 481.
[2] *SDA Bible Dictionary*, pp. 88, 104.
[3] *The SDA Bible Commentary*, vol. 2, p. 480.
[4] 1 Sam. 7:8.
[5] Verse 12.

REJECTING GOD

And the Lord said unto Samuel, Hearken unto the voice of the people in all that they say unto thee: for they have not rejected thee, but they have rejected me, that I should not reign over them. 1 Sam. 8:7.

The years slipped by and Samuel, who had served the people as prophet, judge, and priest, was crowding retirement age. He had appointed his sons to help him in his work, but neither Joel nor Abiah were of the same caliber as their father. It is written of them that they took bribes and perverted judgment. They were more interested in cash than in religious service.

Samuel hadn't really learned from Eli's mistake. He too had been a bit too indulgent with his sons. And this gave the people the excuse they wanted.[1] "You are getting old and your sons do not walk in your ways, so make us a king like the other nations."

It hurt Samuel that they made such a faulty choice. He felt slighted after having been a father figure to the people for so long. But when he took his feelings to the Lord in prayer, God rebuked him for such thoughts. The people had not rejected Samuel, but God!

The Israelites little appreciated the theocracy. Under the kind rulership of the Lord there were never mistakes in judgment and never the complication of taxation. Their best days had always been when God was their king. They really prospered when they followed this order. It didn't take too much intelligence to realize that when they accepted God as their rightful ruler they were superior to any of the surrounding nations. But they had steadily slipped away from His laws until they were so blind as to charge God's rulership for their own failures.

It is sad when God's people fail to accept their uniqueness. The hue and cry to be like others rather than to accept the high destiny God has chosen for His people is ever a danger. The thought pattern that seeks to blend into the woodwork is a choice that ultimately destroys the effectiveness of any real witness by God's people.

---

[1] *Patriarchs and Prophets*, p. 604.

WHEN SAUL WAS GREAT

The fear of the Lord is the instruction of wisdom; and before honour is humility. Prov. 15:33.

When Saul was selected as king he had slipped away and hid among the supplies and baggage at the large assembly. The tremendous burden and responsibility of being the first king of Israel overwhelmed him. So there he was crouched down trying to hide. And when the people finally found him and he stood tall among them, they shouted, "God save the king"![1]

But not everyone shouted. There were those, especially from the larger tribes of Judah and Ephraim, who were miffed that someone from Benjamin, the smallest tribe, was chosen king. Although many of these men had been foremost in clamoring for a king, they, with noses in the air, headed back to their own tribal area. They refused to acknowledge Saul as king.

But then the scene shifted. Suddenly the Ammonites invaded the area of those tribes east of the Jordan, and their cruel king, Nahash, threatened to put out the right eye of all the menfolk of Jabesh-gilead. The people of Jabesh pleaded for a week's respite, and Nahash, thinking the time element would bring more honor to his powerful forces, let them have it.

When Saul heard the dreadful news he killed the oxen he had been using in the field, cut them into chunks, and dispatched the pieces in a meaty telegram to all Israel. Whoever would not show up for his armed forces would have his oxen treated likewise!

The draft worked. Three hundred and thirty thousand came, and Saul led them to a superb victory over a wicked enemy. But now it was suggested that he, as king, should kill those who had previously refused to acknowledge him. But Saul made a magnanimous choice. He shook his head. Nobody would be killed for that. "Instead of taking honor to himself, he gave the glory to God. Instead of showing a desire for revenge, he manifested a spirit of compassion and forgiveness. This is unmistakable evidence that the grace of God dwells in the heart."[2]

---

[1] 1 Sam. 10:24.
[2] *Patriarchs and Prophets*, p. 613.

THE KING WHO COULDN'T WAIT

And Samuel said to Saul, Thou hast done foolishly: thou hast not kept the commandment of the Lord thy God, which he commanded thee. 1 Sam. 13:13.

Saul made a serious blunder in disbanding his army after the defeat of the Ammonites.[1] Flushed with victory, the Israelites could have achieved even greater thrusts against the enemies that surrounded them. Suddenly the Philistines amassed a gigantic force at Michmash. Besides their thousands of chariots and horsemen, the record states that the people were "as the sand which is on the seashore in multitude."[2] Panic-stricken, the few men Saul had left began deserting in droves. Some splashed across the Jordan, while others hid in dens and caves. A quick head count showed that Saul had only about six hundred men left.

This was a time for genuine faith. It was a moment for reflection on how God had delivered Israel with just three hundred men under Gideon's leadership, and to wait patiently for the Lord's direction. But not Saul. Samuel had instructed him to wait a week at Gilgal, and when the prophet arrived, there would be a sacrificial approaching to God in seeking to know His will. With his army shrunk to such a mini-size, Saul simply paced back and forth during the seven days and muttered about the prophet's delay.

Ignoring the fact that only an ordained priest was to officiate, at the end of the seven days Saul stepped forward in full battle armor and offered the sacrifice to the Lord. The ceremony had no more than ended when in walked Samuel. The confrontation that ensued indicated Saul's real spirit. He met the prophet as though he was really satisfied with his actions, and explained that he had forced himself to do such a thing.

Saul's presumptuous choice was based on a faulty character. He was the kind of person who never could bring his own turbulent feelings to submit to God's plan. He had to do things his way. And so in the crisis he buckled.

---

[1] *Patriarchs and Prophets*, p. 616.
[2] 1 Sam. 13:5.

THE BRAVE DECISION

**There is no restraint to the Lord to save by many or by few.
1 Sam. 14:6.**

Those words, spoken by Jonathan, have a ring of fearless bravery to them. He uttered them at a time when his compatriots were cowering in earth holes or deserting to the enemy. That is why Jonathan suggested to his armorbearer that they sneak off and make things happen. They both shared the strong belief that God can accomplish more with a few really dedicated persons than with a vast army of shivering weaklings.

After passing down the gorge that separated the two armies, Jonathan and his armorbearer stepped out from the shadow of the cliff, exposing themselves to the full view of the enemy garrison.

"Behold, the Hebrews come forth out of the holes where they had hid themselves," the Philistines mocked.[1] Then the Philistines challenged the two men, "Come up to us, and we will shew you a thing."[2]

That was the signal, the evidence that God would be by their side. Climbing a steep, unused path, Jonathan and his armorbearer surprised the first sentry and fought their way into the heart of the upland fortress. Then God sent in His angel forces. These unseen, combat-ready agents not only fought side by side with Jonathan and his armorbearer but protected them, as well. Then God produced His earthshaking sound effects. The ground shook as though a whole army of horsemen and chariots were rolling through. In the wild confusion of the moment the Philistines slew one another.[3]

If there is anything God delights in doing, it is honoring the kind of faith Jonathan and his armorbearer displayed. All heaven is on the ready, alert to respond whenever there is a decision to be daring for God.

We may not be faced with physical foes, but the enemy still amasses his armies of stressful situations and depressing circumstances to frighten us. Isn't it time we accepted the challenge with those words of Jonathan? "For there is no restraint to the Lord to save by many or by few."

[1] 1 Sam. 14:11.
[2] Verse 12.
[3] *Patriarchs and Prophets*, p. 623.

LOOKING ON THE HEART

For the Lord seeth not as man seeth; for man looketh on the outward appearance, but the Lord looketh on the heart. 1 Sam. 16:7.

As King Saul continued to disregard the divine commands and blame the people for his disobedience, it was imperative that God change leaders.

Samuel uttered these stinging words to Saul: "The Lord hath rent the kingdom of Israel from thee this day, and hath given it to a neighbour of thine, that is better than thou." [1]

And who was this neighbor? The prophet didn't know at the time, but God instructed him to visit Jesse for a sacrificial feast and have Jesse's sons pass before him. God would make the selection.

When the eldest son passed in review Samuel's pulse quickened. Eliab had that kingly sort of bearing that seemed a sure thing for approval. He had the stature and physical form that most nearly resembled Saul. But Samuel, like many of us, looked only at the outward form. Not a word came from God, and Eliab walked on. Next came Abinadab. He too had some fine features. But God had not chosen Abinadab. Then Shammah walked by, but still God remained silent. Samuel inspected the rest of Jesse's sons one by one, but heaven's selection was not any of the seven young men.

Samuel was baffled. Were there any more boys? One. David was out herding sheep. He was the youngest boy and was not yet considered a man. Now, David's ruddy complexion and well-knit body were not why God selected him. His older brothers looked just as good, and perhaps better. But God saw that the pride and self-esteem hidden from view in his older brothers were not present with David. This lad had early made choices that pleased God.

David was that rare kind of young person who knew the value of looking up through nature to nature's God rather than inward to self and his own pride and passions. Out there herding sheep he daily had decided to respond to the Creator. And because of this, God claimed him as the future king.

---

[1] 1 Sam. 15:28.

A QUESTION FOR GIANTS

Who is this uncircumcised Philistine, that he should defy the armies of the living God? 1 Sam. 17:26.

Whenever we are faced with the giants of discouragement and despair it would be wise to remember the stirring words that David asked about Goliath.

For 40 days the Israelites and Philistines had faced off in a look-fight across the Elah Valley. Every day the enemy's 9½-foot giant had paraded out to shout obscene challenges. His glittering 125-pound bronze armor and 15-pound iron-tipped spearhead—like some shot-put ball—made him seem invincible.[1]

In God's providence David came on the scene just as Goliath stalked out to shout his daily routine.

That was when David asked the question. Just who was this uncircumcised Philistine anyway? This was no boastful or presumptuous query. David was indignant that God's name and honor had been disgraced by this lumbering metal-covered hulk who shouted such arrogant challenges.

Eliab smarted under David's question. After all, he, the eldest son of Jesse, hadn't accepted the challenge. He rebuked his youngest brother openly, but this did not deter David. He would go after Goliath.

The Bible narrative is one of the most thrilling ever recorded because it pits a seeming underdog with the greatest person the enemy could muster. It is written that David *ran* to meet the foe. The best defense is often to attack. He used only one of those five smooth stones in his bag, and as he wound up while he ran, he let fly. And what happened next is the nearest thing to a bullet that was seen in ancient times. The rock struck Goliath right in the forehead, and the giant crashed to earth like a fallen tree.

The forces of evil still send out giants to defy God's people. Often those Goliaths seem invincible, but remember David's decision to do battle with the best the enemy had to offer. God can still topple any giant, anywhere, anytime.

---

[1] *The SDA Bible Commentary*, vol. 2, p. 535.

THE ROTTENNESS OF ENVY

A sound heart is the life of the flesh: but envy the rottenness of the bones. Prov. 14:30.

It all began with antiphonal singing. After the defeat of the Philistines the womenfolk came dancing out into the streets. They beat their little hand drums and chanted back and forth, "Saul hath slain his thousands, and David his ten thousands." [1] It was too much for Saul. As far as he was concerned the music was off-key. It didn't give him the praise he craved. He bristled at the thought that David should be shown more honor than himself.

Saul harbored one basic flaw in his makeup—his deep-seated love for applause. It controlled everything he did. His standard of right and wrong was based entirely on some built-in approbation rating. [2] Popularity was the great driving force in his life, and he chose to measure everything by this distorted rule. When popularity wasn't forthcoming, Saul sulked. It is written, "Saul eyed David from that day and forward." [3]

Even though he loved to hear David sing and play his harp, Saul nursed an increasing hatred for the former shepherd until he finally tried to pin David to the wall with his spear. The more carefully David behaved himself, the more Saul's wrath increased. He became obsessed with destroying David, regardless of the cost. "Envy is the offspring of pride, and if it is entertained in the heart, it will lead to hatred, and eventually to revenge and murder. Satan displayed his own character in exciting the fury of Saul against him who had never done him harm." [4]

The transition from a once humble man to an envious tyrant who bordered on insanity came about by Saul's continual choices to follow the dictates of a carnal clamoring to be number one.

The tragic record of Saul's envious madness is before us in all its stark realism. The Biblical narrative spares nothing in furnishing us with a warning to resist the first satanic suggestion of making our own demands of pride the criterion of success. The choice of following this invariably leads to a living death.

---

[1] 1 Sam. 18:7; *SDA Bible Dictionary*, p. 1086.
[2] *Patriarchs and Prophets*, p. 650.
[3] Verse 9.
[4] *Ibid.*, p. 651.

THE REMEDY FOR STARK TERROR

What time I am afraid, I will trust in thee. . . . In God have I put my trust: I will not be afraid what man can do unto me. Ps. 56:3-11.

David wrote those lines after he had experienced sheer panic. He had begun running from Saul, the infuriated king. He couldn't go back to Samuel because Saul might kill the venerable old prophet.[1] He didn't dare return to his home in Gibeah, or his wife Michal might be in jeopardy, even though she was the king's daughter. So he breathlessly hastened to Ahimelech, the priest.

But when he arrived at Nob he found a sticky situation. There was Doeg, Saul's chief herdsman, paying his vows. David didn't want to tell the priest what really brought him there, so he lied, saying that he was on a secret mission for the king. That was his first mistake. If he had laid out the facts for Ahimelech, the priest would have known what to do, but by lying, David set the stage for Saul's later massacre of Ahimelech and eighty-four others.

"God requires that truthfulness shall mark His people, even in the greatest peril."[2] Heaven has the power to demonstrate miraculous deliverances when faith is active.

But David didn't dare sit around munching on the hallowed shewbread that he had secured from Ahimelech. Grabbing Goliath's sword, which was kept as a museum piece there at Nob, he rushed on to cross the border into Philistia. Gath was less than thirty miles away, and he hoped to find refuge there.[3]

But the Philistines recognized him, so he panicked again and feigned insanity. The madman's act of pounding at the gate and blowing saliva did the trick, but it was his second mistake.[4]

"David ought not to have distrusted God for one moment. . . . If he had but removed his mind from the distressing situation in which he was placed, and had *thought of God's power and majesty,* he would have been at peace even in the midst of the shadows of death."[5]

[1] *The SDA Bible Commentary*, vol. 2, p. 555.
[2] *Patriarchs and Prophets*, p. 656.
[3] *The SDA Bible Commentary*, vol. 2, p. 558.
[4] *Patriarchs and Prophets*, p. 656.
[5] *Ibid.*, p. 657. (Italics supplied.)

THE CURSE OF THE INFORMER
The tongue is a fire, a world of iniquity. James 3:6.

When news reached Saul that David was hiding in the cave of Adullam, a little over sixteen miles (twenty-six kilometers) southwest of Jerusalem, the insanely jealous king was sure he had the son of Jesse trapped.[1] But David escaped, and Saul became suspicious that he had a traitor in the camp. His deranged mind could not fathom anything else. What he did not know or would he have understood was that the prophet Gad had joined David and was providing divine direction.

Saul quivered with such wild emotions that he began lashing out at his own tribesmen, heaping shame upon the men of Benjamin for withholding information about David. Then, taking pity on himself, he cried out, "There is none of you that is sorry for me."[2]

That was when Doeg the Edomite stepped forward. He saw a golden opportunity to lay claim to riches and honor by supplying information that would fortify the rash charges of a conspiracy. Doeg's decision to turn informer was not based on any sense of honesty, but only to satisfy his evil motives. Further, Doeg was still smarting under Ahimelech's rebuke for his sins. By telling his version of what he had seen at Nob that day when David rushed into the scene, he slanted the account to make the priest look as if he were aiding and abetting David.

Saul's anger knew no bounds. He ordered Ahimelech killed. His footmen refused to touch the priest, so Doeg went into action. Not only Ahimelech but eighty-four other priests lost their lives, plus the entire population of Nob and all their livestock. The wholesale massacre stands as a terrible testimony of the curse of the informer.

When we are tempted to turn informer or to pass along some rare piece of gossip dripping with evil suggestions, it would be wise to stop and remember the case of Doeg, whose little fire resulted in the senseless destruction of the innocent because of the satanic fury it generated.

[1] *The SDA Bible Commentary,* vol. 2, p. 559.
[2] 1 Sam. 22:8.

DAVID'S TWO GREAT DECISIONS

The Lord forbid that I should stretch forth mine hand against the Lord's anointed. 1 Sam. 26:11.

About eight miles west of the beautiful Dead Sea oasis of En-gedi twists a steep canyon with innumerable caves that finger back into the white limestone hills.[1] Here David and his small band of six hundred men chose to hide from the fury of Saul. But word reached the king that David was secluded in this wild-goat area, and with three thousand of his best soldiers Saul went on the hunt.

It was an extremely tense moment when Saul unknowingly slipped into the very cave where David and his men were hiding. Coming in from the bright sunlight, Saul could not see David and his men pressed hard against the darkened sides. David's men whispered that God had delivered the king into their hands. The temptation to kill Saul was very real, but the voice of conscience reminded David that Saul was still the Lord's anointed.[2]

After the death of Samuel, David once again found himself in a situation where he could have destroyed the king. This time he and one of his brave soldiers, who had volunteered for a reconnoitering mission, came right into Saul's camp while his soldiers slept. Abishai felt sure that God had delivered Saul into David's hands and asked permission to spear Saul to the ground. "I will not smite him the second time," he whispered.[3] But David shook his head. Once again his magnanimous spirit rose above any desire for revenge. "The Lord shall smite him; or his day shall come to die; or he shall descend into battle, and perish," answered David.[4] David refused to be the one to destroy the king. He would leave that in God's hands.

Whenever the spirit of revenge intrudes into our own lives we should remember its source. "There can be no more conclusive evidence that we possess the spirit of Satan than the disposition to hurt and destroy those who do not appreciate our work, or who act contrary to our ideas."[5]

---

[1] *The SDA Bible Commentary*, vol. 2, p. 568.
[2] *Patriarchs and Prophets*, p. 661.
[3] 1 Sam. 26:8.
[4] Verse 10.
[5] *The Desire of Ages*, p. 487.

THE BEAUTIFUL PEACEMAKER

Blessed are the peacemakers: for they shall be called the children of God. Matt. 5:9.

It was one of those unfortunate incidents that triggers the worst passions. David and his men, who had protected Nabal's shepherds like a wall, requested a few provisions for their round-the-clock patrol duty. But Nabal flatly turned them down. Nabal, a mean miser, not only refused to share his wealth but insulted David's messengers, as well.

When David heard the report, his blood pressure shot up to the flash point of revenge. He and four hundred of his ablest men took off immediately to wipe out Nabal and all his male servants.

Into the midst of this combustible scene entered a woman of great charm. Her calm words and deportment saved her household from certain destruction and kept the future king from rashly staining his hands with innocent blood. The Bible says Abigail was a woman of "beautiful countenance," [1] and her attractiveness went clear to her soul, because she had chosen peace.

One of the hardest of all human relationships is to calm anger. Words can be so inflammatory. It sometimes seems impossible to turn aside people who are obsessed with anger and bent on revenge. Yet Abigail did just that.

"With nothing of ostentation or pride, but full of the wisdom and love of God, Abigail revealed the strength of her devotion to her household; and she made it plain to David that the unkind course of her husband was in no wise premeditated against him as a personal affront, but was simply the outburst of an unhappy and selfish nature." [2]

One of the most revealing characteristics of this cultured and refined woman was in her not assuming to take any credit for calmly reasoning David out of his heated passion. Instead she gave God all the praise and glory.

The only way any of us can become a true peacemaker, as Abigail was, is to partake of the wisdom from above.

---

[1] 1 Sam. 25:30.
[2] *Patriarchs and Prophets*, p. 666.

RIGHT REACTION TO REBUKE
Let the righteous smite me; it shall be a kindness. Ps. 141:5.

When Abigail presented David with the fearful results of his rash course in seeking revenge on Nabal, David had to make a choice. Either his pride could poke through the seams of his leadership or he could graciously accept this gentle woman's counsel. And even on the last count, he could accept it without complaint or he could accept it and bless her for giving him such wise advice. To his credit, David chose the latter. He humbly received the rebuke in harmony with his own words in our text for today.

But why did David make the thankful, humble choice? Was it because Abigail's tone of voice conveyed only honest concern? That helped, of course. Was it because her words gave David time to simmer down? Perhaps. But the words David later penned indicate he took time in those brief moments while Abigail was speaking to view the word picture she displayed of God's character. And that view was enough for him to receive the rebuke and be ever so grateful to her for giving it.

How often we are totally absorbed in some aggravating situation and irritated to the point of wanting to do something similar in heart as David and his men! We may not literally put on a sword and stalk down the hill toward the one who has offended us, but we certainly feel like it! And if we are confronted, the easy, natural thing is to allow pride to take over. And when it does, it will invariably bounce like so much Silly Putty in making excuses and alibis. "We weren't really heading for Nabal's place—just out for a stroll, that's all." And the swords? "Oh, those! Just a quaint old custom we have of wearing them when we walk!"

Worse still would be to fall into the hothead syndrome and angrily flash, "No woman is going to tell me what I'm going to do!"

When some angry course might plunge us over the brink, let's take a moment to do as David did and choose to accept the kind counsel from someone who is truly interested in having us reflect the image of God.

THE WAY OF THE FOOL

A fool's mouth is his destruction, and his lips are the snare of his soul. Prov. 18:7.

Sheepshearing was a time of feasting and celebration. But although Nabal was a very rich sheep owner, this period of thanksgiving only brought out in vivid reality the stark nature of his ugly selfishness. He did not wish to share.

It is hard to imagine any parent naming a child Foolish or Senseless, but that is what the name *Nabal* implies.[1] Perhaps it was a nickname acquired through years of ill-tempered behavior. But what would cause a man like Nabal to slip into such cantankerous behavior patterns? What actually contributed to this faulty trait? Certainly he didn't get it from his ancestor Caleb.[2]

Some might point to his intemperance. That he didn't mind getting drunk certainly could be a factor, but what turned him to drink in the first place? What unhappy feelings made him want to forget it all by being artificially merry at heart? His surly moods didn't come automatically as he was growing up. Somewhere along the way he had to make choices that finally entrenched him into this unhappy attitude and earned him the reputation of bad-mouthing those he contacted. Little by little he allowed his selfishness to exert an influence on his character. Our own unthoughtful words, spoken in haste, often are the strongest means of influencing others—but in the wrong way.

The record states that Abigail waited until Nabal had sobered up before she told him how nearly his mouth had been the means to wipe out his entire household. He probably had a hangover, but this jolted him into a worse headache.

"Nabal was a coward at heart; and when he realized how near his folly had brought him to a sudden death, he seemed smitten with paralysis. Fearful that David would still pursue his purpose of revenge, he was filled with horror, and sank down in a condition of helpless insensibility. After ten days he died."[3] He suffered a stroke because he had chosen the way of the fool.

[1] *The SDA Bible Commentary*, vol. 2, p. 574.
[2] *Patriarchs and Prophets*, p. 664.
[3] *Ibid.*, p. 668.

THE DANGERS OF WEARINESS

My help cometh from the Lord, which made heaven and earth. Ps. 121:12.

It is too bad that David didn't review his own words. He composed Psalms 120 and 121 while hiding in the wilderness of Paran, but afterward he made one of his most serious blunders.[1] In his utter discouragement he chose to flee to the Philistines for safety rather than to continue to allow the Lord to lead him in his own country.

Often Satan approaches us when we are utterly fatigued and long trials have wearied us. That was what happened to David. Before, he had lifted up his eyes to the God who made heaven and earth. He had enjoyed God's guidance through the prophet Gad, and the priest Abiathar, through the Urim and Thummim. But the long haul finally became too much. He began looking inward instead of upward. He started reviewing the negative. And whenever any of us do that, we are headed for deep problems. It is one thing to review how God has led us in the past, but quite another to rehash the accumulated data of our trials.

David looked down that long, dark corridor and just knew he had had it. His own countrymen had shown little sympathy for him. Back when he rescued the people of Keilah from the invading Philistines, the ungrateful men of the city would have turned him over to Saul. Twice the Ziphites informed Saul of his hideout. Everywhere he turned, his own people seemed discourteous and ungrateful. Hunted as outlaws, he and his men had lived on short rations and had hidden in forests and caves, only to be continually tracked down by an insane king. Thus his mind dwelt on the whole string of negative details, which caused him to make a decision to run to the very enemies he had once defeated.[2]

The dangers of weariness are always with us. But when everything seems utterly futile, then is the moment to remember who made heaven and earth. Our patience, then, will not be exhausted, and faith will revive.

---

[1] *Patriarchs and Prophets*, p. 664.
[2] *The SDA Bible Commentary*, vol. 2, p. 580.

THE DESPERATE DECISION

So Saul died for his transgression which he committed against the Lord, . . . for asking counsel of one that had a familiar spirit. 1 Chron. 10:13.

Saul was hunting David with such determined zeal that he failed to protect Israel's frontiers.[1] Suddenly Saul found the Philistine invaders crossing the border and amassing for battle. Worse, he received word that David was marching with them! Saul trembled with fear. But when he turned to his usual sources of communication with God there was total silence. Not by dreams or by Urim or by the prophets could he receive a single word.

And why should God reply? Saul had rejected all Samuel's warnings and had refused to repent. He had tracked David with relentless fury, even though he knew God had selected him as the future king. He had wiped out the priests and he had completely cut himself off from Heaven.

That was when he made a desperate decision to turn to the witch of Endor. While Samuel was alive Saul had commanded that all spiritualists be destroyed, but now in his extreme fright he tried to find a medium who might be hiding out. Up to that time there was still opportunity for him to repent. "But when in his peril he turned from God to obtain light from a confederate of Satan, he had cut the last tie that bound him to his Maker."[2]

Under cover of darkness Saul and two of his men hiked seven miles (eleven kilometers) across the plain where the Philistines camped to the lonely hill home of the sorceress.[3]

Saul hadn't listened to Samuel when he was alive, but now he wanted some word from the prophet. The old seer was asleep, awaiting Jesus' return, but Satan was ready to present his impersonation. The words from this apparition that so resembled Samuel were designed to create total despair. It became a self-fulfilling prophecy that Saul would die in combat the next day.

Saul's suicide is a stern warning to all who might stubbornly cling to their own rebellious ways.

---

[1] *Patriarchs and Prophets*, p. 675.
[2] *Ibid.*, p. 679.
[3] *The SDA Bible Commentary*, vol. 2, p. 586.

MEETING IMPOSSIBLE TRIALS

And David was greatly distressed; for the people spake of stoning him, . . . but David encouraged himself in the Lord his God. 1 Sam. 30:6.

Like so many of us who sometimes make one wrong decision that leads to worse problems, David found himself boxed in. By turning to the Philistines for safety from Saul, he had set himself up for one of those impossible trials where there seems to be no way out, around, or through the situation.

King Achish had protected him, but when the Philistines went to war against the Israelites, David found himself marching along with them for fear of being branded a coward and an ungrateful traitor.[1] But David knew very well that he could not actually fight against his own people, for he would be a traitor to his country and forever barred from the throne.

God in His great mercy sent angels to influence the Philistine princes to send David and his men back to Ziklag for fear he might turn against them in the heat of battle.[2] Suddenly David found himself free, and for three happy days as he returned to Ziklag he sang praises.

But his rejoicing didn't last. He and his men found the town smoldering in total ruins. The Amalekites had ravaged Ziklag and had taken captive all the wives and children and disappeared into the desert. David and his men sat down amid the ashes and wept until there were no more tears to shed. Then their grief gave way to an ugly anger, and his men threatened to stone David for leading them into such a mess.

David could have panicked and slipped into a hand-wringing state. Instead he chose to put his memory to work. He refused to allow himself to be swept away, but reviewed how God had led him in the past. And as he did his courage rose. He turned to the Lord for guidance, which he should have done much earlier, and in the end, after a fast chase and a lightning raid on the Amalekites, all was restored.

---

[1] *Patriarchs and Prophets*, p. 690.
[2] *Ibid.*, pp. 690, 691.

HIGH PRICE FOR DECEIT

The wisdom of the prudent is to understand his way: but the folly of fools is deceit. Prov. 14:8.

One of the surest earmarks of a genuine fool is his fixed concept that by deceiving others he can get ahead.

Our story is about an Amalekite messenger whose deceitful extension of facts brought him the death penalty. He paid the supreme price simply because he chose to lie. The high hopes of favors distorted his decision.

On the third day that David and his men were poking through the rubble of Ziklag as they tried to restore their homes, a stranger with dust on his head and torn clothes came panting into town.[1] Outwardly he showed all the signs of grief. Bowing before David, he told breathlessly how the Hebrews had been beaten in battle and how both Saul and Jonathan had been killed.

Supposing David would undoubtedly enjoy hearing the news of Saul's death, he embellished the account with arm-waving details of how he had followed Saul's advice and killed him before the Philistines came upon the wounded king. Expecting great adulation from David and his men, he waited on tiptoe for the congratulations and reward. But none came.

David and those near him wept at the tragic news of Israel's loss and the sad end of a king who might have been worthy of better things. David and his men remained stunned with profound sorrow until sundown. By then the initial shock had worn off, and David had some questions. Who was this stranger, and why was he not afraid to touch the Lord's anointed? David waited for the first answer, but there was no reply to the second. Without further interrogation David gave the nod to one of his men to execute this stranger. On the testimony of his own words he was worthy of death.

We wonder at the folly of this man who boastfully went beyond the simple facts. Yet those who live by greed invariably expect others to be motivated by their own evil desires.

---

[1] *Patriarchs and Prophets*, pp. 694, 695.

CAUSE OF DEATH: PRESUMPTION

Keep back thy servant also from presumptuous sins; let them not have dominion over me. Ps. 19:13.

For about two decades the sacred ark of God had been quietly stored in the house of Abinadab at Kirjath-jearim, nine miles northwest of Jerusalem.[1] But when David came to the throne he determined to bring it to Jerusalem and place it in a national shrine.[2] Just transporting the ark was to be a gala occasion. The king summoned thirty thousand leading men of Israel, and with a new cart and plenty of music the transfer was to be made with rejoicing.

The problem was that David forgot about the Kohathites whom God had specifically selected to carry the ark on their shoulders whenever it was moved.[3] It was one thing for the heathen Philistines to place it on a cart and return it to Israel years before, but it was quite another to deliberately have it hauled by oxen in the light of divine instruction.

All went well until the procession reached Nachon's threshing floor. The oxen may have reached out to snatch a few pieces of scattered grain, but whatever happened, the ark teetered for a moment.[4] Uzzah, who had been walking beside the cart, reached out to steady the ark. Instantly he dropped dead. The cause of death: presumption. He had made a fatal choice, one based on the false notion that because of his sincerity God would overlook the explicit command. "Transgression of God's law had lessened his sense of its sacredness, and with unconfessed sins upon him he had, in face of the divine prohibition, presumed to touch the symbol of God's presence."[5]

Like Uzzah, many feel that practicing a known sin or neglecting a known duty is permissible as long as religious activities are done with enthusiasm and sincerity. "Presumption is a common temptation, and as Satan assails men with this, he obtains the victory nine times out of ten."[6] Professed Christians would do well to consider this when claiming the promises of God.

[1] *SDA Bible Dictionary,* p. 646.
[2] *The SDA Bible Commentary,* vol. 2, p. 624.
[3] *Ibid.,* p. 625.
[4] *Ibid.*
[5] *Patriarchs and Prophets,* p. 706.
[6] *Testimonies,* vol. 4, p. 44.

MICHAL'S DECISION FOR MISERY

It is better to dwell in the wilderness, than with a contentious and an angry woman. Prov. 21:19.

When Saul's daughter Michal first met David her heart went pitty-pat, but twenty years later it made only a dull thud. She had quickly fallen in love with the handsome exshepherd, and their marriage had glowed with such fervor that she actually helped him escape from her infuriated father.[1] But time eroded those sentiments, and bitter and resentful feelings took over.

Once David was firmly established on the throne of Israel, he sent for his wife. But in the interim Michal had illegally remarried, setting the stage for a domestic trauma that left deep scars. Phaltiel, Michal's new husband, wept and walked sadly behind her as she headed for Jerusalem.[2] It was a touching scene, but Phaltiel was out of bounds in taking another man's wife to himself anyway. Abner, who had made the arrangements for Michal's return to David, finally sent him home. But Michal did not soon forget this.

After three months David had finally decided that he would again try to transfer the ark. The original debacle had taught him that his own heart wasn't right, and this time he would do as the Lord directed. He was so happy that he danced with holy joy.

Michal peered out the window at the king joyfully clapping his hands and dancing, and she sneered. Her lips curled in total contempt and disgust at David's actions. She had chosen to make herself miserable and, like many who refuse to think positively, she determined to share those feelings. "How glorious was the king of Israel today!" she remarked sarcastically.[3]

It had been a high day for David, and now this ugly, discordant note grated on his spirit. Feeling that she despised and dishonored the service of God, he sternly reminded her that "it was before the Lord."[4]

Her brooding pride and arrogance resulted in her going to the grave without ever bearing any children.[5]

---

[1] *The SDA Bible Commentary*, vol. 2, p. 627.
[2] *Ibid.*, p. 613.
[3] 2 Sam. 6:20.
[4] Verse 21.
[5] *Patriarchs and Prophets*, p. 711.

SITTING BEFORE THE LORD
Then went king David in, and sat before the Lord. 2 Sam. 7:18.

It is always a good thing to just sit down and quietly talk to the Lord about our deep feelings whenever we are shattered by some news. David did so because his hopes of building a house for God had suddenly been dashed by the word of the Lord through the prophet Nathan. God had spoken directly to the prophet and had told him that David was *not* to build a house of worship. A son would be born to him, and he would erect an edifice for God.

When Nathan delivered the message David saw his cherished dreams crumble. He had joyfully brought the ark of God to Jerusalem and had temporarily placed it in a tent, hoping to construct a building that would truly bring glory to God. David well knew that such a building would also enhance his own name and elevate the nation. He had already started writing psalms for the music service and he longed to have this one last dream fulfilled.[1] But God denied him this, and that was why he sat down before the Lord that day. David probably went to where the ark rested to chat with God about how he felt. He didn't complain. He chose to accept the news with gratitude and to tell the Lord just how much he appreciated His leading.[2]

"The grateful resignation thus manifested is rarely seen, even among Christians."[3] How often people who have held some cherished dream chafe under God's providence! They long to have their name etched on some brass plate or carved in stone outside some building. They want to do something special for the Lord, yet God has blocked the way so others might finish the task. "But instead of gratefully submitting to the divine direction, many fall back as if slighted and rejected, feeling that if they cannot do the one thing which they desire to do, they will do nothing."[4] How much better to find that same inner joy that David discovered when he decided to sit before the Lord and magnify His name!

[1] *Patriarchs and Prophets*, p. 711.
[2] *The SDA Bible Commentary*, vol. 2, p. 632.
[3] *Patriarchs and Prophets*, p. 712.
[4] *Ibid.*, pp. 712, 713.

THE REWARD OF THE WICKED

The Lord bringeth the counsel of the heathen to nought: he maketh the devices of the people of none effect. Ps. 33:10.

When David heard the news that Nahash, king of the Ammonites, had died, he sent ambassadors across the Jordan with condolences to his son Hanun. David well remembered how Nahash had befriended him when he was fleeing from Saul, and he honestly wished to express his deep sympathies. But when the Hebrew messengers arrived, Hanun's counselors gathered about him and whispered their suspicions. According to them, David had sent spies. It was beyond their comprehension that King David would actually be sympathetic. "When Satan controls the minds of men he will excite envy and suspicion which will misconstrue the very best intentions." [1]

God allowed these Ammonites to carry out their false notions so that their evil purposes might be revealed to David. [2] God did not want Israel to be in any partnership with this treacherous, wicked nation.

Taking David's ambassadors and cutting their beards half off and their clothes down the middle to their buttocks, the Ammonites sent them back home. The news of the embarrassed ambassadors spread rapidly, and when David heard it he told his men to stay in Jericho until their beards grew out.

The decision to insult David's messengers was also backed by a coalition force east of the Jordan. The Ammonites hired the Syrians to join them in battle against the Israelites. It was a tragic mistake. Without waiting to be invaded, the Israelites rushed across the river with a strike force and thoroughly trounced the enemy in their first engagement.

Smarting under this defeat, the enemy gathered even greater forces the next year. This time David himself entered the field, and when the war ended, all the heathen clear to the Euphrates were in subjection to the Hebrews, just as God had promised Abraham centuries before. [3] The outworking of the wicked's evil decision had been rewarded.

---

[1] *Patriarchs and Prophets*, p. 714.
[2] *Ibid.*
[3] *Ibid.*, pp. 715, 716.

FROM LUST TO PANIC

Every man is tempted, when he is drawn away of his own lust, and enticed. James 1:14.

David awakened quite refreshed from his afternoon siesta. Sauntering across the room, he casually walked out onto his palace rooftop. The high-rise view was exhilarating. As his eyes scanned the city spread out before him they suddenly riveted on a beautiful woman bathing in a courtyard below. David already had a harem with a covey of concubines and a selection of wives, including the beautiful Abigail, but this was different. The sinful desire for stolen sweets, the passion for lustful conquest, increased his pulse rate. Now was the moment to decide. Either he was to resist the urge that pulsated through his whole body or he would stand and stare and finally fulfill those clamoring desires.

David had unconsciously set himself up for the tempter to make those alluring suggestions seem almost irresistible. "It was the spirit of self-confidence and self-exaltation that prepared the way for David's fall." [1] Satan didn't pounce on David. He seldom rushes at anyone. He whittles away until little by little concessions are made in adapting to worldly customs and practices that weaken the grip on God. Then when temptation comes, the devil is more sure of success.

It seemed so slick, so neat, right then. But later that brief, shocking note arrived from Bathsheba, "I am with child." [2] David quivered as he stared at those words. Her pregnancy must be covered up, so he sent for her husband, Uriah, who was a soldier on the front lines. But the scheme backfired. Uriah was too patriotic to return home, even after David got him drunk.

Panic—sheer raw panic—set in. The decision to send one of his bravest and most trusted soldiers back to the front, bearing his own death warrant, was based entirely on the terrifying fact that he might be discovered. He who at one time would not stoop to kill Saul, the Lord's anointed, could become so glassy-eyed with fright that he could add murder to his crime of adultery.

---

[1] *Patriarchs and Prophets*, p. 717.
[2] 2 Sam. 11:5.

REAL REPENTANCE

Against thee, thee only, have I sinned, and done this evil in thy sight. Ps. 51:4.

A whole year slipped by, and David had received no outward rebuke from Heaven for his adultery and murder.[1]

Then one day Nathan arrived. The prophet had received a message from the Lord, but like all true prophets it was left for him to present it in his own style. Nathan selected an allegory. He well knew that God's words concerning David were so severe that by delivering the message he could lose his life. Few monarchs would tolerate the kind of rebuke he was about to deliver.

But the story disarmed David. Intently he listened to the tale of the rich man with flocks of sheep and the poor man with only one little pet ewe lamb. When the story ended with the rich man snatching that one pet to make a meal for some traveler because he didn't want to take any from his own flocks, David's anger boiled. The very idea! "The man that did that ought to die!" he cried. The death sentence over a pet lamb was David's verdict.

Nathan fixed his eyes on the king and, lifting his right hand, said forcefully, "Thou art the man"![2] Then with a rapid review of the whole sordid secret, Nathan informed David of God's prediction. The sword would never depart from his household, and what was done in secret would be repeated openly when his own wives would be taken. The days of the cover-up were ended!

At that point David could have reacted violently. His pride could have held him firmly in a viselike grip, and he could have refused to repent. But David chose to turn to the Lord with all his heart. His lips trembled as he cried, "I have sinned against the Lord."[3]

It was in this setting that he wrote Psalm 51. "Against thee, thee only, have I sinned." But what about Bathsheba? Uriah? His children? David rightly sensed that sin reflects on God's character, whose name he had so shamefully misrepresented and dishonored before an onlooking universe.

---

[1] *Patriarchs and Prophets*, p. 723.
[2] 2 Sam. 12:7.
[3] Verse 13.

A FATHER'S FAULTY CHOICE

Restore unto me the joy of thy salvation; and uphold me with thy free spirit. Then will I teach transgressors thy ways; and sinners shall be converted unto thee. Ps. 51:12, 13.

David's prayer in the fifty-first psalm is not only for pardon but for purity. His repentance was profound, and God certainly did lift him up. David wanted to leave with others the truth about sin and its shame. Our text for today is his cry that he be instrumental in reaching those who might get entangled in sin. David honestly wished that he could teach others the way of the Lord.

But something had happened to David. He felt weak and broken. Though forgiven, his own sense of guilt made him silent when he should have spoken out.[1] Like so many who have sinned, he just didn't feel that he could speak out against evil. But he was so wrong. He should have used his own example, especially with his sons, to correct and guide them. Instead, his lips were sealed, and that faulty choice caused a chain reaction of evil that followed him to his grave.

His oldest son, Amnon, who committed incestuous rape against his half sister Tamar, should have received immediate justice. David was angry, but he did nothing. Amnon had been left to grow up selfish and indulgent. Absalom, Tamar's full brother, finally had Ammon treacherously murdered. He too was to become instrumental in marring David's remaining career, all because of silence and a listless, do-nothing attitude.

"When parents or rulers neglect the duty of punishing iniquity, God Himself will take the case in hand. His restraining power will be in a measure removed from the agencies of evil, so that a train of circumstances will arise which will punish sin with sin."[2]

Instead of cringing before accusing fingers, David, who knew he had been forgiven and fully restored by the mercy of God, should have lifted up his voice in making plain the truth that sin does not work. His decision to remain quiet should warn all of us.

---

[1] *Patriarchs and Prophets*, p. 723.
[2] *Ibid.*, p. 728.

PRETTY BOY'S IGNOMINIOUS END

And they took Absalom, and cast him into a great pit in the wood, and laid a very great heap of stones upon him. 2 Sam. 18:17.

According to Absalom's script, that was not how the story was supposed to end. After the death of his three sons, who presumably had died in infancy, he knew there was no chance of his name's being carried on.[1] That is why he erected a costly and beautiful stone monument down in the king's dale about a quarter of a mile from Jerusalem. When people passed his tomb he wanted them to remember his name fondly. Instead, Absalom's remains ended up at the bottom of a huge hole down by the Jordan, with a pile of rocks on top as a monument to his infamous coup.[2]

The problem with Absalom was his persistent turning toward the ego-satisfying route. It wasn't just some onetime decision for him. His life was little more than an accumulation of pride-filled patterns that kept his unscrupulous and ambitious behavior constantly stimulated.

The seeds of Absalom's rebellion against his father's kingdom were planted when David banished him from Jerusalem for murdering his half brother Amnon. For such a high crime it was a flabby punishment, yet David felt he had to do something. But it was dangerous to turn such a person as Absalom away to brood for a number of years.

David's commander finally persuaded the king to bring Absalom back, but David still refused to see his son. By then it was too late for David. All the time he was in Jerusalem, Absalom kept up a charming politician's posture. He turned on the glow. He didn't just glad-hand and kiss the babies. He kissed everyone with a problem down by the city gate and listened intently to their troubles. In that kind of climate it didn't take long for him to establish an antigovernment plot.

People with such motives may not always end up as did Absalom, but they leave behind bad memories of their selfishness.

[1] *The SDA Bible Commentary*, vol. 2, p. 683.
[2] *SDA Bible Dictionary*, p. 645.

THE END OF WISDOM WITHOUT GOD

And David said, O Lord, I pray thee, turn the counsel of Ahithophel into foolishness. 2 Sam. 15:31.

David's prayer seemed to be answered immediately when Hushai appeared with his robes rent and dust on his head in utter sorrow over the plight of the fugitive king. Immediately grasping the possibilities, David sent his wise and true friend back to Jerusalem to thwart the counsel of the crafty Ahithophel.

And just who was this Ahithophel? He had been one of David's chief advisers, a man so gifted in counsel that his very word was considered the ultimate answer to problems. But Ahithophel's wisdom was based on human reasoning. He did not choose to fear God, and thus his brand of wisdom always failed when it came to spiritual understanding.

He defected to Absalom for revenge. Bathsheba was his granddaughter, and the disgrace to the family was more than he could bear.[1] But he knew very well that he would have to make sure of Absalom's victory or he would be the first to die when David returned to reign. That was why he counseled Absalom to pitch a ten on the palace roof, on the very place where David had sinned, and commit incest with all ten of the king's concubines remaining in Jerusalem "to keep the house."[2] He wanted to make sure there was no possibility of reconciliation between Absalom and David.[3]

Further, he advised an immediate attack on the king. That was when Hushai stepped in. He had returned to the capital and was waiting in the wings for Absalom to ask his advice. Since he also was known as a wise counselor, Absalom took the bait. Hushai counseled the opposite. The idea of waiting to gather a greater show of force appealed to Absalom's pride. But Ahithophel knew the coup was lost. Jealous over being snubbed and angry and desperate, he decided to end his own life. He hurried home and hanged himself. Thus ended the life of a highly intelligent and shrewd man who had refused to make God supreme in his life.

---

[1] *Patriarchs and Prophets,* p. 735.
[2] 2 Sam. 16:21.
[3] *Ibid.,* p. 739.

HASTY DECISION AND
TRAGIC COMPROMISE
Teach me good judgment and knowledge. Ps. 119:66.

During the time when David was fleeing Jerusalem something happened that should alert us to the dangers of hasty decisions. David and his entourage were just cresting the Mount of Olives when they came across Ziba on the eastern slope. This high-class servant of Mephibosheth was leading a couple of donkeys laden with all sorts of foodstuff.[1] Ziba, who had seized upon this precious opportunity for personal gain, explained that the beasts were for the royal family to ride, and the food was for the soldiers.

"And where is thy master's son?" David asked.[2]

That most certainly was a good question. Just what was Ziba doing on the road at this time anyway, when the king had assigned him to care for Jonathan's crippled son?

Without flickering his eyes, Ziba told him that Mephihosheth had cast his lot with Absalom and was remaining in Jerusalem. This was a base slander and a lie, but David, without waiting to hear the full facts of the case, told Ziba that he could possess all of Mephibosheth's estate. It was a tragic decision.

When David returned to Jerusalem, who should come hobbling out to meet him but Mephibosheth! And for the first time David heard another version of the story. Mephibosheth had requested Ziba to saddle a donkey so he could make his escape with the king, but Ziba had deceived him and taken off, leaving him helpless in Jerusalem.

David realized that a terrible injustice had been done when he had accepted Ziba's story without verification. Endeavoring to rectify matters, he told Mephibosheth that he could have half his property back. But the compromise only compounded David's snap judgment. If Ziba was right, he should have kept the goods, but if not, then why shouldn't Mephibosheth have all his property back? Mephibosheth didn't complain, but told David that he desired only to be with the king. How much better if David had waited for the true story!

---

[1] *SDA Bible Dictionary*, p. 1211.
[2] 2 Sam. 16:3.

MEETING UNEXPECTED ABUSE

It may be that the Lord will look on mine affliction, and that the Lord will requite me good for his cursing this day. 2 Sam. 16:12.

There is nothing quite so distressing as having someone unexpectedly and vehemently turn against you. David experienced this when fleeing from his son Absalom. He and those loyal to him were hurrying toward the Jordan, but as they reached the village of Bahurim, Shimei, throwing rocks and dust and cursing the king, rushed at them. Not by any word or action during David's reign had Shimei indicated disloyalty, but now in the king's distress he showed his true character.

"Come out, come out, thou bloody man, and thou man of Belial"! he shouted.[1] Shimei went on to call the king worthless and wicked. He claimed that David was responsible for shedding the blood of the house of Saul—an utterly false accusation. Shimei's baseless charges were made because he belonged to the tribe of Benjamin, Saul's tribe, and he was bitter that David had been crowned king.[2] But since God had placed David on the throne, Shimei's slanderous accusations were really against Him. Shimei's behavior betrayed the source of his spirit. Only Satan deals in reviling and distressing people who are under affliction.

David's nephew Abishai had had enough of the tossing of dust into the air, the hurling of rocks, and the shouting. As one of the king's bravest captains, he needed just a nod from David and he would go right over and lop off Shimei's head. That would stop the sound and fury in a hurry. "Why should this dead dog curse my lord the king?" he asked, fingering his sword.[3]

But David refused. "Let him alone, and let him curse," he replied.[4] David chose to leave the matter in God's hands.

When the civil war was over, Shimei came bowing and begging for mercy. Again David showed his nobility by promising that he would not die, though Abishai stood nearby grinding his teeth. David's decision to leave his case in God's hands is a worthy example of how to deal with Shimei types.

---

[1] 2 Sam. 16:7.
[2] *Patriarchs and Prophets*, p. 736.
[3] Verse 9.
[4] Verse 11.

ILL-TIMED TEARS

To every thing there is a season, and a time to every purpose under the heaven: . . . a time to mourn, and a time to dance. Eccl. 3:1-4.

Seldom in Biblical literature can anything be found to match the poignant grief of David over the death of his son Absalom. But his wailing uncontrollably, "Absalom, my son, my son Absalom!" [1] was more than mourning the loss of his son. What made it so difficult for him was the haunting knowledge that this whole tragedy could be traced to his own heinous sin.

But in his extreme anguish he forgot something. The news of Absalom's death had emotionally blocked out the wider picture that the greatest rebellion in Israel's history had just been put down. [2] A long and costly civil war had been averted, and he could safely return to his throne. Instead of rejoicing, he wept, abandoning himself to his suffering.

Joab, the commander in chief responsible for the death of Absalom, was indignant. Brusquely he pushed his way into the king's presence. Fire sparked in his eyes as he spoke. " 'Today you have humiliated your men—the men who saved your life and the lives of your sons and daughters and of your wives and concubines. You oppose those who love you and support those who hate you! You have made it clear that your officers and men mean nothing to you. I can see that you would be quite happy if Absalom were alive today and all of us were dead. Now go and reassure your men. I swear by the Lord's name that if you don't, not one of them will be with you by tomorrow morning. That would be the worst disaster you have suffered in all your life.' " [3]

Joab was blunt and rude, but he was right. His harsh words were a stern reproof to David, but the king did not resent it. Instead he decided to follow Joab's advice. Drying his eyes, he went down to the city gate to cheer his men. And in this he helped himself. There certainly is a time for tears, but choosing to cheer others is better than wallowing in our own woes.

---

[1] 2 Sam. 18:33.
[2] *Patriarchs and Prophets,* p. 745.
[3] Chap. 19:5-7, T.E.V.

BEHIND THE PRACTICE OF COUNTING

And Satan stood up against Israel, and provoked David to number Israel. 1 Chron. 21:1.

Toward the last of David's reign, both the king and the people were increasingly being drawn into the net of pride and self-confidence. Winning wars had expanded Israel's borders and brought in revenue, and the success had sparked a desire for worldly greatness. Prosperity made the Israelites uncomfortable with their unique role as God's representatives. Status among the surrounding nations became their all-consuming passion. Programs and policies were shaped to fit the norm of what others were doing so that they could do even better.

It was in this setting that David made a drastic decision. He called for a census of all able-bodied men. In the Hebrew economy that meant any male of 20 years or older.[1] Invariably when God's people get into status seeking rather than uplifting God's character there is an ever-present desire to count. In this case David called for a draft. But why this, when he already had a capable standing army? What he really wanted was a comparison. His pride and ambition prodded him to show how weak Israel was when he took office, and what it had become under his rule.[2]

Even the hardened Joab could see through this. He remonstrated with the king, trying to persuade him of the stupidity of a body count. But David refused to listen, so Joab was sent out with orders to begin numbering. Usually the priests took the census, but the idea of a draft was no more popular then than now, so it was considered wise to send the military to do the counting.[3] It took Joab nine months and twenty days to finish the task and file his report of 1.3 million men.

But before the count was in, David felt convicted that what he had done was terribly wrong.[4] "I have done very foolishly," he cried.[5] That realization should come to all who are swept up in the pride-inebriated giddiness of counting for wrong reasons.

---

[1] *SDA Bible Dictionary*, p. 196.
[2] *Patriarchs and Prophets*, p. 747.
[3] *Ibid.*
[4] *SDA Bible Dictionary*, p. 196.
[5] 1 Chron. 21:8.

INSPIRATION TO SERVICE

Who then is willing to consecrate his service this day unto the Lord? 1 Chron. 29:5.

The last rebellion had been put down, and Adonijah and those who had conspired to overthrow the government were no more a threat to David. Now the king, old and tired, could turn his attention to the longing of his heart. He would prepare the way for his son Solomon to build the Temple of the Lord. At 70, David sensed the end was not far away, so he called for the princes and representatives of the kingdom to appear for one final assembly.[1] Nobody expected the king, in his weakened condition, to appear in person. But when the Spirit of God came upon David, the old fervor and power returned, and he addressed the VIPs.

He gave Solomon a public charge to remain faithful to the Lord, with the assurance that if he, the new king, would do so, God would be with him. But if not, God would cast him off.

But David wanted to give Solomon and those gathered more than just a public consecration call. He wanted to instill in them a desire to serve with all their heart. That is why he gave a list of material over and above all that he had prepared for the holy house. And it was quite an impressive stockpile, including 113 tons (102 metric tons) of gold, 263 tons (239 metric tons) of silver, and 3,770 tons (3,420 metric tons) of iron.[2]

Then, turning to those assembled, David gave the appeal. Who was willing to consecrate his service to the Lord?

There was no hesitation, no prolonged waiting for music to soften and subdue the waiting assembly. Immediately the princes and captains and rulers offered not only their time but their means, as well. And the list of their own offering is very impressive. Thus by David's own personal example of full and complete dedication, the people were inspired to give. Their choice was based on an example that was more than mere words. And in their decision to give of themselves and their means, they found the joy that is always present when there is a willingness to give to the Lord.

[1] *Patriarchs and Prophets*, p. 750.
[2] *The SDA Bible Commentary*, vol. 3, p. 207.

SHIMEI'S FATAL MOVE

The Lord shall return thy wickedness upon thine own head. 1 Kings 2:44.

Once Solomon was firmly established on the throne, he called for Shimei. He was the man who years before had cursed David during his flight from Jerusalem. Once the threat of civil war was over, Shimei had apologized for his words and actions, and David had promised not to kill him. But before David's death he warned his son Solomon that Shimei was a potential troublemaker.[1] The same old, restless hatred against the house of David might flare up at any time, and he could easily become a party to treason. Since Shimei was under suspicion, his case was one of the first on the new king's docket. Solomon wanted to make a firm agreement with this man to keep him close at hand.[2]

' '' 'Build a house for yourself here in Jerusalem. Live in it and don't leave the city. If you ever leave and go beyond Kidron Brook, you will certainly die—and you yourself will be to blame.'

'' 'Very well, Your Majesty,' Shimei answered. 'I will do what you say.' ''[3]

But three years later a couple of Shimei's servants ran away, and Shimei saddled his donkey and took off clear to Gath to retrieve them. Whether he forgot his solemn oath before Solomon or figured he could slip out without being noticed, we do not know.

Solomon heard about the trip and called in Shimei for a full explanation. The king wanted to know just what Shimei was up to in leaving the city for a heathen country that had often been at war with Israel. Solomon wanted to hear it from the man's own lips before he passed the judgment of the death sentence.[4]

Shimei knew he had a suspicious track record. It was a stupid decision to depart from Jerusalem just to get back some slaves. But people with a temperament like Shimei tend to allow their immediate emotions and desires to override reason. Vows, pledges, and oaths mean nothing. That is why Solomon later wrote, ''But the wicked shall fall by his own wickedness.''[5]

---

[1] *The SDA Bible Commentary*, vol. 2, p. 732.
[2] *Ibid.*, p. 735.
[3] 1 Kings 2:36-38, T.E.V.
[4] *Ibid.*
[5] Prov. 11:5.

DECISION DURING A DREAM

Give therefore thy servant an understanding heart to judge thy people, that I may discern between good and bad: for who is able to judge this thy so great a people? 1 Kings 3:9.

It seems strange to think of making a decision during a dream and having that decision expand into reality. Yet Solomon had such an experience. Most of us are glad God does not judge us by our dreams. These nocturnal meanderings of the subconscious mind far too often border on the bizarre, sending us flying or falling or standing stark nude on some street corner. They do not represent much of what life is really like, nor do they have a great deal to do with our religious experience. The bits and pieces of those fragmentary thought patterns that are mysteriously soldered together to compose our dreams do not form any basis for great decisions. But of the young king it is written, "The Lord appeared to Solomon in a dream by night." [1] This was different.

"Ask what I shall give thee," God said. It was a startling request from Heaven.

Solomon rehearsed God's great mercy to his father, David, and acknowledged that it was the Lord who had placed him on the throne. Then in his dream he said those words of our text for today. He wanted above all else a quick mind that was tender enough to respond to the needs of others.

When Solomon awoke he realized that it was a dream, but his decision was followed through in two solemn religious services.

Shortly after this the case of the argument of the two harlots over one live baby came to Solomon's attention, and we see Solomon's wisdom displayed. Asking for a sword, he ordered the baby cut in half, and each woman who claimed to be the mother would get her share. It worked. The real mother cried out to spare the infant.

People might ask, "Why didn't I think of that?" But they could have. God is no respecter of persons. "He who gave to Solomon the spirit of wise discernment is willing to impart the same blessing to His children today. 'If any of you lack wisdom,' His word declares, 'let him ask of God.' " [2]

[1] 1 Kings 3:5.
[2] *Prophets and Kings*, p. 31.

LETTER FROM A HEATHEN KING

Then Huram the king of Tyre answered in writing, which he sent to Solomon. . . . Blessed be the Lord God of Israel, that made heaven and earth. 2 Chron. 2:11, 12.

This Huram spoken of in our text for today is spelled Hiram in Kings and is the same ruler who responded so favorably to David.[1] Solomon was determined to build the Temple to the Lord and wrote to Hiram to request a skilled workman to lead out in the construction. He also needed timber for the structure. In exchange Solomon promised to ship him food products not found in the coastal areas.

There was not the slightest hesitancy on Hiram's part. His decision to assist was based on a firm conviction that the God of the Hebrews was truly the Creator of heaven and earth. That truth, which David most surely must have established with the king of Tyre, was conveyed in this warm letter to Solomon. That this heathen king should refer to God as the Maker of heaven and earth indicates that the Sabbath observance of the Israelites had impressed on his mind the reason for such a rest day.

In his letter Solomon let the reason he needed the skilled workman and supplies be known. "I build an house to the name of the Lord my God, to dedicate it to him," he wrote. Then he continued, "And the house which I build is great: for great is our God above all gods."[2]

Hiram's decision to do his part reflected a consistent faith on the part of both David and Solomon. Neither father nor son tried to subdue the basic beliefs of the Hebrews.

Often those who claim to be God's people have projected the notion that the good news is about themselves. They want those not of the faith to know all about *their* good works. But the truth is that the most effective witness, and the one that brings the greatest response, is the elevation of God's character, power, and creative genius. When attention is turned away from humanity's achievements and toward God's, we will see letters such as the one Solomon received.

---

[1] *The SDA Bible Commentary*, vol. 3, p. 214.
[2] 1 Chron. 2:4, 5.

PRESSING FOR HIGHER WAGES

For this ye know, that no whoremonger, nor unclean person, nor covetous man, who is an idolater, hath any inheritance in the kingdom of Christ and of God. Eph. 5:5.

The man that Hiram, king of Tyre, sent to Solomon to lead out in the fine arts crafts for the new Temple was also named Hiram.[1] This Hiram was half Hebrew, his mother descended from Aholiab, who had worked with Bezaleel on the tabernacle centuries before.[2] The descendants of Aholiab and Bezaleel inherited a lot of the same talent.

"For a time these men of Judah and Dan remained humble and unselfish; but gradually, almost imperceptibly, they lost their hold upon God and their desire to serve Him unselfishly. They asked higher wages for their services, because of their superior skill as workmen in the finer arts."[3]

Once in a while their demands for more cash were granted, but most of the time they would trot over to the heathen for jobs that paid more. Their spirit of covetousness made them even more grasping, until finally these men were dishonoring God by their construction of heathen edifices that were totally contrary to the high principles they were supposed to hold.

No wonder, then, that Hiram from Tyre demanded the highest wages for his work on Solomon's Temple for God. He had decided long before he ever came to head the work on Mount Moriah that constructing something for God was no different from any other construction. But that decision cost more than just his own high wages. His whole attitude permeated the construction site. And with 153,600 workers that was some influence![4]

David had earlier asked, "Who then is willing to consecrate his service this day unto the Lord?"[5] And Hiram was the kind who would have answered, "I'm willing if the contract carries enough cash!" He was very skillful—if the price was right! But that spirit is not Christ's, and he and all those with that attitude will find themselves outside the kingdom.

[1] *SDA Bible Dictionary*, p. 493.
[2] *Prophets and Kings*, pp. 62, 63.
[3] *Ibid.*
[4] *The SDA Bible Commentary*, vol. 3, p. 216.
[5] 1 Chron. 29:5.

GREATNESS IN HUMILITY

**The Lord is a great God, and a great King above all gods.
. . . O come, let us worship and bow down: let us kneel before
the Lord our maker. Ps. 95:3-6.**

After seven years of construction, about the middle of October
during the rainy season, the magnificent Temple on Mount Moriah
was completed.[1] The great edifice to God's glory was absolutely
unrivaled in splendor. The precious stones, the gold overlay, and
rich furnishings fitly represented the living church of God.[2]

King Solomon did not turn the dedicatory service over to the
priest, but led out himself. He had built a bronze platform about
four and one half feet high (1.4 meters) especially for the
ceremony.[3] Here the great assembly could see and hear the king as
he turned their minds heavenward.

As the trumpets sounded, the cymbals clashed, and the music
sounded, a cloud filled the whole house. Solomon recognized the
significance of this and, turning to the people, told them in solemn
tones, "The Lord hath said that he would dwell in the thick
darkness."[4]

Then, after addressing that vast congregation, he knelt before
the Lord in awe and reverence. With hands outstretched toward
heaven, he prayed a deeply moving prayer that was especially
touching in his appeal for the strangers who might turn their hearts
to the Lord through the sanctuary. At the close of his prayer fire
descended in a burst of awesome brilliance and consumed the
sacrifice.

Solomon had chosen humility, the secret of his greatness.
Even though he was king of Israel and capable of outdoing any of
the surrounding nations for wealth and splendor, he came before
the Lord on his knees. He acknowledged, "I am but a little
child."[5] "True reverence for God is inspired by a sense of His
infinite greatness and a realization of His presence."[6]

So long as Solomon maintained this attitude of reverence
toward God and his own unworthiness, he was a power to turn
people toward the true God.

---

[1] *The SDA Bible Commentary*, vol. 2, p. 753.
[2] *Prophets and Kings*, p. 36.
[3] *SDA Bible Dictionary*, pp. 161, 162, 165.
[4] 2 Chron. 6:1.
[5] 1 Kings 3:7.
[6] *Prophets and Kings*, p. 48.

CHARMED BY HEATHEN BEAUTY

But King Solomon loved many strange women, . . . of the nations concerning which the Lord said unto the children of Israel, Ye shall not go in to them, neither shall they come in unto you: for surely they will turn away your heart after their gods: Solomon clave unto these in love. 1 Kings 11:1, 2.

Solomon thought he was cunning enough to reverse what God had commanded. He tried to make the light-and-darkness blend work. Oh, how he tried! His first step was in marrying Pharaoh's daughter. It wasn't that he had been going steady with her, but simply that by sealing the neat political alliance with Egypt by a marriage he could strengthen his southern border.[1]

Humanly speaking, this marriage seemed such a blessing, not only from a political standpoint but from the fact that Solomon's heathen wife was converted. How nice to have her join him in worship at the Temple! It seems hard to fault that! Yet this very marriage only confirmed others in following the king's example. And it also fortified Solomon in his flattering notion that marrying out of the faith could always be a blessing.

Gradually Solomon's self-confidence gained momentum. He married more wives. In fact, the whole marriage thing got out of hand and no longer had any political bearing. He just loved beautiful women. Beauty contests intrigued him. Attractive women were constantly brought in from surrounding nations. It is hard to imagine one man with seven hundred wives and three hundred concubines, but Solomon had them.[2] And with one thousand women to get moon-eyed over, it doesn't take much imagination to see how the whole course of his life changed.

But other conversions were not forthcoming. These foreign women wanted to retain their own religion. In spite of Solomon's vain hope that he could influence these dark-eyed beauties, it was they who charmed him away from the true God.

That first choice to depart from the explicit command of the Lord led Solomon to make more decisions to satisfy his own desires, until finally he was building all sorts of shrines for idol worship near the beautiful Temple he had constructed for the Lord.

---

[1] *Prophets and Kings,* p. 53.
[2] 1 Kings 11:3.

DECISIONS FOR A DOWNFALL

Trust in the Lord with all thine heart; and lean not unto thine own understanding. In all thy ways acknowledge him, and he shall direct thy paths. Prov. 3:5, 6.

When King Solomon began his reign it was bright with the promise of the grand fulfillment of God's design for Israel. There was peace and prosperity, and those heathen who desired to know about the true God turned toward His people to find the way of life. But the glad dawn turned into a darkness that ended in scheming plots, self-aggrandizement, unbearable taxes, and a king bent on satisfying his own carnal clamorings. Solomon had led his people down into a night of unrest, while he himself became boxed in by staggering evil. He who at one time could be so wise as to return an infant to its rightful mother had degenerated so low that he erected an idol representing a god who demanded the lives of children. The worst sort of heathen rites and gross sin brought the entire nation into the shadows of satanic gloom.

What decisions had led step by step downward to such an abyss? The clue is found in the words he wrote in our text for today. Solomon began to lean on his own understanding and on a pattern of thought that exalted self rather than the Source of wisdom.

Topmost on the list of causes of Solomon's failure was his disregard of the spirit of self-sacrifice.[1] The missionary concept of losing himself in a great cause for God was supplanted by a desire for commercialization. Solomon became totally engrossed in the desire to surpass every person and every nation. This recurring theme dominated so much of his thinking that it consumed both him and the whole nation. The high cost of swallowing up all competition not only exploited the populace but wrecked his and the whole country's influence for saying something beautiful about the character of God.[2]

None of us need to repeat Solomon's steady steps downward. The surest way to keep from such a gloomy descent is to heed his words and to make the Lord's leading paramount in our lives.

[1] *Prophets and Kings*, p. 61.
[2] *Ibid.*, p. 55.

SOLOMON'S REPENTANCE

Remember now thy Creator in the days of thy youth. Eccl. 12:1.

Even with all his accumulated wealth Solomon wasn't happy. He sat on that ivory-and-gold throne, resting his feet on the gold footstool, and brooded. He could select any one of his spirited horses and take a ride in the country, but not one of the thousands of his best fast-lane speedsters interested him anymore. His choirs could sing and sing, and the musicians could play all day and night, but it didn't cheer him anymore. The glitter from all those gold drinking vessels, and the silver, which was reported to be as stones in Jerusalem, simply didn't lift his spirits. Solomon's life had gone flat. The days were filled with jaded feelings, and the nights were shadowed with forbodings. Certainly he found no solace in all those idols he had constructed.

Solomon's apostasy and depths of degradation had reached so low that it really looked as though it would be impossible for him to change. His case seemed absolutely hopeless. But God has a way of reaching people even at their lowest point. In this instance, when all seemed lost, the Lord sent a prophet with a startling message: Solomon's whole kingdom was to be snatched away!

And that did it. Solomon snapped out of his melancholy state as if awakening from a dream. With all his heart he turned to the Lord.[1] Not only did his choice include his own sorrow for the terrible sinful state he had allowed himself to fall into but he sensed that he must do something to warn others, especially the young. He didn't try to paper over his mistakes or devise a scheme to cover up past errors. He laid it all bare so that others might profit from his terrible decision to serve himself.

But of all the lessons Solomon tried to teach, none stands out in such bold relief as does the one about the power of influence over others. Solomon found pardon in his sincere repentance, but he could never retrieve the example of his sin-bent life. The ripples of that terrible example would go on long after he died.[2]

---

[1] *Prophets and Kings*, p. 77.
[2] *Ibid.*, p. 85.

TMTD-5

REHOBOAM'S STUPID CHOICE

Blessed is the man that walketh not in the counsel of the ungodly, nor standeth in the way of sinners, nor sitteth in the seat of the scornful. Ps. 1:1.

After Solomon died "Rehoboam his son reigned in his stead." [1] At least he attempted to reign. He never succeeded in holding the nation together, but he was instrumental in the tragic split of the ten northern tribes.

Rehoboam was only half Jew. His mother, Naamah, an Ammonitess, transmitted to her son a vacillating character that would eventually be his undoing. [2] He was the type who was influenced by the last person he talked to. He never grasped the reality of God's power to overcome all inherited and cultivated tendencies to evil.

Rehoboam's first act was to call an assembly at Shechem, in the central district, for his coronation. It never came off. Instead Jeroboam, a spokesman for the ten northern tribes, wanted to know Rehoboam's future policy for Israel before proceeding. [3] "Your father made our yoke grievous. Now if you will make that heavy yoke lighter we will serve you," he said.

Jeroboam spoke from experience. Working for Solomon, he had heard enough of the complaints and wanted to let Rehoboam know that the people were weary of conscription and taxation.

Rehoboam wanted seventy-two hours to think about it. He sent the people home, then turned to the older, experienced men who understood the national situation. Their advice to Rehoboam was to lighten the taxation and handle matters gently.

But Rehoboam wasn't satisfied with that counsel. So he turned to the young men who had been his associates. Their advice was prompted by the same pride and love of authority that prodded Rehoboam along. They called for a get-tough policy. Let the people know who was boss. Come down harder than Solomon ever thought of doing. Rehoboam's head swelled with the flattering prospects of wielding authority. But it was a stupid choice. His arrogant announcement ruptured the kingdom.

---

[1] 2 Chron. 9:31.
[2] *Prophets and Kings*, p. 88.
[3] *The SDA Bible Commentary*, vol. 2, p. 790.

LEADERSHIP THAT FAILED

And it came to pass, when Rehoboam had established the kingdom, and had strengthened himself, he forsook the law of the Lord, and all Israel with him. 2 Chron. 12:1.

When the ten northern tribes broke away from their allegiance to Rehoboam, the king thought to make some sort of reconciliation and sent Adoram was an ambassdor of peace. It was a poor selection. Adoram had held the unpopular office of superintendent of forced labor. He may have known about the grievances of the people, but the very sight of him stirred anger. His peace mission ended under a heap of rocks.[1]

When Rehoboam heard that Adoram had been stoned he sped back to Jerusalem as fast as his chariot could go. Rounding up 180,000 of his warriors, he planned to quell the insurrection immediately. But the word of the Lord came to him through Shemaiah the prophet, "Ye shall not go up, nor fight against your brethren."[2] And to his credit, Rehoboam accepted the counsel.

For three years Rehoboam did his best to rectify the tragic mistake of his initial harsh policy, and the kingdom of Judah prospered.[3] He fortified the strongholds and built defense cities, but the real strength of the southern kingdom was not in these. The simple fact should have been obvious that the tribes of Judah and Benjamin both recognized God as the Supreme Ruler. Rehoboam, however, did not accept this as the reason for his success. Instead he chose to believe that it was his own doing. Those fortified cities seemed to be the whole answer.

But no man's decisions are confined to himself alone. Rehoboam's wrong example was felt all over the nation. "None perish alone in their iniquity. Every life is a light that brightens and cheers the pathway of others, or a dark and desolating influence that tends toward despair and ruin."[4]

Rehoboam's leadership failed. His decision to follow his own evil tendencies spoiled not only his own life but the lives of many others, as well.

---

[1] *The SDA Bible Commentary*, vol. 2, p. 791.
[2] 1 Kings 12:24.
[3] *Prophets and Kings*, p. 92.
[4] *Ibid.*, p. 94.

JEROBOAM'S FIXATION

Blessed is the man that feareth the Lord, that delighteth greatly in his commandments. . . . His heart is fixed, trusting in the Lord. Ps. 112:1-7.

It is a good thing to keep the heart fixed on God's commandments so that we may see the beauty of His character. It is Satan's studied purpose to keep us from such a fixation, because he knows full well the results of our own character transformation. The enemy would have us lock into some notion that is contrary to God's love, and thus have it become the very means of destroying us.

That is what happened to Jeroboam. When the ten northern tribes placed him on the throne he was in a position to rule Israel wisely and to establish firm reforms away from idolatry. Under Solomon he had shown tremendous skill and talent. But Jeroboam had a faulty fixation. He became obsessed with the notion that if his subjects went to Jerusalem to worship they would reunite with the kingdom of Judah.

That haunting fear caused Jeroboam to make a drastic decision. In one bold maneuver he built two golden calves and placed them in national shrines—one at Dan, north of the Sea of Galilee, and the other at Bethel, on the southern frontier near Jerusalem.[1] "Behold thy gods, O Israel, which brought thee up out of the land of Egypt," he declared to the people.[2] He knew better than that. He had recently come from Egypt himself and had seen firsthand the fallacy of idolatry. When Solomon suspected him to be a leader in rebellion he had fled to that ancient land, and he knew all about heathenism.[3] But it seemed imperative to use these symbols to hold Israel's allegiance. That desire was so strong that he failed to see the basic flaw in his scheme. The Israelites would sink lower and lower until they reached the level of the surrounding nations.

Jeroboam became so fossilized in his determination, however, that he rounded up the dregs of society to act as priests for his new system. We need not be surprised. There is no limit to the level of degradation once a person turns away from the living God.

---

[1] *The SDA Bible Commentary,* vol. 2, pp. 792, 793, and map opposite p. 833.
[2] 1 Kings 12:28.
[3] *Prophets and Kings,* p. 100.

STUBBORNNESS

For rebellion is as the sin of witchcraft, and stubbornness is as iniquity and idolatry. 1 Sam. 15:23.

Men like hardhearted Pharaoh and King Saul, with his perverse will, stand out as bold examples of stubbornness. But Jeroboam should rank right along with them.

Jeroboam wanted to celebrate the dedication of the altar at Bethel by officiating as priest. As self-made religious leader, he hoped to turn the people's minds to his new form of worship.

But on the day of the grand ceremony, a man of God stepped out of the crowd and cried in a loud voice, "O altar, altar, thus saith the Lord; Behold, a child shall be born into the house of David, Josiah by name; and upon thee shall he offer the priests of the high places that burn incense upon thee, and men's bones shall be burnt upon thee." [1]

Seldom does God mention a person's name before his birth, but in this case the prophet gave not only the name of Josiah but also the prediction that he would overthrow the idolatry that Jeroboam was starting. And the prophecy came in words that neither the king nor the people could misunderstand. Then, as proof that God had sent him, the prophet declared that the very altar that Jeroboam had built would be split in two and the ashes poured out. He no more than finished the sentence when the new altar ripped apart and the ashes spilled on the ground.

It was a most convincing testimony. Too convincing for Jeroboam. He didn't appreciate having anyone interrupt his ceremony and the newly formed religious service he had orchestrated. "Lay hold on him"! [2] he shouted, and pointed toward the prophet.

But Jeroboam's outstretched hand immediately withered. In terror the king gaped at his paralyzed hand. "Pray for me, that my hand may be restored me again," he pleaded. [3] The prophet did pray, and the shriveled hand was made whole again. But Jeroboam's heart did not change. Such is the perversity of stubbornness. In spite of God's miracles it will still refuse to yield.

---

[1] 1 Kings 13:20.
[2] Verse 4.
[3] Verse 6.

LISTENING TO A FALSE PROPHET

Beware of false prophets, which come to you in sheep's clothing, but inwardly they are ravening wolves. Matt. 7:15.

The prophet who delivered the stern warning to Jeroboam is identified only as "the man of God." [1] As God's messenger, he unflinchingly rebuked the obdurate ruler, and even prayed to have Jeroboam's withered hand restored.

The king urged this man of God to come home and dine with him and receive a reward. Doing so would undoubtedly have implied that the prophet agreed with Jeroboam's course. But, true to his duty, the prophet refused, telling the king that even if he would offer half his household, he must return by a different route to his home country without stopping for food or drink as God had commanded.

While en route home the man of God stopped to rest under an oak tree. Here a false prophet found him and urged him to come home with him to eat.

The true prophet had to make a choice. Was this really God's word being spoken through this supposed prophet of the Lord? Hardly. God does not send contradictory messages, no matter how smoothly or invitingly they are given. The Scriptures state flatly that "he lied unto him." [2] The false prophet may have heard an angel speak, but it was an evil angel. Satan was trying desperately to thwart God's plan. But the true prophet finally listened to the voice of the false prophet and went home with him without further question.

Now the man of God was actually on the enemy's ground. In the middle of the meal the false prophet came under the inspiration of Heaven and declared that the man of God would never be buried in his own family sepulcher.

The prophecy was quickly fulfilled when a lion attacked the man of God on his way home. If God had allowed him to return in safety Jeroboam would have found an excuse for his own disobedience.[3] The Lord never sanctions departure from right, nor can He protect us when we choose to listen to Satan's emissaries.

---

[1] 1 Kings 13:4.
[2] Verse 18.
[3] *Prophets and Kings*, p. 107.

DETERMINATION TO CHANGE TRENDS

The Lord is with you, while ye be with him; and if ye seek him, he will be found of you; but if ye forsake him, he will forsake you. 2 Chron. 15:2.

While the northern kingdom of Israel was steadily declining into the gloom of national apostasy Judah to the south was having its own problems. Idolatry, with its gross forms of worship, intruded right into the heart of the kingdom.

Then along came Asa, who reigned in Judah forty-one years. And he "did that which was right in the eyes of the Lord."[1] The king decided early in his reign to change the terrible trends that his forefathers had started. During his first reforms he put away the sodomites, the male and female prostitutes that had infested the religion.[2]

Besides religious reformation, Asa also fortified the cities and built up a combat-ready army. It was in the midst of this that Zerah the Ethiopian with a "host of a thousand thousand, and three hundred chariots,"[3] appeared suddenly from the south. The opposing forces were eyeball to eyeball when Asa lifted up his voice in prayer. The king had turned to God in sunny days of prosperity, and he now relied on Him to help in the time of great crisis. This was no panic prayer, but one based on a solid choice that had marked his career.

"The prayer of Asa is one that every Christian believer may fittingly offer. We fight in a warfare, not against flesh and blood, but against principalities, and powers, and against spiritual wickedness in high places. . . . In life's conflict we must meet evil agencies that have arrayed themselves against the right."[4]

Although Asa and his army were outnumbered, the hosts of Heaven stepped in and the Ethiopians fled.

On his return from this great victory, Asa was met by the prophet Azariah, who spoke the encouraging words of our text for today. These words should ring in our own ears as we determine to follow the Lord as did Asa of old.

---

[1] 1 Kings 15:11.
[2] *SDA Bible Dictionary*, p. 253.
[3] 2 Chron. 14:9.
[4] *Prophets and Kings*, p. 111.

ENCOURAGED TO GREATER REFORMS

Be ye strong therefore, and let not your hands be weak: for your work shall be rewarded. 2 Chron. 15:7.

Azariah the prophet spoke these words of encouragement to Asa, urging him to even greater reforms.[1] Few reformations are total. There always seem to be some dark corners that need further light. Asa well knew that there were more things he could do to establish the worship of the true God.

Asa took courage from the prophet's words "and put away the abominable idols out of all the land."[2] He cleansed the altar of the Lord at Jerusalem, which had been polluted with heathen offerings. Finally he called for a national assembly for a renewal of dedication to God.

This super assembly came in the fifteenth year of his reign.[3] Already many Israelites in the northern kingdom had come down because they had heard that God was with Asa. Jerusalem was the focal point, and this grand gathering fairly tingled with the excitement of a united effort to pledge allegiance to the Lord. The worshipers presented such an abundance of sacrificial offerings that it was reminiscent of the day Solomon dedicated the Temple.

Further, it was proclaimed "that whosoever would not seek the Lord God of Israel should be put to death, whether small or great, whether man or woman."[4] Now, how evangelistic can you get! That sort of proclamation would certainly cause the apostasy rate to drop on the annual statistical report! But they were really only enforcing the old law given in Moses' time.

King Asa's full determination came to light in a decision that affected his immediate family. His grandmother, a high-ranking matriarchal type, flagrantly built her own idol. Not just an ordinary idol, but a horribly obscene one that offended even the folk who were used to seeing gross idolatry. Asa did not allow blood relationships to color his thinking, but he removed grandma from being "queen" and burnt her idol.[5] Asa realized that God's blessing does not come to those who play favorites.

---

[1] *The SDA Bible Commentary,* vol. 3, p. 248.
[2] 2 Chron. 15:8.
[3] *Ibid.*
[4] Verse 13.
[5] *Ibid.,* vol. 2, p. 804.

FROM STRENGTH TO FAILURE

For the eyes of the Lord run to and fro throughout the whole earth, to shew himself strong in the behalf of them whose heart is perfect toward him. 2 Chron. 16:9.

God purposes that we go from strength to strength. When our faith fails, it brings disrepute on God's name. The victories and reforms King Asa experienced in the earlier part of his reign offered no assurance that they would continue. Toward the close of his administration his record was marred by a decision that left a blot upon his name and the name of his God.

The influx of Hebrews from the north to Judah aroused Baasha, king of Israel, to march down to Ramah, some five miles (eight kilometers) from Jerusalem. By fortifying the city, King Baasha intended to stop the migration. Instead of trusting in the Lord, Asa hired Benhadad of Syria to attack Baasha.[1] This worked temporarily, because Baasha stopped building Ramah and retreated. But the damage had been done. It was not the Lord's purpose that His people should seek aid from their enemies. The heathen Syrians got the signal that Judah really didn't trust in the Lord their God after all.

Heaven's rebuke was not long in coming. Hanani the prophet paid Asa a little visit. He reminded the king that the huge armies of the Ethiopians had been met while trusting in God, so why had he relied on Syria this time? The words of today's text are right out of Hanani's message to Asa. God delights in showing His power to save. But Asa had done foolishly. Hanani then predicted continual wars for Judah.

Asa did not nod in agreement as he sat on his throne. Instead he rebeled against God's messenger and had him imprisoned. Worse, he became so angry that he oppressed some of his own subjects, as well.

King Asa lost his grip on God. The last few years of his life were miserable, as he nursed a disease in his feet. "Yet in his disease he sought not to the Lord, but to the physicians."[2]

His case should remind us that the triumph of faith can be continual. We need not lapse into a series of failures as we grow older.

---

[1] *Prophets and Kings*, p. 113.
[2] 2 Chron. 16:12.

WEAKLING WITH AN EVIL WIFE

But there was none like unto Ahab, which did sell himself to work wickedness in the sight of the Lord, whom Jezebel his wife stirred up. 1 Kings 21:25.

After Jeroboam started the northern kingdom of Israel on its downhill slide toward idolatry there emerged a series of wicked monarchs to continue the fatal descent. Decade after decade the nation experienced strife and turmoil, yet the people clung to their idolatry. From Jeroboam the scepter passed to Nadab, then Baasha, then to drunken Elah, who was assassinated by Zimri. Zimri ended his week-long reign by burning the palace down on top of himself. Next came Omri, who made Samaria the capital. And after him his son Ahab ruled. The Scriptures say of this man, "Ahab did more to provoke the Lord God of Israel to anger than all the kings of Israel that were before him." [1]

Ahab was a moral weakling. His flabby, irresponsible spiritual nature remained this way because he sought only to satisfy his selfish whims. He never could appreciate or understand the love of God or his obligation to lead the people to Him.

And then he married Jezebel, daughter of Ethbaal, priest of Astarte, and king of the Zidonians. [2] What a choice! Of all the women mentioned in the Bible, she stands out as the one with the most fanatical zeal for idolatry. Jezebel was a hussy who totally dominated her vacillating husband. When she married Ahab she brought with her a whole dormitory of heathen priests to teach the people Baal worship. Ahab's selection of a bride from the coastal country insured him of a built-in Baal worship that would bring the national apostasy to a new low.

Ahab had no idea of the far-reaching results of his decision to marry this heathen woman. Her evil influence helped shape his own destiny and the destiny of many others.

There are still those whose unholy wedlock becomes an agency for Satan to contaminate others with their beguiling concepts in rebellion. We should seek to avoid the friendship of those who turn our heart from God and His love.

---

[1] 1 Kings 16:33.
[2] *SDA Bible Dictionary*, p. 595.

COURAGE FOR THE CRISIS

As the Lord God of Israel liveth, before whom I stand, there shall not be dew nor rain these years, but according to my word. 1 Kings 17:1.

When Ahab's wife Jezebel introduced Baal worship as a national religion, the country found itself in the deepest degradation of its sad history. By importing her own prophets and priests, she assured the Israelites of an education in the mystic rites of deities that were supposed to rule the elements of earth, fire, and water.[1] Ahab himself wavered. Sometimes he gave lip service to God, but most of the time he leaned toward the impious leading of his wife.

The Israelites hadn't gotten into this apostasy by accident. "For many years they had been losing their sense of reverence and godly fear; and now it seemed as if there were none who dared expose their lives by openly standing forth in opposition to the prevailing blasphemy."[2]

Then out of the back country of Gilead, east of Jordan, strode a prophet of God who was destined to burn a message so deeply that its etching is still with us today. From his mountain retreat Elijah the Tishbite had prayed for his people, who continually slipped deeper into the dark shadows of apostasy. He longed to see them brought to repentance before their sins destroyed them. Finally God told Elijah that there would be a drought. If the people would not listen to warnings and rebukes, then God would have to speak to them in judgments. There would be no rain.

But to deliver such a message would take courage. It couldn't be done by running off Xeroxed fliers and sending them to every home. It is so much easier to do things by remote control! But this message from God had to be delivered personally and with enough force to let the king know it was for real. It could well have been Elijah's death warrant, but the prophet had made up his mind. He hadn't sought the job, but when God's hand was laid upon him he decided to deliver the message of stern rebuke without flinching. In this hour Elijah's choice should be ours.

---

[1] *Prophets and Kings*, p. 115.
[2] *Ibid.*

SUPREME TEST OF HOSPITALITY

For thus saith the Lord God of Israel, The barrel of meal shall not waste, neither shall the cruse of oil fail, until the day that the Lord sendeth rain upon the earth. 1 Kings 17:14.

About fourteen miles (twenty-three kilometers) north of Tyre in the coastal town of Zarephath a poverty-stricken widow bent over the parched earth to gather a few sticks for fuel.[1] Elijah's prediction of drought had taken full effect, and she had finally reached the starvation point. There was just a handful of meal left in the barrel and a little oil to bake one last morsel of bread for her and her son.

Suddenly a stranger stood at the village gate and called to her. She had no idea who he was. This was not Israel, but the heartland of Baal worship. The widow didn't realize that an all-points check had been made to find the stranger, because he was a wanted man. All she knew was that he requested that she give him bread before she and her son could partake of their last pitiful meal. Her hospitality had never been slack, but now it was placed on the line for a supreme test. At that precise moment she had to decide.

To help her make the right choice the stranger lettered the words of promise in our text for today. The food supply would not diminish for the remainder of the famine. Elijah had not identified himself, nor had he given any proof of his ministerial credentials. The widow had nothing to go on except the raw promise from a total stranger that this was the word of the Lord God of Israel. The miracle, which was so wonderful that we still enjoy hearing about it, would never have occurred if she had backed away from those words of the man of God. She believed, and that belief was the means whereby God could demonstrate His power.

There was no sense in peeking into the barrel or shaking the jar from time to time to see whether the miracle was happening or to satisfy the curiosity of just how it took place. She accepted the promise just as God intends that we accept all His promises, knowing that Heaven answers faith when we need it the most.

---

[1] *The SDA Bible Commentary*, vol. 2, p. 813.

DECISION AT CARMEL

How long halt ye between two opinions? if the Lord be God, follow him; but if Baal, then follow him. 1 Kings 18:21.

Not one person in that vast assembly on the slopes of Mount Carmel answered Elijah's question. Just why were the people halting between two opinions? The name *Baal* means "lord," [1] and the people had cried, "Lord, lord," for three and one-half years for rain, yet they had received no answer. That is why Elijah directed King Ahab to appear for a special meeting on Carmel. It was to be a final showdown with Jezebel's subsidized clergy.

Mount Carmel, with its 1,742-foot (531 meter) summit, offered a grand promontory for the spectators along its flanks. [2] Elijah determined that Israel would see the contrast between the God of heaven and the false gods who claimed control of the elements. The prophets of Baal were to go first and do their ritualistic maneuvers. "The God that answereth by fire, let him be God," Elijah had said. And the people had responded, "It is well spoken." [3] What else could they say? This was the supreme test.

The false prophets began an all-day stint, dancing and performing their disgusting rites, slashing themselves and working themselves into a frenzy. Elijah watched with tiger-bright eyes, because he well knew that they would love to start a spark to ignite that wood. Hours went by, and still the wild shrieks and chanting continued. Elijah couldn't resist any longer. "At noon Elijah started making fun of them: 'Pray louder! He is a god! Maybe he is day-dreaming or relieving himself, or perhaps he's gone off on a trip! Or maybe he's sleeping, and you've got to wake him up!' " [4]

Finally exhausted, the false prophets retired from the contest. Then Elijah calmly called the people near him as he rebuilt the altar of God. After soaking the sacrifice and the wood and filling the trench with water from a nearby perennial spring, he bowed to offer his eloquently simple prayer. [5] And the fire fell! Now the people chose the real God—the God who retains the same power today.

---

[1] *SDA Bible Dictionary,* p. 104.
[2] *Ibid.,* p. 192.
[3] 1 Kings 18:24.
[4] Verse 27, T.E.V.
[5] *The SDA Bible Commentary,* vol. 2, p. 820.

ACTION AGAINST IDOLATRY

And Elijah said unto them, Take the prophets of Baal; let not one of them escape. And they took them . . . down to the brook Kishon, and slew them there. 1 Kings 18:40.

When the firebolt descended on Mount Carmel in answer to Elijah's prayer, it was seen by the people for miles around. This stunning display of divine power reminded the onlookers of those stories about the pillar of fire in the days of Moses. In response the Israelites fell prostrate. "The Lord, he is the God; the Lord, he is the God!" they cried.[1] "The people recognize God's justice and mercy in withholding the dew and the rain until they have been brought to confess His name. They are ready now to admit that the God of Elijah is above every idol."[2]

But the leaders in Baal worship, the blood-soaked priests who had foamed and danced in their ritual to call down fire, stood staring instead of bowing. It had all been frightfully embarrassing for them, but they still stubbornly refused to budge from their beliefs. In spite of all that the true God could do, they remained adamant. Tenaciously they clung to their falsehoods and deceptive practices, refusing to repent, and making themselves ripe for destruction. Their decision doomed them.

"Let not one of them escape"! commanded Elijah. The repentant people must not ever again be subjected to the priests' false teachings and allurements into idolatry. And at that moment the Hebrews had to make a second choice. It was one thing to acknowledge the true God by voice. It was quite another to break with Baal for good and incur the wrath of Queen Jezebel. Their conviction and conversion must be backed by action.

Today we are prone to get jumpy about anything related to works. Yet it is our deeds that demonstrate the power of God in our lives. Speaking of faith, James nailed the question down by stating, "If it does not lead to action, it is in itself a lifeless thing."[3] Decided action must be taken to separate us from anything that would lead to sin.

[1] 1 Kings 18:39.
[2] *Prophets and Kings,* p. 153.
[3] James 2:17, N.E.B.

CONDITION FOR ANSWERED PRAYER

And Elijah said unto Ahab, Get thee up, eat and drink; for there is a sound of abundance of rain. 1 Kings 18:41.

Elijah gave that weather forecast before he heard even the slightest rumbling of thunder. He heard it in his heart. The cause of God's judgments was now removed, and the repentant people could expect the much-needed moisture. So while the king feasted, Elijah prayed.

In deepest humility Elijah bowed with his face between his knees, seeking the God of the universe to send the rain that had been withheld for three and one-half years. When he finished praying he sent his servant to the crest of Carmel to look out over the Mediterranean Sea. The report came back that there was nothing but the same brassy sky that had by now become so familiar. Again Elijah knelt in prayer, and again the servant brought back a negative report.

At this point many would simply have given up in discouragement. But often God does not answer our prayers immediately. His silence does not always mean that He isn't listening or that He has refused, but that He wants His children to search their own heart and see whether there are any hidden sins. God does not want any of us to become careless in our prayer life so that we will not rely fully upon Him. Elijah knew that. He knew, too, that all the idol barriers had been broken down and that the promised blessing should come. Yet there was silence. Six times after Elijah said Amen his servant returned and reported nothing on the horizon.

Elijah still did not give up in despair, but continued. He made a choice that brought the answer. What was it that brought Elijah to his knees the seventh time?

"Elijah humbled himself until he was in a condition where he would not take the glory to himself. This is the condition upon which the Lord hears a prayer, for then we shall give the praise to Him." [1]

---

[1] *The SDA Bible Commentary*, Ellen G. White Comments, on 1 Kings 18:42-44, p. 1035.

QUESTION FOR THE DISCOURAGED
What doest thou here, Elijah? 1 Kings 19:9.

The pulse-pounding excitement on Mount Carmel had elevated Elijah to a high level of euphoria. But often such elation brings its own reaction, and it came swiftly to the prophet. In a blinding rainstorm he had just finished guiding Ahab's chariot over twenty-eight miles (forty-five kilometers) of treacherous roads to the gate of Jezreel.[1] And now, physically and emotionally spent, he curled up in his mantle to get some much-needed rest.

Suddenly he felt a tap on his shoulder. One of Jezebel's messengers stood over him, bringing him the startling news that the next day he would be slain, just as he had slain her prophets.

Without thinking of how God could easily protect him from this infuriated woman, Elijah cinched up his leather belt again and took off on a dead run. It was a tragic decision. Splashing through mud puddles as fast as his legs could pump, he panted southward through the night. He finally came to Beersheba, about ninety-five miles (153 kilometers) from Jezreel, and then in his panic he pushed a day's journey beyond.[2] No wonder he slumped down at last under a juniper tree! It was here that God sent an angel to serve him two hot meals. On the strength of that food Elijah continued about two hundred miles (322 kilometers) farther, until the discouraged prophet finally climbed the rugged granite peak of Mount Sinai.[3]

It was then that God taught Elijah that spectacular demonstrations are not always the most successful. Wind roared across the face of the cave where Elijah huddled. An earthquake jarred the old mountain. And fire raged along rocks where there was nothing to burn. And then Elijah heard "a sound of gentle stillness."[4] "What doest thou here, Elijah?" The Lord had guided and protected him on other specific errands, but what was he doing here?

When we run and run in utter discouragement, we should once again hear God's still small voice asking that same question. He who rules the universe can still give direction and purpose to our lives, in spite of negative circumstances.

---

[1] *The SDA Bible Commentary*, vol. 2, p. 821.
[2] *Ibid.*, p. 823.
[3] *Ibid.*, p. 824.
[4] 1 Kings 19:12, margin.

ELISHA'S GREATEST DECISION

And Elijah passed by him, and cast his mantle upon him. . . . Then he arose, and went after Elijah, and ministered unto him. 1 Kings 19:19-21.

It is never wise even for a prophet to try to number God's people. Elijah felt sure that he was the only believer remaining in Israel, but God reminded him that at least seven thousand had not bowed the knee to Baal. On that list was a wealthy farmer's son whom God selected to be the next prophet.

Elijah found the son of Shaphat out in the newly plowed fields with twenty-four oxen and servants. It was a beautiful time. The rain had caused the parched earth to flourish once again, and farmers everywhere were out working their fields.[1] But Elijah wasn't interested only in the agrarian activity. He had an errand to perform. Walking past the servants, Elijah came to Elisha and, throwing his camel skin mantle on the young man's shoulders, walked on.[2]

Elisha halted the oxen and ran after the prophet. " 'Let me kiss my father and mother good by, . . . and then I will come with you.'

" 'Go back,' Elijah replied. 'What have I done to you?' " [3] The prophet did not mean for Elisha to refuse the call, but he was simply testing him.

Elisha knew very well what Elijah had done. The prophet had cast his mantle over his shoulders, indicating that Elisha would eventually replace Elijah in the prophetic office. It was a staggering realization, one that must have thrilled this son of Shaphat. Should he remain at home, with all its comforts and pleasures, or should he follow the call of Heaven? It was the greatest single choice he would ever make.

Elisha accepted the call. Killing two of the oxen that he had been using in the field, he boiled their flesh over the fire from the plow and yoke. He would not need them again. God had selected him, and from that moment on he accepted the privilege of being God's man. His faithfulness at home had richly paid off.

---

[1] *Prophets and Kings*, p. 217.
[2] *The SDA Bible Commentary*, vol. 2, p. 826.
[3] 1 Kings 19:20, N.I.V.

LEARNING OF GOD

And whosoever will be chief among you, let him be your servant. Matt. 20:27.

When Elisha was called from the plow to serve as Elijah's apprentice it would be quite natural to suppose that this meant a leap forward in his status. We live today in an environment of status-seeking and conscious desire for advancement. Having been influenced by this type of thinking, we find it hard to conceive of anyone leaving the prosperous farming occupation to pour water over the hands of the prophet Elijah. But that is what Elisha did. Always handy with the water basin, Elisha became a portable spigot for the great prophet! A humble task, to be sure, but Elisha accepted the position gladly, because from his earliest years he had learned to work diligently at the little jobs that needed to be done around his father's farm. This son of Shaphat did not slip into the faulty thinking that simply because his father was wealthy he need not do menial tasks.

"None can know what may be God's purpose in His discipline; but all may be certain that faithfulness in little things is the evidence of fitness for greater responsibilities." [1] There isn't one act in life that doesn't in some way reveal our character, and the person who is willing to do the small jobs can be honored by Heaven with greater tasks in the future.

We must not think that Elisha made just one decision to follow Elijah. There were temptations to go home. It was not easy to think of turning his back on the peaceful agrarian life he had left behind. When the trials of working with Elijah mounted, he had to choose between the hardships of the present and the realization that he could always head home. [2] But Elisha repeatedly refused to turn aside from his God-assigned task. He was willing to become a servant so that he might become acquainted with God's way.

When we move away from the prevailing notion that self is so important that it must always elbow its way forward and are willing to serve others however lowly the task, we will be truly happy.

---

[1] *Prophets and Kings*, p. 218.
[2] *Ibid.*, p. 222.

WOES FOR A POUTING KING

Woe to them that devise iniquity. . . . They covet fields, and take them by violence. Micah 2:1, 2.

From his palace at Jezreel Ahab could look out on the lush vineyards that stretched eastward toward the Jordan.[1] Ahab wasn't so much interested in vineyards as in making an herb garden right next to his palace. The problem was that Naboth owned that piece of property and would not trade or sell it at any price, because he did not want to break the levitical code of transferring his family inheritance.[2]

And that made Ahab pout. Hurrying back to the palace, he flopped down on his bed and refused to eat. Queen Jezebel found him in this sullen mood and asked what was the matter. When he told her she began plotting one of her typically evil schemes.

"Leave it to me," she assured her husband.

At this moment Ahab made a decision that brought down the wrath of Heaven. Instead of listening to the voice of reason and conscience, he chose to give ear to Jezebel. "The influence of Jezebel over Ahab was greater than the influence of the Spirit of God, however powerful and convincing the evidence from heaven."[3]

By a little manipulative scheming and bribery, Jezebel set the stage for Naboth and his sons to be stoned.[4] All she had to do was send out letters under the king's seal, proclaim a fast, and when all were gathered have her hired ruffians accuse Naboth of blasphemy. It worked, and after the deed had been done, with a smirk she told her spoiled husband that now he could take possession of the adjoining property.

But Ahab found someone waiting for him in the vineyard. There among the grapes was none other than Elijah!

" 'Have you found me, O my enemy?' " Ahab stammered.[5]

Elijah was his enemy only because the king refused to listen to God. Elijah's terrible prediction that Ahab's whole house would fall was nothing more than the outworking of Ahab's selfish choice.

---

[1] *The SDA Bible Commentary*, vol. 2, p. 834.
[2] *Ibid.*
[3] *Ibid.*, Ellen G. White Comments, on 1 Kings 16:30, p. 1033.
[4] *Ibid.*, p. 835.
[5] 1 Kings 21:20, R.S.V.

AHAB'S DEATH WARRANT

There is yet one man, Micaiah the son of Imlah, by whom we may enquire of the Lord: but I hate him; for he doth not prophesy good concerning me, but evil. 1 Kings 22:8.

Ahab's words concerning his dislike for God's messenger revealed his weakness. The king of Israel liked to hear only good things about his selfish schemes and plans. None of this negative business for him.

When Jehoshaphat joined Ahab to plan a military alliance against Syria, the king of Judah requested the word of the Lord from a true prophet. Ahab had trotted out four hundred of his own paid prophets, who chorused their approval of the battle. But Jehoshaphat felt uncomfortable. Parroting the king's party line seemed too slick, too polished.

"Is there not here a prophet of the Lord besides, that we might enquire of him?" he asked.[1]

To be sure there was, but Ahab hated him. That is why when Micaiah was ushered in, the prophet mockingly declared, "Yes, by all means, go up." Even Ahab caught the irony and knew that it wasn't really from the Lord. Then Micaiah leveled his cutting words right at the obdurate king and told him that the whole expedition would fail and that Israel would be scattered like sheep.

Ahab's blood pressure shot up, and Zedekiah, one of the leading false prophets, slapped Micaiah on the cheek and asked sarcastically which way the Spirit of the Lord had gone after it left him. But Micaiah stood his ground. He knew what God had said and would not flinch.

Ahab, stubborn to the last, decided not to heed the true prophet, and he ordered Micaiah placed in prison until he returned from battle. But Israel's self-centered king never made it back alive. In the face of divine disapproval, he had determined to go against the will of the Lord and ventured into combat. How tragic for anyone to choose his own will contrary to Heaven's direction!

---

[1] 1 Kings 22:7.

ACCEPTING GOD'S REBUKE

Shouldest thou help the ungodly, and love them that hate the Lord? therefore is wrath upon thee from before the Lord. 2 Chron. 19:2.

Those were not very sweet-sounding words, but that is exactly what Jehoshaphat heard from the prophet Jehu as he entered Jerusalem. With the stern rebuke that the king had not followed God's will when he joined forces with Ahab, Jehu went out to meet Jehoshaphat after the disastrous battle at Ramoth-gilead. It may have seemed right to help Ahab take back a city from Syria, but it was not in God's plan for Jehoshaphat to team up with such a wicked leader.

Instead of allowing the stern rebuke to rankle him, Jehoshaphat let the words sink into his already-downcast heart. Many people react violently to a rebuke from Heaven, but good King Jehoshaphat has left us an example in how he responded to the words from the prophet. He proceeded to carry out some of the best reforms and administrative work after this incident. Jehoshaphat's decision left him with a shining record.

Jehoshaphat set up a system to maintain courts of justice throughout the land. The people must know that God Himself was impartial, and his instructions to the judges he selected were "Let the fear of the Lord be upon you; take heed and do it: for there is no iniquity with the Lord our God, nor respect of persons, nor taking of gifts."[1] Jehoshaphat knew that God was no respecter of persons. He himself had felt Heaven's frown, and he wanted those judges to act accordingly.

The king also set up a court of appeal in Jerusalem, with the priests handling both civil and religious cases.[2] "Deal courageously, and the Lord shall be with the good," he told them.[3] No bribes or gifts that might turn heads from true justice must be accepted. This king, who had felt the sting of divine rebuke, cared enough for his people to pass along the same evenhanded justice. It was a noble decision.

---

[1] 2 Chron. 19:7.
[2] *The SDA Bible Commentary*, vol. 3, p. 261.
[3] Verse 11.

BATTLE HYMN OF PRAISE

Believe in the Lord your God, so shall ye be established; believe his prophets, so shall ye prosper. 2 Chron. 20:20.

It was a fearful time. The combined forces of the Moabites, Ammonites, and Edomites had invaded Judah from the south, and its very existence was in jeopardy.[1] Jehoshaphat himself was afraid, but he refused to succumb to his fears. Instead he immediately turned to the Lord. For years he had been strengthening his army and fenced cities, but now he placed his trust in the mighty deliverance that comes only through Heaven's resources.

After proclaiming a fast he stood before the people in Jerusalem and offered an eloquent prayer. He reminded God that the children of Israel had been forbidden to attack the Moabites, Ammonites, and Edomites when entering the Promised Land, and now these very people were invading their country.

When Jehoshaphat finished praying, Jahaziel, a Levite, stood up and, under the inspiration of God's Spirit, declared: "Be not afraid nor dismayed by reason of this great multitude; for the battle is not yours, but God's."[2]

Early the next morning King Jehoshaphat spoke those ringing words of our text for today. It was time to believe in the spirit of prophecy. Such a belief always establishes people in courage and prospers their activities for God. Then Jehoshaphat made a remarkable decision. He sent a choir ahead of his army! Imagine! The advance guard was nothing more than a group of singers lifting their voices in adoration for what God was about to do. He hadn't done it yet, but they knew He would, so they sang their battle hymn of praise.

The marching choir was God's signal for action. He sent His angels to ambush the enemy, who became so confused that they exterminated each other.

We should remember Jehoshaphat's decision to sing praises during a crisis. "In every emergency we are to feel that the battle is His. His resources are limitless, and apparent impossibilities will make the victory all the greater."[3]

[1] *The SDA Bible Commentary*, vol. 3, p. 263.
[2] 2 Chron. 20:15.
[3] *Prophets and Kings*, p. 202.

SEEKING THE FLY GOD

Is it not because there is not a God in Israel, that ye go to enquire of Baal-zebub the god of Ekron? 2 Kings 1:13.

The upper-story lattice of interlaced wood at the palace of Samaria was not exactly the best place to lean on. But Ahaziah the son of Ahab probably thought it was latched.[1] Suddenly it flew open and he fell. It was quite a tumble for the monarch. Undoubtedly suffering from internal injuries, he remained in serious condition. But instead of turning to the Great Physician, he sent messengers to Ekron to learn his prognosis through Baal-zebub, "lord of flies." Through the hocus-pocus of the Philistine priests, people were supposed to obtain knowledge of future events. But it was nothing more than a direct pipeline from the prince of darkness.[2]

Ahaziah knew better. He had witnessed the amazing power of God during his father's reign, but he had dismissed it as some sort of myth.[3] Like many today who turn to quackery, witchcraft, or any source but the truth through God, Ahaziah decided to cast his lot with this fly god at Ekron.

But his messengers returned quickly. Elijah had intercepted them and had asked them whether no God in Israel was the reason why Ahaziah should go over to the coastal region to seek aid from the stupid god. Without mincing words, the prophet told the king's men to return and inform Ahaziah that he was going to die.

When the messengers described the flowing beard, full head of hair, and the hairy garment, Ahaziah recognized the identification marks immediately.[4] "It is Elijah the Tishbite," he gulped.[5]

Twice the king sent out a force of fifty men to arrest Elijah, but each time the prophet sat atop a hill and called fire down from heaven to wipe out Ahaziah's strong men. But the captain of the third force was unlike the unrepentant king. He pleaded for mercy. The angel of the Lord told Elijah not to be afraid, but to give the king the death message to his face. Ahaziah had chosen to remain stubborn and would suffer the consequences.

---

[1] *The SDA Bible Commentary*, vol. 2, p. 846.
[2] *Ibid.*, Ellen G. White Comments, on 2 Kings 1:2, 3, p. 1036.
[3] *Prophets and Kings*, p. 209.
[4] *The SDA Bible Commentary*, vol. 2, p. 847.
[5] 2 Kings 1:8.

ELISHA'S SPECIAL REQUEST

And Elisha said, I pray thee, let a double portion of thy spirit be upon me. 2 Kings 2:9.

Their day started at Gilgal, near the oaks of Moreh. From there Elijah and Elisha hiked more than seven miles (eleven kilometers) southward to Bethel, where they visited another of the schools of the prophets.[1] Then these two, who had traveled together for several years, took the steep route down through the ravines to the last of the training centers at Jericho, twelve and one-half miles (twenty kilometers) beyond Bethel.[2] These schools had fallen into decay after Samuel had established them, but after the Mount Carmel event, Elijah had reestablished them as a legacy of leadership in Israel. Today he would pay his last visit, and both Elijah and Elisha knew it.

Elijah did not know that God had revealed the secret of his forthcoming translation to Elisha. That is why each time Elijah urged the younger man to stay behind, Elisha had refused.

The nearest bend of the Jordan River is five miles (eight kilometers) from Jericho.[3] When they reached the river Elijah wrapped his mantle together and smote the waters. No bridge spanned the Jordan, but God provided a miraculous path for His servants. And as they walked on, Elijah wanted to know what Elisha really wanted before he was taken to heaven.

Elisha did not hesitate. The younger man made a choice based on a tremendous need. "Elisha asked not for worldly honor, or for a high place among the great men of earth. That which he craved was a large measure of the Spirit that God had bestowed so freely upon the one about to be honored with translation."[4]

Suddenly they were parted by a brilliant burst of fire as a chariot and horses swept down and picked up the older prophet in a blinding whirlwind. And Elisha watched Elijah's ascent to glory. It was the signal that God had granted his request. Now Elisha knew that he would be fitted for service. God is eager to answer any request based on the desire to serve.

---

[1] *The SDA Bible Commentary*, vol. 2, p. 850.
[2] *Ibid.*, p. 851.
[3] *Ibid.*
[4] *Prophets and Kings*, p. 226.

THE SENSELESS DECISION

Hear counsel, and receive instruction, that thou mayest be wise in thy latter end. Prov. 19:20.

Fifty students from the school of the prophets at Jericho watched Elisha and Elijah head for the Jordan. They too had been told by Heaven that Elijah would be translated, so they watched from the heights above the town. Yet they saw only half the show. Elijah and Elisha walked across the Jordan through the divinely engineered path, but only Elisha returned.

The young men went out to meet him, recognizing that he now possessed more than just Elijah's mantle. Elisha truly had the spirit and power of his predecessor.

But these fifty couldn't contain themselves. Where was Elijah? Maybe he was on top of some mountain or down in some far-off valley. "Can't we go look for him?" they begged.

Elisha shook his head. It was an immature request based on curiosity. It is one thing to experiment, seeking to discover truth, but this had no virtue, only a childish determination to refuse counsel from someone who knew better.

Again and again they asked Elisha for permission to go hunt. "Let us go search," they pleaded

Finally, weary with their persistence, Elisha reluctantly let them go. For three days those fifty young men combed the area, climbing mountains and poking down ravines in their search for the translated prophet. At last, weary and exhausted, they returned shamefacedly to campus. It was embarrassing, because Elisha met them with a question they didn't want to hear: " 'Didn't I tell you not to go?' " [1]

Hopefully these young men learned from this senseless decision of following their own curiosity rather than listening to wisdom. Some youth seem to have a penchant for learning the hard way. With a determination worthy of a better cause, they continue to be hurt or embarrassed. Happy are those who quickly respond to mature counsel.

---

[1] 2 Kings 2:18, N.I.V.

EVEN RABBLE CAN LEARN

When thy judgments are in the earth, the inhabitants of the world will learn righteousness. Isa. 26:9.

Mild-tempered Elisha preached such a message of quiet assurance that he became known as a prophet of peace. On his first tour of duty he retraced his steps to Bethel. Just as he entered the city something happened that would forever settle the question of his role as Elijah's successor.

A local gang of youth were milling around, and, typical of riffraff, one of them suggested one thing and one another until a collective irreverent behavior fomented that gave vent in a loud chorus of jeers and ridicule at Elisha.

" 'Go up, you baldhead! Go up, you baldhead!' " [1]

The news of Elijah's translation was still fresh, and they thought it great sport to make fun of Elisha by suggesting that he too depart. These smart-mouthed youngsters had never learned reverence or respect for God's messengers.

At that precise moment Elisha had to make a decision. Either he could ignore the hooting mob and act as if he hadn't heard them or he could take quick and decisive action. Even though he was naturally a kind person, Elisha demonstrated that he could choose to be stern and forceful. Wheeling about to face the jeering crowd, under the inspiration of God he "cursed them in the name of the Lord." [2]

"Even kindness should have its limits. Authority must be maintained by a firm severity, or it will be received by many with mockery and contempt. The so-called tenderness, the coaxing and indulgence, used toward youth by parents and guardians, is one of the worst evils which can come upon them." [3]

We have no record of what Elisha said in that curse, but immediately God sent two growling and snarling she-bears out of the woods. Before the dust had settled in the wild scramble, forty-two youngsters had been ripped up. The word got around fast. And it stayed around, too. For fifty years Elisha passed back and forth throughout the land, and never again did anyone mock him. [4]

---

[1] 2 Kings 2:23, R.S.V.
[2] Verse 24.
[3] *Prophets and Kings*, p. 236.
[4] *Ibid.*

BLAMING GOD, AND MIRACLES

And Elisha said, As the Lord of hosts liveth, before whom I stand, surely, were it not that I regard the presence of Jehoshaphat the king of Judah, I would not look toward thee, nor see thee. 2 Kings 3:14.

There are always those who blame God when trouble emerges. Jehoram the son of Ahab was one of those kind. He made plans to attack Mesha, king of Moab, for rebelling against Israel, but he had not asked for divine guidance. But the moment he and his allies, the kings of Judah and Edom, found themselves trapped in the southern desert without water, it was all God's fault.

Jehoshaphat, who had come to Ahab's aid at one time, was a God-fearing man and immediately requested a prophet of the Lord. One of Jehoram's servants knew of Elisha's presence in the district, and so the three kings immediately made their trek to the prophet's place.[1]

" 'What have I to do with you?' " Elisha asked when he saw Jehoram. " 'Go to the prophets of your father and the prophets of your mother.' "[2]

Jehoram wasn't quite as bad as his father. He had instituted some reforms, but his attitude of blaming God and his inability to choose the right despite the circumstances bothered Elisha. Why not go back and see the court prophets who invariably spoke on cue? Jehoram had chosen to blame God, and Elisha gave him this sharp rebuke in the presence of the other kings. It was timely and necessary, because God was about to reveal to Elisha the outcome of this apparently disastrous expedition.

Elisha told the three kings to dig ditches in the valley and the Lord, without wind or rain, would fill them with water. Further, God would destroy the enemy at the same time. The next morning the valley ran with water, but the Moabites thought it was blood. They charged to the fray, only to be suddenly defeated.

The experience should have left some impression on Jehoram's vacillating mind, as it should on the minds of those who read this inspired, dramatic narrative.

---

[1] *The SDA Bible Commentary*, vol. 2, p. 861.
[2] 2 Kings 3:13, R.S.V.

BORROWING WITH BELIEF

Trust in the Lord, and do good; so shalt thou dwell in the land, and verily thou shalt be fed. Ps. 37:3.

It was one of those frightfully stressful financial situations. A widow of one of the "sons of the prophets" was confronted by her husband's creditor, who claimed the right to take her two sons for service to pay off the family debt. People tend to panic when creditors come knocking. Debts do strange things to them. Some begin nagging at their loved ones. Others kick the dog or throw things. Others try to run away. But this widow decided her best counsel would be to turn to Elisha, the man of God. He, friend of both kings and common folk, would know what to do.

"Go borrow all the containers you can from your neighbors, and then shut the door and start pouring," he advised her.

Now, the widow could have doubted these instructions. She knew how little oil she had in her own jar, so why borrow more vessels? After all, just how many of us would go so far as to borrow pots and pans and jars and jugs to pay off a debt anyway? Doubt has an obnoxious way of elbowing forward and shoving faith aside with all sorts of solid "reasons" why something won't work. It invariably demands full and adequate explanations. Rational scientific proof is a top priority. But this widow didn't need all those plausible possibilities. She chose to act on faith, not even sensing how far God would go in the matter. When she started pouring, the oil kept coming in a steady stream. And when she called for more vessels, one of her sons answered, "Mother, there just isn't one jar left."

The record states, "And the oil stayed." [1] It was enough. God provided not only enough to pay off the debt but enough to care for her other needs, as well. How like God to go beyond our requests in fulfilling His promises when we believe!

---

[1] 2 Kings 4:6.

REWARD OF HOSPITALITY

Be not forgetful to entertain strangers: for thereby some have entertained angels unawares. Heb. 13:2.

We think of this text in conjunction with Abraham and the visiting angels at the oaks of Mamre, but Biblical hospitality is certainly not limited to that one instance. The wealthy woman living at Shunem who saw Elisha traveling through town and offered him a meal is another fine example. She did not allow her possessions to make her self-centered or forgetful of others. She was sensitive to the needs of this stranger and invited him home. Not until later did she sense that he was a man of God. And with Elisha, as with all God's children, the accompanying angel came along too.

This Shunammite woman wasn't satisfied with providing just a routine meal each time Elisha came to town. She told her husband that it would be fine to do a little remodeling and add a room to their home just for the prophet. Further, she suggested furnishing it just for his needs. It was a gracious choice, and a decision that would later prove very rewarding.

Hospitality is one of those traits that invariably returns to the giver. One day while Elisha was resting on his bed in the new apartment he began thinking about a gift for this very gracious woman. Surely he could provide some token of appreciation for all she had done in making life more comfortable for him. Since he had some influence in the court, could he speak to the king for her? But she told Elisha that all was at peace and she really didn't need anything. That was when Gehazi, Elisha's servant, suggested something that would be very special to any Hebrew woman. "She hath no child, and her husband is old." [1]

Ah! That was it! Elisha informed the woman that next year at this same time she would hold a baby boy in her arms. It was such a surprise to her that she didn't want Elisha to hold out any false hopes. But Elisha spoke the truth. She did have a son. And undoubtedly both Elisha and his guardian angel rejoiced with her.

---

[1] 2 Kings 4:14.

TENACIOUS FAITH

Be of good courage, and he shall strengthen your heart, all ye that hope in the Lord. Ps. 31:24.

The Shunammite woman did not reveal to her husband just why she wanted a donkey and driver in the middle of the harvest. He was puzzled, since it wasn't a religious holiday. Why should she ride the long, hard journey of sixteen miles (twenty-six kilometers) from Shunem to Mount Carmel, where Elisha was staying, if it weren't for the purpose of worship?[1] The woman's only answer was "It shall be well."[2]

Literally she said, "Peace." Peace? Her young son had just died on her lap and was now lying on the bed in Elisha's apartment. But this woman of faith did not give way to grief. Tenaciously she clung to the hope that the prophet who had prayed for the gift of a little boy in the first place would bring him back to life. She had no telephone or means of sending a telegram, but she would ride as fast as she could to tell Elisha. This was a decision of firm faith.

The prophet saw her approaching a long way off. The Lord had not revealed to him the exact problem, but the fact that she was in such a hurry was not a good sign. And even when she clung to his feet, this anguished mother only cried out, "Did I desire a son of my lord? did I not say, Do not deceive me?"[3] She hadn't asked for a child in the first place. In answer to the prophet's promise God had given her this treasure. She had known a mother's love, and now her son was gone. We Westerners would have blurted out the whole story in a jumble of words. We would have told the prophet how the boy had cried, "My head, my head"![4] and then later died of sunstroke. But Elisha understood the simple pleading questions, and he sent his servant ahead to lay his staff on the boy's face.

Gehazi returned with the message that nothing had happened. The boy was still dead. When Elisha arrived he put both his servant and the mother outside while he prayed for the lad, just as Elijah had for a dead boy many years before. Suddenly the child sneezed seven times. God had mercifully restored to life this son of promise.

---

[1] *The SDA Bible Commentary*, vol. 2, p. 869.
[2] 2 Kings 4:23.
[3] Verse 28.
[4] Verse 19.

A LITTLE GIRL'S HIGH DESTINY

Would God my lord were with the prophet that is in Samaria! for he would recover him of his leprosy. 2 Kings 5:3.

These words from a little Hebrew slave girl have a ring of triumph in them. We have no record of her name, but Heaven certainly has it on file. She carried out in a far-off heathen home exactly what God had in mind for all Israel. She gave to those who knew not Israel's God the testimony that nothing was impossible for Him. Curing Naaman's leprosy would be easy!

This charming little girl had been captured during one of Syria's border raids, and she found herself far from family and friends, under the care of Naaman's wife. She was required to serve in the home of the commander of the Syrian forces, who would undoubtedly be responsible for more invasions of her land. She could have been sullen about that. She could have cowered from fear or turned rebellious as she thought about her terrible fate. She had no recourse to any Hebrew ambassador in Damascus, nor could she see some attorney about getting the minimum wage. Nothing was available to her but board and room and the long, uncertain future of being a slave in a foreign land. Yet this little girl chose to be cheerful and to share her faith with her mistress.

That says something special about her early training. It tells us that somewhere this sweet maiden learned the truth about God. She did not wish Naaman ill. She wanted only the best.

But we cannot speak of her decision without thinking about her parents, whoever they were. They too had made a choice to serve God in the midst of considerable apostasy. "The parents of that Hebrew maid, as they taught her of God, did not know the destiny that would be hers. But they were faithful to their trust; and in the home of the captain of the Syrian host, their child bore witness to the God whom she had learned to honor." [1] Naaman learned of a possible cure, as did the king of Syria himself, all because of one little girl who was willing to speak for God.

---

[1] *Prophets and Kings*, p. 246.

THE NEGATIVE OUTLOOK

O Lord of hosts, blessed is the man that trusteth in thee. Ps. 84:12.

When Benhadad the king of Syria heard that a prophet in Israel could cure Naaman's leprosy, he immediately wrote a letter to Joram the king of Israel and requested a miraculous healing. Undoubtedly he thought the prophet worked under a state-controlled system and would have to be approached through the king.[1] Naaman hand delivered the message, and also brought sufficient funds and gifts to pay for such a cure.

When Joram read the letter, his eyes snapped in anger. He saw only gloom and doom. " 'How can the king of Syria expect me to cure this man? Does he think that I am God, with the power of life and death? It's plain that he is trying to start a quarrel with me!' " [2]

Joram realized that leprosy was such a living death that only God could cure it, and it was far beyond his faith to believe that any such miracle could take place. Joram chose the negative outlook because he had such a wobbly faith in God. Instead of seeing a wonderful opportunity to share the power of God, he decided that this was only a scheme against his country. People with little faith often turn this direction and read their own dark viewpoint into matters.

We are not told how the news of Naaman's arrival at Joram's court reached Elisha, but the prophet soon sent for the Syrian captain. Joram may have looked on the whole delegation from Damascus as a catastrophe, but Elisha saw it as a tremendous opportunity to turn this heathen's attention to the God of heaven.

Joram need not have been so paranoid about the letter from Benhadad. If he had responded to God's love and had turned from his own evil ways he would have seized upon Naaman's need as an indication of the kind hand of Providence.

---

[1] *The SDA Bible Commentary,* vol. 2, p. 876.
[2] 2 Kings 5:7, T.E.V.

NAAMAN'S CONVERSION

Behold, now I know that there is no God in all the earth, but in Israel. 2 Kings 5:15.

For a moment Naaman blinked in disbelief. Then ever so slowly the red appeared in his neck and moved upward. When he found his voice he spoke in hot anger.

"I thought, He will surely come out to me, and stand, and call on the name of the Lord his God, and strike his hand over the place, and recover the leper." [1]

The very idea that Elisha should send out a messenger to tell him that he, the captain of the entire Syrian army, should go dip seven times in the muddy Jordan was a bit much!

"Are not Abana and Pharpar, rivers of Damascus, better than all the waters of Israel? May I not wash in them, and be clean?" he snorted. [2]

And with that he wheeled his chariot around and started to leave. But Naaman's mounted servants pressed their horses around his chariot and urged their leader to follow the prophet's advice. [3] Why not give it a try? It was such a simple command.

Right at this moment Naaman's pride struggled for the mastery. It would be a most humiliating experience to wash in the Jordan, when his own country had clear streams pouring from the mountains. [4] Further, the whole water treatment idea didn't keep pace with his own notions of how he ought to be treated as a VIP. A decision had to be made. His servants, still looking to their leader, waited. Naaman had to bring himself to the place where he would recognize that Elisha was God's spokesman and would willingly obey the prophet's orders. It was a crucial moment. But finally, after looking at his skin, Naaman decided it would be worth everything to put aside his pride and prejudice.

Imagine the look on Naaman's face as he came out of that murky water the seventh time! His flesh was smooth and clean like that of a little child. No wonder he made the arduous trip back to Elisha to give the testimony of his new faith!

---

[1] 2 Kings 5:11.
[2] Verse 12.
[3] *The SDA Bible Commentary*, vol. 2, pp. 876, 877.
[4] *Ibid.*, p. 877.

TMTD-6

THE GRASPING CHOICE

Take heed, and beware of covetousness: for a man's life consisteth not in the abundance of the things which he possesseth. Luke 12:15.

Naaman was so thrilled that God had replaced his ugly leprosy with new skin that he wanted to pay the prophet for the miraculous healing. But Elisha refused his offer. Naaman could load two mules with dirt to carry back to Syria if he thought the God of Israel could be worshiped only on Israel's soil, but Elisha would not consider accepting Naaman's gifts.[1]

Gehazi, Elisha's servant, listened to the conversation with keen interest. He watched Elisha shake his head, and then he looked at the packtrain loaded with all sorts of gold, silver, and fancy clothes. His mind went stomping along in giant strides as he thought of all he could do with the riches.

Once Naaman was out of sight, Gehazi went into action. It was a choice based on an inner drive of covetousness that had propelled him for a long time. Now it thrust him into lying that he might achieve his goal. Minds caught up in greed can be diabolically creative. Panting to catch up, Gehazi babbled on about how two young men from the schools of the prophets had just arrived and were in dire need. Would Naaman be so kind as to help these poor young men? Naaman, of course, consented.

Loading down two of his servants, Naaman directed them to follow Gehazi back. But Gehazi didn't want them to go too far. He halted them near a hill out of Elisha's sight and sent them on their way, and he stashed away the gifts. Then he nonchalantly sauntered back to Elisha as if nothing had happened.

"Where did you come from, Gehazi?" Elisha asked.

With a fake smile Gehazi told Elisha that he hadn't gone anywhere. Lying usually leads to more lying, but this time the prophet stopped the vicious cycle and told Gehazi of God's disapproval. He would contract Naaman's leprosy for life! The centuries have not eroded Heaven's stern warning of Gehazi's grasping choice.

---

[1] *The SDA Bible Commentary,* vol. 2, pp. 877, 878.

ELISHA'S LEADERSHIP

I am a companion of all them that fear thee, and of them that keep thy precepts. Ps. 119:63.

Today we often picture a leader or some administrator sitting behind a large mahogany desk. A battery of telephone lines is at his finger tips, and he is far removed from any real action or contact with underlings. But Elisha was different. He was the kind of leader who wanted to stay in close proximity to the action. We find him down at the Jericho school. Conditions had become overcrowded, and the young men asked permission to go to the Jordan woodlots so they could cut timber for a larger assembly hall.[1] He granted permission.

Then one of the students turned to Elisha. "We'd be pleased to have you come along with us."

It would have been easy for Elisha to tell the young man that he had sorely pressing business to attend to at the other schools, but Elisha didn't use the old calendar-and-clock excuse to slip out of duty. His simple answer reveals much. "I will go," he said.[2]

Elisha chose to be close to those students who were unafraid of hard work. He would be a companion to those who had dedicated their lives to learning how to be leaders. And that very choice opened the way for God to reveal how much He loves to become involved in even the daily chores and sometimes unglamorous enterprises.

One of the young woodcutters lost an axhead in the muddy Jordan. We might pass this off as a trivial thing, yet these youth were poor, and this axhead happened to be borrowed.

"Where did it drop?" Elisha asked.

The young man pointed at the spot. A stick was cut and cast into the river, and suddenly the axhead floated. The miracle leaves us with a charming view of a prophet and his God working closely with those who love Him and love to serve.

---

[1] *The SDA Bible Commentary*, vol. 2, p. 882.
[2] 2 Kings 6:3.

ANGEL FORCES

Fear not: for they that be with us are more than they that be with them. 2 Kings 6:16.

Time and again Benhadad tried to ambush Joram, but the king of Israel always slipped away from the trap. It was frustrating to the king of Syria! It could be dismissed as a coincidence if it had happened only a couple of times, but after the careful scheming with his military leaders behind closed doors, invariably all would come to nought. Who was leaking information to Israel? How could Joram be tipped off so many times? Benhadad sensed a traitor in his midst.

But then the truth came out. One of his officers reported that there were no Hebrew sympathizers. The prophet Elisha was informing Joram of every Syrian move. "He tells the king of Israel what you speak in your bedchamber."

In an Oriental palace the bedchamber was the most inaccessible and best-guarded place.[1] And if this was so, Benhadad would have to silence Elisha. Benhadad sent out spies to locate the prophet, and soon word came back that he was residing at Dothan, a town on the regular caravan route between Gilead and Egypt.[2]

To awaken to the bright dawn, expecting a fresh new day of sunshine and peace, is one thing. But to arise and find your city surrounded by war chariots and soldiers is quite another. Elisha's servant gulped. His eyes bulged in fear. Although he was undoubtedly one of the prophet-disciples, his faith had just not matured enough to react in complete confidence in the Lord. He panicked.

"What are we going to do?" he cried to Elisha.

Elisha didn't need to see anything. He knew God was there all the time. So he prayed—not for himself, but for the young man. "Open his eyes, that he may see," Elisha requested.[3] Suddenly the young man saw the whole mountain full of Heaven's own forces.

Whenever we are prone to panic, it would be well to choose faith instead, for our God still has at His command all the help we need.

---

[1] *The SDA Bible Commentary*, vol. 2, p. 884.
[2] *Ibid.*
[3] 2 Kings 6:17.

COALS OF FIRE

If thine enemy be hungry, give him bread to eat; and if he be thirsty, give him water to drink: for thou shalt heap coals of fire upon his head, and the Lord shall reward thee. Prov. 25:21, 22.

Elisha prayed that his servant's eyes might be opened to see angels, and he prayed that the Syrian army surrounding Dothan be inflicted with blindness. Then Elisha stepped out. "This is not the way, neither is this the city," he said. "Follow me, and I will bring you to the man whom ye seek." [1]

Now, it sounds as if he were lying. Of course this was the city the Syrians wanted to besiege, and Elisha was the man they sought. But we must remember that the whole story begins with the king of Syria, who wanted to take Joram, not Elisha. And the king of Israel resided in Samaria. We have no record that God revealed to Elisha why the enemy forces were there, but the prophet knew that his God could smite them with blindness and bring them to a startling realization of Israel's God.

This was probably not a total physical blindness or Elisha could not have led them eleven miles (eighteen kilometers) over mountainous terrain to Samaria. God must have struck them with an illusionary blindness so they would have no idea where they were going. [2]

It must have been a shocker when Joram looked out and saw the prophet of Israel leading the Syrian army into town. King Joram just itched for revenge. "My father," he called respectfully to Elisha, "shall I smite them, shall I smite them?" [3]

But Elisha had already made a choice based on extending the full measure of God's mercy to the heathen. No, Joram must not smite his enemy. Elisha reminded him that it would be reprehensible to kill in cold blood those whom he had captured. Instead of bloodshed, Elisha ordered a banquet. The Syrian army was given a royal feast and treated as friends. The "coals of fire" began to work. No wonder they went back to Syria as men changed from combat-ready to be peaceful and with no heart to return.

[1] 2 Kings 6:19.
[2] *The SDA Bible Commentary*, vol. 2, p. 885.
[3] Verse 21.

BLAMING THE PROPHET

The wicked plotteth against the just, and gnasheth upon him with his teeth. Ps. 37:12.

It was no minor border raid this time. The whole Syrian force besieged Samaria with devastating effectiveness. The years had slipped by, and the enemy had forgotten all about the special banquet Elisha had ordered. And now the Israelites in Samaria were in such dire straits that they were paying eighty pieces of silver for a donkey's head and five pieces of silver for a little more than a dry quart of dove's dung.[1] Not exactly the most appetizing menu, but that was all that seemed available in the barren marketplace.

King Joram was inspecting the battlements on the wall when he heard a woman cry out, "Help, my lord, O king." [2]

"If the Lord doesn't help you, how can I?" Joram replied.

But he paused a moment to hear the woman's awful story. She had boiled her son and had shared the sickening meal with her neighbor. And now this other woman refused to share her son, whom she had hidden away. The gross account was too much even for King Joram. He tore his clothes in utter anguish, and in so doing revealed to those who saw him that he had sackcloth under his outer garment. But it was meaningless; he was not repentant.

Joram, with all the Hebrews who were caught in this siege, was paying the price for turning away from God. This was a direct fulfillment of Moses' prophecy that if God's people departed from the Lord they would actually eat their sons and daughters.[3] Yet the king refused to turn to the Lord for help even in this extreme emergency. He chose to blame Elisha instead! That decision was fired by a determination to behead the prophet immediately.

Fortunately, the murderous intent was never carried out. Elisha bolted the door before the executioner arrived. Yet Joram's reaction when the going got rough betrayed how the carnal mind lashes out at God's messengers rather than repenting.

---

[1] *The SDA Bible Commentary*, vol. 2, p. 886.
[2] 2 Kings 6:26.
[3] *Ibid.*, p. 887.

STAMPEDING THE SCOFFER

Then Elisha said, Hear ye the word of the Lord; Thus saith the Lord, to morrow about this time shall a measure of fine flour be sold for a shekel, and two measures of barley for a shekel, in the gate of Samaria. 2 Kings 7:1.

Elisha's startling prediction made exciting news. Within twenty-four hours the same amount of money that would purchase only garbage to sustain life would buy 120 times as much of the best flour.[1] There would be no more scrounging in the sewer, because the siege of Samaria would be over!

"Even if the Lord would make windows in heaven this couldn't happen!" scoffed one of the king's officers.

With Elisha's consistent heaven-sent miracles on record, it would seem that this officer would have chosen to believe. Instead, he decided to scoff. Skeptics often are driven by their own pride of opinion and cling to their stubborn doubts.

"You'll see it with your eyes," predicted Elisha, "but you won't eat of it."

All the Lord had to do was to amplify some sound effects around the Syrian camp at twilight. It worked. The rumbling chariot noise, the pounding hoofbeats, and the tramp of a vast host scared them silly. Leaving their tents and all their belongings, the Syrian soldiers fled to the Jordan as fast as their feet could churn.

Meanwhile, four lepers outside Samaria figured they might as well cast their lot with the Syrians rather than starve. It must have been a weird sensation as they stumbled from tent to tent, only to find them empty except for food and riches. When they reported back to the city, a quick check was made, and sure enough the Syrians had fled.

The scoffing officer had been put in charge of opening the city gate, but as the hungry masses surged forward they stampeded him into the ground. The skeptic's horrible death served as a fresh reminder that the word of God was indeed accurate.

---

[1] *The SDA Bible Commentary,* vol. 2, p. 890.

UNSEEN WICKEDNESS

O Lord, thou hast searched me, and known me. Thou knowest my downsitting and mine uprising, thou understandest my thought afar off. Ps. 139:1, 2.

Word spread quickly throughout Damascus. Elisha had actually come to the Syrian capital! King Benhadad, who had previously tried to kill the prophet, now sought his counsel. He was ill and desperately needed to know the prognosis, so he sent his high-ranking officer Hazael with a forty-camel train of presents.

"Go, meet the man of God, and enquire of the Lord by him, saying, Shall I recover of this disease?" [1]

This amazing command from a heathen king shows that he really believed Israel's God capable of knowing his condition. It was a marvelous testimony to Elisha's influence.

Elisha informed Hazael that the king would surely recover. He did not have a fatal disease, yet he would die. It was a strange pronouncement.

Then, looking Hazael squarely in the eye, he stared intently at him until Hazael was ashamed. Tears streamed down Elisha's face. What was the matter?

"I know the evil that you will do to the children of Israel," Elisha explained. "You will set on fire their strongholds, slay their young men with the sword, dash their children, and rip up their pregnant women."

"Am I a dog that I should do this great thing?" Hazael asked.

He didn't know the full extent of the evil within himself. None knows unless he is willing to allow the Holy Spirit to direct his attention away from self to Christ. Hazael was blinded by his own carnality. Step by step Hazael made choices that would lead him down to degradation beyond his own capacity to realize at the moment.

Hazael's first act after leaving Elisha was to suffocate King Benhadad with a thick wet cloth. After that he was pronounced king of Syria, and all of Elisha's predictions came to pass.

---

[1] 2 Kings 8:8.

MOVING WITH DISPATCH

And the watchman told, saying, . . . The driving is like the driving of Jehu the son of Nimshi; for he driveth furiously. 2 Kings 9:20.

The sentinel on the tower of Jezreel could look down the sharp descent above which the city was strategically located and see the whole Valley of Jezreel clear to the Jordan.[1] Away off in the distance a cloud of dust curled up as a contingent of horses with a lead chariot approached at top speed. Were they coming in peace? King Joram already had sent out two horsemen to check, but neither had returned. Instead, each had fallen behind the fast-moving column. However, the watchman had a hunch who it was. The furious driving was characteristic of Jehu, Israel's army commander.

Some folk are inveterate procrastinators. But not Jehu. We may not respond favorably to his fast-lane driving or his barbaric manners, but we cannot fault his decision to do things with dispatch. He was a man of action. There was never any dillydallying with him. He didn't wait for something to happen; he made it happen.

Elisha had sent a young prophet to Ramoth-gilead to anoint Jehu as the new king of Israel. It was dangerous business, because Joram had gone to Jezreel to recuperate from wounds he had suffered during the battle with the Syrians. The young man anointed Jehu with oil, then told him that God had chosen him to be king and executioner of the house of Ahab and all Baal worshipers. Then he fled. Jehu himself didn't waste time. He went in immediately and told his fellow officers, who, on the spot, proclaimed him king.

Without hesitation Jehu gave his first orders. "If you're with me, then don't let anybody slip away to warn the king in Jezreel."

Timing is very important. "The most signal victories and the most fearful defeats have been on the turn of minutes. God requires promptness of action. Delays, doubtings, hesitation, and indecision frequently give the enemy every advantage."[2]

---

[1] *The SDA Bible Commentary,* vol. 2, p. 906.
[2] *Gospel Workers,* p. 134.

THE PAINTED FACE

And when Jehu was come to Jezreel, Jezebel heard of it; and she painted her face, and tired her head, and looked out at a window. 2 Kings 9:30.

When the wicked queen mother Jezebel heard that Jehu had just killed her son Joram and her grandson Ahaziah, king of Judah, she realized that her final hour had come.[1] What was her decision when she sensed what was coming next? Certainly it was not one of repentance and humility. Defiant to the last, she chose to use cosmetics for her final appearance, which says something about this abandoned woman. The decorated eyebrows and lashes, the headdress in a "tire," were not intended to enhance nature, but were signs of her arrogant rebellion against God's prediction through the prophet Elijah that the whole Baal-worshiping Ahab clan would eventually collapse. Her last appearance provided an index to her character.

"Had Zimri peace, who slew his master?"[2] she shouted down at Jehu as he entered the gate.

She referred to the Zimri whose reign had lasted only a week, the exterminator of the house of Baasha. Literally Jezebel asked, "Peace, you Zimri, murderer of your master?" as she tauntingly called Jehu "Zimri."[3]

It mattered not to Jehu. Neither her contemptuous words nor her appearance altered his determination to carry out his ordained purpose of wiping out Ahab's household. He wouldn't even wait for a formal execution, but ordered her attendants to throw her down. In utter contempt for this vile woman, Jehu drove his chariot over her body.

We cringe at such barbarism, yet out of this ancient story we may learn a lesson in human nature. Jezebel's attitude was one of stubborn resistance to God and His people. Defiance can take many forms, but none reflects so graphically its utter failure as that painted face which was trampled in the bloody dust of Jezreel so many centuries ago.

---

[1] *The SDA Bible Commentary*, vol. 2, p. 909.
[2] 2 Kings 9:31.
[3] *Ibid.*

TAINTED ZEAL

But Jehu took no heed to walk in the law of the Lord God of Israel with all his heart. 2 Kings 10:31.

If awards for zeal had been offered, Jehu undoubtedly would have won a blue ribbon. His dashing record remains a breathlessly bloody series of actions in destroying the house of Ahab as well as Baal worship. Although Ahab had been dead twelve years, a large posterity still remained in Samaria, and Jehu ordered Ahab's seventy sons beheaded, their heads placed in baskets and delivered express to Jezreel within twenty-four hours.[1] That order was carried out with dispatch, and the gory monument to his ardor was placed in two ugly heaps outside the city gate. Next Jehu wiped out all high officials and influential pro-Ahab personnel.

In the midst of this activity he held out his hand to Jehonadab, who had come out to meet him while he was en route for further destruction.

"Come with me," Jehu said, "and see my zeal for the Lord."[2]

Jehonadab climbed aboard Jehu's chariot, and away they went on a nonstop killing spree until "he slew all that remained unto Ahab in Samaria."[3]

Jehu next ordered a one-day camp meeting for all Baal worshipers, and when he had them assembled, he ordered that every one of them be destroyed. Once the slaughter was finished, he broke the Baal images and burned them. Then, with an added touch of his own zealous ingenuity, he remodeled the Baal shrine into a public toilet, making it a wee bit difficult for latent future Baal lovers to find their religious house very worshipful.[4] In all, Jehu left a breathless chronicle of deeds that fulfilled Elijah's earlier prophecy.

Outward manifestations of ardor have always had a certain appeal. We are duly impressed with religious activity. Yet this is no criterion for success. Jehu's zeal was tainted with his consistent decision to be a law unto himself. His actions had no permanent results. Outwardly Baal worship seemed stamped out, yet Israel remained just as corrupt, dishonest, and immoral as before.

[1] *The SDA Bible Commentary*, vol. 2, p. 913.
[2] 2 Kings 10:16.
[3] Verse 17.
[4] *Ibid.*, p. 916.

A BRAVE, RISKY DECISION

And he brought forth the king's son, and put the crown upon him, and gave him the testimony; and they made him king, and annointed him; and they clapped their hands, and said, God save the king. 2 Kings 11:12.

The Lord had promised David that someone from his lineage would always be sitting on the throne of Judah. But Satan had other plans. Through his evil agent Athaliah, Jezebel's daughter, he nearly succeeded in thwarting that promise.[1]

When this wicked woman, who possessed all the diabolical traits of her mother, heard that Jehu had killed her son Ahaziah, she quickly ordered all of David's descendants massacred. Her marriage to Jehoram, king of Judah, gave her a foothold in the southern kingdom and allowed her to usurp the throne. She was determined to destroy David's whole bloodline at one time.

Athaliah would have succeeded except for the brave decision of Jehosheba and her husband, Jehoiada, the priest. Secretly they snatched away the infant Joash and hid him in the Temple. It was a risky choice, but one that eventually placed Joash on the throne. Six years later Jehoiada brought the lad out, but not until he had carefully planned a coup that would surely overthrow the rule of the hated Athaliah and her pro-Baal party.

With ranks of carefully selected soldiers to guard the youngster, Jehoiada assembled the people at the Temple one Sabbath and crowned Joash king of Judah. Athaliah heard the commotion and came scurrying to the sacred precincts shouting, "Treason! Treason!" but it was too late. Jehoiada ordered the soldiers to escort her outside the Temple and execute her. Then this brave priest made a covenant between the Lord, the king, and the people "that they should be the Lord's people."[2]

A genuine reform followed this revolt against wickedness in high places. Yet none of it could have transpired if Jehosheba and Jehoiada had not been willing to risk so much for God.

---

[1] *The SDA Bible Commentary,* vol. 2, p. 918.
[2] 2 Kings 11:17.

FUNDS FOR REPAIRING

**And Joash did that which was right in the sight of the Lord
all the days of Jehoiada the priest. . . . And it came to pass after
this, that Joash was minded to repair the house of the Lord. 2
Chron. 24:2-4.**

During the short, vicious reign of Queen Athaliah there was a
concerted effort to establish Baal worship in Judah. This wicked
woman even orchestrated diabolical schemes to wreck the house of
God. The Temple was deliberately brokendown. Although funds
had been collected to restore the house of the Lord, nothing was
done for twenty-three years after Joash was crowned king.[1] The
Levites who had collected the funds for Temple repair had kept the
money for their own use.

"Why haven't you required the Levites to bring in the
collection?" the king asked his mentor Jehoiada.

Dear old Jehoiada was more than 90 years old when Joash was
crowned king at age 7, and he now possessed little vigor to head a
levitical reform.[2] Undoubtedly he was delighted that the youthful
king was willing to spark the move for the Temple repair.

Joash made a decision that would stir the liberality of the
people. He ordered a chest constructed for collection purposes.
Jehoiada bored a hole in the top and placed the chest on the right
side of the altar of burnt offering. Worshipers were encouraged to
drop their money in when they came to the Temple court. When
the chest was full the king's scribe, along with the high priest,
counted out the cash and placed it in bags to be set aside for
payment to the carpenters, masons, and other workers responsible
for repairing the Temple. This collaboration between the king's
officer and Jehoiada in supervising the funds assured that there
would never again be any misappropriation.

The liberality of the people far exceeded the cost of repair.
Enough was left over to supply Temple items as well. And it all
came about because Joash chose to move matters off dead center.
Whenever we do great things for God, people respond accordingly.

---

[1] *The SDA Bible Commentary*, vol. 3, p. 275.
[2] *Ibid.*, p. 276.

INGRATITUDE PERSONIFIED

And the Spirit of God came upon Zechariah the son of Jehoiada the priest, which stood above the people, and said unto them, Thus saith God, Why transgress ye the commandments of the Lord, that ye cannot prosper? because ye have forsaken the Lord, he hath also forsaken you. 2 Chron. 24:20.

The venerated high priest Jehoiada lived to be 130 years old. The Scriptures contain no record of anyone else's living that long after the Exodus.[1] For more than a decade he had virtually held the office of king until the young Joash was old enough to reign on his own. Because of his spiritual leadership and devotion, Jehoiada was shown unusual honor in being buried "among the kings."

But after the funeral something terrible happened. Joash, who should have been foremost in following Jehoiada's example in carrying out spiritual reforms, made an about-face. When some of the princes of Judah came to him in obeisance, he listened to their request to turn away from serving the Lord. It was a tragic decision. Joash proved to be an idolater at heart.

God in His mercy sent prophets to warn the king and his people of the dangers of their course. Finally Zechariah took a position above the people so that he could be heard, and he asked the question of rebuke. This appeal, coming from Jehoiada's own son, should have reached Joash's heart. As king, he above all others should have been quick to respond. Instead he made another choice that proved his base ingratitude, not only to Jehoiada, who had saved him from certain death as an infant and had placed him on the throne, but also to God, who had been his real protector through the years. Joash ordered Zechariah stoned. The prophet met his death by a nod from this insensible king.

Joash was later assassinated in his own sickbed. He who had started life with such great promise was refused burial in the royal sepulchers. His tragic record is a stark reminder of the ungrateful choice.

---

[1] *The SDA Bible Commentary*, vol. 3, p. 276.

NOT QUITE ENOUGH FAITH

They that trust in the Lord shall be as mount Zion, which cannot be removed, but abideth for ever. Ps. 125:1.

There was another king by the name of Joash. He ruled the northern kingdom of Israel. This Joash greatly admired Elisha, but at heart he remained an idolater. He revered the old man of God, and when paying him a final visit broke down and cried at the thought that Elisha would soon die. Although he was far from righteous, Joash recognized in Elisha a true father in Israel who was more valuable in a crisis than all the horses and chariots in the country.

Joash was the kind of person who never committed himself to God, but who was strangely drawn to someone who was. God in His providence led Joash to visit the dying prophet that he might rectify his own mistakes.

The belligerent Syrians were again rattling the sword. If Joash would trust in God he would be victorious.

"Take your bow and arrow," Elisha ordered. "Now open the lattice window to the east." Propping himself up in bed, Elisha placed his wrinkled old hands on the king's hands. "Shoot!" Elisha commanded. The arrow sped out the window, and Elisha exclaimed, "The arrow of the Lord's deliverance." [1]

"Now take the arrows and strike the ground," Elisha continued. It was to be another symbolic act. If the king would be aggressive and persevere, total victory would be his. It was left with him to decide how many times he would strike the ground.

Joash picked up his arrows and chose to strike the ground only three times. It was a halfhearted approach to the command. This upset Elisha greatly, and he told the young king that now he would have only three victories instead of many more he would have had had he struck five or six times.

Often, like Joash, we fail to obtain the victory over the enemy's onslaught of temptation because we are unwilling to extend our faith to the limit.

---

[1] 2 Kings 13:17.

SEEING GOD WITHIN THE SHADOWS

As for me, I will behold thy face in righteousness: I shall be satisfied, when I awake, with thy likeness. Ps. 17:15.

It certainly was not easy for Elisha to lie in bed day after day, knowing that he was growing weaker and weaker. The lonely days of his lingering illness could have been the means to unravel his faith and send him moaning into self-pity. Elisha could have muttered about the unfairness of his dying condition as he compared himself with his predecessor, Elijah, who had been swept heavenward in a fiery chariot and had never tasted death. He could have allowed his mind to dwell on his unfortunate situation, but he didn't. Elisha chose to keep a firm grip on his God. He never allowed his mind to slip into that agonizing hole of despair.

Elisha chose not to complain. And that says something special about this man of God. It reveals to all of us that Elisha understood the force of the will in choosing not to turn inward in thoughts, but outward to God. All of us experience those moments when God seems hidden in the shadows and His kind providence obscured by dreaded circumstances that seem to blot out all thoughts of faith. At such a time Elisha's decision should be ours also. Instead of trying to penetrate the darkness, we need to recall God's past dealings with us and look beyond the gloom to the glory.

Elisha didn't need to see the angels hovering over his bed. He already knew. The years of active faith did not permit him to be blinded by the present.

"As on the heights of Dothan he had seen the encircling hosts of heaven, the fiery chariots of Israel and the horsemen thereof, so now he was conscious of the presence of sympathizing angels, and he was sustained. Throughout his life he had exercised strong faith, and as he had advanced in a knowledge of God's providences and of His merciful kindness, faith had ripened into an abiding trust in his God, and when death called him he was ready to rest from his labors." [1]

---

[1] *Prophets and Kings*, p. 264.

HIS OWN WORST ENEMY

When pride cometh, then cometh shame: but with the lowly is wisdom. Prov. 11:2.

It is written of Amaziah, son of Joash the king of Judah, that "he did that which was right in the sight of the Lord, but not with a perfect heart." [1] His on-again, off-again religious experience led him into pitfalls of pride that eventually caused his undoing.

One of his first acts as king of Judah was to hire 100,000 soldiers from Israel to bolster his own army for a battle against Edom. God sent a prophet to warn him that this expedition would fail. The Lord was not with Israel. Amaziah should send the troops from the northern kingdom home. Amaziah had laid out hard currency for these warriors, but he obeyed this command. But Amaziah's refusal to use these men made them so angry and upset that as they marched back home they raided the border area in retaliation. Amaziah suffered a double loss because he had chosen not to consult the Lord first.

When he was victorious against the Edomites it went to his head. First off, he borrowed some captured Edomite idols and bowed down to them. Again a prophet appeared, warning him that his base defection would bring down the wrath of God. But Amaziah wouldn't listen. Instead he sent a message to the king of Israel stating that he would like to meet him face to face in combat. Back came a letter from the north likening him to a thistle, while the king of Israel was a cedar of Lebanon by comparison.

"Just because you are boasting of victory over the Edomites, why do you want to meddle to your own hurt?" the king of Israel asked.

That was a good question. But Amaziah made another faulty decision and persisted in going into battle against Israel.

Not only was his own army routed in a precipitous retreat but the walls of Jerusalem were smashed and he himself was captured. His wavering religious behavior, prompted by pride, has left an ugly warning track smeared across the pages of Scripture. Shouldn't we learn to be consistent in our dedication to God?

---

[1] 2 Chron. 25:2.

RUNAWAY PROPHET

But Jonah rose up to flee unto Tarshish from the presence of the Lord. Jonah 1:3.

When God calls someone to carry out a particular mission, He provides enough divine resources for success. But Jonah failed to realize this. He allowed his emotions to sweep him along. His decision to run away was prompted by an imagination that considered the whole command unreasonable. Jonah simply did not stop to think that God could fulfill His obligation in the matter.

But before we shake our heads and wonder why this prophet should buy a ticket on a ship headed for Spain instead of going eastward to Nineveh as directed, we must remember that the Assyrian city was known for its wickedness.[1] Nineveh carried an ID of being the "bloody city."[2] Monuments were erected in that heathen metropolis that depicted captives being whipped, decapitated, tortured by hanging by their limbs, or impaled alive.[3] The Ninevites boasted of their cruelty. Atrocities brought rejoicing in the city.

So with these news reports consistently tucked away in his mind, Jonah felt that God simply had made a mistake and that it was better to flee than to follow His orders. After all, what good could ever come of preaching to such a bloodthirsty city as that? And if he fled, wouldn't that enable him to do better work for God? At least he'd be alive!

So Jonah hurried to the Joppa travel agency. Choosing to flee rather than obey is such a part of humanity's reaction to God's commands that Jonah reflects much truth about all of us. The Christian life requires a discipline that means making choices contrary to feelings, knowing that God will provide the power to fulfill. Once that is firm in the mind, there is no need for traumatic experiences.

---

[1] *The SDA Bible Commentary,* vol. 4, p. 998.
[2] Nahum 3:1.
[3] *Ibid.,* p. 1042.

DECISION FROM THE DEPTHS

When my soul fainted within me I remembered the Lord: and my prayer came in unto thee, into thine holy temple. Jonah 2:7.

Sometimes the Lord has to use extreme means in order to turn people in the right direction. Jonah had been running away from God, but when he found himself in the belly of the fish, he decided to run to Him. Not literally, of course. He really couldn't budge. Down there in that suffocating soft tomb with seaweed wrapped about his head, Jonah could only pray silently for deliverance.

Did you ever pray like that? Have you ever felt, as Jonah did, that the only way out was to turn to God? As we enter into Jonah's experience we may see that God sometimes does allow circumstances to arise that will seemingly crush us. But even then He is there, waiting patiently for us to decide for the right. And when we make that choice, He is ready to provide a way of escape.

In the darkness of that awful stomach, the runaway prophet could not even make out his hands in front of his face. There wasn't even the comfort of reading Bible promises. He couldn't talk to anyone. No human could hear his choking cries. All he heard was the gurgling of gastric juices and those abdominal sound effects that convinced him the end was upon him. Indeed he later wrote, "I went down to the bottoms of the mountains; the earth with her bars was about me for ever." [1] Jonah was on this squishy ride for three days and three nights, which in the Hebrew reckoning might be much shorter, but to Jonah it seemed forever—a hopelessly open-ended time slot. [2]

And then he prayed. As our verse for today says, "I remembered the Lord." How much better had he remembered earlier! Jonah could have avoided the submarine ride had his memory been activated the moment God called him. We can all avoid much hardship if we first remember God's care.

[1] Jonah 2:6.
[2] *The SDA Bible Commentary,* vol. 4, pp. 1000, 1003.

A CITY ON ITS KNEES

So the people of Nineveh believed God, and proclaimed a fast, and put on sackcloth, from the greatest of them even to the least of them. Jonah 3:5.

After Jonah dried off, the word of the Lord came to him the second time. He must start preaching in Nineveh. God uttered no rebuke, but Jonah's feet began churning eastward as fast as he could go. He wanted no more submarine rides or being belched onto the beach. He had run away from God. Now he was running with Him.

God knew all along about Jonah's persuasive powers. When the Lord selects a person for a special task, He knows precisely what the results will be. He gave His prophet one dominant theme: In forty days Nineveh will be overthrown. Jonah walked up one street and down the next and preached.

According to Jonah, Nineveh was "an exceeding great city." [1] Not by our standards, of course. It was actually only seven and one-half miles (twelve kilometers) in circumstance.[2] But Jonah had come from Palestine, and in ancient times even Israel's capital city of Samaria was only nineteen acres (eight hectares).[3] Yet Jonah had help while he paced up and down all those winding streets. Word of mouth is always rapid. And with Heaven's resources ready to bring penetrating conviction, Jonah's preaching produced amazing results.

"The message was not in vain. The cry that ran through the streets of the godless city was passed from lip to lip until all the inhabitants had heard the startling announcement. The Spirit of God pressed the message home to every heart and caused multitudes to tremble because of their sins and to repent in deep humiliation." [4]

Decisions were made quickly. From the king on his throne to the farmer bringing his produce to market, all made a consistent choice that they had better turn to the Lord with all their heart. The king issued a strange decree that included even the flocks and herds in a fast. The seriousness of their response should encourage us as we warn cities today.

---

[1] Jonah 3:3.
[2] *The SDA Bible Commentary*, vol. 4, p. 1000.
[3] *SDA Bible Dictionary*, p. 226.
[4] *Prophets and Kings*, p. 270.

ANGRY PROPHET

For I knew that thou art a gracious God, and merciful, slow to anger, and of great kindness. Jonah 4:2.

Jonah prayed those words, but they came from lips hot with anger. He reminded God that it was because he knew all about His loving nature that he had fled toward Tarshish in the first place. He had a suspicion that something like this would happen. The Ninevites would repent, and God would not destroy the city after all.

After his forty-day evangelistic campaign Jonah went east of the city to sit down and watch the fireworks. But nothing happened. All his persuasive preaching had come to nought, as far as he was concerned. Repentance was not what Jonah had in mind. He wanted action. He had predicted destruction in forty days, and the time was up. So he sat there pouting and steaming. The very idea that the Ninevites should not sizzle incensed him. His pride was wounded. And when pride gets in the road, people try to protect their reputation. Jonah simmered because news would reach home that his prophecy had not come to pass. He would be considered a false prophet, and that would be terribly embarrassing. Now Jonah was running ahead of God. His choice to be angry was prompted solely by selfishness.

God had a city full of repentant sinners, and one angry prophet hunched down out there in the desert, fuming all the while about the whole thing. That was why the Lord miraculously caused a gourd to grow. Jonah was extremely happy for the leafy shade. But when the Lord permitted a worm to chomp away on the gourd so that it withered, Jonah sweated it out, not realizing just how foolish his priorities had been. Sitting there in that hot sun with an east wind about to drop him in a faint, he felt more sorry about the gourd than for all the people in Nineveh. His story ought to jolt all of us into remembering how our own decisions can become distorted when we put self first.

HONEST OR CHARMING
Woe to them that are at ease in Zion. Amos 6:1.

Under the leadership of Jeroboam II, the northern kingdom of Israel reached its zenith of power.[1] Militarily the boundaries were secure, and peace prevailed in the land. But along with all this came a prosperity that bred pride, luxury, and the oppression of the rich grinding down the poor.

The sins of selfishness continued at a gallop. Gross immorality, drunkenness, extortion, bribery, and perversion of judgment did not abate, yet the people carried on an active form of religious exercise with a vigor that belied their inner decay. Church attendance was high. Offerings, songs, and elaborate ceremonies made great performances, but the moral fiber of the nation was so rotten that it was about to collapse. It was time for the voice of a prophet to be heard.

Down among the rough limestone hills of the little town of Tekoa, about five miles (eight kilometers) south of Bethlehem, God found His man.[2] Amos was herding sheep and gathering sycamore figs when the Lord laid His hand upon him to preach in Bethel, right in the king's chapel. Amos would bear a warning message against specific sins.

But how could he ever capture the attention of such smug people? God never overrides a prophet's own choice in how to present the message. Amos selected God's messages against the border nations as an attention-getting step. Once he got the people at Bethel nodding their approval and saying Amen, then he could proceed. But should he be honest or charming? Humanity enjoys playing verbal games. People would rather talk in generalities than about specific sins.

Fortunately, Amos chose to be honest. Once he had their attention, he delivered his searing broadside attack against popular sins. His decision to be absolutely frank without any unnecessary verbiage has provided us with some of the plainest and best in Hebrew literature. His penetrating words are still valid today and worth placing against the backdrop of contemporary complacency.

---

[1] *The SDA Bible Commentary*, vol. 4, pp. 953, 954.
[2] *Ibid.*, p. 956.

COURAGEOUS PROPHET

Then answered Amos, and said to Amaziah, I was no prophet, neither was I a prophet's son; but I was an herdman, and a gatherer of sycamore fruit: and the Lord took me as I followed the flock, and the Lord said unto me, Go, prophesy unto my people Israel. Amos 7:14, 15.

It was a classic encounter. Amaziah, the priest of Bethel, faced Amos, the prophet from Judah. The straight, hard-hitting preaching of this countryman of God had aroused Amaziah's animosity. He had already written to Jeroboam II and accused Amos of treason. He wanted to nail the prophet for conspiracy.

That Amos had been outspoken could not be denied. He had called the voluptuous, ease-loving women " 'cows of Bashan,' " [1] and in stinging irony had said, "Come to Bethel, and transgress." [2] But he could not honestly be accused of any attempt to overthrow the government.

Like all weak men in high places, Amaziah derived his security from his office and his connection with government. He assumed a tone of intellectual and moral superiority as he addressed the prophet. He even insinuated that Amos was being paid to prophesy. We can almost hear the rising pitch in his voice as he spoke.

"Visionary, be gone!" he ordered. "Go off to the land of Judah and earn your bread and play the prophet there. But don't prophesy again at Bethel, for it is the king's chapel and it is the king's court."

And this brings us to our text for today—Amos' answer. His words are based on a choice not to back off, but to stand firm for the Lord. No person who has a "thus saith the Lord" need flinch or be defensive. We should take heart from this courageous prophet, who demonstrated firmly that God's people need not be apologetic when under attack by false shepherds or by those who would seek to destroy their mission.

---

[1] Amos 4:1, R.S.V.
[2] Verse 4.

June 25

HEARTBROKEN PROPHET
My people are destroyed for lack of knowledge. Hosea 4:6.

With tears streaming down his face, the prophet Hosea wrote those words, for he knew just how God felt. Out of his own dark domestic troubles he understood how God experienced rejection by His own people. His own wandering wife, Gomer, never knew him personally. She was insensitive to his tender, loving nature and left home to seek out her lovers.

Some people, of course, have a problem as they read Hosea's book. It is written, "And the Lord said to Hosea, Go, take unto thee a wife of whoredoms and children of whoredoms." [1] On the surface it sounds as if God were ordering a man to transgress the law and commit adultery. But God's law is a transcript of His character. He cannot violate Himself, nor would He contribute to Satan's charges that the law of God is invalid. Thus this passage must be approached the same way as those startling texts that seem to show the wicked burning forever.

Nowhere does Scripture establish that Gomer was of questionable character when Hosea married her.[2] "Of whoredoms" may simply be describing her ancestry, not necessarily her personal character, or it may be projecting her future status after she left Hosea. The whole idea is that Hosea's tragic experience illustrates that God found Israel pure and clean when He chose His people as His bride. Hosea had such high ideals of marriage and such strong convictions against infidelity that we cannot imagine his choosing an impure woman for his wife.

But he did make a choice that demonstrates a love that will not let go. After their first child, he suspected the next two were not his own.[3] He urged the children to plead with their mother to return home and not to run around.

Gomer finally slipped so low that Hosea found her being sold on the slave block. There and then he decided to buy her back, and in so doing he left us a picture of God's care for us.

---
[1] Hosea 1:2.
[2] *The SDA Bible Commentary*, vol. 4, p. 888.
[3] *Ibid.*, p. 889.

PENALTY FOR PRESUMPTION

But when he was strong, his heart was lifted up to his destruction: for he transgressed against the Lord his God. 2 Chron. 26:16.

Uzziah was only 16 when he began to reign in Judah, but it is written that "he did that which was right in the sight of the Lord." [1] Not having to run a political campaign every few years to hold his office, he could settle back and rule for the next fifty-two years with ease. And during those years the nation really prospered. Not since the days of Solomon, nearly two centuries before, had Judah seen anything like it. Uzziah rebuilt and fortified the cities, making them safe from marauding bands of Bedouins.[2] Trade flourished, and the marketplaces hummed with activity.

But all this prosperity did not bring corresponding spiritual strength. To be sure, church attendance was high. People crowded the sanctuary, but humility and sincerity took a back seat.[3] People came out of habit and went through the motions of worship, which is easy to do in the setting of prosperity.

A presumptuous attitude prevailed. Even King Uzziah was afflicted with the problem. That is why he entered the Temple with his retinue, fully intending to burn incense on the altar. It was a rash and reckless choice. Azariah and eighty of his associates remonstrated with the king, urging him to cease and desist from his unlawful act.

Uzziah became hot with anger and stood defiantly resisting the priests. How dare anyone try to stop the king! At this point God cooled him down. Suddenly smitten with leprosy, Uzziah was escorted out of the precincts, to spend the rest of his days under quarantine.

We would do well to remember how Heaven feels about such matters. "Neither his exalted position nor his long life of service could be pleaded as an excuse for his presumptuous sin by which he marred the closing years of his reign." [4]

---

[1] 2 Chron. 26:4.
[2] *The SDA Bible Commentary,* vol. 3, p. 283.
[3] *Prophets and Kings,* pp. 303, 304.
[4] *Ibid.,* p. 304.

DECISION IN VISION

Also I heard the voice of the Lord, saying, Whom shall I send, and who will go for us? Then said I, Here am I; send me. Isa. 6:8.

The same sins that were bringing Israel to the brink of ruin were fast spreading throughout Judah. Gross drunkenness, social injustices, and idolatry ran rampant. The remaining God-fearing folk who stood firm for principle were appalled by the lowering standard of righteousness. They were tempted to give up in discouragement that God's purposes for His people would ever be fulfilled.[1]

It was at this time, when leprous King Uzziah was passing from the scene, that God called a young aristocrat to the prophetic office. Isaiah, whom tradition says was cousin to the king, shrank from this ministry. It was not easy telling the hypocrites that they really weren't the beautiful people they thought they were. It was not pleasant to write that God considered their fertile country a wasteland, their proud towns and cities nothing more than ash heaps, and their magnificent capital city like a shack in the midst of a cucumber patch. That kind of straightforward writing and preaching is never popular.

But in the year Uzziah died Isaiah had a vision that changed his whole outlook.[2] He had been wondering whether he shouldn't just leave Judah undisturbed in its idolatry and ask God to relieve him of his mission. But suddenly, while standing under the portico of the Temple, he saw the gate and inner veil withdrawn, and right before his eyes sat God upon His throne in the Holy of Holies. God's awesome majesty and glory overwhelmed Isaiah with a sense of his own impurity.

Whenever we sense the purity and holiness of God we will respond as Isaiah did. We will want nothing more than to extend God's character to those around us. Our choice will be "Here am I; send me."

[1] *Prophets and Kings*, p. 306.
[2] *Ibid.*, pp. 307, 308.

REAPING THE WHIRLWIND

Turn ye from your evil ways, and keep my commandments
. . . which I sent to you by my servants the prophets.
Notwithstanding they would not hear. 2 Kings 17:13, 14.

The problem in the ten northern tribes started when Jeroboam introduced calf worship in Israel. While Judah to the south had some good kings, Israel produced nothing but bad leadership. The nation continually chose idolatry, despite all that God could do through His servants the prophets. Through the man of God who prophesied at the altar at Bethel; through Elijah, the prophet of fire; and then through Elisha, the man of miracles, opportunity after opportunity came to turn the people back to the true God.[1] Still they sustained a steady decline in love for Him. Finally, God sent Amos, whose voice thundered of approaching doom. Hosea quickly followed, uttering loving appeals that were broken only by sobs. But at last even this sensitive man of God had to pen those dread words "Ephraim is joined to idols: let him alone."[2]

The Assyrians swept down upon apostate Israel, scattering them to lands far beyond Palestine. Only a remnant remained. At this time good King Hezekiah invited all, both those in Judah and whoever remained in Israel, to come to Jerusalem for the Passover. Riders went out with the gracious invitation that all might join in turning to the Lord. The people of Israel should have recognized this appeal and repented. But again most of them stubbornly refused or were indifferent. Some even treated the messengers with total contempt and "laughed them to scorn."[3] Only a small number responded.[4]

It was Israel's last chance. Two years later the Assyrians once again surged down upon them and finished them off as a nation. Hosea's prophecy had come to pass: "For they have sown the wind, and they shall reap the whirlwind."[5]

The nation's tragic choice should alert all of us to similar dangers. Rejection of God's gracious offers is always a most serious matter.

---

[1] *Prophets and Kings*, p. 281.
[2] Hosea 4:17.
[3] 2 Chron. 30:10.
[4] *Ibid.*, p. 291.
[5] Hosea 8:7.

HEZEKIAH'S CHOICE

Be strong and courageous, be not afraid nor dismayed for the king of Assyria . . .: with him is an arm of flesh; but with us is the Lord our God to help us, and to fight our battles. 2 Chron. 32:7, 8.

In the fourteenth year of Hezekiah, the great Assyrian juggernaut rolled into Judah, crushing all who stood in its cruel path. Sennacherib, the arrogant king of Assyria, claimed forty-six walled cities of Judah and then pounded at the gate of Jerusalem. Hezekiah bought a little time by paying a high ransom, temporarily saving the city.[1]

But Hezekiah knew that Sennacherib would return so he ordered the outside springs stopped up and the water channeled through his now-famous tunnel to the city. But all the clever and careful construction and preparations would avail nothing if the people did not have God with them. The Assyrians seemingly could not be stopped.

Rabshakeh, the boastful spokesman for Sennacherib, warned the people of Jerusalem not to listen to Hezekiah or to trust in their God to deliver them. But after a special prayer meeting with his high officials, including Isaiah the prophet, Hezekiah spoke the encouraging words of our text for today. And it is written, "The people rested themselves upon the words of Hezekiah."[2]

After Sennacherib went down to cut off any aid coming from the Egyptians, he sent an ultimatum to Hezekiah. Surrender or die. This was it! When Hezekiah received the letter he went into the Temple and spread it before the Lord. That was a wise decision. It is always good to take our problems directly to God. He knows precisely what course to take and He is ever eager to send divine aid whenever we turn to Him in time of need.

Sennacherib would eat his arrogant words. That night the Lord sent one angel, who wiped out 185,000 Assyrians. Word spread that the God of heaven could still answer prayer.

---

[1] *The SDA Bible Commentary,* vol. 3, p. 300.
[2] 2 Chron. 32:8.

HEZEKIAH'S PSALM

For the grave cannot praise thee, death can not celebrate thee: they that go down into the pit cannot hope for thy truth. The living, the living, he shall praise thee, as I do this day. Isa. 38:18, 19.

These words come from the psalm of Hezekiah. What had really distressed the king was that he could not praise God if he were dead. This is a profound statement on the condition of man in death, yet it reveals much more. Hezekiah refused to accept Isaiah's prophecy that he would soon die. Instead of resigning himself, as most would, he turned his face to the wall and wept and prayed. He did not consider the prediction as absolute, but conditional.

While we may wince at Hezekiah's reminding God how he had walked before Him with a perfect heart, we can respond to his choice to trust the Lord completely and to stay by Him in faith. Hezekiah has left us with the tremendous truth that God can often begin to work when we pray. In the light of the great controversy, prayer is the means whereby God can step in and thwart the enemy. We often let go the arm of the Lord too soon.

Isaiah, who had prophesied that Hezekiah would die, had to turn around and go back to reword his prediction. Hezekiah would get fifteen more years of life! The prophet ordered a fig poultice for the boil to bring down the inflammation that had undoubtedly spread frightfully. This simple means was in accordance with God's will, and Hezekiah did go down to the Temple on the third day to praise God, just as Isaiah had predicted.

The mature Christian may not need a particular sign that prophecy will be fulfilled, but God graciously answered Hezekiah's request and had turned the sun back ten degrees. It would serve to call attention to the God who could perform miracles. That is why Hezekiah praised the Lord with such fervor, leaving us with a lesson in laying claim to His promises and not letting go.

DISASTROUS DECISION

What have they seen in thine house? 2 Kings 20:15.

The miracle of the sundial's shadow going backward ten degrees was not done only in some remote Jerusalem city park. It occurred as far east as Babylon, as well. The astronomers and scholars of that far-off heathen land were greatly astonished and puzzled by the strange phenomenon. When one of the caravan messengers brought back the news report that this was God's sign to Hezekiah, Merodach-baladan, king of Babylon, immediately dispatched ambassadors to Judah. He wanted to congratulate Hezekiah and find out more about this God who could do such wonders.

It was a wonderful opportunity for Hezekiah. Here these representatives of a powerful heathen nation had traveled that long, hard route to Judah to learn more about the God of heaven. What changes could have been wrought had they taken back with them the truth concerning a gracious God! But no. Instead they returned with nothing more than a report of a guided tour through the treasury vault. They would come back some day, and this time not for any spiritual uplifting. For them the gold glittered far greater.

Hezekiah's pride had shoved aside all desire to show these heathen representatives anything more than his own accomplishments. That is why Isaiah asked that searing question "What have they seen in thine house?" Fortunately Hezekiah humbled himself and repented of his blunder, but that same question should resound in our own ears.

"The last rays of merciful light, the last message of mercy to be given to the world, is a revelation of His character of love." [1] But when inquiries are made concerning our message, how often we rattle off an achievement list! We would rather tell folk about our accomplishments as a church than the truth about God. Press releases paralyze us into believing that this is promulgating the message. It remains a disastrous decision.

---

[1] *Christ's Object Lessons,* p. 415.

REMARKABLE REPENTANCE

And when he was in affliction, he besought the Lord his God, and humbled himself greatly before the God of his fathers. 2 Chron. 33:12.

Of all the remarkable turnarounds in Scripture, none can quite compare with the case of Manasseh's conversion. Here was the king who brought the nation so low it is written of him that he "made . . . the inhabitants of Jerusalem to err, and to do worse than the heathen." [1] Yet this wicked ruler decided to turn to the Lord, and God graciously accepted his humble repentance and even permitted him to be restored from bondage to king.

The conversion part makes nice copy. We enjoy reading about people who are transformed by God's grace. Yet the long years of evil leadership would make most of us recoil so violently to Manasseh's rule that we would probably have written him off as an impossible case. It would be hard to imagine a man being converted who had ordered his own children offered as burnt offerings to the gods and who had revived the ancient heathen cult worship within the Temple precincts. Perhaps it was Manasseh who permitted apartments for the sodomites to be built next to the Temple. [2] These female and male prostitutes were used in the grossest forms of worship. Then to add to his wickedness, he turned to witchcraft and sorcery for direction in the affairs of the nation. But that wasn't all. When those who had remained stalwarts for God spoke out against his evil reign, he persecuted them with a vigor that caused the blood of the righteous to flow in the streets of Jerusalem.

Yet in spite of his horrible track record, Manasseh repented while in captivity. When he was down he looked up, and his conversion should encourage us all never to give up on anyone. We must never forget the power of the Holy Spirit to bring conviction and conversion. Manasseh's choice is evidence of that power.

---

[1] 2 Chron. 33:9.
[2] *The SDA Bible Commentary*, vol. 3, p. 304.

EARLY CHOICE FOR GOD

Josiah was eight years old when he began to reign. . . . And he did that which was right in the sight of the Lord. 2 Kings 22:1, 2.

It would seem that Josiah didn't have a chance. His grandfather Manasseh had left a heritage of evil that caused the whole nation to reek with the stench of corruption. Even though Manasseh later repented, there was no way to stop the moral decay. Since his grandfather had been responsible for killing off many of the righteous, including dear old Isaiah, the lad could find few good counselors.[1]

Not only that, but Amon, Manasseh's son, had followed hard on the same evil course. At age 16 he had fathered Josiah and had left the child with no worthy role model.[2] Amon was assassinated after a short two-year reign, and thus Josiah was thrust upon the throne at the tender age of 8.[3]

The words of warning given by such prophets as Habakkuk and Zephaniah undoubtedly influenced young Josiah.[4] "Warned by the errors of past generations, he chose to do right, instead of descending to the low level of sin and degradation to which his father and his grandfather had fallen."[5]

When he turned 16, Josiah decided it was time to make his commitment to the Lord more than verbal. He rededicated his life to God. When he was 20, he set out to destroy the images and evidences of idolatry wherever their disgraceful figures were present. It was the beginning of the greatest single reformatory movement ever instituted by anyone in the long, sad history of God's people.

In the thirteenth year of his reign, one year after he started his reforms, God called Josiah's friend Jeremiah to the prophetic office.[6] Thus at the right time the young king had Heaven's support for his decided determination to be firm for the Lord. In the light of contemporary spiritual irresponsibility, we should be greatly encouraged by Josiah's early choice.

---

[1] *Prophets and Kings*, p. 382.
[2] *Ibid.*, p. 383.
[3] *The SDA Bible Commentary*, vol. 2, p. 973.
[4] *Prophets and Kings*, p. 389.
[5] *Ibid.*, p. 384.
[6] *The SDA Bible Commentary*, vol. 3, p. 310.

STIRRED BY WORDS

And he read in their ears all the words of the book of the covenant which was found in the house of the Lord. . . . And all the people stood to the covenant. 2 Kings 23:2, 3.

King Josiah had ordered extensive repairs on the Temple, which his grandfather had allowed to fall into terrible neglect. Besides clearing the area of idols, the young monarch was determined to restore the house of God as much as possible.

During this time Hilkiah, the priest, stumbled across an ancient dusty scroll. "I have found the book of the law"! he cried.[1]

Hilkiah immediately handed the sacred writings to Shaphan, the scribe, who hurried away to Josiah with the tremendous news of the discovery. For many years the people had been deprived of hearing those words Moses had written long centuries before. As Shaphan read those encouraging words of God's blessings on obedience and warnings of judgments to those who transgressed, Josiah was deeply affected. He had already started a reform to destroy idolatry, and this moved him to inquire of the Lord just what else he should do.

That was when the delegation from the king sought out Huldah, the prophetess who lived in the new, or outer, portion of the city.[2] Since Josiah had deeply humbled himself, the awful judgments to come would be delayed until he had died. Josiah did not give up in despair, but he sensed that God had left open the way for repentance and reformation.

Immediately he decided to call for a holy convocation to read aloud those words that had stirred him so much. His personal choice of believing God affected his own emotions. The words and the pathos of his voice deeply moved the people. Whenever we are stirred by God's Word, others will also respond to the truth.

---

[1] 2 Kings 22:8.
[2] *The SDA Bible Commentary*, vol. 2, p. 974.

TMTD-7

JOSIAH'S FAILURE

Wherefore let him that thinketh he standeth take heed lest he fall. 1 Cor. 10:12.

Josiah's long record of reforms sweeps through the pages of sacred history like a whirlwind. He knocked over idols and ground images to powder. He destroyed the houses of the sodomites, rid the country of witchcraft and idolatrous priests, and smashed every vestige of heathen worship he could find. The Temple was repaired and the sacrificial offerings restored. And he gave the people the most lavish Passover since the days of Samuel. According to the prediction of Huldah, the prophetess, he was to die in peace. But he died in battle at age 39.[1]

Pharaoh Necho had warned Josiah not to meddle in his affairs. The Egyptian army was pressing northward to assist the Assyrians against the Babylonians. " 'I am not coming against you,' " Necho urged.[2]

But Josiah was determined to go into battle against him. It was a pride-filled decision. Necho had no quarrel with the king of Judah. All he wanted was to get to the Euphrates to engage his forces with Babylon.[3] But Josiah disguised himself and took up a position with his forces where the southern road crosses the pass into the Plain of Esdraelon.[4] It was an ill-fated decision. The Egyptians mortally wounded him at Megiddo.

"Because Josiah died in battle, who will charge God with denying His word that Josiah should go to his grave in peace? . . . To turn back with his army would have been humiliating, so he went on. And because of this, he was killed in battle, a battle that he should not have had anything to do with. . . . He went against the word of God, choosing to follow his own way, and God could not shield him from the consequences of his act." [5] We should not be surprised at the results when we follow our own desires.

---

[1] *SDA Bible Dictionary,* p. 623.
[2] 2 Chron. 35:21, R.S.V.
[3] *The SDA Bible Commentary,* vol. 2, p. 980.
[4] *SDA Bible Dictionary,* p. 624.
[5] *The SDA Bible Commentary,* Ellen G. White Comments, on 2 Kings 23:29, 30, p. 1039.

WHEN GOD CALLS

Be not afraid of their faces: for I am with thee to deliver thee, saith the Lord. Jer. 1:8.

About two and one-half miles (four kilometers) northeast of Jerusalem, in the little town of Anathoth, lived a young man whom God called to stand for right against tremendous opposition.[1] Jeremiah was a priest by birth, but God selected him also as a prophet in the days of Josiah. He wanted Jeremiah to raise his voice pleading with the people against the rising iniquity. Josiah's reforms had not taken root, and God needed someone to speak out in warning and counsel.[2]

The word of the Lord came to Jeremiah with the startling revelation that he had been chosen even before he was born! Jeremiah could, of course, have refused to accept his role as prophet.[3] Although he decided not to turn God down, he did shrink from that high calling. He reminded God that he was but a mere child compared with the graybeards around him.[4] He was possibly only in his late teens, and the thought of his speaking for God when he was such a timid and naturally retiring person made him shudder. How could he speak eloquently for God? How could he preach to those angry Jews in Jerusalem?

God told Jeremiah not to mention his youth as a disadvantage. He promised to give him words to speak. And then those reassuring words of our text came thundering from heaven, ''Be not afraid of their faces''! Whatever scowls or sneers or facial expressions that were possible in a hostile audience, God would stand right beside Jeremiah. And then the Lord touched the young man's mouth and promised to give him words to speak.

God may not call us to the prophetic office as He did Jeremiah, but we would do well to learn the lesson of his decision to accept God's calling for any task, realizing that ''all His biddings are enablings.''[5]

---

[1] *The SDA Bible Commentary*, vol. 4, p. 354.
[2] *Prophets and Kings*, p. 410.
[3] *The SDA Bible Commentary*, vol. 4, p. 354.
[4] *Ibid.*, p. 355.
[5] *Christ's Object Lessons*, p. 333.

THE QUESTION FOR SIN LOVERS

An appalling and horrible thing has happened in the land: the prophets prophesy falsely, and the priests rule at their direction; my people love to have it so, but what will you do when the end comes? Jer. 5:30, 31, R.S.V.

There will always be those who make religious activity a substitute for repentance. This is a most dangerous decision, yet it happens frequently to professed Christians.

God instructed Jeremiah to preach a warning message about such choices. "Diminish not a word," God said.[1] The Lord knew that the young prophet might shrink from delivering such a sermon.

We have Jeremiah's notes today. He preached his sermon in the Temple and told the people that if they did not repent, God would make that house like Shiloh. Back in the days when Eli lightly passed over the sins of his sons, God had allowed the site of the ancient sanctuary to be destroyed. "Israel had vainly thought that, notwithstanding their sinful practices, the presence of the ark would insure them victory over the Philistines. In like manner, during the days of Jeremiah, the inhabitants of Judah were prone to believe that a strict observance of the divinely appointed services of the temple would preserve them from a just punishment for their wicked course."[2]

The priests, and especially the false prophets, screamed their hatred of Jeremiah and all that he stood for. "You shall surely die!" they vehemently responded.

Would Jeremiah's message be accepted any better today? Are we allowing energetic evangelistic activity to substitute for genuine practical godliness in the home and in business? The very notion that anyone should speak out against a God-ordained activity creates problems for those who use that activity as a cover to keep from any real cleansing. "A neglect to repent and to render willing obedience will bring upon men and women today as serious consequences as came upon ancient Israel."[3]

---

[1] Jer. 26:2.
[2] *Prophets and Kings*, p. 416.
[3] *Ibid.*, pp. 416, 417.

NEVER BACKING DOWN

But the Lord is with me as a mighty terrible one: therefore my persecutors shall stumble, and they shall not prevail: they shall be greatly ashamed; for they shall not prosper: their everlasting confusion shall never be forgotten. Jer. 20:11.

The news of Jeremiah's warning sermon quickly reached the ears of the princes, and they hurried over from the palace to hear for themselves.[1]

"This man is worthy to die"![2] shouted the priests and false prophets, giving vent to the same old hue and cry of those who cannot abide with truth.

But Jeremiah staunchly stood up and flatly told them all that it was God Himself who had called him to preach. "Amend your ways and your doings, and obey the voice of the Lord your God," he urged.[3]

And then in a swift, bold move he decided to put his own life on the line. That choice actually saved his life. "I am in your hand," he declared.[4] They could kill him if they chose, but he reminded them that if they did, they would be shedding innocent blood, because God had told him to preach.

Had Jeremiah flinched in the slightest or had he been in the least bit intimidated by the scowling faces and grinding teeth, his whole message would have been ineffective and he would have lost his life.[5] Instead he chose to stand his ground, and the princes were impressed. They chose to defend him and spoke in his favor. The elders also united with the princes and persuaded the false prophets, priests, and people that Jeremiah was in good company with other prophets who had preached similar messages.

How could a timid, retiring person like Jeremiah muster such courage? The secret lies in his grasp on the Terrible One, who stood beside him as a warrior against all opposition. There is no substitute for trusting in the God of the universe.

---

[1] *Prophets and Kings*, p. 417.
[2] Jer. 26:11.
[3] Verse 13.
[4] Verse 14.
[5] *Ibid.*, p. 418.

DECISION TO QUIT

Then I said, I will not make mention of him, nor speak anymore in his name. But his word was in mine heart as a burning fire shut up in my bones. Jer. 20:9.

It is quite easy for any preacher to feel courageous and energetic in his ministry when people glad-hand him and give their smiling approval. But let stony glares and frowning disapprovals come, and depression sets in. Jeremiah felt so low and so much a failure that he even complained to the Lord that He had deceived him. We must not react to Jeremiah's complaint too harshly, though. He had just spent a whole night in a terribly cramped position because a priest by the name of Pashur, who opposed the prophet, had provided the indignity of smiting him and then placing him in the stocks.

When Jeremiah was released the next morning, he prophesied that Pashur and his family would die in Babylonian captivity, along with the rest of his unrepentant friends in Judah. But then the prophet slumped down into a depression that brought him to the decision to quit. He was through, as far as he was concerned. Failure ground its way into his very heart and left him with only the jarring complaint. He decided right then and there to close his ministry. He would not speak for God again.

Jeremiah made his decision during a moment of depression, and that is never a good time to make a choice. Later, a quieter moment, Jeremiah knew that God had not deceived him or failed to fulfill His promises. And when he pondered the promises of God's word, they became like a burning fire, and he literally said, "I could not stand it!" He had to go on speaking for the Lord.[1]

Into the life of every Christian, low points are bound to come. But when they do come, we should remember Jeremiah and his plaintive cry "I am in derision daily." [2] He was about to quit, but God's burning word sustained him.

---

[1] *The SDA Bible Commentary,* vol. 4, p. 431.
[2] Jer. 20:7.

JEHOIAKIM'S LAST CHANCE

The heart is deceitful above all things, and desperately wicked: who can know it? Jer. 17:9.

The answer to that penetrating question flashes back in the very next verse: "I the Lord search the heart." Only through the operation of the Holy Spirit can we know ourselves.

But Jehoiakim, king of Judah, was the kind who refuses to allow the Lord to reveal the truth about his perverse character. Jehoiakim didn't want to know. Instead he chose to remain cloaked in his own stubbornness.

While Jeremiah was still in prison God instructed him to write out the warnings of impending doom against an unrepentant nation.[1] The prophet dictated the message and told his secretary, Baruch, to go read it to the multitudes.

The princes also wanted to hear Jeremiah's words, but when Baruch repeated his reading they suggested that the secretary hide himself because the words would certainly arouse the king's wrath.

When Jehoiakim got wind of all that had happened he ordered the scroll to be brought in and read in his presence. It was winter, and he was seated before an open hearth. When the royal attendant started to read, the king leaned forward, snatched the scroll, cut it with his penknife, and threw the parchment into the flames.

"Scorning the unusual privileges granted him, Judah's king willfully followed a way of his own choosing. . . . Within a few years he closed his disastrous reign in ignominy, rejected of Heaven, unloved by his people, and despised by the rulers of Babylon . . . and all as the result of his fatal mistake in turning from the purpose of God as revealed through His appointed messenger."[2] It was Jehoiakim's last chance.

Those who seek to destroy the effectiveness of God's Word will find in the end that they have only destroyed themselves.

---

[1] *Prophets and Kings*, p. 433.
[2] *Ibid.*, p. 438.

THE END OF A FALSE PROPHET

Behold, I am against them that prophesy false dreams, saith the Lord, and do tell them, and cause my people to err by their lies. Jer. 23:32.

One of the main reasons the people of Jeremiah's time continued their spiritual decline was the powerful influence of the false prophets.[1] These corrupt, self-styled prognosticators were ever on a popularity-seeking binge. They would do or say anything for applause.

Jeremiah's prophecies that Babylon would be used by God to chastise the rebellious nation never brought any great cheers from the crowds. Jeremiah insisted that the lightest punishment God could inflict on His people for their evil ways was to allow their captivity, and that it would be much easier on them if they would submit to the rule of the Babylonians. If they fought back, it would bring the wrath of the heathen nation down on them in full fury.[2]

The false prophet Hananiah, the chief opponent of Jeremiah, simply could not tolerate that kind of talk. During one of Jeremiah's illustrated sermons, when the prophet wore a yoke about his neck to demonstrate how the surrounding nations and Judah should submit to the yoke of Babylon, Hananiah offered a daring challenge. It was a stupid decision that soon cost him his life. Jerking the yoke from Jeremiah's neck, he smashed it to the ground and proclaimed that God would release those taken in captivity in two years.

Two years, as opposed to Jeremiah's seventy! It is not difficult to imagine the effect this had on the people. Jeremiah simply walked away. He had had enough. But then God told him to go back and level a prophecy against Hananiah. He would soon die as a result of his bad influence.

Hananiah actually dropped dead in two months, leaving us a warning of how God feels about listening to such false prophets, who would smooth over messages He sends to His people.[3]

---

[1] *The SDA Bible Commentary*, vol. 4, p. 414.
[2] *Prophets and Kings*, p. 444.
[3] *SDA Bible Dictionary*, p. 455; *Prophets and Kings*, p. 446.

REWARD FOR A GALLANT CHOICE

For I will surely deliver thee, and thou shalt not fall by the sword, . . . because thou hast put thy trust in me, saith the Lord. Jer. 39:18.

The Babylonians temporarily lifted the siege of Jerusalem to meet the advancing Egyptian army marching up from the south.[1] Jeremiah felt that his long years of service for God and his people was completed, and he quietly headed for his home village of Anathoth, three miles (five kilometers) to the northeast of the doomed city.[2]

He was just going through the Sheep Gate when he was apprehended and accused of slipping off to join the Babylonians.[3] It was a false charge, but the princes were so angry that they beat the poor old prophet and threw him into prison. Weak-kneed King Zedekiah secretly sent for Jeremiah and provided him with bread, yet when the princes heard that Jeremiah had told the king to surrender, they became even more determined than ever. Jeremiah should die, they urged, and the vacillating king allowed these evil men to lower Jeremiah into an empty cistern to starve to death.

Enter Ebed-melech, an Ethiopian who was one of the king's favorite servants. "These men have done evil," he said.[4] And then with compassionate tones he urged the king to allow him to release the aged prophet from the foul-smelling mire that Jeremiah had sunk into at the bottom of the pit. It was a gallant choice, a choice to stand for God's true prophet in the face of all the threatening actions of the bad-tempered princes and false prophets.

With the king's consent Ebed-melech took thirty men with him, and after tossing down some old rags to place under the prophet's armpits for protection from the ropes, this noble servant hoisted Jeremiah to safety.

God marked his kind action, and in our text for today God assured Ebed-melech that He would not forget him. Our God puts His reputation on the line for those who trust Him.

---

[1] *The SDA Bible Commentary*, vol. 4, p. 485.
[2] *Ibid.*, vol. 2, p. 734.
[3] *Ibid.*, vol. 4, p. 485.
[4] Jer. 38:9.

SLAVE TO PUBLIC OPINION

Obey, I beseech thee, the voice of the Lord, which I speak unto thee: so it shall be well unto thee, and thy soul shall live. Jer. 38:20.

Those words of Jeremiah to wavering King Zedekiah still hold meaning for those who have made no firm commitment to the Lord. From the prophet's final pleading with the vacillating monarch we may learn something of the terrible consequences of yielding to public opinion.

After the prophet cleaned himself up from the awful pit experience, Zedekiah wanted a private interview with him.[1] The king covered up the real purpose of his meeting, however, because he feared a violent reaction from the princes and false prophets. In that interview Jeremiah pleaded with the king to surrender to the Babylonians, who by now had returned and were at the height of the siege.[2]

"If you will go to the Babylonians, you will save yourself and the city," Jeremiah urged. "But if you won't surrender, then you will never escape, and this city will be burned."

Tears streamed down Jeremiah's face during his final appeal to the king. It was now or never for Zedekiah. It was the moment to decide. "But the king had started on the wrong course, and he would not retrace his steps. He decided to follow the counsel of the false prophets, and of the men whom he really despised, who ridiculed his weakness in yielding so readily to their wishes. He sacrificed the noble freedom of his manhood and became a cringing slave to public opinion."[3]

Zedekiah was under conviction to follow Jeremiah's counsel, but he didn't have the backbone to accept God's leading. The end was more terrible than his worst fears. The beautiful Temple and the city were destroyed, his own sons were killed in front of him, and his eyes were put out before the invaders led him away to die miserably in captivity.[4]

---

[1] *The SDA Bible Commentary*, vol. 4, p. 488.
[2] *Ibid.*, p. 487.
[3] *Prophets and Kings*, pp. 457, 458.
[4] *Ibid.*, pp. 458, 459.

JEREMIAH'S LAST CHOICE

Greater love hath no man than this, that a man lay down his life for his friends. John 15:13.

There is a persistent tradition that Jeremiah was finally stoned to death by his own people at Daphnae, in Egypt.[1] Considering the negative attitude his own countrymen took toward the prophet, we can surmise that Jeremiah did not quietly pass to the grave in peace. This tender, timid man, who since his youth had faithfully preached God's message to a recalcitrant crowd, undoubtedly met his doom by the very people who dragged him down to Egypt in spite of his pleas to remain in Palestine as God had directed.[2]

But it must be remembered that Jeremiah did not have to stay with his people. He had a chance to leave and to live comfortably under the full protection of Nebuchadnezzar, who appreciated the prophet.

Bound in chains, Jeremiah had been led away to the Babylonian prisoner station in Ramah, where Nebuchadnezzar's captain of the guard found him among the captives and released him.[3]

"I am loosing you this day from your chains. If you would like to come to Babylon, you may; or if you choose to stay, that is fine too. It is your choice."

Jeremiah decided to remain with the remnant of his people. He would urge them to cooperate with the Babylonians in restoring some semblance of government in his native land. But the perversity of his people prevailed, and they rejected his God-given counsel. In the end he laid down his life for those whom he considered to be his friends, but who treated him as an enemy.

Why would Jeremiah exchange a pleasant retirement for tears and heartache? Only because of the driving force of love! He had come so close to the Lord that His life was reflected in Jeremiah's decision.

---

[1] *SDA Bible Dictionary*, p. 567.
[2] *Ibid.*
[3] *The SDA Bible Commentary*, vol. 4, p. 491.

DECISION IN THE DINING HALL

But Daniel purposed in his heart that he would not defile himself with the portion of the king's meat, nor with the wine which he drank. Dan. 1:8.

When Nebuchadnezzar swept through Judah during his first invasion of the western lands, he took captives from the royal line of that unhappy country. Among those who sadly trekked eastward to the conqueror's land was a young aristocrat who was destined to take his place among the galaxy of prophets.

During his first nineteen years in Babylon, Daniel saw his own country wiped out as a kingdom.[1] Although he had received his fundamental education in his Judean homeland, he studied three years in the University of Babylon.

Attending the university was an ordeal that was calculated to subvert those who would vacillate between principle and inclination. It required familiarization with courtly grandeur, hypocrisy, and paganism.

There was an additional problem in the dining hall. Although Daniel and his companions understood the relationship between the principles of health and the activity of the mind, they certainly could have found a plausible excuse for departing from their strict temperate habits. After all, they could have argued, if they chose to follow their religious training it might offend the king. Then they would lose their positions in court, and could possibly even lose their lives. Compromise would enable them to get in good with the king so that they could share their faith. Compromise always has a logical appeal.

"But Daniel did not hesitate. The approval of God was dearer to him than the favor of the most powerful earthly potentate—dearer than life itself. He determined to stand firm in his integrity, let the result be what it might."[2]

How few are willing to make a similar choice today! How few experience the freedom that such a choice affords!

---

[1] *The SDA Bible Commentary,* vol. 4, p. 745.
[2] *Prophets and Kings,* p. 483.

CONFIDENCE IN HIS GOD

I thank thee, and praise thee, O thou God of my fathers, who hast given me wisdom and might, and hast made known unto me now what we desired of thee. Dan. 2:23.

Nebuchadnezzar was angry. The so-called wise men of his realm were stalling, and he knew it. They wanted him to relate the mysterious dream that he had had, but he told them that the whole nocturnal experience had escaped him. If these men were supposed to have communication with the gods and if they were holding out on him, he would have them all destroyed.

The problem with his death decree was that it included the Hebrew graduates. The king had been so infuriated with the hemming and hawing that he had ordered the entire learned class of his society wiped out.[1] It wasn't a matter of reading some checklist on the bulletin board. The death squad had arrived to slay Daniel and his friends.

Under such circumstances many of us would quiver with fear, fall on our knees, and beg for mercy, or panic into a mumbling, incoherent prayer circle. But not Daniel. He chose to face Arioch, the captain of the guard. "Why is the decree so hasty from the king?" he asked.[2]

When Arioch explained the circumstances, Daniel immediately requested a personal interview with the great monarch. He would plead for just a little time. This was no stalling tactic. He needed to be still and hear God speak His special mysteries to him personally.

And the answer came. It always will when we trust God. That is why Daniel prayed those words of our text for today. He was thankful that God had opened to him the truth about the king's dream.

But Daniel held no special edge on God. We may all have what he had. "Those who accept the one principle of making the service and honor of God supreme will find perplexities vanish, and a plain path before their feet."[3]

---

[1] *The SDA Bible Commentary*, vol. 4, p. 768.
[2] Dan. 2:15.
[3] *The Desire of Ages*, p. 330.

BOW-OR-BURN CEREMONY

If it be so, our God whom we serve is able to deliver us from the burning fiery furnace, and he will deliver us out of thine hand, O king. Dan. 3:17.

The grand day of dedication for Nebuchadnezzar's giant image of gold arrived. There it stood, eighty-seven and one-half feet (twenty-seven meters) tall, gleaming in the sunlight.[1] The plain of Dura buzzed with activity as courtiers and VIPs from the Babylonian realm scurried about the monarch. When the orchestra sounded, it was not just a matter of every head bowing and every eye closing but all were to prostrate themselves in reverence before the golden statue.

But when the orchestra began to play, some in the vast crowd peeked. Just as the jealousy-inspired antagonists of the Hebrews figured, the three Jews remained on their feet. The music hadn't stirred them to reverence at all. Quickly feet began churning to make the report.[2] And the finger-pointing produced the desired effect. Nebuchadnezzar grew furious. But he would give the young men another chance, reminding them that when the music swelled to a crescendo, they were to bow, or they would burn in the brickkiln that had been used to make the image.

But the three Hebrews did not need to huddle for a private conference. They had already made their decision. If they had been afraid of the king's decree they wouldn't have stood in the first place. That was when Shadrach, Meshach, and Abednego uttered those words of our text for today. God could deliver them. But if in His providence He did not see fit to bring them through the fire, they still would not buckle to the king's demands.

"As in the days of Shadrach, Meshach, and Abednego, so in the closing period of earth's history the Lord will work mightily in behalf of those who stand steadfastly for the right."[3] But knowing Him personally is the key to making courageous decisions.

---

[1] *The SDA Bible Commentary*, vol. 4, p. 780.
[2] *Ibid.*, p. 783.
[3] *Prophets and Kings*, p. 513.

A DECREE TOO FAR

Therefore I make a decree, That every people, nation, and language, which speak any thing amiss against the God of Shadrach, Meshach, and Abednego, shall be cut in pieces, and their houses shall be made a dunghill. Dan. 3:29.

Of course Nebuchadnezzar was impressed. Who wouldn't be? The brickkiln had been fired with a mixture of crude oil and chaff until it had blazed seven times hotter than usual.[1] Even his own officers who threw the three Hebrews into the fiery opening were scorched, their singed bodies lying as grotesque proof that it was hot down there.

But suddenly Nebuchadnezzar arose from his throne. "Did not we cast three men bound into the . . . fire?" he asked, his voice rising with excitement. "Lo, I see four men loose, walking in the midst of the fire, and they have no hurt; and the form of the fourth is like the Son of God."[2]

Now how did Nebuchadnezzar know what the Son of God looked like? Few realize the impact of the Hebrews' testimony to this heathen monarch. They had told the king about the Redeemer to come, and when he saw the fourth Man walking about, he recognized the Son of God.[3]

After he called for the three young men to come out and the fourth Man had disappeared, he made a public confession. Never had he or anyone else seen anything like this. Not even the smell of smoke lingered on the men, yet the cords that had bound them were burned off!

But then Nebuchadnezzar made a wrong decision. It was a choice that was designed to make believers in a hurry, but it was not after God's order. "It was right for the king to make public confession, and to seek to exalt the God of heaven above all other gods; but in endeavoring to force his subjects to make a similar confession of faith and to show similar reverence, Nebuchadnezzar was exceeding his right as a temporal sovereign."[4]

---

[1] *The SDA Bible Commentary,* vol. 4, pp. 782, 783.
[2] Dan. 3:24, 25.
[3] *Prophets and Kings,* p. 509.
[4] *Ibid.,* pp. 510, 511.

INSANITY TO CONVERSION

"Now I Nebuchadnezzar praise and extol and honour the King of heaven, all whose works are truth, and his ways judgment: and those that walk in pride he is able to abase. Dan. 4:37.

The last official act of Nebuchadnezzar's life of which we have record was those words.[1] He finally acknowledged publicly that the authority of God was supreme in his life.

But it hadn't always been that way. After he had had that peculiar dream in which he saw a lofty tree cut down, God allowed him time for repentance. The interpretation Daniel gave was clear. Either Nebuchadnezzar would turn from his pride and arrogance or he would be cut down in a most embarrassing fashion.

The months passed slowly, but instead of turning repentant Nebuchadnezzar indulged in his same old proud habits. A whole year slipped by, and one day while walking on one of his rooftop palaces, he scanned the city before him. And as he breathed in that Babylonian air a thought just struck him with great force: Everywhere he looked he saw reminders of his power and clever management. The hanging gardens, the walls, the temples, and the palaces were impressive. Everywhere his eye drifted he saw full evidence that he had achieved the greatness of a world empire and city that was renowned. The tender nerve endings of pride transmitted the message, and he basked in the thought. It was a fatal choice.

"Is not this great Babylon, that I have built?"[2]

While the words were fresh in his mouth God removed Nebuchadnezzar's reason, and he became a maniac crawling about like some animal. Removing him from office, his supporters led him out to pasture, where he munched on grass and grunted for seven years.

But the insanity treatment did the job. "The once proud monarch had become a humble child of God."[3] Never again did Nebuchadnezzar soar away on the clouds of ego. He had learned that humility is the essence of real greatness.

---

[1] *Prophets and Kings,* p. 521.
[2] Dan. 4:30.
[3] *Ibid.*

BELSHAZZAR'S FATAL CHOICE

Thou art weighed in the balances, and art found wanting. Dan. 5:27.

From his youth Belshazzar chose to follow his own inclinations.[1] He cared not that his grandfather had committed his life to the God of heaven. For him the power and glory of the Babylonian kingdom gave free license to satisfy all the clamoring of the flesh. His whole being was wrapped up in wine, women, and song. Weakened by constant partying, he plunged recklessly ahead with little thought about tomorrow. He felt secure behind the massive walls of the city, and his last feast only accentuated the doom that was about to descend upon him.

The decision to bring in the sacred vessels captured from the Jews many years before was the signal that Heaven could wait no longer. Right at the height of all the toasting to the gods, that mysterious hand began tracing those cryptic words on the banquet-hall plaster.

Belshazzar came unhinged. It is written, "His thoughts troubled him, so that the joints of his loins were loosed, and his knees smote one against another."[2] Conscience was aroused. "When God makes men fear, they cannot hide the intensity of their terror."[3] All those beautiful women, the princes, and the statesmen were shaking with fright too. They were a part of the whole inebriated scene.

When Daniel was called in to interpret the mysterious message which remained on the wall, he let the king know that his waywardness had caught up with him. Without hesitation Daniel made plain the cause of God's final verdict. Belshazzar had crossed the boundary. He was finished. Already the alien armies had penetrated the walls of the great city.

Belshazzar lost his life and his kingdom that night because he was consistently satisfied with impulses and passions. In an age when the very atmosphere is tainted with the Belshazzar mentality, his case needs constant reviewing as a reminder of the futility of such life-destroying decisions.

---

[1] *Prophets and Kings,* pp. 522, 523.
[2] Dan. 5:6.
[3] *Ibid.,* p. 524.

CONSISTENT UNDER PRESSURE

Now when Daniel knew that the writing was signed, he went into his house; and his windows being open in his chamber toward Jerusalem, he kneeled upon his knees three times a day, and prayed, and gave thanks before his God, as he did aforetime. Dan. 6:10.

When Darius promoted Daniel to the highest civil position in the Medo-Persian Empire it triggered a tremendous jealous reaction among the Median and Persian dignitaries.[1] The fact that a Jew and a former minister under the Babylonian government should hold such an office above them was too much. They huddled for a plot to ensnare Daniel, but they finally decided that nothing could be found wrong with him except his relationship to his God. That was quite a testimony!

So playing on the king's vanity and using the unbending restrictions of the legal system, they sprang their envious trap. Darius signed a decree stating that nobody could pray to any god except the king for a thirty-day stretch. Gleefully rubbing their hands and nodding their smiling approval, the dignitaries knew that the trap had snapped shut. Daniel was doomed to the lions' den.

But when the law went into effect Daniel did not go into some fluttering, nervous hand-wringing cycle of high-pitched prayer. He simply knelt in his usual way, with the windows open toward his beloved Jerusalem, and calmly prayed as he always did. It was a decision of high faith that offered proof of his integrity before God and his grip on Heaven's promises. "A man whose heart is stayed upon God will be the same in the hour of his greatest trial as he is in prosperity, when the light and favor of God and of man beam upon him. Faith reaches to the unseen, and grasps eternal realities."[2]

There are always those who would suggest some sort of compromise. At least be discreet and shut the windows so the snoopers can't peek. But Daniel refused to change his worship to save his life, leaving us a worthy example for times when we are under pressure.

---

[1] *The SDA Bible Commentary*, vol. 4, p. 810.
[2] *Prophets and Kings*, p. 545.

LODGING WITH LIONS

**My God hath sent his angel, and hath shut the lions'
mouths, that they have not hurt me. Dan. 6:22.**

Satan, of course, was behind the jealous plot to destroy Daniel.
The enemy gets very fidgety when someone truly represents the
character of God. But he felt especially nervous with Daniel in his
high place right in the midst of a heathen court, so he inspired those
snooping dignitaries to manipulate a decree out of Darius that
would seal Daniel in the lions' den.

The king woke up to their scheme too late. When he
discovered that he had become the tool for destroying his faithful
servant, he tried every legal means possible to release Daniel. But
the revengeful dignitaries were waiting in the wings to remind him
of the unalterable law of the Medes and Persians. So before the day
was done Satan had his wish, and Daniel went into the pit.

Now, our God has a real flair for the dramatic. At least it turns
out that way, because His deliverances are precisely timed to
counteract the work of the enemy and to demonstrate His power to
save. Daniel understood that. He knew that his God could deliver
him. So did the king. In fact, Darius said, "Thy God whom thou
servest continually, he will deliver thee." [1]

That constant communion with his God enabled Daniel to
remain calm amid a most trying situation. He chose to stay close to
God and not to panic. And that kind of faith comes only after long
hours of consistent communion. It is never built in haste.

For a man in his mid-eighties to spend the night in the worst
"hotel" in Babylon wasn't exactly easy. [2] Down there in that dark,
smelly dungeon, those big snarling cats were anything but cozy. It
could be hard on the nervous system, especially when you are
tired. But Daniel was relaxed. He knew about God's angels.

One was sent with a mouth clamp and claw paralysis especially
to thwart Satan's evil purpose. The words of our text for today so
thrilled Darius that he brought the prophet up and threw the
dignitaries and their families down into the den.

---

[1] Dan. 6:16.
[2] *The SDA Bible Commentary*, vol. 4, pp. 810-812.

INTERCESSORY PRAYER

O my God, incline thine ear, and hear; open thine eyes, and behold our desolations, and the city which is called by thy name: for we do not present our supplications before thee for our righteousnesses, but for thy great mercies. Dan. 9:18.

The seventy years of captivity were approaching the finish line when Daniel received the remarkable 2300-day prophecy.[1] The vision staggered him. He feared that, because of impenitence, it might imply an extension of the time.[2] The aged prophet well understood the conditional nature of many of God's promises, and with the most profound heart-searching and intense desire to turn to God, he prayed for his people. It was a decision based entirely on the kind of love that God accepts.

"Daniel knew that the appointed time for Israel's captivity was nearly ended; but he did not feel that because God had promised to deliver them, they themselves had no part to act. With fasting and contrition he sought the Lord, confessing his own sins and the sins of the people."[3]

Just reading his prayer in Daniel 9 is an encouragement. It gives us insights into the heart of a man who was, according to the angel Gabriel, "greatly beloved" in heaven. There is absolutely no self-righteousness in his prayer. None of the "they have sinned" approach, but "we have sinned." Daniel fully identified himself with his people. Further, his prayer provides a glimpse into the heart of a man who knew that all righteousness comes from God. We have no self-generating good deeds to offer as a means of getting attention. Daniel's entire prayer overflows with a profound longing to represent God's gracious character before an onlooking world.

As we approach the end of the time we have promises concerning the latter rain of God's Holy Spirit. The whole world is to be enlightened with God's glory. Should we not gather from Daniel's decision the desire to pray for the fulfillment of God's promises with the same intensity and heart-searching?

---

[1] *The SDA Bible Commentary*, vol. 4, p. 849.
[2] *Ibid.*
[3] *Ibid.*, Ellen G. White Comments, on Dan. 9:3-19, p. 1172.

EMPATHY IN ACTION

Then I came to them of the captivity at Telabib, that dwelt by the river of Chebar, and I sat where they sat. Eze. 3:15.

Among those transported to the bleak wastelands of Babylon was a 25-year-old captive named Ezekiel.[1] For five years he resided with the exiles along the banks of the Chebar irrigation canal, which branched off the Euphrates River. Out there in the shimmering desert the future looked very uncertain, yet the people clung to their false hopes of an early return. But back in Jerusalem and elsewhere the children of Israel persisted in their love of heathenism.

And then at age 30 Ezekiel saw an awesome vision of God's majesty, power, and order.[2] Suddenly he was thrust into the dignified role of a prophet.

Ezekiel's assignment was strictly as a home missionary. Unlike Daniel, who had to learn a difficult new language in the court of Babylon, Ezekiel was told, "For thou art not sent to a people of a strange speech and of an hard language, but to the house of Israel."[3] That was the good news. The uncomfortable part was the Lord's description of the people themselves. He called them "briers," "thorns," and "scorpions." Not exactly the most encouraging type of audience, to be sure. But the Lord continued, "Be not afraid of their words, nor be dismayed at their looks, though they be a rebellious house."[4]

Before Ezekiel could proceed fully into his ministry to his own people he decided to do something. His was a wise choice indeed: He sat where they sat. It is not possible to reach those who need help unless this is first done.

Now, the context of the scriptural passages suggests that during Ezekiel's week-long sitting God waited patiently for his mute prophet to speak.[5] Ezekiel needed to be a faithful watchman. Yet this does not negate the worthy example Ezekiel has left us of empathy in action, especially when given a most difficult assignment with obstinate people.

---

[1] *SDA Bible Dictionary*, p. 353.
[2] *Ibid.*
[3] Eze. 3:5.
[4] Chap. 2:6.
[5] *The SDA Bible Commentary*, vol. 4, p. 586.

FAITHFUL IN SPITE OF THE ODDS

And, lo, thou art unto them as a very lovely song of one that hath a pleasant voice, and can play well on an instrument: for they hear thy words, but they do them not. Eze. 33:32.

We must never accept the notion that the role of a prophet is an easy one, that somehow these mouthpieces for God simply live apart from human decision-making and act only on Heaven's orders. In reviewing Ezekiel's experiences with the captives in Babylon, we can catch a glimpse of the ordeal that a prophet faces when choosing to stay by his task in spite of the odds.

Fresh new captives kept pouring into camp, and Ezekiel continued preaching his warning messages to turn to the Lord. He was an eloquent speaker and a truly cultured Hebrew. His writings indicate his superior grasp of the language. People liked to hear him. His diction and delivery were superior. With upturned faces the captives sat before him and listened with rapt attention, as if enjoying some musical concert. Yet God told Ezekiel that they would not respond with any spiritual action. They came just to listen.

It would be hard to keep preaching with that sort of information available. Yet Ezekiel stayed by and offered his people the truth in the best way he knew how. This was a very personal decision on his part. More than this, he refused to allow his emotions to interfere with his preaching.

God told him in the ninth year of his captivity, when he was only 34 years old, that "the desire of thine eyes" would die of a stroke.[1] And when she did, he must not lament publicly. God would use Ezekiel's controlled behavior as an example of how the people must react when they learned that the Temple had been destroyed. That evening his beloved wife died, and although the grief must have lacerated him within, outwardly he remained calm.

We should take courage from the example Ezekiel left us, knowing that such faithfulness can be ours, too, in spite of the odds. Our emotions need not govern our faith.

---

[1] *SDA Bible Dictionary*, p. 353; Eze. 24:16.

DANIEL'S FAR-REACHING INFLUENCE

Thus saith Cyrus king of Persia, The Lord God of heaven hath given me all the kingdoms of the earth; and he hath charged me to build him an house at Jerusalem, which is in Judah. Ezra 1:2.

Now, why should a heathen king so far removed from the ruins of Jerusalem decide to restore the Temple and acknowledge the Lord as the God of heaven? The answer, of course, lies in Cyrus' marvelous contact with Daniel.

"The deliverance of Daniel from the den of lions had been used of God to create a favorable impression upon the mind of Cyrus the Great. The sterling qualities of the man of God as a statesman of farseeing ability led the Persian ruler to show him marked respect and to honor his judgment." [1]

Daniel introduced the monarch to the prophecies of Isaiah, which actually name Cyrus and predicted the Babylonian overthrow and the restoration of the Jews a century and a half before he was even born. [2] What thoughts flooded into the Persian ruler's mind as Daniel explained those prophecies can only be imagined. As God's Spirit moved forcefully upon Cyrus, the impact must have been profound. His decision to fulfill his divinely appointed mission as God's agent was a delight.

But Cyrus went even further. The act of recognizing the rights of the Jews carried also to other conquered peoples who wished to worship their gods. The influence of Daniel's contact with this ruler was so far-reaching that it eventually became a general policy of the Persian government to grant the right of worship to those nations that had suffered so cruelly at the hands of the Babylonians. [3]

God has ever sought to have a people glorify His name. The impact of one man like Daniel is staggering. What would have happened had all Israel done the same? What could happen today if the church were crowded with Daniels? The impact on society of a people who had firmly decided to live only for God's glory would be tremendous. It would bring the world to its final decision for or against God.

---

[1] *Prophets and Kings*, p. 557.
[2] *The SDA Bible Commentary*, vol. 4, p. 265.
[3] *Ibid.*, vol. 3, pp. 327, 328.

SOUR NOTES AT THE SERVICE

And all the people shouted with a great shout, when they praised the Lord. . . . But many . . . who were ancient men, that had seen the first house, . . . wept with a loud voice. Ezra 3:11, 12.

It should have been a day of rejoicing. The long seventy-year captivity was ended, and the remnant that had returned from Babylon were ready to lay the cornerstone for the new Temple. Many of those at the service that day in Jerusalem realized God's overruling providence and were glad they had an opportunity to begin again. They now had their priorities straight and they were putting the Lord first in their lives.

Only fifty years had elapsed since the Temple that Solomon had built was destroyed, but some of the older ones in that crowd reflected on something else.[1] They chose to dwell on the former grandeur and extravagant display rather than on God's leading. This caused them to moan and groan instead of shouting for joy. The sour effects created such a mingled noise that it was hard to distinguish between the glad and the sad.

All this negative influence weakened the hands of the builders. Why should they continue with any zeal when the whole Temple project was being criticized so heavily?[2] It may have been quite natural for the older men to weep as they thought of the comparison, but to do so publicly hurt the cause tremendously. Their failure to see anything more than the difference in size and magnificence should alert us to the need of being careful about giving vent to negative sentiments.

We tend to think numerically. This is a seductive temptation that often brings sour notes. God is not honored by the big count. But how does God view His people and their projects?

"He values His church, not for its external advantages, but for the sincere piety which distinguishes it from the world. He estimates it according to the growth of its members *in the knowledge of Christ, according to their progress in spiritual experience.*"[3]

---

[1] *The SDA Bible Commentary*, vol. 3, p. 341.
[2] *Prophets and Kings*, p. 564.
[3] *Ibid.*, pp. 565, 566, emphasis supplied.

REFUSING HELP

Ye have nothing to do with us to build an house unto our God; but we ourselves together will build unto the Lord God of Israel. Ezra 4:3.

Those words, spoken by the Jewish leaders to the Samaritans, seem to have a ring of bigotry in them. Why should this small remnant, struggling to rebuild the Temple out of the ruins of old Jerusalem, refuse help from their nearest neighbors? When these Samaritans presented themselves for service they said, "Let us build with you: for we seek your God, as ye do." [1] How could the Jews turn down such an offer?

Out of the sad experience of the Babylonian Exile the Jews had learned one thing very well. They must resist the temptation to join with idolaters in any kind of project. The Jewish leaders detected the insincerity of the Samaritans. But is it ever possible to sense insincerity? Absolutely. Based on the Samaritan track record of mixing idolatry with the worship of the true God, the Jewish leaders decided that it would be only inviting trouble to associate with them in the enterprise. Any advantage gained would be worthless compared with Heaven's blessing in remaining true to God.

Their decision to refuse assistance, when outwardly it seemed sensible to accept it, should warn us today when many claim to be worshiping the same God. Just claiming to worship God is no criterion. [2] The Samaritans, for instance, were a mixed race, with a mixed religion that tended downward spiritually. For all their profession, they were a real menace to pure religion. [3]

"There is constant danger that professing Christians will come to think that in order to have influence with worldlings, they must to a certain extent conform to the world. But though such a course may appear to afford great advantages, it always ends in spiritual loss." [4] Always! People may scream and call it bigotry, but the true believer cannot afford compromise with principle in any kind of alliance with unbelievers.

[1] Ezra 4:2.
[2] *Prophets and Kings,* p. 567.
[3] *The SDA Bible Commentary,* vol. 3, p. 342.
[4] *Prophets and Kings,* p. 570.

FIRST THINGS FIRST

Then came the word of the Lord by Haggai the prophet, saying, Is it time for you, O ye, to dwell in your cieled houses, and this house lie waste? Haggai 1:3, 4.

For more than a year the Temple project had been stalled. The people who had returned to Palestine from their long years in exile were simply too discouraged to continue the noble venture that they had begun with such enthusiasm. Not only had there been far too much criticism but the Samaritans had done their best to thwart the Jews, even to the extent of inducing an impostor king to issue a decree to stop the work.[1]

It seemed better to build their own houses and seek to gain some temporal prosperity first. But that was a faulty choice. It always is. Then an old man, who had undoubtedly seen the first Temple but who was not discouraged by the thought of building a lesser one, stepped forward with a prophetic message.[2] Haggai preached for only three and one-half months, but in that time the people responded so well that the Lord did not need his services anymore. He could be considered one of the most successful of the prophets, because those who heard him chose to respond to his searching question of our text for today. They stopped their own work and began putting their energy into God's house.[3]

The decision to put first things first came at the right time. Despite their efforts to establish their own homes and get ahead financially, everything had gone wrong. The harder they worked, the less they had. Haggai himself preached, "He that earneth wages earneth wages to put it into a bag with holes."[4]

When those who profess to love the Lord must consistently face reverses in their lives, perhaps they would do well to listen again to the counsel from this aged prophet, "Consider your ways."[5] In seeking to satisfy our own needs first, we actually hold back the Lord's blessings.

---

[1] *Prophets and Kings*, pp. 572, 573.
[2] *SDA Bible Dictionary*, p. 450.
[3] *The SDA Bible Commentary*, vol. 4, p. 1074.
[4] Haggai 1:6.
[5] Verse 7.

MORDECAI IN THE GATE

And all the king's servants, that were in the king's gate, bowed, and reverenced Haman: for the king had so commanded concerning him. But Mordecai bowed not, nor did him reverence. Esther 3:2.

The great bulk of the Jews did not heed the warnings of the prophet Zechariah to leave Babylon for their homeland.[1] Instead they settled down and thus left themselves open for a crisis. The Medo-Persian Empire changed rapidly, and after Darius died, Xerxes the Great, or Ahasuerus as he is known in the Bible, ruled. This king was a weakling who was strongly influenced by his servants.[2]

Thus Haman, the prime minister, was able to secure a decree that all should bow before him in due reverence. Haman was Satan's agent in a deeply laid plot to thwart God's purpose to reestablish His people as His representatives in Palestine.[3]

Mordecai was one Jew who retained his hold on God. It mattered not to him that Xerxes the Great had given the command for Haman to receive reverence. He chose to remain true to his God and to bow only to Him. He saw that Haman wanted something more than just the usual Oriental custom of bowing before superiors in polite recognition and honor. He demanded reverence as some deity, and that Mordecai could not give. So he stood. And standing when everyone else is bowing does make a person rather conspicuous. The rest of the servants peeked and reported. And that set the stage for a confrontation, because Haman was the type of man who wanted not only Mordecai's neck but all the Jews, as well.

There is a coming parallel to this. "The Protestant world today see in the little company keeping the Sabbath a Mordecai in the gate. His character and conduct, expressing reverence for the law of God, are a constant rebuke to those who have cast off the fear of the Lord and are trampling upon His Sabbath; the unwelcome intruder must by some means be put out of the way."[4]

[1] *Prophets and Kings,* pp. 599, 600.
[2] *SDA Bible Dictionary,* p. 23.
[3] *Prophets and Kings,* p. 600.
[4] *Testimonies,* vol. 5, p. 450.

MORDECAI'S CHALLENGE

And who knoweth whether thou art come to the kingdom for such a time as this? Esther 4:14.

It would be difficult to find a more dramatic challenge requiring raw courage and faith in God than this question. Mordecai put this penetrating query to his surrogate daughter, Esther, when the news reached him that all the Jews were slated for extermination on a set date. Everything rested on this young woman's decision to use all the tact and faith she had in presenting her cause before the king. Not only her life but the lives of all her people, as well, were at stake.

Haman had been granted blanket permission for genocide. Mordecai's insulting behavior in refusing to bow before him had made him determined to rid the earth of all Jews. He was even willing to back up his request to the king with his own personal bank account, which amounted to ten thousand talents of silver. Based on the light Babylonian talent, that would mean 377 tons of the precious metal.[1] His hatred extended that far!

Haman was eager to get the news out to the kingdom as quickly as possible. The most remote regions of the empire could hear any news within a month, or two at the very most, with the famous Persian postal system, which was akin to our pony express.[2] Mordecai saw the need for quick and decisive action on Queen Esther's part. She was the only person who could legitimately see the king in behalf of the Jewish people.

Esther's response indicates that she understood the importance of communion with God. She directed Mordecai to gather the Jews for a three-day fast while she and her maidens also fasted. Then, and only then, would she appear before the king. "And if I perish, I perish," she concluded.[3] Her decision to respond to the challenge and place herself on the line remains to this day an electrifying choice.

---

[1] *The SDA Bible Commentary,* vol. 3, p. 473.
[2] *Ibid.,* p. 475.
[3] Esther 4:16.

SECOND CALL TO THE LEVITES

And I sent them with commandment . . . that they should bring unto us ministers for the house of our God. Ezra 8:17.

Ezra was driven by a compulsion to teach the people the ways of God.[1] His life was totally submerged in the desire that they should revive an interest in the sacred writings. Those writings indicated that God had a special place for His people, and that place was Jerusalem, the crossroads of the Middle East. This was why he told King Artaxerxes of his longing to see the Holy City restored.

Between the sixth and seventh chapters of Ezra is a span of about fifty-eight years.[2] During that time the story of Esther and how God protected His people from annihilation transpired.[3] Now it was time for God to move again. Two decrees already had been issued, but when Artaxerxes signed his decree in 457 B.C. it gave the fullest measures for the Jews to go back and restore Jerusalem.

Ezra persuaded nearly two thousand families to head westward with him, but before the caravan started he gathered everyone at the Ahava River to make a final head count.[4] To his surprise, not one Levite was in the crowd.[5] They should have been the first to respond, but they had chosen to remain in the comfort of their Babylonian homes instead of pioneering back in Palestine. The Temple at Jerusalem had been built, and there was a pressing need for ministers to teach the people. Yet even with the clearance from Artaxerxes, not one Levite was present for the roll call.

So Ezra made a special plea, sending representatives for a second call. About forty Levites decided to accept the challenge this time, and about 220 Nethinim, the Temple workers, also volunteered.[6] They came willingly to the embarkation camp in response to Ezra's final appeal.

We should never be ashamed of repeating the needs of God's cause to those who have at first hesitated to respond. Ezra's second appeal for ministers was effective as the Levites saw more clearly the indications of God's providence.

---

[1] *Prophets and Kings*, pp. 608, 609.
[2] *The SDA Bible Commentary*, vol. 3, p. 364.
[3] *Ibid.*, pp. 326, 327 (chart, between 515 B.C. and 457 B.C.).
[4] *Ibid.*, p. 376.
[5] *Prophets and Kings*, p. 612.
[6] *Ibid.*, p. 615.

RUNNING THE RISK

For I was ashamed to require of the king a band of soldiers and horsemen to help us against the enemy in the way: because we had spoken unto the king, saying, The hand of our God is upon all them for good that seek him; but his power and his wrath is against all them that forsake him. Ezra 8:22.

In an age of insurance forms and governmental protection agencies this sort of refusal by Ezra seems tinged with presumption. In that caravan destined for Palestine was a collection of treasure and bars of silver and gold amounting to more than $1 million.[1] And it was no imaginary enemy who lurked out there among the rocky desert reaches either. The Samaritans might intercept them at any time in their fired-up hatred of the Jewish enterprise. There were also roving bands of Arabs who certainly owed no allegiance to the Persian Empire and who could easily ambush and plunder. But Ezra turned down the military protection that Artaxerxes would have willingly provided, and in so doing he left us a worthy example.

"Ezra would run the risk of trusting his cause with God. He well knew that if they failed in their important work, it would be because they had not complied with the requirements of God and therefore He could not help them."[2]

But running that risk was a decision based on a principle. Ezra saw a wonderful opportunity to give God the credit before the heathen. The whole Persian Empire was aware of what was happening as the Jews headed back to their homeland, and Ezra did not want to suggest in the slightest manner that they depended on anyone but God.[3]

Before departing, Ezra called for a fast and a time for heart-searching. If there were any secret sins, they must be dealt with immediately or the success of the mission would be in jeopardy. Only as we seek to abide in God's law because we desire to give Him the glory can we realize His full protection.

---

[1] *The SDA Bible Commentary*, vol. 3, p. 377.
[2] *Ibid.*, Ellen G. White Comments, on Ezra 8:22, p. 1134.
[3] *Prophets and Kings*, p. 615.

EZRA'S RED FACE

O my God, I am ashamed and blush to lift up my face to thee, my God: for our iniquities are increased over our head, and our trespass is grown up unto the heavens. Ezra 9:6.

It had taken four months to make the journey from Babylon, but Ezra and company finally arrived at Jerusalem.[1] Ezra took only a brief three-day rest, and on the fourth day presented the Temple treasury with the gifts from Artaxerxes. Thanksgiving was in the air until the princes came to him with shocking news. Some of the priests and people who were already living in Jerusalem had married heathen women! On an average, three out of every one thousand men were involved in this departure from the law.[2]

But Ezra didn't think of averages. His thought was that the leadership especially had given license to sin. Intermarriage had been one reason for the captivity in the first place. It made him sick. In typical Oriental fashion he responded with visible embarrassment. "When I heard this, I tore my tunic and cloak, pulled hair from my head and beard and sat down appalled."[3]

Shortly after this he fell on his knees in prayer and uttered those words of our text for today. He was red-faced before the Lord. Ezra's colleagues shared his profound pangs of sorrow over the guilt of a people who were supposed to represent God's character.

Shechaniah, one of the influential men, suggested that those men involved should put away their wives and that all should make a covenant with the Lord. Ezra agreed. It may seem harsh to us today, but it was a decision intended to spare the people and to begin a reformation that would permit God's people to build solidly for the future. Ezra was a true leader.

"The compassion and tenderness that he revealed toward those who had sinned, either willfully or through ignorance, should be an object lesson to all who seek to bring about reforms."[4]

[1] *The SDA Bible Commentary,* vol. 3, p. 378.
[2] *Ibid.,* p. 387.
[3] Ezra 9:3, N.I.V.
[4] *Prophets and Kings,* p. 623.

INSTANT PRAYER

Then the king said unto me, For what dost thou make request? So I prayed to the God of heaven. Neh. 2:4.

Three or four months had elapsed since Nehemiah had heard from his brother Hanani the bad news about conditions in Jerusalem.[1] The Samaritans had broken down part of the city wall just when it seemed that the city would be fully restored.[2] The shock had left Nehemiah numb. Long hours of prayer and tears had left their visible mark of concern on his face. But as cupbearer he was always to be pleasant before the king.

Monarchs in those days were so fearful of being poisoned that they used only very trusted servants to serve them drinks.[3] That a Jew should be engaged in such a position in the Persian palace speaks well of Nehemiah's character.

But now he was sad, and the king had spotted the concern on his countenance and wanted to know the reason. Nehemiah frankly told Artaxerxes the truth. And that in itself was a dangerous thing to do. Servants just did not carry their personal feelings with them on the job. He could lose his life for negative behavior. Yet Artaxerxes listened sympathetically and desired to know exactly what could be done for Nehemiah.

It was a high moment to decide. Just how should he tell the king of the longing of his heart to see Jerusalem's walls built once again? He wanted so much to lead out in the enterprise, but how could he ever ask for time off? There sat Artaxerxes with the queen, ready to hear his request, and in that moment Nehemiah prayed silently.[4]

"To pray as Nehemiah prayed in his hour of need is a resource at the command of the Christian under circumstances when other forms of prayer may be impossible."[5] In times of stress or sudden difficulty we may send a prayer heavenward with the assurance that God does hear our cry for help. We may not have time to kneel or even close the eyes, but God has pledged His aid to His trusting servants.

In this instance Nehemiah said the right words, and the king released him for active duty in Jerusalem.

---

[1] *The SDA Bible Commentary*, vol. 3, p. 394.
[2] *Ibid.*, p. 392.
[3] *SDA Bible Dictionary*, p. 168.
[4] *The SDA Bible Commentary*, vol. 3, p. 395.
[5] *Prophets and Kings*, p. 631.

NEHEMIAH'S DETERMINATION

The God of heaven, he will prosper us; therefore we his servants will arise and build. Neh. 2:20.

Nehemiah carried with him the royal commission to rebuild Jerusalem's walls. While Ezra had rightly declined military protection, Nehemiah wisely accepted this addition of dignity and authority to his work.

Everything seemed to fall into place. He arrived safely, and after a night's secret reconnaisance of the wall's condition, he was able to present to the people an accurate picture of the need. His full knowledge of the situation and his earnestness aroused the people to cooperate fully. With one voice they pledged their support.

But no mission for God ever runs without opposition. Satan always has his agents primed, and the Samaritans began a scoffing campaign. That was to be expected, but what was nettling were those who stood aloof from the project. The Tekoite nobles left a slothful example. These would-be leaders refused "to put their necks to the work of their Lord," as Nehemiah wrote.[1] Yet there was such enthusiasm for the work that their example held little weight.

But the steady bombardment of ridicule from the Samaritans was picked up by some of the leading Jews. They sounded a discouraging note, exaggerating the difficulties.[2] Then the Jews who lived nearby and who hadn't been doing anything toward the project started circulating negative reports as well. The Samaritans saw their chance and threatened violence against those who would continue building. It was a dark hour indeed, and one calculated to discourage the best of men.

Nehemiah quickly armed his workers. He simply would not be cowed by threats, nor would he stoop to argue. His inspiring decision to trust God comes ringing down to us in today's verse: "The God of heaven . . . will prosper us."

---

[1] Neh. 3:5.
[2] *Prophets and Kings*, pp. 642, 643.

TMTD-8

DEFENDING THE POOR

For the poor shall never cease out of the land: therefore I command thee, saying, Thou shalt open thine hand wide unto thy brother. Deut. 15:11.

Right in the midst of the wall-building program, Nehemiah's attention was diverted to meet the pressing issue of the poor.[1] Their pitiful cries demanded justice. Instead of being blessed, those with large families were burdened with too many mouths to feed and not enough food. They were obliged to buy on credit at frightfully inflated prices. Others had been forced to mortgage their property to meet the Persian taxes. Still others had turned to the moneylenders to meet the same government taxes, and the rate of interest soared accordingly. Children were being sold as servants to help meet the high demands. It was hard to take. They had come from Babylonian captivity only to find themselves in a new kind of bondage. This time it was worse because much of the exaction came from their own people![2]

"I was very angry when I heard their cry and these words," Nehemiah said. "Then I consulted with myself."[3]

He held a one-man committee meeting! As a result of that private session, he had to make a decision. Many today would vote to ignore the situation because the wealthy folk were the big givers who helped finance the wall building.[4] But this did not influence Nehemiah.

Instead of taking the soft, noncommittal stance that has such an appeal when money is at stake, this man of God sharply rebuked those nobles and rulers who were involved in the extortion. Then he called for a general assembly to present God's requirements. Moses had written centuries before that no usury should ever be charged to God's people, and Nehemiah felt it was time to review God's ways before the people.

The fraudulent practices ceased because Nehemiah chose to stand for justice despite the obvious pressure to go easy on the financial backers of the wall-building program.

---

[1] *Prophets and Kings*, p. 646.
[2] *The SDA Bible Commentary*, vol. 3, p. 413.
[3] Neh. 5:6, 7.
[4] *Prophets and Kings*, p. 648.

THWARTING ENEMY PLOTS

I am doing a great work, so that I cannot come down: why should the work cease, whilst I leave it, and come down to you? Neh. 6:3.

Nehemiah had lost himself in a great cause for God, and he was not about to be distracted by little men in high places.[1] Sanballat, governor of Samaria, and his cohorts had schemed and plotted to halt the work on the wall, but to no avail. When the project reached the point where the gates were about to be set in place, the enemy became desperate and sent a message urging Nehemiah to meet them in one of the villages on the plain of Ono, seven miles (eleven kilometers) southeast of Jaffa.[2] Although this was a Jewish district, Nehemiah could easily be attacked on the road crossing Samaritan territory. He refused to be lured into any false sense of security. Furthermore, why should he meet with them when they had persistently ridiculed and harrassed him about the building program? Four times the same message came, and each time Nehemiah gave the same answer.

Next came an open letter. This very technique alerted Nehemiah, because the letter, which all could read, suggested that the heathen were reporting rebellion among the Jews and that Nehemiah himself was hiring prophets to preach that he would be king in Jerusalem. Nehemiah rushed back a reply, "There are no such things done as you say. You have made them up in your own heart."

Shemaiah the prophet next stepped into the scene, suggesting that Nehemiah hide himself in the Temple. Assassins were on the prowl. But Nehemiah would not succumb to paranoia either. He knew that Sanballat had hired the prophet to urge the hiding. "Should such a man as I flee?" he asked.[3]

Nehemiah's decision to remain on duty keeps sharply in focus our own need for solid commitment to God, regardless of Satan's persistent distractions. We should never be turned aside from God's cause because of the devil's agents.

---

[1] *The SDA Bible Commentary,* vol. 3, p. 396.
[2] *Ibid.,* p. 417.
[3] Neh. 6:11.

JOY AT THE WATER GATE

For this day is holy unto our Lord: neither be ye sorry; for the joy of the Lord is your strength. Neh. 8:10.

Even though the walls around Jerusalem were finished, sadness hung over the city. A large section of Jerusalem still lay in ruins, a gaunt reminder of their earlier rebellion.[1]

It was now New Year's Day of the civil calendar and time for the Blowing of Trumpets, which announced a coming holy convocation. This would correspond to our early fall. It was a time when all Israelites examined their lives as the Day of Atonement approached on the tenth day of the month.[2] But when the people gathered this time, they came "as one man into the street that was before the water gate."[3] They urged Ezra to read to them from the book of the law. This was a remarkable request, because in spite of their own transgressions they chose to hear what God had to say to them personally.[4]

Ezra, now an aged man, stood high on a wooden platform to read from those ancient writings. Beside him were Levites, and below was a sea of people waiting to hear from God's law.

As a result of intermarriage, the Hebrew language had been corrupted. Ezra and his helpers had to be extra careful in explaining the meaning of God's Word.[5]

We get a bit uneasy if the preacher speaks beyond noon. After all, we have dinner to eat, and being famished for physical food always seems to take precedence over anything spiritual. But these folks did not glance at the sundial or shake the hourglass. With upturned faces they listened intently for five or six hours.[6] It is written that amens could be heard throughout the assembly. Tears streamed down their faces as they learned how far they had departed from the Lord. But Ezra and company urged the people to respond with rejoicing instead. "For the joy of the Lord is your strength," Nehemiah said.[7] This is still true today.

---

[1] *Prophets and Kings*, p. 661.
[2] *The SDA Bible Commentary*, vol. 3, p. 338.
[3] Neh. 8:1.
[4] *Ibid.*, p. 425.
[5] *Prophets and Kings*, pp. 661, 662.
[6] *The SDA Bible Commentary*, vol. 3, p. 425.
[7] Verse 10.

MAN OF ACTION

Be ye doers of the word, and not hearers only, deceiving your own selves. James 1:22.

Nehemiah was the kind of man who could translate the Written Word of God into action. During his first twelve years as governor of Judea, he organized the wall building and placed the people on a solid moral foundation. He was a true reformer. But after he returned to Persia for a while, things in Jerusalem began to slip. Upon his return for a second term of office he immediately went into action again.[1]

Eliashib the high priest had formed a friendship with Tobiah the Ammonite, one of Israel's bitterest enemies. This all came about because of intermarriage, but regardless of this, Eliashib should never have allowed Tobiah to move into an apartment next to the Temple. When Nehemiah learned of this he was incensed. "It grieved me sore," he said.[2] After all, the plain words of God through Moses declared that because of the cruel treachery of the Ammonites and Moabites toward Israel, none of their tribes should ever be allowed to join the congregation of His people. And here Tobiah was, living in the storehouse that had been used for tithes and offerings![3]

Nehemiah did not sit around pondering what he should do. Without waiting for a committee meeting, he threw out all of Tobiah's belongings and cleaned house in a hurry.

Nehemiah soon found that heathen traders had induced many of the Israelites to carry on their business during the Sabbath. Immediately he swung into action again and ordered the gates shut over the Sabbath. When the merchants stayed around, hoping to generate some business activity, Nehemiah gave them a stern warning.

Next Nehemiah turned his attention to the intermarriage problem, and with full backing from God's Word he ordered this to cease. Those who refused to put away their wives were to leave.[4]

Nehemiah's consistent decisions to take action were based not on personal preference, but entirely on the Word of God. This kind of decision always corresponds with genuine faith.

---

[1] *The SDA Bible Commentary*, vol. 3, pp. 450, 322.
[2] Neh. 13:8.
[3] *Prophets and Kings*, pp. 669, 670.
[4] *Ibid.*, p. 674.

A FAITH THAT DID NOT FAIL

For I know that my redeemer liveth, and that he shall stand at the latter day upon the earth. Job 19:25.

Like a lone figure standing atop a lofty mountain, Job is revealed against the skyline of history. He was totally free from political, military, and ecclesiastical background.[1] He was one of those rare worshipers of God outside the realm of the Israelites. His story, coming to us out of the Arabian Desert, has all the earmarks of a very early setting. Yet it matters not about the time or place. His experience of remaining faithful to his God despite every negative influence has left us with a remarkable example of the power of such a decision.

We are given a peek behind the scenes in the longstanding controversy between God and Satan. The devil, as instigator of all Job's troubles and heartaches, is shown to be what he really is—an enemy. At his hand Job lost much, even his own children, and was then struck with boils. His own wife suggested that he curse God and die, which says something very tragic about a woman who should have supported her husband in his hour of need.

Then his friends arrived and harped on the theme that all his calamities came as punishment for his sins.[2] Yet in spite of all this, Job maintained his integrity throughout the protracted harangue. (The remarkable thing about this whole narrative is that Job was never given a clue as to the reason for his troubles. He had no hint that it was a test and that the entire universe was watching to see whether he would keep his grip on God.) His faith increased steadily until he could declare the words of our text for today. He knew that his Redeemer lives, and that He would return to the earth. Further, Job declared in his next breath that, because of this, he would be resurrected to see Him. This kind of decision to remain faithful to God is still needed today.

---

[1] *The SDA Bible Commentary*, vol. 3, p. 494.
[2] *Ibid.*, p. 496.

PRAYING FOR CRITICAL FRIENDS

And the Lord turned the captivity of Job, when he prayed for his friends. Job 42:10.

Job felt the sting of constant criticism from his friends. In his terrible distress he was forced to listen to these would-be companions who tried to lay guilt on him despite his innocence. They felt sure that he had sinned or he certainly would not be suffering the horrible calamities that had befallen him. Their cold, persistent logic ran a weary circuit of accusations that were enough to make any well man cringe. Job did show discouragement and despair in his trouble, but he never lost his basic trust in God.

Then out of the whirlwind God spoke. Thundering from heaven, He revealed to Job a progressively elevating thought pattern that broke the gray sameness he had been hearing.[1] Using nature as a medium, God lifted Job to a level of understanding that made him repent. "I abhor myself," Job declared.[2]

Turning to Job's so-called friends, God told them that they were dead wrong in their philosophy of suffering. They themselves were the ones who needed to repent.

At this point Job made a wonderful decision. After seeing God and His ways, he determined to offer an intercessory prayer for his friends. It seems hard to pray for someone who is set in his ways and determined to lay some guilt on you. But the knowledge of God turns folk into the likeness of the Saviour. Job may not have been able to answer his accusers, but he could pray for them.

And right then God halted the test. Satan had been defeated. The enemy's opening charge that Job served God only because He had built a hedge about him was proved to be a lie. "Though he slay me, yet will I trust in him"[3] was Job's ringing declaration of faith. When we listen to God as Job listened we too will be able to choose to pray—even for our critics.

---

[1] *The SDA Bible Commentary,* vol. 3, p. 496.
[2] Job 42:6.
[3] Chap. 13:15.

IN CONTRAST WITH
THE COMPLAINERS

Then they that feared the Lord spake often one to another: and the Lord hearkened, and heard it, and a book of remembrance was written before him for them that feared the Lord, and that thought upon his name. Mal. 3:16.

The contents of the last book of the Old Testament bear a marked similarity to the Laodicean message of Revelation.[1] The people of Malachi's day were totally insensitive to their true spiritual condition. The Babylonian captivity had forever cured the Israelites of idolatry, but it had plunged them into an exclusiveness that led to a staggering smugness.[2] So long as they kept up the rituals of worship they felt sure of God's blessings. They could not fathom why God regarded obedience without love unacceptable. When God through Malachi asked hard questions about their hollow round of service, they replied with a pretense of injured feelings, demanding from God just why their religious activity wasn't acceptable.

The people failed to distinguish between the sacred and the common, and this was invariably followed by an inability to tell the difference between good and evil.[3] So long as they went through the motions, why should God care? With that attitude they missed the whole point of their existence.

But a few did understand. These were the truly righteous. And when Malachi passed the word along from God that "I have loved you,"[4] their hearts leaped forward in true obedience. They delighted in discussing His character. Today's text indicates how Malachi encouraged them.

Heaven's judgment record will reveal the truth of a choice to reverence and love the Lord. That record will be in sharp contrast with the complainers who murmur against God for His refusal to accept their pretended piety.

---

[1] *The SDA Bible Commentary*, vol. 4, p. 1123.
[2] *Prophets and Kings*, p. 705.
[3] *The SDA Bible Commentary*, vol. 4, p. 1122.
[4] Mal. 1:2.

ZEAL WITHOUT KNOWLEDGE

For I bear them record that they have a zeal of God, but not according to knowledge. For they being ignorant of God's righteousness, and going about to establish their own righteousness, have not submitted themselves unto the righteousness of God. Rom. 10:2, 3.

Century after century slipped silently away, and still the promised Messiah did not appear. When all the prophets finally died it seemed that their echoing voices mocked those long-looked-for promises. As the Israelites departed steadily from God their hopes for the future were nearly crushed by the reality of Roman oppression. Yet in heaven the great prophetic clock inched forward with the surety that Jesus would come.

Satan had done his homework well. He had taken those very promises of the ancient prophets and had distorted them to suit his own diabolical purposes.[1] It was his carefully laid plot to establish firmly in the minds of the Israelites that the Redeemer was coming for the sole purpose of national greatness, and not to reveal the truth about God's gracious, loving character.

"For more than a thousand years the Jewish people had waited the coming of the promised Saviour. Their brightest hopes had rested upon this event. For a thousand years, in song and prophecy, in temple rite and household prayer, His name had been enshrined; and yet when He came, they did not recognize Him as the Messiah for whom they had so long waited."[2]

It was not just one choice, but a continual series of choices which fostered their pride and false concepts of God, concepts that fit Him into the mold of their own distortion of His character. To this they bent every energy with a zeal that was totally without the true knowledge of God.

The same danger still exists. Whenever the church is more zealous over presenting its own accomplishments than the truth about God, it is doomed to recycle the history of the Jews.

---

[1] *Prophets and Kings*, pp. 686,687.
[2] *Ibid.*, p. 710.

REBUKED FOR DOUBTING

Blessed be the Lord of Israel; for he hath visited and redeemed his people. Luke 1:68.

With such a firm affirmation of faith it would seem that there had always been no doubt about God's power. Yet these words of the aged priest Zacharias were spoken after his son, John, was born. It is an implied announcement that the Messiah would soon appear, after nearly four hundred years of prophetic silence.[1] Deliverance was on the way! But the inspirational note then sounded was not the same as it was the day the angel Gabriel informed the old man that he would become the father of the forerunner of Christ.

Zacharias had been selected to officiate at the golden altar in the Temple at Jerusalem for one week.[2] This high privilege usually came only once in a lifetime for a priest,[3] and undoubtedly Zacharias left his hill country in Judea with a sense of exalted duty.

For years Zacharias and Elisabeth had been praying for a son. It was a real stigma to be childless in those days, because the Jews felt that such a situation implied sin.[4] But even more than for their own child, Zacharias had been praying that the Redeemer would soon come.

We can only imagine the shock as Zacharias looked up during the service and saw the bright form of Gabriel fresh from the heavenly courts. The position of the angel on the right side of the altar should have alerted the old priest to God's approval, but he never noticed.[5] Instead, he just gulped as Gabriel announced that he and his wife would have a son, whom Heaven had already named John. Infirmity clutched at the old man, who was now crowding 70, and in that instant he chose to doubt.[6] Even with the full knowledge of Abraham's experience, he decided not to believe.

Since his faith could not rise to the occasion, God struck him dumb until the baby was born. The heavenly rebuke served as a lingering reminder that nothing is impossible with God.

---

[1] *The SDA Bible Commentary*, vol. 5, p. 690.
[2] *The Desire of Ages*, p. 97.
[3] *The SDA Bible Commentary*, vol. 5, p. 672.
[4] *Ibid.*
[5] *The Desire of Ages*, pp. 97, 98.
[6] *The SDA Bible Commentary*, vol. 5, p. 676.

MARY'S SONG

And Mary said, My soul doth magnify the Lord, and my spirit hath rejoiced in God my Saviour. Luke 1:46, 47.

Six months after Gabriel visited Zacharias he appeared to Mary in the hill town of Nazareth. But what a different reception the angel received! There was no doubt, no hesitancy, on this young woman's part. She chose to believe, and that belief allowed her humbly to accept the greatest secret ever committed to any mortal. That she should bear the Son of God undoubtedly thrilled her through and through. We can sense that peace in total trust when she quietly answered the angel, "Behold the handmaid of the Lord; be it unto me according to thy word." [1] Her simple childlike faith grasped the truth that Heaven selected her to become the special link with humanity.

We can only imagine how eager Mary was to share this news with someone who would truly understand. And that is why she hurried the some eighty or more miles (130 kilometers) down to Hebron, south of Jerusalem, to visit her relative Elisabeth, who was now six months pregnant. [2] More than anyone on earth, this older woman would understand and could share in Mary's inmost feelings. Elisabeth showed no envy, but gave Mary her heartfelt congratulations for her faith and high honor.

That is when Mary burst into one of the most sublime and elevated Hebrew poems. Her heart swelled with the desire to exalt God. She herself, a mortal of lowly birth, recognized at least some of the meaning of what Gabriel had said to her, so she sang what has become known as the Magnificat. We have the opening words of Mary's song in our text for today. It is an expression from the depths of the heart. No happiness can compare with the rejoicing that comes from a sense of God's majesty and power, yet knowing how He is so gracious as to include even the lowliest person in His plans and purposes.

Mary's song reveals God's character and what He considers to be greatness. It is for all who, like Mary, choose to believe.

---

[1] Luke 1:38.
[2] *The SDA Bible Commentary*, vol. 5, pp. 684, 685, 214 (map).

JOSEPH'S KINDNESS

Then Joseph her husband, being a just man, and not willing to make her a publick example, was minded to put her away privily. Matt. 1:19.

The tenderness displayed here reveals much about the character of Joseph. He was "not willing" to expose Mary or to cause any further embarrassment when he learned of her pregnancy.

In ancient times an engagement constituted a legal relationship. Even though the prospective husband and wife did not live together, they were bound by law, and any covenant broken would mean a divorce.[1]

From what we can gather, Joseph was a widower with at least six children of his own at the time he was engaged to this young virgin of Nazareth.[2] When Mary looked up at him with wide-eyed wonder and whispered her secret, we can only imagine the shock and disbelief he must have felt. To have Mary tell him that she was pregnant by the Holy Spirit would indeed be hard for him to swallow. Yet Joseph chose not to make a public example of her, and he intended to divorce her privately, without causing any pain of exposure. That decision demonstrates a consideration that is godlike and worth remembering. Undoubtedly Joseph may have questioned whether or not it would be morally right to marry someone who appeared to be an adulteress. In those days he could legally put her away simply by declaring that she did not please him. Or he could expose her. But today's verse demonstrates his kindness in protecting Mary.

Fortunately the angel soon stimulated a dream that gave Heaven's stamp of approval to Mary's condition. Her story was true. But it would still require an act of faith on Joseph's part.

Joseph's kind choice should always be ours. There are times when all outward appearances seem to dictate the need for justice, but may we learn to temper this with mercy as he did. May we see how faith and love go hand in hand.

---

[1] *The SDA Bible Commentary,* vol. 5, p. 282.
[2] *Ibid.*

GOING TO BETHLEHEM

And it came to pass, as the angels were gone away from them into heaven, the shepherds said one to another, Let us now go even unto Bethlehem, and see this thing which is come to pass, which the Lord hath made known unto us. Luke 2:15.

Not until Jesus comes again will humanity see or hear anything like what the shepherds experienced the night Christ was born.[1] Their decision to hurry to the stable in Bethlehem was prompted by the audio-visual impact that had left them breathless. No pride or prejudice could hold them back.

When Gabriel suddenly appeared, illuminating the sky and ground around them, they truly were "sore afraid." Seldom is the veil between men and the invisible world of angels lifted, and when it is, humanity is so startled and so undone by the glory that fear becomes the natural reaction. Yet Gabriel came with the reassuring words "Fear not: for, behold, I bring you good tidings of great joy."[2] The Messiah they had been talking about through the long hours had just been born!

But the shepherds, like the masses in Israel, expected the Messiah to come in power. Their King would triumph over the hated Roman enemy. Gabriel did not try to correct their theological misconception, but he did seek to prepare them for the poverty and humiliation of the Saviour. They would find Him, just like any other Hebrew infant, bathed in water, rubbed in salt, and placed diagonally on a square cloth with three ends folded over the body and feet, and tied loosely in place with strips of cloth.[3] He would not be lying in silks, but wrapped in "swaddling clothes." And they need not check the rooms at the local inn. They would find Him a stable. They were used to stables, but their expectations might be jarred by the fact that He would be there.

We may not see angels as the shepherds did, but we can rehearse the exhaustless theme of His birth. Then we too shall catch the glory and in spirit go to Bethlehem and afterward carry with us the exciting good news.

---

[1] *The Desire of Ages*, p. 48.
[2] Luke 2:10.
[3] *The SDA Bible Commentary*, vol. 5, p. 698.

A SETTLED HATRED

When Herod the king had heard these things, he was troubled, and all Jerusalem with him. And when he had gathered all the chief priests and scribes of the people together, he demanded of them where Christ should be born. Matt. 2:3, 4.

The shepherds' story of the angels soon became the hottest news item in Palestine. It jarred Jerusalem. Next came the Wise Men, who had trekked in from the east, with their persistent query regarding the whereabouts of the newborn King. Their search brought Herod to his feet. Ever suspicious of some sinister plot, he questioned the leading theologians about the prophecy of the Messiah's birthplace.

The scholars halfheartedly unrolled their ancient scrolls. It stung them to think that a king of non-Jewish descent who had been influenced by a few heathen strangers should order them to do some Biblical research.

Their foot-dragging aroused even more suspicion. Now Herod was sure there was a massive cover-up. In an authoritarian voice they could understand, he commanded them to find the prophecy or else. Winding through their ancient scrolls, they quickly found Micah. Amazingly they had the answer. Bethlehem, in Judah, was the spot!

Now why weren't those scholars out front, zealously trying to locate the baby Jesus in the first place? They weren't as ignorant as they pretended.[1] These would-be guardians of truth should have rushed to Bethlehem, but they chose to remain aloof. The problem was their pride. "It could not be, they said, that God had passed them by, to communicate with ignorant shepherds or uncircumcised Gentiles. They determined to show their contempt for the reports that were exciting King Herod and all Jerusalem. They would not even go to Bethlehem to see whether those things were so. . . . Here began the rejection of Christ by the priests and rabbis. From this point their pride and stubbornness grew into a settled hatred of the Saviour."[2] Thus their pride-filled decision became their final downfall.

---

[1] *The Desire of Ages*, p. 62.
[2] *Ibid.*, pp. 62, 63.

AROUSING A HEATHEN KING

Then Herod, when he saw that he was mocked of the wise men, was exceeding wroth, and sent forth, and slew all the children that were in Bethlehem, and in all the coasts thereof, from two years old and under. Matt. 2:16.

When the Wise Men did not return on schedule, Herod surmised a plot to take his throne. All the pieces fit together. First the theologians were reluctant to tell him precisely the birthplace of the Messiah. Then these Eastern strangers failed to report back to him. Something was afoot. So if he could not win one way, he would use the surest method he knew.

Herod's record was stained with blood. Any man who could kill three of his sons and one of his ten wives certainly would have no qualms about slaughtering the babies of Bethlehem.[1] We shudder in horror at the thought of wiping out an estimated twenty-five or thirty male children.[2] Yet his decision came because of the people he was ruling. "This calamity the Jews had brought upon themselves. If they had been walking in faithfulness and humility before God, He would in a signal manner have made the wrath of the king harmless to them."[3]

What had gone wrong? The key lies in Israel's refusal to follow God's will. They chose to listen to their own selfish clamorings. Often when they studied the Scriptures they did it only to bolster their exalted ideas of themselves and to demonstrate how God hated the surrounding nations. Out of such distorted Bible study came a boast that when the Messiah came He would appear as a conquering king to crush all opposition in His wrath against the heathen.[4] Is it any wonder that Herod responded as he did? Popular misconceptions had excited his worst fears.

There is a lesson here that we would do well to ponder. Choosing to bend the Word of God to suit our own selfishness invariably sets the stage for a curse far beyond our own power to control. Bible study should ever be motivated by the desire to know the truth about God.

---

[1] *SDA Bible Dictionary*, p. 479.
[2] *The SDA Bible Commentary*, vol. 5, p. 291.
[3] *The Desire of Ages*, p. 65.
[4] *Ibid.*, pp. 65, 66.

THE DANGER OF SUPPOSING

But they, supposing him to have been in the company, went a day's journey; and they sought him among their kinsfolk and acquaintance. Luke 2:44.

At the end of the Passover, Joseph and Mary joined the large caravan that headed back to their Galilean home. In the bustle and confusion of travel it would be quite natural to be distracted. The pleasures of traveling with relatives and old friends could easily have swept them along in a happy montage of companionship. Yet a decision should have been made. At least one of them should have checked to see whether Jesus was in the company. Since women customarily traveled in the lead part of the caravan, Joseph and Mary may have been temporarily separated, each supposing Jesus to with the other.[1]

That evening, when camp was being set up for the night, their supposing halted. As they scurried from one relative and acquaintance to another and He was not to be found, the stark truth sent shudders through them. They well remembered how Herod had tried to kill the infant Jesus. This was the first time He had visited Jerusalem since His dedication, and they suddenly had all sorts of anxious thoughts. They certainly couldn't have slept much that night.

The caravan likely was taking the Jordan route to avoid Samaritan country, so the next day Joseph and Mary had to climb the seventeen miles (27 kilometers) from Jericho back to Jerusalem. They had little chance of finding Jesus that evening. But on the third day they did find Him—right where they had left Him, in the Temple. He had not run away. They had walked off without Him.

It is always dangerous to suppose that Jesus is with us. We need to check constantly; otherwise in the bustle of our everyday schedule we will neglect Him. "We may in one day lose the Saviour's presence, and it may take many days of sorrowful search to find Him, and regain the peace that we have lost."[2]

---

[1] *The SDA Bible Commentary*, vol. 5, p. 708.
[2] *The Desire of Ages*, p. 83.

THEIR GOLDEN OPPORTUNITY

They found him in the temple, sitting in the midst of the doctors, both hearing them, and asking them questions. And all that heard him were astonished at his understanding and answers. Luke 2:46, 47.

His first Passover service was an intensely moving experience for the boy Jesus. New emotions welled up within Him as He began to sense the mystery of His mission.[1]

It was quite natural, then, that He tarried in the Temple and seated Himself on the ground with the other youngsters who came to be instructed by the great rabbis of the time. These learned doctors usually sat on benches on the Temple terrace or in an apartment, with their pupils seated about them. The one great theme was the coming Messiah and how He would elevate the Jewish nation.[2] But a puzzlng frown crossed Jesus' face. How could the Messiah come as a conquering hero when Isaiah had depicted Him as a lamb led to the slaughter? His hand was raised in question. The scholars were amazed at the depth of His knowledge of the Scriptures. Again and again they discussed the ancient prophecies with this Youngster from Galilee and pondered His amazing questions and answers.

It was God's method of reaching these proud men. Jesus had come to learn and had caught them in an unguarded moment. They were totally unconscious of the fact that before them sat the Lord of glory, who had given the Scriptures in the first place. Yet, like every child of humanity, Jesus had learned by studying, and from that study He was able to develop a depth of understanding that startled the greatest minds in Israel. It was their golden opportunity to accept the truths about the Messiah that would prepare their hearts for receiving Jesus when He began His ministry some eighteen years later. The choice was theirs if they did not resist the Holy Spirit. God seeks to reach us in our most unguarded moments when the barriers of pride are down.

---

[1] *The Desire of Ages*, p. 78.
[2] *The SDA Bible Commentary*, vol. 5, p. 709.

DAILY DECISIONS OF JESUS

And Jesus increased in wisdom and stature, and in favour with God and man. Luke 2:52.

That favor with God and man was bought with the price of daily decisions that met Heaven's standard of righteousness. Jesus would have nothing to do with the artificial requirements that man had set up as the criteria for acceptance. From His earliest years He had had to make decisions that invariably countered the current notions of correct behavior. For instance, at the close of their twelfth year, all Jewish boys were required by rabbinical tradition to wear phylacteries at the prescribed hours of prayer.[1] Why should Jesus wear on His forehead or arm the strips of parchment with written passages from the law? The rabbinical literalists who had interpreted the law of Moses in this fashion were ignoring the truth that God wants to write His law in the heart.

But it wasn't just the wearing of such outward adornment to demonstrate some man-made custom of righteousness that Jesus condemned. He would not do anything that did not follow the Word of God itself. Jesus was not ashamed of being different. He knew that the blessing of His heavenly Father was more precious than the smiling approval of the priests or His peers. So we can only imagine the days of conflict at home and wherever He went. He was out of step with the religious leaders, the community in general, the children of Joseph, and sometimes His own mother.[2] His gentle and tender life was a constant irritant because it was in such sharp contrast to the selfishness all around Him.

So our text says more than what appears on the surface. "In favour with God and man" came about by hard decisions of high integrity, which all of us may have as He did if we cherish that loving intent to abide only by the Word of God.

Silently Christ's childhood and youth passed in Nazareth, the skid row of Palestine. Yet out of those quiet years came an example for all who daily desire to choose, as He did, the peaceful atmosphere of heaven rather than to conform to self-seeking standards.

---

[1] *The SDA Bible Commentary,* vol. 5, pp. 706, 707.
[2] *The Desire of Ages,* p. 90.

JOHN'S CHOICE

And the child grew, and waxed strong in spirit, and was in the deserts till the day of his shewing unto Israel. Luke 1:80.

While Jesus quietly grew up in the village of Nazareth, His cousin John, who was six months older, spent his time in the wilderness of Judea.[1] Since his parents were well-advanced in years, they undoubtedly passed away while he was still young. But the Nazirite vow they had made on his behalf became "his own in a lifelong consecration."[2] Far removed from village or city, John turned to the things of nature for his schooling.

"It was a lonely region where he found his home, in the midst of barren hills, wild ravines, and rocky caves. But it was his choice to forgo the enjoyments and luxuries of life for the stern discipline of the wilderness."[3]

John made such a decision because he did not trust his own humanity. If he was to be the forerunner of Christ, he knew that his mind must be highly honed for the task of detecting the very early advances of the enemy. Out there in that semiarid country, far away from the hustle and bustle of daily traffic, John could focus on the depth of God's providence and hear, through the quiet stillness of nature, the real thunder of His power.

It is only then that any human can better perceive the truths about God's character. For most of us, being alone in nature is absolutely essential for spiritual growth. When we are willing, as John was, to be alone with God amid the things He has made, then we shall enter that same school that John did so many centuries ago. John was afraid to come too close to sin lest his own perceptions become blurred.[4] From his quiet life apart from the rush of things we may learn how he prepared himself for that important task of turning the attention of sensuous, world-loving people to Jesus.

We need to understand the value of Nature's ability to strengthen our own heart in these last days, when sin seems to saturate every fiber of life.

---

[1] *The SDA Bible Commentary*, vol. 5, p. 694.
[2] *The Desire of Ages*, p. 102.
[3] *Ibid.*, p. 101.
[4] *Ibid.*, pp. 101, 102.

WITHOUT MINCING WORDS

But when he saw many of the Pharisees and Sadducees come to his baptism, he said unto them, O generation of vipers, who hath warned you to flee from the wrath to come? Matt. 3:7.

John the Baptist did not fit into any official ministerial role. Dressed in his coarse camel-hair robe, which he tied at the waist by a leather belt, he looked for all the world like some prophet who had stepped out of the ancient past.[1] Even in his day he was a singular individual. John never rented a hall, distributed handbills, or urged folk to invite their friends and neighbors to his wilderness evangelistic meetings. He never sought a crowd, but they came to him!

And when the people pressed their way to the Jordan, what did they hear? Certainly not some ego-inflating words to flatter the sinner. God's great preachers invariably lay heavy burdens on the consciences of those who rest smugly satisfied in their sinful ways. But such preaching is a choice. God does not override a person's selection of words or his tone of voice. So John chose to speak in a language that thundered at hypocritical piety. Repentance was his keynote.

And when he saw the richly robed leaders from headquarters, he cared not whether they were liberals or conservatives. The Pharisees were sticklers for the law, yet they used their conservative stance to cover their sins. And the Sadducees, who didn't believe in a real heaven or hell or angels or anything that might interfere with their convenient worldly ways—all received his penetrating denunciation. "John declared to the teachers of Israel that their pride, selfishness, and cruelty showed them to be a generation of vipers, a deadly curse to the people, rather than the children of the just and obedient Abraham."[2]

We may not think that such an approach would be acceptable today, yet God still seeks those who by their words and actions fearlessly proclaim the urgent need for repentance.

---

[1] *The SDA Bible Commentary*, vol. 5, p. 296.
[2] *The Desire of Ages*, p. 106.

A TIME TO CHANGE PROFESSIONS

Then cometh Jesus from Galilee to Jordan unto John, to be baptized of him. Matt. 3:13.

No communication is quite so effective as word of mouth. John the Baptist's announcement of a coming Messiah and his appeal for repentance to prepare His way were so powerful that people mistook him for the Messiah.[1] Word spread to every quarter of Palestine. From the fisherman's wharf on the shore of Galilee to the coastal cities to the little villages tucked away in the hill country—all heard the report that something significant was happening down at the Jordan. The strange wilderness prophet had captured the imagination and hearts of all ranks of people.

It was now the fall of A.D. 27.[2] Up there in the town of Nazareth the villagers heard the story. Someone entered Joseph's carpenter shop and excitedly poured forth the news. Immediately Jesus knew that His time had come. He had never met His cousin John, but He knew from His study of the ancient scrolls that Daniel's prophecy would soon meet its fulfillment.[3] Putting His tools away for the last time, He cleaned up the shop and locked the door behind Him. Then, bidding His mother goodbye, He headed with others of His countrymen to the Jordan. His was a decision based on the sure word of prophecy. He knew where He was in the stream of time, and without delay He followed the dictates of the Holy Spirit.

Jesus did not choose to leave when He was 18 years old, nor did He consider packing away the carpenter's tools even when He turned 25. He remained there in Nazareth and built solid furniture for the citizens until He caught the signal that the right moment had come to change professions.

As we approach the Second Coming, the great prophecies of Scripture should become an integral part of our lives. If we stay alert to God's leading, we will know the right moment to decide matters that will keep us ready for His appearance.

[1] *The SDA Bible Commentary,* vol. 5, p. 719.
[2] *Ibid.,* p. 301.
[3] Dan. 9:25.

DEFEATING SATAN WITH THE WORD

Then saith Jesus unto him, Get thee hence, Satan: for it is written, Thou shalt worship the Lord thy God, and him only shalt thou serve. Matt. 4:10.

Immediately following His baptism Jesus climbed the steep, rugged route to the back country beyond Jordan to be alone. There in the wilderness haunts He could meditate and pray in preparation for His divine mission.

At the end of His forty-day fast a bright angel appeared as if God had answered His prayers. By all appearances Satan surely looked as if he had come straight from glory. But when he opened his mouth he betrayed himself.

"If You really are the Son of God, then make these stones into bread," he said as he pointed to the rocks.

That "if" rankled with a bitterness that suggested that surely God would not leave His Son to look so emaciated. Perhaps Jesus was the fallen angel!

It would have been no trick at all for Jesus to speak and turn those rocks into loaves of bread. It might even settle the question of His divinity. But instead, Jesus chose to meet the temptation with the words He Himself had given Moses some fifteen centuries earlier:[1] "Man shall not live by bread alone, but by every word that proceedeth out of the mouth of God."[2] He would not work a miracle for Himself then or at any other time.

The devil then whisked Jesus off to a high turret of the Temple and, using a memory verse himself, quoted from Psalm 91. He suggested that Jesus do a little sky-diving stunt, because the angels would easily provide Him with a soft landing. Jesus refused to take the presumptuous bait, and He met the temptation with another "It is written." He did the same for Satan's last effort, when the enemy urged Him to bow down and worship him. Jesus chose to use only the Word of God, and we too may find this our source of power in defeating the enemy.

---

[1] *The SDA Bible Commentary,* vol. 5, p. 311.
[2] Matt. 4:4.

LEARNERS, NOT CRITICS

Blessed are they which do hunger and thirst after righteousness: for they shall be filled. Matt. 5:6.

Twice John the Baptist pointed out Jesus to the crowds down by the Jordan, and under inspiration he declared, "Behold the Lamb of God!" [1] The first time the people heard this their eyes followed the outstretched hands of John. They noticed Jesus mingling with the multitude, and they were stunned. Jesus, with His unassuming and gentle attitude, certainly did nothing to arouse their emotions and expectancy of the Messiah. Perplexed and disappointed, many could not fathom what John meant. [2]

The next day John singled out Jesus again, and when John made the same pronouncement, two young men immediately began following Jesus. Andrew and his friend John were irresistibly drawn to Jesus. Each wondered to himself whether He was truly the Messiah. Jesus knew that these two were trailing Him, and turning around, He asked, " 'What are you looking for?' "

" 'Rabbi . . . , where are you staying?' " they asked. [3]

Andrew and John wanted more than just a brief chat in public. They longed to be alone with this Man, to understand what John the Baptist meant by the words "the Lamb of God." They were thrilled and wanted to learn more. Since it was now about 4 P.M., Jesus encouraged them to follow Him to the place where He was staying. [4]

We have no record of the conversation that evening, but we can be assured that Jesus led them into grand themes that would later bear fruit in these two becoming full disciples. But they would have missed this opportunity had they not chosen to seek for truth.

"If John and Andrew had possessed the unbelieving spirit of the priests and rulers, they would not have been found as learners at the feet of Jesus. They would have come to Him as critics, to judge His words. Many thus close the door to the most precious opportunities." [5]

[1] John 1:29, 36.
[2] *The Desire of Ages*, pp. 137, 138.
[3] Verse 38, N.E.B.
[4] *The SDA Bible Commentary*, vol. 5, p. 910.
[5] *The Desire of Ages*, p. 139.

SHARING THE JOY

He first findeth his own brother Simon, and saith unto him, We have found the Messias, which is, being interpreted, the Christ. And he brought him to Jesus. John 1:41, 42.

Andrew was the first disciple to introduce someone to Jesus.[1] It was a decision prompted by the profound impression that Jesus had made on his heart. He just had to share his joy! He couldn't wait to tell his brother Simon the exciting news!

In the unfolding Gospel story following this event, we spot Andrew only a few times. Simon Peter's image looms larger and larger, while Andrew, by comparison, recedes into the background. We have no books written by Andrew, we know of no great miracles that he performed—nothing that would make him stand out above the other disciples. Nothing of any certainty is known about his later life either. Tradition has left us only with an obscure account of his traveling as far as Scotland and being martyred in Greece.[2] Yet this was the man who brought Peter to Jesus, and Peter left us with some of the most exciting accounts of the gospel in action that we have on record.

How important, then, was Andrew's sharing! Yet we would not have this whole account if it were not for his decision. And what was it that prompted Andrew's choice? Surely it was not to make some statistical report to the church, because there wasn't any Christian church yet! Nor did he hope that his fellow fishermen of Galilee would notice his missionary activity. He brought Simon Peter to Jesus because he loved his brother and longed to have him enter that same joy he had experienced. He didn't rattle off some prepared speech to Peter, because his words tumbled out in the excitement of discovery.

"Our influence upon others depends not so much upon what we say as upon what we are. Men may combat and defy our logic, they may resist our appeals; but a life of disinterested love is an argument they cannot gainsay."[3]

---

[1] *The SDA Bible Commentary*, vol. 5, p. 910.
[2] *SDA Bible Dictionary*, p. 46.
[3] *The Desire of Ages*, p. 142.

OVERCOMING PREJUDICE

And Nathanael said unto him, Can there any good thing come out of Nazareth? Philip said unto him, Come and see. John 1:46.

Nathanael had mingled with the crowds down by the Jordan, listening to John the Baptist. He was there when John had singled out Jesus as the Lamb of God, but Jesus did not have the slightest attraction to him as the Messiah of his dreams. The careworn look and obvious poverty were a disappointment to Nathanael. Yet the words of John cut deeply into his consciousness.

Nathanael felt that he needed time to meditate and pray. If Jesus really was the one whom God had sent, he wanted to know it. So he went to his favorite secluded spot under a fig tree. And here his friend Philip found him. They had often come to this quiet green haunt to be alone.[1]

"We have found him, of whom Moses in the law, and the prophets, did write," exclaimed Philip.[2]

His words seemed like a direct answer to Nathanael's prayer. But Philip added his own doubtful remark, which betrayed a shaky faith, "Jesus of Nazareth, the son of Joseph."

Nathanael had been fighting off the prejudice that was pushing against his belief, and this seemed too much.[3] His own hometown was Cana, about eight miles (thirteen kilometers) north of Nazareth, and he knew all about the wicked little hill village.[4]

"Can there any good thing come out of Nazareth?" he asked. Philip didn't argue with him. "Come and see," he replied. Right at that point was the moment to decide. Should he go with Philip and judge for himself or should he be swayed by the prejudice that shadowed his thinking? Obviously the rabbis in Israel would not be interested, so why should he? But deep inside, the Holy Spirit had found a responsive chord, and Nathanael was willing to see and judge for himself.

How many have missed the opportunity to find Jesus because they refuse to make their own discovery! They are turned off by what they think is Christianity, and they never find the Saviour.

---

[1] *The Desire of Ages*, p. 140.
[2] John 1:45.
[3] *SDA Bible Dictionary*, p. 779.
[4] *The SDA Bible Commentary*, vol. 5, p. 921.

BELIEVING ANYWAY

**His mother saith unto the servants, Whatsoever he saith
unto you, do it. John 2:5.**

It was now about December, two months after Jesus' baptism.[1]
He and five of His new disciples, John, Andrew, Peter, Philip, and
Nathanael, had returned from the Jordan to Galilee and had headed
for Cana, "the place of reeds," a town near a marshy area north of
Nazareth. They arrived in time for the wedding of a couple who
were relatives of both Mary and Joseph.[2]

Little knots of guests soon began whispering together and
glancing toward Jesus and His disciples. If the stories were true
Jesus might be the promised Messiah!

Mary had longed for the moment when Jesus would manifest
His calling. Now, with the natural tug of a fond mother's longing,
she waited on tiptoe for Him to perform a miracle. She had never
seen Him perform a miracle, but her implicit faith was so strong
that she just knew He could.

Suddenly the servants crowded excitedly around her with
whispered concerns. The wine supply was depleted! Since she
had been assisting with the catering, it was partially her
responsibility to provide enough food and drink for the guests.
And then the thought struck her. Why not tell Jesus?

But Jesus only replied, "Woman, what have I to do with
thee?"[3] His words sound rather brusque to our Western ears, but it
was a proper way of addressing a mother in Oriental custom.[4] Jesus
told her frankly that His time had not yet come. What He meant
was that before He was to be proclaimed the Messiah, He was to be
"a man of sorrows."[5]

Mary didn't understand the full import of what He said, nor did
she grasp the significance of His mission. But she chose to believe
anyway. And that belief set the stage for Christ's first miracle. To
honor Mary's faith and establish His disciples' confidence He
turned the water to wine, and the servants were able to pour out
about eighty-seven gallons (330 liters) of fresh grape juice.[6]

---

[1] *The SDA Bible Commentary*, vol. 5, p. 921.
[2] *The Desire of Ages*, p. 144.
[3] John 2:4.
[4] *Ibid.*, p. 146.
[5] Isa. 53:3.
[6] *The SDA Bible Commentary*, vol. 5, p. 922.

FLEEING HYPOCRITES

And when he had made a scourge of small cords, he drove them all out of the temple. John 2:15.

At the Passover of A.D. 28, Jesus entered the Temple for the first time since He began His ministry.[1] He was about to announce His mission as the Messiah. And what an announcement it was to be!

As Jesus stood at the top of the stairs His eyes swept over the whole unfair and unholy traffic in the courtyard below. Not only were the poor people required to purchase the animal sacrifices at exorbitant prices but, worse yet, it was impossible to buy anything without exchanging their currency for Temple money at frightfully high rates.[2] Even though some were so poverty-stricken that they barely had enough food for themselves, the greedy priests, who were growing fat on the whole religious business, were totally unsympathetic. The sight of this marketplace atmosphere in God's house of worship—the cacophony of bleating sheep, lowing cattle, and cooing doves, amid the sharp bargaining at the tables—was too much for Jesus.

For a moment He just stood there, His face filling with indignation. Steadily the sound effects died out as every eye came to be riveted on His searching gaze. In that painful silence His voice lifted like a trumpet, ''Take these things hence; make not my Father's house an house of merchandise.''[3]

Then, raising that small scourge of cords, which now looked like some flaming sword to those hypocrites, He went into action. Nobody bothered to count the receipts or to gather up the coins as He turned the tables over. Priests, officers, and brokers decided it was time to move. Hoisting their skirts, they and their sheep and cattle stampeded to the nearest exit. It was a fantastic flight to behold.

But why did they decide to run when the poor chose to remain for a blessing? Remember, hypocrites detest exposure! They would rather run than allow Christ to cleanse the soul temple of all selfishness and corruption.

---

[1] *The SDA Bible Commentary,* vol. 5, p. 923.
[2] *The Desire of Ages,* p. 155.
[3] John 2:16.

THE DELAYED CHOICE

And as Moses lifted up the serpent in the wilderness, even so must the Son of man be lifted up. John 3:14.

When Christ drove the money changers from the Temple for the first time, one Pharisee watched intently from the sidelines. Rich, talented, and highly educated, Nicodemus had studied the prophecies and concluded that Jesus was the promised Messiah.

During the strategy committee's secret meeting to decide the fate of Jesus, Nicodemus had voted on the side of moderation. He felt the leadership might bring fresh calamities on the nation if they followed a hawkish policy.

But his less-embarrassing arrangement to meet Jesus at night didn't go as he had planned. His private conversation with Jesus immediately shifted into an area that he hadn't counted on. Jesus refused to be taken in by his flattering salutation and went quickly to work on Nicodemus' own heart.

In spite of his seeming ignorance of Jesus' terminology, the idea of being born again wasn't really new to Nicodemus. The priests used such terminology themselves. But the fact that Jesus was probing for a personal commitment confronted his own pride. Nicodemus was a great giver. Charity was his thing. He had heard the preaching of John the Baptist. But the notion of personal repentance had never crossed his mind. After all, he served on the highest ecclesiastical board in Israel!

That night meeting left him stunned. He could not shake the conviction that Jesus was the Saviour and that he personally must be born again. For three long years Nicodemus tossed this disturbing thought around. And he watched Jesus even more intensely.

That Friday afternoon when Christ hung on the cross, the whole picture finally snapped into place. As Jesus was lifted up Nicodemus caught the full, personal meaning of the Sin Bearer, and just how Moses' lifting up the serpent in the wilderness related to it. The event that shattered the disciples' faith only strengthened his. He became a full-fledged follower of Jesus from that moment on.

THE JOY OF SELF-DENIAL
He must increase, but I must decrease. John 3:30.

It all began over an attendance record. The disciples of the Baptist felt jealous of Jesus' rising popularity. But what made it seem worse to them was that Jesus had authorized His own disciples to baptize. The situation reached the flash point. John's disciples were ready to criticize Christ's work, and Satan was prepared with the right spark.

The Jewish authorities had avoided attacking John because of his strong influence over the people, but they had tried the less-conspicuous method of hindering his work by questioning the purification of John's baptism. Jews baptized Gentile proselytes, but John was baptizing Jews![1] Theological hassles have a way of growing out of minor points, and soon questions were raised regarding the essential difference between the baptism of John and the baptism of Jesus. Next came the dispute over the actual words to be spoken at the ceremony, and finally John's disciples questioned whether Jesus' disciples had any right to baptize.[2] It became such a hot issue that they hurried to the Baptist himself.

" 'Rabbi, that man who was with you on the other side of the Jordan—the one you testified about—well, he is baptizing, and everyone is going to him.' " [3]

At this point John could have chosen to feel sorry for himself and express hurt over his waning popularity, or he could rise to the very heights of self-denial and find his joy in Jesus. How often the gospel has been hindered by little men who have been interested only in self-exaltation rather than in lifting up the Saviour before the people! John would have no dissension. He knew he could speak words that would create a great hindrance to Christ's work, but he refused to follow Satan's suggestions.

John's decision should always be ours. He found his joy and happiness in exalting Christ, while his own selfish interests decreased. As Christ's followers "We can receive of heaven's light only as we are willing to be emptied of self." [4]

---

[1] *The SDA Bible Commentary*, vol. 5, p. 932.
[2] *The Desire of Ages*, p. 178.
[3] John 3:26, N.I.V.
[4] *Ibid.*, p. 181.

TESTIMONY OF THE WAITING WATERPOT

The woman then left her waterpot, and went her way into the city, and saith to the men, Come, see a man, which told me all things that ever I did: is not this the Christ? John 4:28, 29.

When she first saw Jesus, He was resting on the curbstone of Jacob's well. She had no idea that He may have hiked between fifteen and twenty miles (twenty-four and thirty-two kilometers) that morning, but she soon learned that He was thirsty.[1] It had shocked her that this stranger should speak to her, even to request a drink. It was not proper for a Jewish rabbi to speak to a woman in public anyway, and this woman was a Samaritan at that![2]

Obviously Jesus had no equipment to draw water from the one-hundred-foot well, but He spoke to her about "living water."[3] As the conversation proceeded she became dimly aware that this water Jesus spoke of was figurative, satisfying the thirst of the soul. "Give me this water"! she exclaimed.[4]

But before Jesus could supply her with His gift, He had to lead her to recognize her need of a Saviour. That is why He abruptly changed the conversation to her marital status. For her this was a sticky subject. She had had five husbands, and the man she presently had was only a live-in. Genuine commitment had not marked her life.

Uncomfortable with this turn of the conversation, she acknowledged Jesus as a prophet but then quickly changed the conversation to a theological argument to avoid further personal discussion. It was then that Jesus opened the truth to her about real worship of the true God. It was His call for a decision, and she took it.

She knew that the Messiah would be coming, and when Jesus told her that He was the Messiah, she left her waterpot and hurried back into the city. That empty waterpot stood as mute testimony of the effect of Jesus' words on her life. She forgot her errand and the Saviour's thirst. With her heart overflowing with joy, she just had to share the good news.

---

[1] *The SDA Bible Commentary*, vol. 5, p. 937.
[2] *Ibid.*, p. 941.
[3] John 4:10; *ibid.*, p. 938.
[4] Verse 15.

BELIEVING WITHOUT MIRACLES

Now we believe, not because of thy saying: for we have heard him ourselves, and know that this is indeed the Christ, the Saviour of the world. John 4:42.

When the Samaritan woman rushed back to the village with her face aglow from having discovered Jesus, she went directly to the men of Sychar. They knew her! And for her to be so excited about anything spiritual was enough to arrest their attention.

" 'Come, see a man who told me everything I ever did,' " [1] she said, pointing back toward Jacob's well.

This was something of an exaggeration, but she apparently thought that if Jesus could reveal her deep, dark secrets, He could easily tell her more. Then she very tactfully asked a question that aroused further interest: " 'Could this be the Christ?' " [2]

That did it! It must have been quite a sight, the men of Sychar coming to meet Jesus. We can only imagine that the woman came following behind, because she had left her waterpot at the well and certainly wanted to hear more of what Jesus had to say.

One brief visit would not suffice for these people. They wanted more, and Jesus stayed with them for two days. He ate with them and slept under their roofs and showed them the consistent, gracious kindness of God. They had many questions to ask Him, and in His own style He opened before them the truths they most needed to hear.

Not one miracle did He perform, except in revealing the woman's secret. He healed no one, and no special sign was given, yet these people chose to accept Jesus on His word. Unlike the Pharisees, who sneered at Jesus' simple methods and totally ignored His miracles, these Samaritans decided that Christ's words were enough to convince them that He is the Saviour of the world.[3] It was not because of the woman's sayings, but because of Christ's own testimony. How important that we examine things for ourselves!

---

[1] John 4:29, N.I.V.
[2] Verse 29, N.I.V.
[3] *The Desire of Ages*, p. 192.

BELIEVING TO RECEIVE

The nobleman saith unto him, Sir, come down ere my child die. John 4:49.

Those words were wrenched from the lips of the Jewish nobleman when he realized that his conditional belief in Jesus could cost his son's life. He had come from Capernaum to Cana when he learned that Jesus was back in the district. Pressing through the throngs, he had approached Jesus with the request to come down to Capernaum to heal his boy. It is the first recorded instance of anyone asking Jesus for healing, yet it is tainted with unbelief.[1] This official from Herod's court would accept Jesus as the Messiah *if* He would heal his son. " 'Unless you people see miraculous signs and wonders,' Jesus told him, 'you will never believe.' "[2]

The precise moment had come for the king's courtier to make up his mind. The words of Jesus flashed in bold contrast to his own selfish motives. He realized that he was standing before Someone who could read his heart, and he cried out for help. It was a decision that saved him from the folly of unbelief and spared his little child from certain death.

" 'You may go,' " Jesus told the nobleman. " 'Your son will live.' "[3]

It was enough. The nobleman believed without reservation. In fact, he didn't even head home that afternoon. Capernaum was only sixteen miles (twenty-six kilometers) away, and he could have easily made the downhill trip in four or five hours.[4]

The next morning when he arrived home, his servants rushed out to greet him with the news he already knew awaited him. When they told him the fever had left his son at one o'clock the day before, the father knew it was the time that Jesus had spoken the word. This miracle turned not only the nobleman into a believer but his whole household, as well.

His decision is for us, also. We should ask, believe, then thank the Lord ahead of time that the promised blessing will be ours when we need it most.

[1] *The SDA Bible Commentary,* vol. 5, p. 943.
[2] John 4:48, N.I.V.
[3] Verse 50, N.I.V.
[4] *Ibid.,* p. 944.

ACTING WITHOUT HESITATION

Jesus saith unto him, Rise, take up thy bed, and walk. John 5:8.

Jerusalem's Pool of Bethesda wasn't a public swimming pool or recreation center. It was really a double pool, fifty-five feet (seventeen meters) long and twelve feet (four meters) wide, spread under five arches and designated as the place for the impotent to be cured.[1] The atmosphere around the place hung heavy with legend. It was commonly believed that an angel periodically agitated the waters. At that precise moment, the first person to step into the pool would be healed, regardless of his malady. Such a myth surely testified to the low esteem the people placed on God. Would He encourage the weaker, suffering humanity to be trampled and crushed by the stronger?

One Sabbath when Jesus was strolling beside the pool, He spotted a paraplegic who had put up with this wretched condition for thirty-eight years. Jesus longed to heal all the poolside patients, but this man in particular was so helpless and in such misery that He compassionately bent over him.

"Would you like to be made whole?"

It was a rhetorical question that would quicken the hope of any person in such a condition. But the cripple's hope soon faded. He explained to Jesus that nobody was willing to put him into the pool when the waters rippled. Jesus did not stop to discount the legend. Neither did He offer any physical therapy. He simply told him to rise, pick up his rug and blanket, and walk. Jesus did not ask the man to exercise faith in Him. He didn't even identify Himself. He just gave the command.[2]

At that point the man could have taken time out to discuss the condition of his atophied muscles or the impossibility of paralyzed nerves responding to such a command. Instead, he chose to act without hesitation, and that decision sent him leaping on his way.

Spiritual healing is accomplished the same way. "Do not wait to feel that you are made whole. Believe His word, and it will be fulfilled. Put your will on the side of Christ."[3]

---

[1] *The SDA Bible Commentary*, vol. 5, p. 948.
[2] *The Desire of Ages*, p. 202.
[3] *Ibid.*, p. 203.

CHOOSING A FALSE LEADER

I am come in my Father's name, and ye receive me not: if another shall come in his own name, him ye will receive. John 5:43.

Jesus had deliberately selected the worst case at the Pool of Bethesda. If He had healed all the poor people waiting around the pool that Sabbath, the Jews would have become so excited about His transgressing the law, as they interpreted it, that His work would have been cut short.[1] But by healing the man who had been crippled for thirty-eight years, Jesus intended that the discussion of Sabbath healing should be brought up so that all could understand the real purpose of the Lord's day. Having the man carry his bed through the streets would automatically advertise the miracle and trigger the discussion.

When Jesus was summoned to appear before the Sanhedrin for Sabbathbreaking, the Jewish leaders hoped to pin the charge of blasphemy and treason upon Him. But the whole procedure backfired. Before it was through, Jesus was accusing them of transgression by turning their backs on God. Before the highest tribunal in Israel, Jesus declared Himself one with the Father in the work of salvation. He denied them the right to interfere with His mission. Before that august assembly stood the Lord of the Sabbath, and they supposed themselves authorized to judge Him? It was a thrilling moment in their own lives. Never had they heard such words from any person. They were stunned. But they had to make up their minds. Would they choose Jesus and His way to salvation, or would they cling to their own system of works?

Christ told them in our verse for today that they would rather have a false teacher than have Him. It was a decision based on self-exaltation. "To such appeals the Jews could respond. They would receive the false teacher because he flattered their pride by sanctioning their cherished opinions and traditions."[2] People are still exchanging the Saviour for a man-made system, and they will choose any leader or religious activity that fits their carnal minds.

---

[1] *The Desire of Ages,* pp. 201, 202.
[2] *Ibid.,* pp. 212, 213.

DRIVEN BY INFATUATION

For Herod himself had sent forth and laid hold upon John, and bound him in prison for Herodias' sake. . . . For John had said unto Herod, It is not lawful for thee to have thy brother's wife. Mark 6:17, 18.

In the spring of A.D. 29, John's ministry abruptly halted.[1] Herod Antipas arrested the prophet and placed him in his Jordanian fortress to satisfy the revengeful sentiments of his new wife, Herodias. It is a sad commentary on this morally flabby ruler's life, who would go cross-grained to his own conscience because of the demands of this woman to whom he was unlawfully married.

Herod had listened to John preach. He felt the awesome sense of the coming judgment and the need for repentance. In fact, the Scriptures tell us that he feared John and heard him gladly. Why, then, did he arrest the Baptist? His infatuation with Herodias prompted his decision to send his soldiers. He had tried feebly to break the chains that she had forged around his life, but the lustful passions were too much, and Herodias held him firmly in her grasp.

That phrase "for Herodias' sake" holds a warning. It speaks to us of the power of infatuation and it shouts the cry to turn from the evil that so entrances us that we will decide against all sense of justice. Herod knew very well that he was out of bounds in divorcing his wife and laying claim to his halfbrother Philip's wife, who was also his own niece.[2] They both had living spouses and were drawn together only because of lust. Yet infatuation has a sinister technique of overriding all reason just to clamor onward in its quest for desired expression. That decision to cast the faithful prophet in prison solely to satisfy the anger of an evil woman jarringly reminds us of the insidious evil of lust. The so-called "falling in love" experience often is nothing more than an unlawful infatuation that effectively drowns out the Holy Spirit's plea for repentance.

---

[1] *The SDA Bible Commentary*, vol. 5, p. 614.
[2] *SDA Bible Dictionary*, p. 481.

NO GREATER PROPHET

For I say unto you, Among those that are born of women there is not a greater prophet than John the Baptist. Luke 7:28.

For someone who had always known the freedom of the wilderness, the incarceration in Herod's gloomy dungeon was especially excruciating. John had been locked up for about six months when some of his disciples brought him fresh reports of the large crowds flocking to Jesus.[1] Ordinarily the visiting hours would bring some cheer, but John was distressed with the obviously growing animosity his own disciples had toward Jesus.

"If Jesus is really the Messiah, how can He permit you to be left in prison?" they asked.

Their question haunted John. He would never have asked such a thing, and it made his imprisonment even harder on him.[2] Often our well-meaning friends do that to us. Yet John did not give way to unbelief. He wanted his own disciples to find out for themselves about Jesus, and at the same time maybe he would receive some word for himself. So he sent two of his trusted disciples to Jesus with the question Are You the One to come, or are we to look for another?

Jesus didn't answer John's disciples when they came to Him with that question.[3] Instead He kept healing and caring for the needy. The disciples of John watched and listened all day, until finally Jesus called them to Him and told them to return to the prison and tell John what they had witnessed. " 'And happy is the man who never loses his faith in me,' " Jesus told them.[4]

Those words were not lost on John. It was a gentle rebuke that opened to John even more fully the real mission of the Messiah. He decided more firmly to keep a tight grip on God, regardless of whether he was freed or died in the dungeon. John had chosen to lose himself in the great cause of glorifying God. It was his joy. That is why Jesus said that there was no greater prophet. He knew that John could endure anything, because he had found the secret of eternal life.

---

[1] *The SDA Bible Commentary,* vol. 5, p. 758.
[2] *The Desire of Ages,* p. 215.
[3] *Ibid.,* p. 217.
[4] Luke 7:23, Phillips.

DRUNKEN DECISION

Wine is a mocker, strong drink is raging: and whosoever is deceived thereby is not wise. Prov. 20:1.

It would be hard to fault Herodias' timing. She waited for Herod's birthday party before springing the trap of revenge against John the Baptist. She well knew that her husband really wanted to free John and would have done it earlier had it not been for her threatening vigilance.[1] But a dungeon wasn't enough for John, as far as she was concerned. She wanted the prophet dead—silenced forever. So she waited, knowing that when Herod was off his guard her diabolical scheme would work.

Waiting in the wings for the precise moment, she sent her voluptuous daughter Salome in for the main attraction, just when the VIPs were glassy-eyed with wine, and the laughter was getting silly.[2] To have a princess dance, instead of some hired dancer, was so unusual that it created a stir even before Salome really got under way.[3] But when she uncoiled in her sensuous dance, those dignitaries stared goggle-eyed at the floor-show performance. The flickering torchlights only accentuated every undulating movement as her shadows danced with her. Salome had no idea of her mother's hatred against John the Baptist. All she knew was the power in her body to hold those high officials spellbound.

When the applause died away, Herod arose—just as Herodias knew he would—and promised before all his chiefs that the dancing girl could have any gift. Heady with wine, the king felt very reckless at the moment.

And mother had her gift order all ready. Salome was to ask for the head of John the Baptist on a platter! The grisly request stunned Herod. It silenced the whole party. He had to decide then and there. It couldn't be postponed. Herod waited in vain for someone to speak up for John. All the guests respected him and had even traveled long distances to hear him preach.[4] But their intoxicated silence finally held Herod to his oath and sealed the doom of God's prophet.

---

[1] *The Desire of Ages*, pp. 220, 221.
[2] *Ibid.*, p. 221.
[3] *The SDA Bible Commentary*, vol. 5, p. 615.
[4] *The Desire of Ages*, p. 221.

HOMETOWN REJECTION

The Spirit of the Lord God is upon me . . . , to proclaim liberty to the captives, and the opening of the prison to them that are bound. Isa. 61:1.

In the late spring of A.D. 29 Jesus returned to His hometown of Nazareth for the first time since He had begun His ministry.[1] Since He was now quite famous, He was requested to take the Sabbath service as a guest rabbi.

For the Scripture reading Jesus selected the first verse and a half from Isaiah 61. If He used one of the common scrolls of the day it meant that He had to unroll nearly thirty feet of scroll before He found the spot.[2] Custom required that Jesus stand and read from the ancient prophets. Then He sat down in a special minister's chair, called the seat of Moses, to deliver His sermon.[3] His commentary captured the attention of His listeners. All eyes were fixed on Jesus as He graciously explained the meaning of the Messiah's role. His delivery and style charmed the hometown folk. But then something happened.

"This day is this scripture fulfilled in your ears," He said.[4]

Suddenly all His charm vaporized. The very idea that they were in some sort of bondage and in need of release was too much. And not only that, but He claimed to be the Messiah! This was inconceivable to them. They had known Jesus since His childhood. " 'Isn't this Joseph's son?' " they asked.[5]

Unconsciously they were making decisions that would seal them off from any demonstration that Jesus was what He claimed to be. Their pride was wounded, and when that happens the door of faith slams shut. Their choice left them in darkness and restricted Jesus from working many miracles.

The whole synagogue service broke up, not with hymn singing and a beautiful benediction, but with a mob that brusquely escorted Jesus to the top of the local limestone cliff. The Nazarenes were so angry that they intended to kill Him.[6]

Doesn't His truth often produce the same proud reaction today?

[1] *The SDA Bible Commentary*, vol. 5, p. 726.
[2] *Ibid.*, p. 113.
[3] *Ibid.*, p. 729.
[4] Luke 4:21.
[5] Verse 22, N.I.V.
[6] *Ibid.*, p. 732.

OF FISH AND FAITH

And Simon answering said unto him, Master, we have toiled all the night, and have taken nothing: nevertheless at thy word I will let down the net. Luke 5:5.

It had been a discouraging night. The disciples had not caught a single fish, which is quite remarkable. Peter and his fishing partners couldn't even succeed at the old trade that they knew so well!

The nocturnal conversation during the long hours had only added to Peter's downcast feeling. The growing hatred of the religious leaders against Jesus, the gloomy fate of John the Baptist (who at that time was still in prison), and the dark prospects for the future accentuated defeat.[1]

We are not told how much Jesus' sermon by the sea that morning lifted the spirits of the disciples. We do know that immediately after His discourse from his boat, Jesus told Peter to launch out into the deep and cast his net.

Our text tells us of Peter's choice to obey. From this fishing master's point of view, however, the command was futile. After all, he and his partners had fished all night and had come up empty. Fishing in the clear waters of the Sea of Galilee *had* to be done at night.[2] Daytime was for washing and mending nets, not fishing. Jesus was a carpenter by trade, not a fisherman, and Peter could have argued that carpenters should stay in the building trade and let fishermen tend to their fishing. Instead he chose to launch his boat and promptly start fishing again. He did this, not because he felt like it, but because he loved Jesus. His feelings still lingered in the shadows, and his common sense told him that it was a useless venture, but he obeyed anyway. And that kind of obedience makes all the difference in the world.

The huge catch not only started to break the net but, when secured, nearly sank two boats. Peter was overwhelmed. "This miracle, above any other he had ever witnessed, was to him a manifestation of divine power."[3] Christ longs to have us experience that same power.

[1] *The Desire of Ages*, p. 245.
[2] *The SDA Bible Commentary*, vol. 5, p. 737.
[3] *The Desire of Ages*, p. 246.

DISSOLVING THE FISHING PARTNERSHIP

And he saith unto them, Follow me, and I will make you fishers of men. And they straightway left their nets, and followed him. Matt. 4:19, 20.

The great catch of fish was such an awesome miracle that Peter fell down at Jesus' feet. While holding Him firmly in those big fisherman's hands of his he cried out, "Depart from me; for I am a sinful man, O Lord." [1] He was totally overwhelmed with the sense of his own unworthiness, yet out of love for Jesus and the very sense of his need to be near the Lord, he held on. Whenever men see their own sinfulness in contrast with infinite purity, they invariably cry out in dismay at their own unholy deficiency and are then prepared to let God use them.

"Fear not," Jesus told Peter. "From henceforth thou shalt catch men." [2]

When they reached shore Jesus turned to Andrew, James, and John and said, "Follow me, and I will make you fishers of men."

Peter had already accepted the call, and now the other three responded too. [3] No one showed the least hesitation. These four fishermen willingly dissolved their fishing partnership in exchange for a full-time ministry with Christ. They didn't ask for time to think things over or to call a business meeting. And this decision was made right at the point of supreme success in their lifelong trade. They had never seen so many fish in one catch.

Two autumns before, these four had received the call down by the Jordan to accept Jesus as the Messiah, but then they were only part-time disciples. [4] Now, however, Jesus called them to unite with Him fully and to leave their fishing boats for good. [5] The miracle of the great catch assured them that Jesus could supply their needs. But more than this, it showed them that "He whose word could gather the fishes from the sea could also impress human hearts, and draw them by the cords of His love, so that His servants might become 'fishers of men.' " [6]

---

[1] Luke 5:8.
[2] Verse 10.
[3] *The Desire of Ages,* p. 249.
[4] *The SDA Bible Commentary,* vol. 5, p. 740.
[5] *The Desire of Ages,* pp. 246, 247.
[6] *Ibid.,* p. 249.

DELIVERED FROM THE DEVIL

Let him take hold of my strength, that he may make peace with me; and he shall make peace with me. Isa. 27:5.

It is one thing to have a Sabbath service interrupted by a crying infant. It is quite another to have some madman come shrieking down the aisle. Such a demonical demonstration most certainly would grab people's attention. The best speaker in the world couldn't hold a congregation with every head snapped around in unison as the people watched, transfixed at some menacing maniac rushing toward the front of the church.

Jesus Himself couldn't continue His discourse at Capernaum during such a devilish diversion. The deep interest in Christ's charming love had tenderly held the congregation. But when this madman interrupted the service by crying out in terror, " 'What do you want with us, Jesus of Nazareth? Have you come to destroy us? I know who you are—the Holy One of God!' " [1] All eyes were riveted on this crazy wild-eyed demoniac. All Satan can offer is distraction, and it was his purpose to lead his victim to this Sabbath service to disrupt Christ's sermon. [2]

Without going through some incantations or great display of dialoging with the devil, Jesus authoritatively ordered the demon to hold his peace and come out of the man.

The congregation was stunned. Never before had they witnessed such transformation. Right before their wondering eyes they saw the captive of Satan set free, and soon he was praising God for deliverance.

The former victim had made a series of choices in his life that had led him toward total control by demons. He had thought of life as nothing more than fun and games. Hedonism was his driving goal. But finally his intemperance caught up with him, and Satan took charge. [3]

"Every man is free to choose what power he will have to rule over him. None have fallen so low, none are so vile, but that they can find deliverance in Christ." [4] In today's verse the Saviour invites us to accept that deliverance.

---

[1] Mark 1:24, N.I.V.
[2] *The Desire of Ages*, p. 255.
[3] *Ibid.*, p. 256.
[4] *Ibid.*, p. 258.

ALONE WITH GOD IN NATURE

And in the morning, rising up a great while before day, he went out, and departed into a solitary place, and there prayed. Mark 1:35.

It wasn't that Jesus had a problem with insomnia. He could use sleep just like the rest of us. But He did have His priorities straight. In the midst of His active ministry He felt that it was essential for Him to spend time alone with God in nature.

This verse comes after the record of a very exciting Sabbath and busy Saturday night. After Jesus had healed the demoniac, He left the awestruck congregation and went to Peter's house. There Jesus had healed Peter's mother-in-law. The physician Luke had diagnosed her disease as "a great fever," [1] which could well have been malaria, since Capernaum was so near the marshlands. [2]

Then as soon as the sun went down, the people began crowding the doorway. They came in droves, bringing their sick with them. They would have come earlier except for the rabbis, who frowned on any healing service on the Sabbath. It was long after bedtime when the last person left and the house finally settled down for the night. But after only a few hours of sleep Jesus slipped out of bed and headed for a quiet retreat where He could talk alone with His heavenly Father. [3]

We should all make a similar choice. Jesus would often choose either morning or evening for time alone with God. [4] We place a high premium on being go-getters and measuring success by countable achievements. We think we can participate full force in the travail of the world without suffering thus. We pace ourselves by those worldly standards which are totally out of sync with the quietness that Jesus sought in nature. In this particular case, He left at predawn because of popular public excitement that might cause Him to lose the object of His mission. He needed to be alone with God to get a proper perspective. Shouldn't we do the same, especially when our emotions are running high?

---

[1] Luke 4:38.
[2] *The SDA Bible Commentary*, vol. 5, p. 570.
[3] *The Desire of Ages*, p. 259.
[4] *Ibid.*, p. 260.

REACHING FOR DELIVERANCE

Behold a man full of leprosy: who seeing Jesus fell on his face, and besought him saying, Lord, if thou wilt, thou canst make me clean. Luke 5:12.

We can only imagine what Luke, the physician, meant by his description of a man "full of leprosy." The dread disease had undoubtedly left a hideous disfigurement. The poor victim not only knew that he was in a state of living death but that he was banished from the rest of society by an inflexible law.

Not since the days of Elisha, about eight centuries before, had anyone heard of someone's being cured of leprosy.[1] That in itself would have made his situation seem hopeless to most people.

But there was another hurdle greater than this. The Jews considered leprosy to be a curse from God. They generally believed that it was wrong to interfere with God's judgment. Would Jesus try to heal him? And even if Jesus would consent to heal him, how could he ever get close enough for such a cleansing?

Considering the extent of the obstacle course, this leper had seemingly insurmountable odds against ever receiving help. Yet on the day that he finally spotted Jesus down by the lake and healing people, his faith leaped forward.[2] He edged closer. And as he watched the sick rise in fresh vigor, the lame walk, and the blind see, that spark of faith was fanned into a flame. He decided that Jesus could heal him and rushed forward unmindful of the crowd. He didn't bother to shout the prescribed words, "Unclean! Unclean!" as he closed in on the group. His decision to reach Jesus drove him on. He didn't even notice the ugly looks people gave him or the fact that they crawled all over one another trying to get away. He just kept running until he reached Jesus.

And with compassion the Saviour reached out and touched him, and that contact brought instant healing. The very disease symbolized sin, and Jesus desired to show that when we choose to come to Him just as we are, His power to deliver is immediate. Answers to other prayers might be delayed, but never the cry for deliverance from sin.

---

[1] *The SDA Bible Commentary,* vol. 5, p. 573.
[2] *Ibid.*

THE DANGER OF PARTIAL OBEDIENCE

**And [he] saith unto him, See thou say nothing to any man.
. . . But he went out, and began to publish it much, and to blaze
abroad the matter, insomuch that Jesus could no more openly
enter into the city. Mark 1:44, 45.**

Insistence marked Jesus' voice when He instructed the healed
leper to go directly to the religious authorities before any rumors
about His miraculous cure could reach them.[1] The Saviour knew
that pride could prevent the priests from giving an honest report.
They could deny the former leper a health certificate simply on the
basis that the cure had come through Christ. Jesus also wanted to
reach these leaders that they might recognize Him as their Saviour.
The fact that the healed man obeyed the command of Jesus and
obtained a certified public pronouncement of the cure was one
reason many of the priests later turned to Jesus. Their official
recognition of an actual cure was a standing testimony for Christ.[2]

But the man only partially obeyed Jesus. He decided on his
own that any gag order simply revealed Jesus' modesty and was
not really essential. But Jesus knew all along that curing leprosy
would be big news, and once the word spread, the lepers would
come en masse to His meetings. This would give the authorities a
real opportunity to raise the hue and cry that the people might
become contaminated. Further, it would demonstrate before the
populace that Jesus was indeed, so the Jewish leaders charged,
breaking down the restrictions of the Mosaic law. Jesus also knew
that many of the lepers who might come would not rightly use their
gift of health.[3]

But the ex-leper chose to second-guess Jesus, and that very act
temporarily halted His ministry. Obedience in going directly to the
priests did not justify the man's disobedience in not remaining
silent about the miracle. Whenever we take it upon ourselves to
only partially obey Christ's commands, we invariably hinder His
work in some way.

---

[1] *The SDA Bible Commentary*, vol. 5, p. 573.
[2] *The Desire of Ages*, p. 265.
[3] *Ibid.*, p. 264.

DESPERATE ENTRANCE

When Jesus saw their faith, he said unto the sick of the palsy, Son, thy sins be forgiven thee. Mark 2:5.

Peter's place was packed. When the news spread that Jesus was back in town, the people scurried from every quarter of Capernaum to be near the Saviour. The crowd was so tightly pressed together in the house that they spilled out into the street. With no loudspeakers, every ear strained to hear the words of the Saviour.

Suddenly Jesus stopped speaking and looked up. Dust filtered down from the ceiling, and the commotion on the roof signaled a desperate entrance. Sunlight spilled into the room as the tile was torn loose. Then steadily a poor paralytic was lowered to Jesus, who watched the whole faith action with compassion. His great heart had sensed the man's need long before the paralytic had urged his four friends to take him to Jesus. The people standing outside knew that four men carrying a stretcher had tried to push their way through several times, but they had no idea that they would go to such lengths as running an elevator service for the stricken man.

But the paralytic was desperate. He knew that his wild life style had brought on his condition, and the knowledge nearly dragged him to despair.[1] He sensed that Jesus was his only hope. He decided that if there was no other way to reach the Saviour, then he would have to come in through the ceiling.

We have no record of Peter's reaction as he saw his roof being torn up. But we do catch the joy of the man when he heard those words of forgiveness. In reality he longed for the peace of forgiveness as much as for physical healing. "In simple faith he accepted the words of Jesus as the boon of new life. He urged no further request, but lay in blissful silence, too happy for words."[2]

But he didn't lie there long. When Jesus told him to take up his bed and walk, he sprang to life. Suddenly there was room to move, as the crowd parted to let him out. His desperate entrance had paid off. Whenever the same urgency drives us to come to Jesus He will respond just as He did then.

---

[1] *The Desire of Ages*, p. 267.
[2] *Ibid.*, p. 268.

ENTRENCHED IN UNBELIEF

Whether is easier, to say, Thy sins be forgiven thee; or to say, Rise up and walk? Luke 5:23.

The religious dignitaries never answered the question Jesus asked. Jesus answered it Himself by telling the paralytic to get off his mat and use his legs.[1] The Pharisees and doctors had come to Peter's house not only from the local Galilean district but from Judea and as far south as Jerusalem. Their growing hatred of Jesus spurred them to greater spying activity. And although they sat there closed-mouthed that day, they watched the whole proceedings with tiger-bright eyes.

The very man who entered the room vertically was a case they knew well. They had condemned him as a great sinner. No one could deny his profligate track record. But these so-called religious leaders had shown no sympathy toward him, nor had they offered any help. They were nothing more than sanctimonious icicles. Their chilling pronouncement that the man's malady was a judgment from God only added to his torment.

Christ's ability to read their minds was always frightfully disturbing, and as they glanced at each other their eyes told the same story. This young Galilean must be stopped at all costs! Only God can forgive sins! So they tagged Jesus with blasphemy. Their theology was correct up to a point, but they would not recognize Jesus as the Son of God.

Yet when Jesus told the man to pick up his bed and walk, those same faces that had just shown such knowing glances registered total defeat. They were overwhelmed. Yet they still refused to confess Him as the Saviour. And thereby they made a collective and drastic choice. The healing of the paralytic was proof of Christ's creative power for both body and soul, but their pride prevented them from rejoicing in that power. "The stronger the evidence that Jesus had power on earth to forgive sins, the more firmly they entrenched themselves in unbelief. From the home of Peter . . . they went away to invent new schemes for silencing the Son of God."[2]

---

[1] *The SDA Bible Commentary*, vol. 5, p. 581.
[2] *The Desire of Ages*, pp. 270, 271.

CALL TO THE TAX COLLECTOR

And as he passed by, he saw Levi the son of Alphaeus sitting at the receipt of custom, and said unto him, Follow me. And he arose and followed him. Mark 2:14.

In the days of Christ the publicans were more than collectors of internal revenue for the Roman government. They were legalized swindlers. The Romans were smart enough to auction off to Jews the privilege of collecting their taxes. The person winning the right to this IRS system was assigned a given area, and in turn he hired agents for the actual work of collecting taxes.[1] Along with regular rip-offs, these publicans often trumped up false charges of smuggling to extort hush money. A Jew who became a publican was considered a tool of the enemy and a traitor. And to use his office for fraud and extortion was considered the lowest form of vice. Thus they were seldom seen in any worship service at the Temple or in the synagogues. Their only real friends were of the same hated occupation.

But Jesus saw something special in one publican working from his seaside office. Levi-Matthew undoubtedly was collecting for Herod Antipas revenue from the caravans and travelers from the East.[2] Matthew had heard Jesus and was already under conviction from the Holy Spirit. God's Spirit had instilled in his heart a deep longing to turn his life around. Yet it seemed too hard for him to break free from the lucrative occupation that held him so tightly.[3] But when Jesus passed by that day, the grip of his occupation loosened. That the Saviour even noticed him touched his heart. When Jesus spoke those words "Follow me," it was enough.

Levi-Matthew did not hesitate. His decision was prompt. Whatever cash receipts were on hand, whatever other business seemed to be pressing—someone else could handle it from that time on.[4] Matthew resigned. Closing his books, he left his office for good. Just to be with Jesus was his greatest joy. Whenever the call of Jesus moves us as it did Matthew, then we too will become as devoted as he was.

---

[1] *SDA Bible Dictionary*, pp. 915, 916.
[2] *The SDA Bible Commentary*, vol. 5, p. 582.
[3] *The Desire of Ages*, p. 272.
[4] *Ibid.*, p. 273.

OFFENDING THE PHARISEES

But go ye and learn what that meaneth, I will have mercy, and not sacrifice: for I am not come to call the righteous, but sinners to repentance. Matt. 9:13.

Like all who have found Jesus as the center of joy, Matthew longed to show Him honor and to share Him with his friends. And since he was a man of means, he could afford the large banquet to which he invited many of his former associates and others he knew.[1] The problem, of course, was that these "others" had just as dubious reputations as did the publicans.

So Jesus had to make a decision. By calling Matthew to become a disciple He had already cut across religious, social, and national customs.[2] And by accepting an invitation to eat with these outcasts of society, He and His cause would most certainly fall into disrepute. But Jesus did not hesitate to accept the invitation. "He well knew that this would give offense to the Pharisaic party, and would also compromise Him in the eyes of the people. But no question of policy could influence His movements."[3]

Some would argue that Jesus should have refused the invitation on the basis of avoiding even the appearance of evil. But who said it was evil? Certainly the Pharisees, who disdained all those who did not fall in line with their narrow concepts of righteousness, would consider it evil. But in accepting this invitation Jesus in no way compromised with sin. He did not attend for any personal gratification. What appealed to Him were those who hungered for real righteousness.[4]

It didn't take long for the rabbis to accuse Jesus. Instead of a direct personal attack, they worked through the disciples. But Jesus didn't wait for the disciples to answer the question as to why He ate with publicans and sinners. He told those self-sufficient bigots to go do their homework and learn what Hosea 6:6 meant about showing mercy to those who needed the most help. When we understand the meaning of Scripture we too will choose to be where we can call the sinner to repentance.

---

[1] *The SDA Bible Commentary,* vol. 5, p. 583.
[2] *The Desire of Ages,* p. 273.
[3] *Ibid.,* p. 274.
[4] *Ibid.*

SABBATH CONFLICT

And he said unto them, The sabbath was made for man, and not man for the sabbath: Therefore the Son of man is Lord also of the sabbath. Mark 2:27, 28.

One Sabbath during the spring of A.D. 29 Jesus and His disciples were returning from worship. They were walking along a path that wound through a grainfield. Since the disciples were hungry, they picked a little of the grain and rubbed the hulls off in their hands. Ordinarily this would have been acceptable, but the snooping rabbis knew all about the special Sabbath codes. They had them all memorized, right down to the page and paragraph. The disciples were guilty of both harvesting and threshing! And that was a no-no. The multiplied rules had encrusted God's rest day with so many regulations that even if someone should spit on the ground, it would have been considered a form of irrigation.[1]

"Why do they do that which is not lawful on the Sabbath?" these professional nitpickers asked haughtily.

It is worth noting that Jesus never got defensive. Nor did He taunt them with the stupidity of their traditions, even though their man-made laws had reduced God's commandments to absurdity. He chose, however, to answer them with a question right from the Scriptures. His decision to meet such constricted thinking ought to teach us something about meeting narrow-mindedness.

" 'Have you never read what David did?' " Jesus asked.[2]

They prided themselves in knowing the Scriptures, but Jesus rebuked their vaunted knowledge by reminding them of the time David had actually eaten the shewbread, which only the priests were supposed to eat. If David could satisfy his hunger by eating the bread set aside for holy use, then surely it was right for His disciples to eat a little grain on the Sabbath.

Jesus never stooped to argue, but He ever kept before His friends and enemies alike the truth about God's law. He closed the discussion on the Sabbath accusation by reminding them that He is Lord of the Sabbath, "One above all question and above all law."[3]

---

[1] *The SDA Bible Commentary,* vol. 5, p. 587.
[2] Mark 2:25, R.S.V.
[3] *The Desire of Ages,* p. 285.

SULLEN SILENCE

And he saith unto them, Is it lawful to do good on the sabbath days, or to do evil? to save life, or to kill? But they held their peace. Mark 3:4.

The Pharisees chose not to answer Christ's questions. But their decision to sit there in sullen silence was an admission of defeat. They didn't dare answer Him for fear another display of their own untenable arguments would further embarrass them.

A man with a withered hand stood in front of the whole congregation. Jesus had deliberately told the man to stand up so that all could see what He would do next. But before He restored the withered hand, Jesus fired those questions in our text for today at the religious leaders. The Pharisees had been eager to know whether Jesus would heal on the Sabbath, and now they were just as eager to slip out the back exit. Jesus had met them on their own turf, and He had turned their own rule of conduct against them. It was commonly taught that any failure to do good was tantamount to doing evil.

The Scriptures record that Jesus looked on them ''with anger.'' [1] It was an anger filled with absolute hatred for the evil that prevented these would-be guides from seeing that their own hardness of heart was preventing them from accepting the truth about real Sabbath observance and the basics of God's love.

The rabbis knew that Jesus had spoken the truth. But their minds were locked into a position of thinking that it would be better to allow this poor man to suffer than to break their own tradition. [2] They would lift an ox out of the ditch on Sabbath, but they would not consider helping a fellow human being. Worse still, they were right then plotting to kill Jesus. Was this more righteous than healing on the Sabbath?

Without further hesitation Jesus healed the man's hand, and in so doing He shattered the traditions of the Jews but firmly let the Sabbath commandment stand.

---

[1] Mark 3:5.
[2] *The Desire of Ages,* p. 286.

SELECTION FOR TRANSFORMATION

And when it was day, he called unto him his disciples: and of them he chose twelve, whom also he named apostles. Luke 6:13.

After spending a night in prayer Jesus came down from the mountain and called His disciples to a private ordination service. His choice of disciples covered a broad spectrum of personalities.

There was the flabby-faithed Philip, who received the first call to follow Jesus.[1] Then came the Galilean fishermen—Andrew and his impetuous, impulsive, but generous brother Peter; and the hot-tempered Zebedee boys, James and John. The childlike, trusting Nathanael was added, along with the ex-tax collector Levi-Matthew and the timid, doubting Thomas.

Somewhere along the line Jesus picked up Simon the Zealot, who apparently had only one string on his guitar—he hated Romans.[2] A couple of others—James the son of Alphaeus, and Thaddeus—filtered quietly into the background.[3] And then came Judas Iscariot. Jesus never really called him. He just imposed himself on the group, in hopes of becoming a part of the inner circle.[4] As far as the rest of the disciples were concerned, Judas was the most likely to succeed. He had so much going for him as far as culture and education were concerned! "They were surprised that Jesus received him so coolly."[5] But there they stood that morning, ready for His laying on of hands in ordination as apostles or ambassadors for the new little church He was forming.

Jesus did not choose unfallen angels, but these imperfect men with a list of negative qualities that would not make a very attractive portfolio. Why did He select such unlikely personalities with all their glaring faults? Jesus knew that as they connected themselves with Him, something profound could happen. If they would allow Him the touch of His power, He could transform them into His own image. He would take all those negative traits and channel them into energy devoted to His service. He would utilize the positive traits by honing them into even greater good.

---

[1] *The Desire of Ages*, p. 292.
[2] *Ibid.*, p. 296.
[3] *The SDA Bible Commentary*, vol. 5, p. 593.
[4] *The Desire of Ages*, pp. 293, 294.
[5] *Ibid.*, p. 294.

WIDE AUDIENCE, CAREFUL PRESENTATION

And seeing the multitudes, he went up into a mountain: and when he was set, his disciples came unto him: and he opened his mouth, and taught them. Matt. 5:1, 2.

Hidden in these verses is a double choice. The first is the Saviour's wider audience appeal. Rarely did He gather His disciples alone for private tutoring. "He did not choose for His audience those only who knew the way of life. It was His work to reach the multitudes who were in ignorance and errors." [1]

This is the setting for the famous Sermon on the Mount. Since the narrow beach afforded little standing room, Jesus headed up the mountain flank to a wide grassy area. [2] With His disciples pressed tightly around Him and the crowds spread out all over the grass before Him, He began His talk on the kingdom of God. His disciples knew they were supposed to be near Jesus because He would sometimes send them out to carry the same message, and they did not want to miss a word.

But Jesus had a problem in the presentation of His sermon. Everyone, including the disciples, expected the promised kingdom to be nothing more than a dominant Jewish state in which the hated Romans would be subjugated. The low-income folk saw the kingdom as a means by which they could finally make ends meet. The wealthy saw the same kingdom as an avenue by which they could gain substantial power far beyond anything they presently knew. Rich and poor alike held such high expectations and were so eager to learn about the new kingdom that Jesus could easily catch their attention. But He knew that He would have to dash their hopes of all worldly greatness.

Instead of lashing out against popular misconceptions, Jesus simply chose to show the conditions for entrance into His kingdom. Then He let the people draw their own conclusions. [3] His choices of an audience and methodology are still valid today.

---

[1] *The Desire of Ages*, p. 298.
[2] *Ibid.*
[3] *Ibid.*, p. 299.

WHEN JESUS MARVELED

When Jesus heard it, he marvelled, and said to them that followed, Verily I say unto you, I have not found so great faith, no, not in Israel. Matt. 8:10.

The Bible never tells his name, but the Roman centurion in command of an army post in Capernaum was truly a quality person. In an age when slaves were bought and sold like so much cattle, this officer had developed a tender, sympathetic bond with his servant. When he learned that the Saviour had arrived back in town, he felt totally unworthy to enter Jesus' presence. But if the Master would only speak the word, then he just knew his critically ill servant would be healed.

The centurion was a rare find. Despite Jewish bigotry and prejudice, and despite their ritualistic formalism, he had seen something in the Jews' religion that was far superior to any of the heathen religions.[1] There was a constancy to the God of the Hebrews that appealed to him, and he sincerely wanted to know this God better.[2] And that is why he chose to respond to Jesus. He had never met Jesus, but he certainly had heard of Him.

Since Jesus had made Capernaum His headquarters during His Galilean ministry, it was impossible to keep the stories of His healing and words away from even the Roman soldiers.[3] The centurion sent a delegation of Jewish elders first, and later some friends, to tell Jesus just to speak the word for healing.

But Jesus came anyway. A year before, a nobleman who had come to Jesus and who had requested healing for his son had felt that he needed some sign that Jesus could actually perform the miracle. But this Roman officer needed none.[4] He had made his decision. He knew about a chain of command. He knew how to receive and obey orders, and how to give them. All the Son of God had to do was to speak the word and his dying servant would be healed.

Jesus marveled. He had not seen faith like this. The centurion's choice to believe had leaped the barriers of heathen background and education. It brought Jesus the greatest joy.

---

[1] *The Desire of Ages*, p. 315.
[2] *The SDA Bible Commentary*, vol. 5, p. 62.
[3] *Ibid.*, p. 752.
[4] *Ibid.*, p. 755.

HOW THE ELDERS MISSED THE GOSPEL

Not by works of righteousness which we have done, but according to his mercy he saved us. Titus 3:5.

When the Jewish elders met Jesus with the centurion's request to heal his servant, they recommended the Roman officer to Christ on the basis that he loved the Jewish nation and had built them a synagogue. "He is worthy that you should do this," they said.

The centurion was obviously pro-Hebrew. He desired to know the true God, and out of his own expense account had built a synagogue in Capernaum.[1] But the Jewish elders' recommendation revealed a glaring fault in their decision to turn to Jesus for help. "They did not recognize that our great need is our only claim on God's mercy. In their self-righteousness they commended the centurion because of the favor he had shown to 'our nation.' "[2] This basic flaw demonstrated that their choice in seeking Jesus was far from the spirit of the gospel.

The centurion had said, "I am not worthy."[3] He realized that there was nothing good in himself that could recommend him to Jesus. The argument for his request was solely his great need. He saw more in Jesus than just some miracle worker. From what he had gathered, Jesus was truly the Saviour of the world and ready to help all, both Jew and Gentile.[4] The elders had missed the point, and in missing this they could never grasp the reasons for Christ's actions.

Our text today reveals how we may come to Jesus. No list of good deeds can recommend any of us. But we do have a strong plea that our utter helplessness gives God the opportunity to save.

How often the attitude of the Jewish elders still prevails! Whenever someone not of the faith shows favor, especially financially, to the church, it seems to bring out all the latent good-works concepts in so-called soul-winning efforts for them, which misses the meaning of the gospel.

---

[1] *The SDA Bible Commentary*, vol. 5, p. 754.
[2] *The Desire of Ages*, p. 317.
[3] Luke 7:6.
[4] *Ibid*.

THE MOST DANGEROUS DECISION

Wherefore I say unto you, All manner of sin and blasphemy shall be forgiven unto men: but the blasphemy against the Holy Ghost shall not be forgiven unto men. Matt. 12:31.

Jesus uttered this warning not only for the benefit of the stubborn Pharisees but for anyone—clear to the end of time—who might steel himself against the promptings of the Holy Spirit.

Jesus had just healed a poor wretch who was not only a demoniac but blind and dumb, as well. The healing touch of Jesus had turned this sufferer into a sane, seeing, articulate believer. Yet this fantastic miracle only further exasperated the Pharisees. They so disdained Jesus that they wouldn't even take His name on their lips.[1]

"This fellow," they hissed, "casts out devils by Beelzebub, the prince of devils."

Not one of those haughty men really believed their own charge. It was prodded solely by pride.[2] They were feeling the tug of the Holy Spirit to turn to Jesus and publicly acknowledge Him to be the Messiah, yet this would have been too humiliating. So they stubbornly braced themselves against the compelling force of God's Spirit and attributed the work of Jesus to that of Satan. It was a most dangerous decision!

Jesus reduced their argument to complete absurdity. " 'Any kingdom divided against itself is bound to collapse, and no town or household divided against itself can last for long. If it is Satan who is expelling Satan, then he is divided against himself—so how do you suppose that his kingdom can continue?' "[3]

Then Jesus warned them that to resist even one ray of light can lead to resisting another, until finally spiritual blindness sets in and the work of the Holy Spirit is attributed to the devil. Then there is nothing more that God can do. Tragically, the person has finally run out of choices and is left in darkness.

[1] *The SDA Bible Commentary,* vol. 5, p. 394.
[2] *The Desire of Ages,* p. 322.
[3] Matt. 12:25, 26, Philips.

BELONGING TO THE FAMILY OF GOD

For whosoever shall do the will of my Father which is in heaven, the same is my brother, and sister, and mother. Matt. 12:50.

The sons of Joseph by a former marriage claimed Jesus as their younger brother, but they were constantly embarrassed by Him.[1] That He should even claim to be the Son of God was crazy, as far as they were concerned. And for Him to reprove the rabbis exceeded their comprehension. When they heard how He spent whole nights in prayer and the next day allowed throngs of people around Him, taking no time for food or rest, they felt sure He had slipped a cog. They were totally out of harmony with His mission and could not comprehend even a little of His inner torture and trials.[2]

Often they tried to influence Mary to do something to stop Him. If He rejected their counsel, maybe He would listen to her.[3] They knew she believed in Him, but they personally chose not to accept Him. For them it seemed the wisest decision. After all, they wanted the rabbis to accept them.

These older brothers would trot out the tradition-bound Pharisee party line that time had worn smooth, and they would do their best to teach Jesus what they considered to be right and wrong.[4] "They freely condemned that which they could not understand. Their reproaches probed Him to the quick, and His soul was wearied and distressed. They avowed faith in God, and thought they were vindicating God, when God was with them in the flesh, and they knew Him not."[5]

Right after Jesus had warned the Pharisees about committing the unpardonable sin, Jesus' brothers stood outside the gathering and wanted to see Him. When He heard that they were there, along with His dear mother, He stretched His hands toward His disciples and uttered the words of today's verse. He made it plain that the family of God means far more than any blood relationship. It has to do with choosing to accept the will of God as a part of one's personal life.

[1] *The SDA Bible Commentary*, vol. 5, p. 400.
[2] *The Desire of Ages*, p. 326.
[3] *Ibid.*, p. 321.
[4] *Ibid.*, p. 326.
[5] *Ibid.*

PANIC INSTEAD OF PEACE

And his disciples came to him and awoke him, saying, Lord, save us: we perish. And he saith unto them, Why are ye fearful, O ye of little faith? Then he arose, and rebuked the winds and the sea; and there was a great calm. Matt. 8:25, 26.

It was nearly dusk when Jesus told His disciples to cast off and head for the opposite shore.[1] All day He had ministered to the needs of the people, and at that moment He felt extremely worn out from His constant labor. He had finally reached the saturation point. The incessant daily harrassment of the Pharisees and the demands of the people had drained Him, and He needed rest. Utterly exhausted, He took the coarse leather steerman's pillow, curled up in the stern, and went to sleep.[2]

The evening was calm at first, but suddenly a wind roared out of the mountain gorges and whipped the lake into a froth. Several of the disciples were expert seamen, having spent their lives on the lake. But they hadn't seen a storm like this one for a long time. In fact, all their combined expertise could do nothing to keep the little craft from swamping in the wild storm.[3] Most of the disciples had no fishing background, and we can imagine that they must have sat there white-knuckled, feeling totally helpless. Matthew may have wished for the stability of his old tax booth right then. The boat, tossed like a cork, would plunge into a trough, and the sea would rush in with a vengeance. Bailing produced no appreciable good. It was a desperate moment. They were sinking.

The disciples, like many of us when facing the storms of life, forgot that Jesus was on board. It was an unconscious decision, but in their panic they lost their peace and began doing everything they humanly could.

Jesus was calmly resting in the care of His heavenly Father. When they shouted to Him that they were going down, He awakened and quieted the storm. Yet, had they chosen to trust in Him earlier, they could have had the same peace that He possessed.

---

[1] *The SDA Bible Commentary*, vol. 5, p. 367.
[2] *Ibid.*, p. 601.
[3] *The Desire of Ages*, p. 334.

AFRAID OF SANITY

Then they went out to see what was done; and came to Jesus, and found the man, out of whom the devils were departed, sitting at the feet of Jesus, clothed, and in his right mind: and they were afraid. Luke 8:35.

Actually there were two demoniacs.[1] Matthew, an eyewitness to the terror that morning after the storm, records a double threat as both madmen rushed toward Jesus and the disciples. While Jesus held His ground, the disciples churned back to the boat. The sight of those bloodied demoniacs with their wild eyes and long disheveled hair convinced them that the best place was back in the boat and rowing toward the opposite shore.

One of the demoniacs identified himself to Jesus as Legion, because there were so many demons in him. He was the fiercer of the two and spoke through lips entirely controlled by the demons within. The quick exchange of words between Jesus and the demoniacs indicated that the demons were willing to depart only if they could go into a nearby herd of swine. It was the enemy's purpose to distract from Jesus. Devils don't drown. And pigs, like most animals, are good swimmers. But the devils knew how to hold the squealing porkers underwater long enough. The sight of two thousand pigs plunging madly down the steep bank into the water sent the swineherds rushing back to town with the alarming news.

When the local folk hurried back to the beach, the two former wild men, dressed in clothing borrowed from the disciples, were sitting at the feet of Jesus and listening intently.[2] Their eyes no longer glared with the insanity of demon possession, but were clear and bright with the eagerness to learn from Jesus.

But the local folk were not properly impressed. What crowded their attention was the cash loss. They would rather have had the pigs back, even if it would have included the screaming madmen. If such a supernatural display produced so much loss, they decided that this stranger must leave. How often a similar choice to reject Jesus is made because of some superstitious fear of possible financial ruin.

---

[1] Matt. 8:28; *The SDA Bible Commentary,* vol. 5, p. 603.
[2] *Ibid.,* p. 605.

FROM MANIACS TO MISSIONARIES

Go home to thy friends, and tell them how great things the Lord hath done for thee, and hath had compassion on thee. Mark 5:19.

If there was one thing the former demoniacs desired more than anything else, it was to remain with Jesus. They begged to be allowed to stay with Him so they could hear His words, but Jesus shook His head. No, they must return home and tell their friends and relatives the good news about the compassionate God who had freed them from the demons. In this way they would find the security and peace they craved.

Ordinarily Jesus requested folk to keep quiet about His miracles. The Jewish authorities could easily clamp down on His ministry if they found the slightest trace of anything that might lead to a popular uprising.[1] But He was in Gentile territory now. These men needed to enjoy relating their exciting experience.

It would seem easy for some to rationalize away such a request from Jesus. These men hadn't heard one sermon. Jesus never even gave them any key texts for substantial Bible study. Neither was there any local seminary where they could secure some educational credits to qualify them for the mission of sharing their faith. So they could have backed off, clinging tenaciously to their miraculous freedom and talking only between themselves. But they chose to do exactly as Jesus told them. They could recount their experience from maniacs to missionaries.

"If we have been following Jesus step by step, we shall have something right to the point to tell concerning the way in which He has led us. . . . This is the witness for which our Lord calls, and for want of which the world is perishing."[2]

When Jesus returned to Decapolis about ten months later, in the spring or summer of A.D. 30, thousands flocked to hear Him because of the witness of these two ex-madmen. No longer were the people afraid. The memory of the big pig plunge had been marvelously displaced.

[1] *The SDA Bible Commentary,* vol. 5, p. 606.
[2] *The Desire of Ages,* p. 340.

BELIEVING IN SPITE OF DEATH

Thy daughter is dead: why troublest thou the Master any further? As soon as Jesus heard the word that was spoken, he saith unto the ruler of the synagogue, Be not afraid, only believe. Mark 5:35, 36.

Although he belonged to a class who despised and hated Jesus, Jairus, ruler of the local Capernaum synagogue, swallowed his pride and pressed his way into the presence of the Master. It didn't matter that he had to go down the street to Levi-Matthew's house, where Jesus had gone for a publican banquet in His honor. The point was that his little 12-year-old daughter lay deathly ill. Falling humbly at Jesus' feet, he pleaded with Him to come immediately. " 'My little girl is dying,' " he explained.[1]

Jairus had heard the consistent reports of people being healed all over town. Capernaum buzzed with the glad news of Jesus' power to restore people to health. And Jairus just knew that if Jesus would only come and touch his girl, she would be perfectly whole again. But there wasn't much time.

Jesus could not turn down a faith like this, and immediately He headed toward the elder's nearby home.[2] But Jesus was locked into the pressing crowd that wished to be relieved of some suffering, and He paused often along the way. The anxious father could only wring his hands and inch along at the agonizingly slow pace.

Then a messenger, elbowing his way through the mass of humanity, reached the ruler and privately gave him the word that it was all over. There was no point in bothering the Master any further. The professionally hired mourners were already doing their mechanical, unfeeling thing.

Jairus suddenly found himself thrust into a precise moment of decision: Either he would sink into the despair of unbelief or he would press closer to the Saviour. Since he chose the latter, we have the glad record of his little girl's being raised to life.[3]

---

[1] Mark 5:23, Phillips.
[2] *The Desire of Ages*, p. 342.
[3] *Ibid.*, p. 343.

WITH ONLY A TOUCH

When she had heard of Jesus, . . . she said, If I may touch but his clothes, I shall be whole. Mark 5:27, 28.

Weakened by twelve long years of hemorrhaging, her savings exhausted on physicians who had accomplished nothing, this woman of Capernaum focused her thoughts on her only hope. She decided that at all costs she must find Jesus, and if it was possible to touch only His garment, she knew she would be healed. But how could she act on her decision? When she tried to reach Him down by the lake, the crowds prevented her from getting close enough.[1] When He moved to Levi-Matthew's house for a banquet, she couldn't get near the door.

Then suddenly Jairus appeared, and as Jesus slowly made His way down the street to the ruler's house she realized that her moment had come. The jostling crowd jerked her back and forth, but in desperation she reached out and barely touched the hem of His garment. "In that one touch was concentrated the faith of her life, and instantly her pain and feebleness gave place to the vigor of perfect health.[2]

Jesus stopped, and the flow of the foot traffic surged around Him. "Who touched Me?" He asked.

In such a setting the question seemed oddly incongruous.

"Master," Peter blurted out, "the crowd is pressing all around You, and You ask who touched You?"

"Somebody touched Me, for I sense that power went out of Me."

The woman realized that she could not stay hidden any longer. Trembling, she came forward and fell at Jesus' feet. Then it all tumbled out. As tears of gratitude ran down her cheeks she told the story of how she had suffered for a dozen years from this terrible malady. She could not endure the awful sense of being considered unclean. And now she was healed!

Whenever we choose to concentrate every ounce of our energy in reaching Jesus, we too will find Him willing to make us whole.

---

[1] *The Desire of Ages,* p. 343.
[2] *Ibid.*

THE NEEDED BREAK

And he said unto them, Come ye yourselves apart into a desert place, and rest a while. Mark 6:31.

Jesus never unduly hurried. Yet His movements were calculated to accomplish as much as possible while on this earth. His life was regulated by His heavenly Father, who operates in the lofty circle of no haste and no delay. Thus Jesus never knew any frenzy.

The words of our text come to us right after the disciples had returned from their first missionary tour. Naturally, they had all sorts of success stories to relate, as well as some tales of bungling and errors.[1] But most of all they were just plain exhausted. Working with people is tiring. And the last half of today's verse says that "they had no leisure so much as to eat." They had become so busy that there wasn't even time for a lunch break!

Jesus' choice to get away and rest should say something to us today. We have the habit of overscheduling. And still there are those who, like the rabbis of Jesus' time, make a savior out of religious activity. Placing a high premium on bustling and a good performance record still lures us, but it produces problems. "As activity increases and men become successful in doing any work for God, there is danger of trusting to human plans and methods. There is a tendency to pray less, and to have less faith."[2] Once we begin to pride ourselves as pacesetters and go-getters, we lose sight of God. We forget that it is the power of the Holy Spirit that does the work.

And the choice to rest awhile does not mean some hyped-up, fast-paced vacation. Notice that Jesus said to "come . . . apart into a desert place." There is great therapy in nature. By choosing to take time to be alone with God, we give Him the opportunity of helping us sort things out. The meditation and prayers in such a setting invariably strengthen us for even greater work. It is never time lost.

---

[1] *The Desire of Ages*, p. 359.
[2] *Ibid.*, p. 362.

PHILIP'S FAILURE MAY BE OURS

When Jesus then lifted up his eyes, and saw a great company come unto him, he saith unto Philip, Whence shall we buy bread, that these may eat? And this he said to prove him. John 6:5, 6.

Philip was never very quick to seize faith and run with it. His slowhearted response to Jesus' ministry plagued him. In spite of all the miracles he had seen, he retained that awkward element of not catching the impact of what Jesus really could do.[1] And that day when more than five thousand men, besides women and children, followed Jesus into the countryside outside Bethsaida, he was staggered at the thought of throwing a picnic for that crowd.

Jesus stretched Philip's imagination and put him to a test. Just where would he buy bread for all the multitude? Immediately Philip made a decision. We seldom think of it that way, but he did. He chose to see only the impossibility of paying for such a spread. Bethsaida was his hometown, and he knew enough about food prices there to realize that with the sea of heads before him it would take just about two hundred average days' wages to feed the crowd.[2]

Jesus singled out Philip to prove him, but all the disciples were bent on sending the crowd home before it got too late. Philip, however, exemplified the type of choice that cannot see the possibilities with Jesus in command.

Philip's friend Andrew found a lad with a small lunch of five barley loaves and two small pickled or dried fish for relish.[3] This only confirmed Philip's belief that there was no way around the problem. Andrew couldn't see it either. There wasn't even enough for a few nibbles, so they had best dismiss the crowd and go get some food for themselves.

How often Jesus brings us some test of trust that will afford Him the opportunity of satisfying both our spiritual and our physical needs! And like Philip we fail the test because we forget the magnitude of His miracle-working power. We choose to think only of impossibilities.

[1] *The SDA Bible Commentary,* vol. 5, p. 960.
[2] *Ibid.,* p. 617.
[3] *Ibid.,* p. 961.

RELUCTANT OBEDIENCE

And straightway Jesus constrained his disciples to get into a ship, and to go before him unto the other side, while he sent the multitudes away. Matt. 14:22.

At first glance there doesn't seem to be any decision-making in this verse except on the part of Jesus. Yet the background of this passage unfolds a dramatic turn of events that placed the disciples squarely in confrontation with their Master.

When the grand picnic was over and all those thousands realized that Jesus had fed them solely with five small barley loaves and a couple of dried fish, the whole picture snapped into focus. Jesus was the long-looked-for Messiah! That conviction had been growing all day for both the disciples and the crowd, but the afternoon dinner miracle did the trick.[1] Now they knew He must be crowned king. He could heal soldiers wounded in battle, feed the armies, and smash the Romans or anyone else in Israel's path. But Jesus saw what was happening and commanded His disciples to get into the boat. Then He ordered the crowd to disperse.

This was the first time Jesus found it necessary to speak to His disciples with such force and authority.[2] They griped and complained about the dismissal, but it was useless.[3] His firmness held, and silently they turned and headed for the boat. But they only reluctantly obeyed. Like sullen children the disciples stood around the beach and pouted. If only they had followed through with the idea of crowning Him king! Caught up in the popular movement, they saw themselves cut off from the chance to present Jesus as king of Israel at the upcoming Passover.

In this muttering, mumbling mood they finally set out across the lake. That was when the Lord sent a storm to preoccupy their minds. "God often does this when men create burdens and troubles for themselves." [4] Whenever we choose to be obstreperous while going through the motions of obeying, we can expect God to allow a chain of circumstances to arise so that we may see how childishly foolish we have been.

---

[1] *The Desire of Ages*, p. 377.
[2] *The SDA Bible Commentary*, vol. 5, p. 415.
[3] *The Desire of Ages*, p. 378.
[4] *Ibid.*, p. 380.

A SOAKING LESSON IN
SELF-CONFIDENCE

**But when he saw the wind boisterous, he was afraid; and
beginning to sink, he cried, saying, Lord, save me. Matt.
14:30.**

If the disciples had obeyed Jesus they probably would have
reached Capernaum before the storm struck. But they delayed their
lake crossing until nearly dark[1] and were caught by a strong head
wind that blew them off course to the south. After eight hours of
hard rowing they had covered only three miles when Jesus
overtook them.[2] He had been watching them all along. At the
precise moment when they were subdued and humbled by the
violence of nature and prayed for help, He came to their rescue.[3]

But when they saw Him they were sure He was a ghost. We
need not wonder at their fright. After all, how often do you see
someone strolling on a storm-tossed lake at night?

Peter was delirious with excitement when he realized that it
was Jesus. He asked permission to come to Him right then. And at
one word from Jesus, Peter climbed over the side of the boat and
headed straight for his Master. In the excitement he forgot all about
the whitecaps and the wind in his face.

Then he forgot Jesus. His newfound skill in walking on water
intrigued him, and he turned around to see whether the rest of the
crew were watching. It was a split-second choice that nearly cost
him his life. The question "How am I doing?" was torn from his
lips. When he turned back, Jesus wasn't where he had last seen
Him. But something else was there. In that deep trough he saw
only waves surrounding him. Peter was a good swimmer, but this
was not swimming weather. In desperation he cried, "Lord, save
me"!

Jesus immediately reached out and took Peter by the hand, and
the two walked back to the boat. Peter was soaked, silent and
humbled by the experience. The choice of taking our eyes off Jesus
in self-confidence, if only for a moment, is always highly
dangerous.

---

[1] *The Desire of Ages*, pp. 379, 380.
[2] *The SDA Bible Commentary*, vol. 5, pp. 415, 416.
[3] *The Desire of Ages*, p. 381.

TMTD-10

THE DECISION ABOUT JESUS

From that time many of his disciples went back, and walked no more with him. John 6:66.

When Jesus returned to shore after the night's experience on the lake, He reached the critical period of His ministry. There in the synagogue in Capernaum He knew the crisis had come, and He did nothing to avert it. The people must not be deceived regarding His kingdom.[1] They must understand that He spoke of spiritual matters, and those caught up in the earthly-kingdom notion of pride and aggrandizement must have their dreams shattered.

Up to that point Jesus had many followers. But, as He pointed out, they sought Him only for the loaves and fishes. When He told them that He was the bread from heaven, it pushed their minds forward along a path that they did not wish to take. To these followers it was a great mystery why He could not proclaim Himself king when He could work so many miracles.[2] They could not fathom His purpose or understand His mission. But Jesus wanted to press the issue even further and separate those who were captivated only by selfish ambition.

" 'I tell you the truth, unless you eat the flesh of the Son of Man and drink his blood, you have no life in you.' " [3]

" 'This is a hard teaching. Who can accept it?' " they replied.[4]

It was not really so difficult. They had all sorts of similar symbolisms. But when unbelief takes hold, it always seeks for some excuse and will invariably find reasons for rejection no matter how positive the proof. For these followers it was enough. Jesus was not offering them anything that would satisfy their own carnal pride and passions, so they got hung up on literalism.

"They had made their choice—had taken the form without the spirit, the husk without the kernel. Their decision was never afterward reversed; for they walked no more with Jesus." [5]

How often people make similar decisions! When they find that Jesus does not offer their kind of self-centered life style, they immediately reject Him.

[1] *The Desire of Ages*, p. 383.
[2] *Ibid.*, p. 385.
[3] John 6:53, N.I.V.
[4] Verse 60, N.I.V.
[5] *Ibid.*, p. 392.

THE DECISION TO REMAIN WITH JESUS

Then said Jesus unto the twelve, Will ye also go away? Then Simon Peter answered him, Lord, to whom shall we go? thou hast the words of eternal life. John 6:67, 68.

There is no grief quite so poignant as rejection. As Jesus saw the bulk of His followers turn from Him with disdain, His sorrow was inexpressible.

But added to their rejection of Him was the fact that now they would join the ranks of His worst enemies. These ex-disciples would twist His words to suit their own distortions, lie about His teachings, and place a false coloring to His motives.[1] They would gather every tidbit of information against Him that they could, and armed with this, they would stir up all sorts of evil reports. The popularity Jesus had enjoyed in Galilee vanished, as these same people now hated Him.

Jesus didn't try to stop these disciples from leaving. He didn't beg them to reconsider. They wanted to hear praise and flattery, but all He could give them was the truth. And this they didn't want to hear.

With pathos in His voice Jesus wanted to know whether the twelve also wished to leave. The original Greek is very touching: "You do not wish to go away also, do you?"[2] It was not for His information that He asked this, but to bring out an affirmation of faith from His disciples.

Peter's answer in behalf of the whole group was a declaration of a decision to remain with Jesus. Certainly they didn't want to go back and be a part of the constant squabbling between Pharisees and Sadducees.[3] Why become embroiled in the old conservative-liberal arguments? And who among them ever wanted to get involved in the minutia of religious ceremonialism again? They had found far too much joy and peace in being with Jesus. They made their choice. They would stay with Him because, as Peter added, "we believe and are sure that thou art that Christ, the Son of the living God."[4] May this be our personal decision, too!

---

[1] *The Desire of Ages*, p. 392.
[2] *The SDA Bible Commentary*, vol. 5, p. 973.
[3] *The Desire of Ages*, p. 393.
[4] John 6:69.

TURNING POINT FOR JUDAS

Jesus answered them, Have not I chosen you twelve, and one of you is a devil? He spake of Judas Iscariot the son of Simon. John 6:70, 71.

Peter, acting as spokesman for the disciples, had just firmly declared his faith in Jesus. But Judas did not share this consecration, and Jesus knew it. At first glance today's text seems only to point to Jesus' choice in selecting His disciples. But there is more to these verses. They speak of one within the ranks of that little group who had reached a turning point in his life.[1] Satan had a direct pipeline to the sharpest and most talented of all the disciples.

Jesus' sermon in the Capernaum synagogue on the bread from heaven stopped Judas short. While the rulers were caught up in the literalism of eating Christ's flesh and drinking His blood, Judas perceived its significance. He saw clearly that Jesus was talking about a spiritual kingdom. And that jolted him. There was no way he or any of the disciples could achieve any status in that kind of kingdom. There would never be any of the grandeur and power of political position. Nothing was going to happen as he had hoped it would. So Judas made a choice. "He determined not to unite himself so closely to Christ but that he could draw away. He would watch. And he did watch." [2]

From the moment he decided that he didn't want any part of this spiritual kingdom, Judas began his in-house confusion tactics. He was generally the one who excited most of the arguments on who would be the greatest. By taking Christ's words and mixing them with key texts out of context, he continually confused the rest of the disciples. He kept up his theological maneuvering under a guise of real religion, but he had set out to mold the minds of the disciples into thinking of a worldly kingdom as he had envisioned. His decision to back away from the spiritual opened the door for the devil to infuse those dark thoughts that would consume him in the final betrayal of Jesus.

[1] *The Desire of Ages,* p. 719.
[2] *Ibid.*

WHY JESUS CHOSE A CRISIS

No man can come unto me, except it were given unto him of my Father. John 6:65.

When Jesus preached that jarring sermon on the bread of life, He essentially ended church growth in Galilee. His followers left in droves. Some might suggest that it would have been better to show some discretion in the choice of subject matter rather than to lose all those folk. Jesus should have included an interesting parable or two so the congregation could later think about what He had said. But Jesus deliberately chose to trigger a crisis by using the graphic expressions of eating His flesh and drinking His blood. What lay behind His decision to speak so bluntly?

Through this crisis in Galilee He wanted to separate the true from the false believer. He saw Calvary down the road, and with it the severe test for His beloved disciples. If the false followers still professed to believe at that time, He knew they could not endure the pressure of their peers and would join those shouting, "Crucify Him!" He wanted to separate them now while He was still with His true disciples.[1] Jesus knew that their dark hour would be hard enough without the added burden of the undermining effect of seeing these professed believers turn against Him.

Popularity is ever the driving force behind the self-centered. Jesus knew that this type would crumble under the anti-Jesus hysteria, and thus He allowed this crisis to develop. He still makes decisions like this for His church today. He deliberately allows a lesser crisis to develop in order that separation can take place in advance of an even greater crisis which would be most discouraging if the false professors were still attached to the main body of believers.

If Jesus chose to show that much compassion in helping His disciples meet their trial, then we can rest assured His love has not lessened today. Jesus still tenderly regards all those who truly are His disciples, and He strengthens them for the days ahead when every earthly support will be cut off.

---

[1] *The Desire of Ages*, p. 394.

MAJORING IN MINUTIA

Well hath Esaias prophesied of you hypocrites, as it is written, This people honoureth me with their lips, but their heart is far from me. Mark 7:6.

The religious leaders had a trap ready for Jesus when He showed up at the third Passover of His ministry.[1] But this time He stayed away. Knowing their purpose, Jesus remained in Galilee to minister to the needs of the people.[2] Since Jesus didn't go south to Jerusalem, a delegation from the faultfinding committee went north seeking Him. The official snoopers just had to find some accusation to bring against Jesus. It didn't take long for them to find it.

" 'Why is it that your disciples do not follow the teaching handed down by our ancestors, but instead eat with ritually unclean hands?' " [3]

These sticklers for tradition did not complain about any lack of sanitary measures. What they were concerned about were the prescribed washings required for ceremonial purposes. In their minds it was absolutely unthinkable to eat without going through the rite of pouring a small amount of water upon the fingers and palm and tilting the hand just so, with the water running down to the wrist but no farther, then repeating the performance on the other hand.[4] The minimum amount of water to be used was exactly that which one and one-half egg shells could hold. Such a ritual seemed so neat! It fit perfectly into their type of ecclesiastical thinking.

Jesus didn't even bother to answer their charge, but quickly unmasked their life styles by pointing out how they bypassed the law of God with their traditions. He showed them how they had chosen to remain locked into the habit of majoring in minutia.

This same dangerous decision still exists. "Whenever the message of truth comes home to souls with special power, Satan stirs up his agents to start a dispute over some minor question. Thus he seeks to attract attention from the real issue." [5]

---

[1] *The Desire of Ages*, p. 395; *The SDA Bible Commentary*, vol. 5, p. 198.
[2] *The SDA Bible Commentary*, vol. 5, pp. 621, 622.
[3] Mark 7:5, T.E.V.
[4] *Ibid.*, p. 622.
[5] *The Desire of Ages*, p. 396.

COMMENDATION FOR
PERSISTENT FAITH

Then Jesus answered and said unto her, O woman, great is thy faith: be it unto thee even as thou wilt. And her daughter was made whole from that very hour. Matt. 15:28.

She had come from the obscurity of the heathen coastal region. After having heard the reports of this remarkable Jewish Teacher, this unnamed Canaanite woman decided it was worth the effort to leap all barriers of pride and prejudice. But when she met Him there, these obstacles loomed very high.

The disciples were still very much into the mind warp of Jewish bigotry. The fact that they had come north to the borders of Phoenicia to get away for a while didn't help matters. For them she was just an annoyance. She kept begging Jesus to heal her demoniac daughter. It was embarrassing to have this stranger following them, and to top it off she was a woman! At this point the disciples had no time for strange alien women.

Even Jesus seemed aloof. What the disciples didn't realize was that He wished to show them just how cold and heartless the Jews really were. He had come all the way north to place Himself in the path of this woman so that not only could she receive help but also that the disciples could learn a lesson.[1]

Despite the disciples' urging Jesus to send her away and despite His own apparent lack of interest, she persisted. Even after Jesus explained that He was come only to the lost sheep of the house of Israel, she continued to plead with Him. Throwing herself at His feet, she cried, "Lord, help me!"

"It just is not right to take the children's bread and throw it to the dogs," explained Jesus.

"That's the truth, Lord, yet even the dogs eat the crumbs from their masters' tables," she countered.

It was enough. She had passed the highest test of persistent faith, and she had proved that nothing but our own choice can prevent us from receiving the promised blessings of the gospel.[2]

---

[1] *The Desire of Ages*, p. 400.
[2] *Ibid.*, p. 403.

MIRACLES IN GENTILE COUNTRY

Then Jesus called his disciples unto him, and said, I have compassion on the multitude, because they continue with me now three days, and have nothing to eat: and I will not send them away fasting, lest they faint in the way. Matt. 15:32.

Who was this multitude who stayed with Jesus on a three-day camp-out? They were none other than the heathen folk from the region of Decapolis. About nine or ten months before, in the late autumn of A.D. 29, these same people had insisted that Jesus leave.[1]

Losing two thousand pigs over the steep bank had settled the matter then. They wanted Jesus out of their country. But now they flocked to Him. They brought their sick and crippled and they stayed with Him until He had healed every one of them. They crowded around Him by day and slept in the open at night in this mini-camp meeting setting.[2] What had made the difference? Why had they chosen to see Him now, when their decision in the fall had seemed so final?

The secret lies in the two former demoniacs, who had done their work well. They told what Jesus had done for them, and it is written that "all men did marvel."[3]

That was miracle number one. That these heathen should decide to turn to Jesus because of the witness of these two men demonstrates the power of the gospel through those who have had Jesus touch their lives.

But finally the food ran out. All the baskets of supplies got down to seven loaves of bread and a few fishes. This was the setting for Jesus' miracle of feeding the four thousand men, besides women and children. And incidentally, the disciples, even though they had seen Him feed five thousand Jews, didn't catch the power present to perform this miracle.[4] After all, these were Gentiles and heathen. They could not figure out how Jesus could supply their needs. But miracle number two took place because of these heathen people's choice to see Jesus. And that choice came about because of the testimony of two men who were left behind at the beach near Gergesa.

---

[1] *The SDA Bible Commentary,* vol. 5, pp. 605, 606.
[2] *The Desire of Ages,* p. 404.
[3] Mark 5:20.
[4] *Ibid.*, p. 405.

EVIL COALITION

The Pharisees also with the Sadducees came, and tempting desired him that he would shew them a sign from heaven. Matt. 16:1.

For the first time the Sadducees joined the Pharisees in an attempt to silence Jesus.[1] It was a strange but evil coalition.

The Sadducees belonged to the liberal aristocratic wing that felt compelled to orchestrate every political possibility in courting the favor of the Romans in order to maintain their own power and prestige.[2] The Pharisees, on the other hand, encouraged the popular anti-Roman fervor and longed for the time when the Jewish nation could be in total control of its fate.

And the two parties were just as much apart religiously as they were politically. The Sadducees did not believe in angels, a resurrection, a heaven, or a hell. They were essentially skeptics and materialists.[3] These rich religionists disdained the narrow-minded conservative Pharisees, who constantly bickered over the nitty-gritty of tradition, the resurrection, and the law.

Yet for all their differences these two parties decided to unite forces. What could possibly drive them to such a decision? "Like seeks like; and evil, wherever it exists, leagues with evil for the destruction of the good." [4] It had now become a necessity for them to unite in stopping Jesus.

They came to Him demanding some sort of external evidence of His claim to be the Messiah. But instead of offering them a spectacular demonstration of His power, Jesus called this coalition delegation nothing but hypocrites. He told them frankly that, while they could forecast the weather, they did "not discern the signs of the times." [5] His continuing miracles offered more than enough proof of His claim. He would do nothing to satisfy the demands of their pride and unbelief. We should remember Jesus' method when meeting similar evil coalitions during the forthcoming events of the last days.

---

[1] *The SDA Bible Commentary*, vol. 5, p. 426.
[2] *The Desire of Ages*, p. 405.
[3] *Ibid.*, p. 603.
[4] *Ibid.*, p. 405.
[5] Matt. 16:3.

JESUS' CHOICE TO SUFFER

From that time forth began Jesus to shew unto his disciples, how that he must go unto Jerusalem, and suffer many things of the elders and chief priests and scribes, and be killed, and be raised again the third day. Matt. 16:21.

During the latter part of the summer of A.D. 30 Jesus began instructing His disciples more fully about His mission.[1] They had retreated to Caesarea Philippi, about twenty-five miles north of Galilee, to avoid the continuing conflict with the religious spies that were assigned to harass Jesus.[2] Now He could be alone with His twelve men to unfold the future.

It was a difficult task to reveal the forthcoming agony of the cross.[3] Jesus prayed about this. He wanted them to see the real role of the Messiah. They, of course, recoiled in stunned horror when they heard the description of Christ's future. They simply could not reconcile the Messiah of their dreams with what Jesus was telling them. Yet Jesus saw it all.

The scenes of His suffering were revealed in detail before He ever left heaven. He saw the path from the manger to Golgotha, yet He came anyway.[4] But now that He had taken upon Himself humanity, He felt the tremendous tug of the desire to be free of suffering.

Many long to look into the future. They seek out some palmist or crystal gazer for a clue. Devouring the daily astrology predictions is still popular. But one wonders whether the eagerness would be there if every detail of the life down to the last gasping agony of some excruciating death were revealed. Would the lovers of the future keep going then?

But Jesus did. Through His close connection with the Father He saw the whole wrenching ordeal before Him, yet He kept going. Even with the knowledge that the weight of all the sins of humanity would press down upon Him, He still chose to suffer as a lost sinner for the joy of seeing those who would respond to His love.

---

[1] *The SDA Bible Commentary,* vol. 5, p. 433.
[2] *Ibid.,* p. 428.
[3] *The Desire of Ages,* p. 411.
[4] *Ibid.,* p. 410.

PETER'S DOUBLE DECISION

But he turned, and said unto Peter, Get thee behind me, Satan: thou art an offence unto me: for thou savourest not the things that be of God, but those that be of men. Matt. 16:23.

This is one of the sternest rebukes Jesus ever uttered.[1] Literally He told Peter, "Get out of my sight!"[2] The sharp severity had all the overtones of the language Jesus had used when He repulsed the devil in the wilderness.

How quickly Peter had switched sides in the great controversy! Just prior to this he had confessed that Jesus is "the Son of the living God."[3] While others might doubt that Jesus is the Christ, Peter accepted Him. Jesus told Peter that he was blessed of Heaven for making that choice, because flesh and blood had not revealed this truth to him. Peter had professed the very foundation of the Christian faith.[4] It was a choice made possible only by a willing response to the moving of God's Spirit.

But when Peter heard Jesus tell about His future persecution and death in Jerusalem, he took the Saviour aside and privately rebuked Him in his own vigorous style. " 'Never, Lord!' he said. 'This shall never happen to you!' "[5]

Peter decided that Christ's self-sacrificing way was not to be. While he loved Jesus, this personal rebuke to the Master was only a sentiment whispered by Satan. The enemy was using Peter to discourage Jesus and instill in the disciple the yearning for earthly glory. It was essentially the same temptation that Jesus faced in the wilderness, and He would have none of it. "The words of Christ were spoken, not to Peter, but to the one who was trying to separate him from his Redeemer."[6]

How often we may give some exalted testimony of our faith in Christ, only to turn around and mouth some self-seeking suggestion from Satan! Whenever we turn from Jesus and His way of the cross to satisfy our own selfish ends in an easier way, we repeat Peter's double decision.

[1] *The Desire of Ages*, pp. 415, 416.
[2] *The SDA Bible Commentary*, vol. 5, p. 434.
[3] Matt. 16:16.
[4] *The Desire of Ages*, p. 412.
[5] Verse 22, N.I.V.
[6] *Ibid.*, p. 416.

RESTING AT THE WRONG TIME

But Peter and they that were with him were heavy with sleep: and when they were awake, they saw his glory, and the two men that stood with him. Luke 9:32.

Many years after that radiant night on the Mount of Transfiguration, Peter wrote that he and his companions "were eyewitnesses of his majesty." [1] They were privileged to see the Second Coming in miniature, with a glorified Christ surrounded by Moses, who represented the resurrected saints, and Elijah, who represented the translated ones. [2]

But today's text suggests that they could have seen and heard much more. Instead of resisting their drowsiness, they yielded to soporific symptoms and rested at the wrong time. It might have been a natural choice, but it was a tragic one. "Through being overcome with sleep, the disciples heard little of what passed between Christ and the heavenly messengers. Failing to watch and pray, they had not received that which God desired to give them—a knowledge of the sufferings of Christ, and the glory that should follow. They lost the blessing that might have been theirs through sharing His self-sacrifice." [3]

That conversation between Jesus, Moses, and Elijah was lost for good. But worse than that, their nap deprived them of the fullest knowledge of Christ's forthcoming trial. They went down to Jerusalem without the fortification that God intended.

But Jesus had fully prepared them for this magnificent time. A week before, He had predicted that some of the disciples would see His second coming in type. [4] And when they hiked up that lonely mountain with Jesus, these three should have known that He hadn't come just to look at stars. At least they should have caught the significance of His prayers in their behalf. But instead they decided to sleep. If they had resisted the drowsiness it would surely have left them.

Whenever God sets aside some special moment for our benefit it is never wise to excuse our lethargy on the basis of workload. Like these three disciples, we will always miss Heaven's great blessings by such a decision.

[1] 2 Peter 1:16.
[2] *The Desire of Ages*, p. 422.
[3] *Ibid.*, p. 425.
[4] *The SDA Bible Commentary*, vol. 5, p. 436; Matt. 16:28-17:2.

NO LACK OF POWER

Jesus said unto him, If thou canst believe, all things are possible to him that believeth. Mark 9:23.

It was one of those extremely embarrassing moments when the frustrations of impotence stared directly at the disciples. While Jesus and the three disciples were climbing down from the Mount of Transfiguration the other nine were doing their best to cast out a demon from a possessed boy. A desperate father had brought his son for healing, but instead of the demon's obeying their command, it sent the lad into wild spasms.

The haughty scribes on hand heckled the disciples about their attempts to heal the boy. These hostile theologians made the most of the occasion and implied that Jesus and His disciples were impostors. Pointing to the wretched young demoniac, they sneeringly claimed that the disciples were powerless.

When Jesus approached, their haughtiness vanished and they quickly retreated.[1] It was then that the father hurried forward and explained that he had brought his son to the disciples but that so far nothing had happened. When Jesus asked for the lad to be brought to Him the demon threw the boy down in frightful convulsions. Jesus permitted the enemy to display his power before he brought deliverance.

"Jesus asked the boy's father, 'How long has he been like this?'

" 'From childhood,' he answered. 'It has often thrown him into fire or water to kill him. But if you can do anything, take pity on us and help us.' "[2]

Even then the father questioned if Jesus had the power.[3] That is when the Saviour uttered the words of our text for today. The father had to decide. There was no lack of power on Christ's part. Bursting into tears, the father cried out, " 'I do believe; help me overcome my unbelief!' "[4]

His cry indicated his choice. Faith always gives Jesus the opportunity to deliver us from the enemy, regardless of his apparent strength.

---

[1] *The Desire of Ages*, p. 427.
[2] Mark 9:21, 22, N.I.V.
[3] *Ibid.*, p. 428.
[4] Verse 24, N.I.V.

WHY THE DISCIPLES FAILED

His disciples asked him privately, Why could not we cast him out? And he said unto them, This kind can come forth by nothing, but by prayer and fasting. Mark 9:28, 29.

The nine disciples had come face to face with the devil in the form of the possessed boy, and they should never have known defeat. Christ had authorized them to cast out demons, and in His name was power. There was no need to engage in some protracted conversation with the evil spirits in order to exorcise them. Jesus' method was to give the command, and the demons would depart. But the power that Jesus had imparted now seemed to have departed. When they were alone with Him they asked the obvious question: What went wrong?

Jesus did not refer to an immediate prayer in connection with casting out demons, but to the whole life dedicated to prayer. He spoke of an attitude. His answer shows that a decision must be made to permit Christ to fill the life. The disciples, instead of meditating on Christ's words and strengthening themselves with prayer, chose to simmer with jealousy instead. They were miffed that Jesus had selected Peter, James, and John to accompany Him up the Mount of Transfiguration.[1] Instead of praying, they had pouted. And in this attitude they attempted to meet the enemy.

Why they failed was no secret. It never is a mystery when professed believers come short of God's glory. The devil cannot be defeated while we choose to indulge in his own evil attitudes of pride and envy. Jesus wanted to make it plain to His disciples for all time that they must be emptied of self before they can be filled with the Holy Spirit. When we are entirely consecrated to Jesus, the Holy Spirit will bring His divine resources to bear in the battle with the wicked one. Jesus said that faith even the size of a grain of mustard seed could grow by laying hold on God's power. And all the mountains of difficulty Satan could ever pile up would disappear on the demands of such faith.

---

[1] *The Desire of Ages*, p. 431.

DECISION TO AVOID CONTROVERSY

Lest we should offend them, go thou to the sea, and cast an hook, and take up the fish that first cometh up; and when thou hast opened his mouth, thou shalt find a piece of money: that take, and give unto them for me and thee. Matt. 17:27.

This is the only instance in the New Testament where anybody caught a fish with a hook.[1] But Jesus sent Peter on this strange fishing trip for a very special reason.

Peter had fallen for the trap set by the Temple tax collector who asked whether Jesus paid the annual fee. This tax came due around February or March, and it was a rabbinical custom prescribed for all free male Jews 20 years of age and older.[2] The tax collector waited until the late summer to mention it, which indicates that the rabbis hadn't thought of the scheme until just now. Peter, caught off guard, voiced his assurance that his Master did pay the revenue. He should have consulted Jesus before making such a quick reply. In stating that his Master paid this Temple tax, he indicated that Jesus was not a prophet or a true teacher, since they were exempt from this requirement.[3] Unwittingly Peter had placed Jesus in the common-person class.

The tax collector and his colleagues were sure they had Jesus where they wanted Him now. If He paid the tax they would quickly seize on His right to claim divinity. If He refused they were ready to scream that He was disloyal to the Temple, and thus they would justify their rejection of Him as a prophet.

That is when Jesus sent Peter fishing. This was a decision that left its mark. He would pay the tax under protest, but He would show His divinity by the miracle used to obtain the tribute money.[4] He would meet their arbitrary demand, but He denied the distorted claim upon which it was founded.

Jesus left His disciples a lesson clear to the end of time. When possible we should always choose to avoid controversy while persisting in our commitment to remain true to principle.

[1] *The SDA Bible Commentary,* vol. 5, p. 443.
[2] *Ibid.,* pp. 441, 442.
[3] *The Desire of Ages,* p. 433.
[4] *Ibid.,* p. 434.

October 23

CHOOSING REAL GREATNESS

Verily I say unto you, Except ye be converted, and become as little children, ye shall not enter into the kingdom of heaven. Matt. 18:3.

Jesus had hoped to stimulate a conversation with the disciples regarding their forthcoming test of faith when He would die and be resurrected.[1] But they remained silent. Their guilt when He asked them what they had been arguing about behind His back sealed their lips. Finally one of them got the courage to ask, "Who is the greatest in the kingdom of heaven?"[2]

That was it! The all-consuming topic was out. Whom would Jesus select for the top position? Jesus realized that it wasn't enough to tell them the nature of His kingdom. They had heard that before. But even if He spelled it out in greater detail it would stifle the argument only for a while.

The disciples didn't realize that strife over greatness was really the underlying principle that started the great controversy in the first place. Lucifer had clamored for a position like the Most High. To be like God sounds noble. Yet "Lucifer desired God's power, but not His character."[3] And once that desire firmly establishes itself in the mind, wrangling and arguments will inevitably follow. Satan's entire establishment is based on using force. If others block the road to personal self-seeking, push them aside to get ahead.

So the disciples had to come to a decision about the kingdom. That is when Jesus called a youngster to Him. Taking the child in His arms, He stated the words of our text for today. The disciples needed a genuine change of heart, and that could happen only if they chose to be molded by the Holy Spirit. The little child was a living symbol of an essential attitude. "The simplicity, the self-forgetfulness, and the confiding love of a little child are the attributes that Heaven values. These are the characteristics of real greatness."[4]

[1] *The Desire of Ages*, p. 435.
[2] Matt. 18:1.
[3] *Ibid.*
[4] *Ibid.*, p. 437.

304

THEIR CHOICE OF THE WORLD

The world cannot hate you; but me it hateth, because I testify of it, that the works thereof are evil. John 7:7.

Jesus spoke these words to His own unbelieving brothers. These sons of Joseph urged Jesus to attend the fall Feast of Tabernacles, claiming that the time had come for Him to present Himself as the Messiah in Jerusalem. But Jesus would not give them any definite plans regarding His going to this annual harvest feast. Furthermore, He let them know that He did not include them among His disciples, but rated them with the world.[1] And the world with all its clamoring for pride and pomp was doomed to perish. Jesus was not about to fulfill some self-aggrandizing claim to the kind of kingdom they envisioned. He would not go right then to the annual feast or follow their directions, because their motives were wrong.

Jesus' brothers could not fathom Him. He was a total enigma to them. When He could perform such wonderful miracles and had swept the whole district of Galilee with Him in a popular movement, why did He do and say things that lowered His prestige? Why did He keep neglecting the religious services in Jerusalem when this was the place where He must be shown and accepted in order to achieve the status of the long-looked-for Messiah?[2] It bothered these brothers of Jesus that He mingled freely with the outcasts of society and yet continually antagonized the ruling religious authorities. He kept exalting the law and talking about the blessings of keeping it, yet He did everything He could to counter the keeping of the traditions of the elders, which in their minds was equally as essential.

His brothers had spoken to Him with a tone of authority, insisting that He abide by their wishes. But Jesus returned their rebuke by informing them that they had chosen the world and that, because of their choice, the world would accept them.[3] But His life and the lives of His true followers would always be out of sync with the world and its self-exalting, self-centered desires.

---

[1] *The Desire of Ages,* p. 451.
[2] *Ibid.,* p 450.
[3] *Ibid.,* p. 451.

TEMPLE POLICE WITHOUT A PRISONER

Then came the officers to the chief priests and Pharisees; and they said unto them, Why have ye not brought him? The officers answered, Never man spake like this man. John 7:45, 46.

As the Feast of Tabernacles approached, all Jerusalem buzzed with rumors about Jesus. While those who had traveled long distances waited to see Him the authorities hoped He would show up so they could condemn Him.[1] But as the annual thanksgiving feast neared, Jesus was nowhere to be found.

By taking a back route Jesus had slipped into the city unnoticed. Suddenly, when the excitement about Him was at its height, He entered the Temple court and began teaching. It was a dramatic moment. Every voice was hushed. The people could not understand how He was so knowledgeable about the Scriptures when He had never attended the rabbinical schools. "If any man will do his will, he shall know of the doctrine," Jesus declared.[2]

The reason so many misunderstood the Scriptures was that the religious teachers slanted the Word of God to suit their own purposes.[3] And those texts that didn't appeal to them personally they ignored.

Day after day Jesus taught, and the authorities didn't dare to touch Him for fear of the people. But when the spellbound people said, "When Christ cometh, will he do more miracles than these which this man hath done?"[4] it was too much for the Pharisees, who hurried away to call the arresting committee together. A quick vote and they sent the Temple police to arrest Him on the spot.

Later these same officers returned empty-handed. They had made a decision. As hardhearted as they were, they felt the conviction of His words. They chose to face the wrath of the Pharisees rather than to take Him who had so deeply touched the need of their souls.

---

[1] *The Desire of Ages*, p. 451.
[2] John 7:17.
[3] *Ibid.*, p. 459.
[4] Verse 31.

THE BOLDEST PHARISEE

Nicodemus saith unto them, . . . Doth our law judge any man, before it hear him, and know what he doeth? John 7:50, 51.

Like some jolting crack of thunder Nicodemus asked a question the Sanhedrin didn't want to hear. They had called an emergency session to condemn Jesus and they had expected the officers to bring Him before them. But when there was no arrest the meeting evolved into a determined discussion on how to silence this Galilean.

Right at the height of the discussion Nicodemus spoke up.[1] Earlier he had secretly found Jesus at night, but now he spoke for Him in broad daylight. It was a bold decision. He could not just sit there and listen to his colleagues harangue against Jesus, who was giving more and more evidence that He truly is the Messiah. To make such a decision took courage. It is never easy to speak up for someone when the tide of popular opinion runs high against him. Nicodemus could have sat there in silence and refrained from voting. That would have been the polished, political, noncommittal approach. But silence isn't always golden; sometimes it's just plain yellow. So Nicodemus, the Pharisee in full and regular standing, spoke up. It was a courageous choice backed by centuries of God-given instruction. Moses had written under inspiration, "Ye shall not respect persons in judgment; but ye shall hear the small as well as the great." [2] Nicodemus was pleading only for fairness and justice in Jesus' case.

The council members sat stunned. In silence they stared at Nicodemus. That he dared to ask the question was bad enough, but the fact that one of their own ruling members should speak in favor of justice shocked them. When they regained their speech they cut Nicodemus down with sarcasm. "Are you also from Galilee? Search and you'll find that no prophet comes from Galilee."

They were wrong, of course. Jonah, for one, came from the district.[3] But right then they were confused. Nicodemus' question served to stall the proceedings. His boldness remains a worthy example.

---

[1] *The Desire of Ages*, p. 460.
[2] Deut. 1:17.
[3] *The SDA Bible Commentary*, vol. 5, p. 983.

DUST WRITING AND CONVICTION

But Jesus stooped down, and with his finger wrote on the ground, as though he heard them not. . . . And they. . . , being convicted by their own conscience, went out one by one, beginning at the eldest, even unto the last. John 8:6-9.

For the first and only time on record Jesus wrote something.[1] He wrote it not on parchment, neither did He chisel it in stone; but He wrote in the dust, which eventually would blow away. But what He wrote served its purpose well.

The Pharisees and scribes had come to Him with all the apparent piety they could muster. Dragging a frightened woman with them, they had thrust her in front of Jesus and demanded a verdict. Disregarding their own court system and the right of the husband to bring charges of adultery, their diabolical minds had set up this case, which seemed to be such a foolproof trap.[2] Jesus had to commit Himself now! And if He forgave the woman, as they suspected He might, they were all fired up to denounce Him for despising the law. But if He should condemn her according to the law of Moses and order the death sentence, they were all set to run and report it to the Romans, pointing out that He was trying to usurp Roman authority.[3] It seemed to be such a neat package!

But Jesus acted as though He hadn't heard their clamoring demands. Stooping down, He began finger-writing in the dust. What He wrote was not the outline for the next week's Sabbath school lesson, nor was it some vague generality. What He wrote pinpointed specific sins. He may have even written the dates. At any rate, what He wrote certainly caused some rapid decision-making. These would-be guardians of the law crowded around, craning their necks to look. But once they saw what Jesus had written on the ground, the voice of their own consciences screamed at them. When Jesus stood up and asked for the first sinless stone thrower to proceed and then stooped to continue writing, they chose to exit one by one.

Pharisaical behavior often ends in public humiliation.

---

[1] *The SDA Bible Commentary,* vol. 5, p. 986.
[2] *The Desire of Ages,* p. 461.
[3] *Ibid.,* pp. 460, 461.

THE BEGINNING OF A NEW LIFE

Woman, where are those thine accusers? hath no man condemned thee? She said, No man, Lord. And Jesus said unto her, Neither do I condemn thee: go, and sin no more. John 8:10, 11.

She had fully anticipated death.[1] It was a heart-pounding moment for her when she heard Jesus say, "He that is without sin among you, let him first cast a stone."[2] She just knew that at least one of those self-righteous, scowling-faced men would pick up a rock and hurl it at her. And then would come the avalanche of boulders. Cowering and terrified, she expected the pain to begin any moment.

There had been no need for the Pharisees to make a public show of her impure sex life. To be caught in a frame-up was bad enough, but to be brought right down to the Temple with all those people around was terribly shameful. She dared not look up. With clammy hands and terror gripping her whole body, she suffered through those long, agonizing minutes.

But then the harsh, angry voices subsided. She heard the shuffling of feet, and all was quiet. She was alone with Jesus. When she heard His gentle voice say, "Neither do I condemn thee: go, and sin no more," her decision was final. She had no desire to defend her adulterous actions or to try to hide her past. "Her heart was melted, and she cast herself at the feet of Jesus, sobbing out her grateful love, and with bitter tears confessing her sins."[3]

From that moment on she chose to love and follow Jesus. It was the beginning of a new life for her. Jesus had not said, "Go and taper off." He had told her to turn around completely. And His words of mercy were packed with the power of His creative genius to provide the means of living free from the old sinful life style.

To lift this woman from degradation to newness of life was a far greater miracle than healing someone of a dread disease. It meant transforming the whole current of thought patterns and turning passions into purity in preparation for eternal life.

---

[1] *The Desire of Ages,* p. 462.
[2] John 8:7.
[3] *Ibid.*

THE QUIBBLER'S CHOICE

He that is of God heareth God's words: ye therefore hear them not, because ye are not of God. John 8:47.

To the Pharisees, Jesus' claim to be the light of the world was an audacious assertion. It was intolerable because they ranked Him right along with the rest of humanity.

But Jesus, in one of His classic confrontations with them, spoke also to those bystanders who were drawn to Him. " 'If you hold to my teaching, you are really my disciples. Then you will know the truth, and the truth will set you free.' " [1]

This was too much for the rulers. Without recognizing that they were in the most abject bondage of sin, as well as being physically under Roman jurisdiction, they boastfully claimed that as Jews they had never been in bondage to any man. "We be Abraham's seed," they smirked. [2]

Their boastful claim of freedom had absolutely no foundation. All through their history the Jews had known bondage. Had they forgotten the Egyptians, Philistines, Assyrians, Babylonians, and others? But by their nit-picking they went blind. They claimed Abraham as their father, but Jesus told them frankly that with their hatred and bigotry they were of their father the devil.

" 'Can any of you prove me guilty of sin? If I am telling the truth, why don't you believe me?' " [3]

Not one of those critics could convict Jesus of sin. Their silence on the subject testified of His claim to be the Son of God. They were totally irrational in their arguments, yet they would not recognize Him as the very one whom God had sent. By choosing to quibble they missed the reality of God's character right before their eyes.

Whenever anyone is bent on assuming a critical attitude toward the things of God, he invariably loses the capacity to appreciate or recognize His character. [4] Thinking themselves highly independent and clever, the Pharisees ended up with nothing but the quibbler's choice of darkness.

---

[1] John 8:31, 32, N.I.V.
[2] Verse 33.
[3] Verse 46, N.I.V.
[4] *The Desire of Ages*, p. 468.

REFUSING TO BE CONFUSED

Since the world began was it not heard that any man opened the eyes of one that was born blind. If this man were not of God, he could do nothing. John 9:32, 33.

Instead of rejoicing that someone had regained his sight, the Pharisees seethed with hatred. Jesus had healed a blind man. And worse than that, He had healed him on the Sabbath. The miracle violated their theology. They had perverted the truth about the results of sin to mean that every disease and death was a curse from God.[1] They were prepared to reject Jesus becaue He did not fit into their theology of God's retributive punishment. And the fact that He healed on the Sabbath only confirmed their false notion that Jesus was a sinner.

The former blind man was hailed before a council to be interrogated. These hypocrites desperately tried to confuse the man with questions, hoping that he might think himself deluded. But in the midst of their discussion they themselves became divided. One segment hammered away with the idea that Jesus could not be of God because He healed on the Sabbath, while another group asked, "How can a sinner perform such miracles?"

The former blind man finally picked up on this division of the Pharisees and met them on their own ground. He refused to be confused and chose to stay by the facts. There was no historical record of anyone's ever having been healed of congenital blindness. "If this man were not of God, he could do nothing," he reasoned. And his logic was absolutely irrefutable.[2] It took the Pharisees a few moments to recover from the shock, and then all they could do was to shout their abusive denunciations and finally excommunicate him.

Satanic forces are ever seeking to confuse and depreciate Jesus' miraculous work. When we personally have felt the touch of His divinity we should decide as did this former blind man not to be confused. Nothing should ever shake our confidence or faith in Jesus' power manifested in our lives.

---

[1] *The Desire of Ages*, p. 471.
[2] *Ibid.*, p. 474.

EVADING THE TRUTH

The Jews had agreed already, that if any man did confess that he was Christ, he should be put out of the synagogue. Therefore said his parents, He is of age; ask him. John 9:22, 23.

These verses speak of a lost opportunity to speak up for Jesus. The Pharisees had summoned the parents of the former blind man, hoping they could intimidate them into saying something that would condemn Jesus for healing on the Sabbath. But the parents shifted all responsibility to their son and did a fast shuffle past the truth.

The Pharisees had a couple of questions. " 'Is this your son, who you say was born blind? How then does he now see?' " [1]

The parents willingly answered the first question, which cleared the matter of identity. The former blind man did look different, because now his face was so radiant.

" 'We know that this is our son,' " they replied, " 'and that he was born blind; but how he now sees we do not know, nor do we know who opened his eyes. Ask him; He is of age.' " [2]

They may not have been present when their son came home seeing after having washed in the Pool of Siloam in southern Jerusalem, but they certainly heard the facts from their neighbors on just how his sight had been restored.[3] The great work Jesus had done for their son brought conviction, yet they chose to evade the truth for fear of excommunication.[4] Those grim faces of the Pharisees sent chills through them, and they were truly frightened.

It is always tragic when people choose to evade the truth out of fear and intimidation. It is even more tragic when this is done with a full knowledge that the name of Jesus should be glorified. Whenever, because of some threat, we back off from acknowledging what Jesus has done we lose the special blessing of God's presence during the time of pressure. The only way any of us can remain firm for Christ under threatened persecution is to develop a solid relationship of love which will stand any test.

---

[1] John 9:19, R.S.V.
[2] Verses 20, 21, R.S.V.
[3] *The SDA Bible Commentary*, vol. 5, p. 998.
[4] *The Desire of Ages*, p. 472.

THE LAWYER'S EVASION

If a man say, I love God, and hateth his brother, he is a liar: for he that loveth not his brother whom he hath seen, how can he love God whom he hath not seen? 1 John 4:20.

It was one of those typical entanglement setups for Jesus. The Pharisees and rabbis prompted one of their lawyers to question Jesus, hoping He would say something about the law that they could use to condemn Him.[1] They had systematically accused Jesus of treating the law of God lightly, so the lawyer's question was heavily loaded with the sense of earning salvation. "Master," he asked, "what shall I do to inherit eternal life?"[2]

The large congregation assembled to hear Jesus was hushed. Everyone wanted to hear His answer. Jesus, however, refused to engage in polemics. It was appropriate that the lawyer, who was supposed to be a specialist in religious law, should answer his own question. "What is written in the law?" Jesus asked.

The lawyer immediately quoted from Deuteronomy 6:5. Every morning and evening each devout Jew recited those words about loving God with all the heart.[3] The lawyer had those words down pat.

"You've answered correctly," Jesus told him. "Do this and you will live."

A mere ceremonial religion had not satisfied the lawyer. He honestly wanted to know the basis of eternal life, but now he squirmed because those words about loving God and neighbors, as well, indicated that he was really a lawbreaker. But at that moment he decided to evade conviction, and instead tried to vindicate himself before all the onlookers. "Who is my neighbor?" he asked.

It was at this point that Jesus related the story of the good Samaritan. But as far as the lawyer was concerned there was no such thing as a "good" Samaritan. In his evasion of the truth about his neighbor, he missed the whole meaning of God's love.

---

[1] *The Desire of Ages*, p. 497.
[2] Luke 10:25.
[3] *The SDA Bible Commentary*, vol. 5, p. 782.

THREE MAJOR ROAD DECISIONS

If we love one another, God dwelleth in us, and his love is perfected in us. 1 John 4:12.

When Jesus told the story of the good Samaritan, both the priest and the Levite involved were in the audience.[1] This was no parable. Everyone had heard the news report of the robbery. But the story actually relates three major decisions that unfold the truth of each man's religion that day on the Jericho road.

Out there in those wild, rocky reaches of the Judean wilderness a robbery victim lay half dead. Both the priest and the Levite had just finished their official religious duties at the Temple in Jerusalem and were heading home to Jericho.[2]

The priest saw the poor man first, stripped and bleeding, but only glanced in his direction. Since the man might be already dead, it would be unlawful for him to touch him. But even if the man were not dead he might be a Samaritan or some other Gentile. Whatever passed quickly through his sanctimonious priestly mind, he checked off the reasons for unconcern with a flare for the official policy excuse record.

When the Levite came along he at least showed some concern and went over to where the victim lay moaning. The sights and sounds made the Levite wish he hadn't come that way. He too made a decision to keep going after his curiosity had been satisfied.

The scene shifted dramatically when the Samaritan came along. His actions, at considerable risk to himself in that robbers' retreat, showed how much his compassion resembled the Saviour's. His choice was immediate. He knew that if the roles had been reversed, he would not have received any help from a Jew, yet he pushed all this aside because a fellow human being was in terrible need. The Samaritan paid in his time, his strength, his supplies, and his cash. His choice was the only one of the three that will stand the test of time and eternity.

[1] *The Desire of Ages*, p. 499.
[2] *The SDA Bible Commentary*, vol. 5, p. 783.

THE CHOICE OF RICHES

Jesus said unto him, If thou wilt be perfect, go and sell that thou hast, and give to the poor, and thou shalt have treasure in heaven: and come and follow me. Matthew 19:21.

One onlooker who watched Jesus bless the little children felt such a strong tug toward the Saviour that he came running to Him.[1] He was rich, young, influential, and totally sincere in his request to find some good thing he could do to inherit eternal life.

Jesus did not engage him in any discussion about faith, as we might like to hear, but told him frankly that obedience to the commandments of God was absolutely essential. To us who are so sensitive to any works in religion, this seems out of harmony with righteousness. But Jesus never thought so. He invariably turned people toward the great standard of all righteousness in the commandments. He even quoted a few for the rich young ruler as a reminder.

"I've kept these ever since my youth. What am I lacking?"

It was a delusion, of course. This young man had a checklist religion. He hadn't robbed any caravans or had an affair or lied in his business dealings. He was Mr. Clean.

It was because of this attitude that Jesus laid bare the real idol of his life. If he really wanted eternal life he must focus his affections totally on God and not on his possessions. Jesus never told the disciples that they had to sell their fishing boats and nets before they could follow Him, because these did not stand in the way. But in telling the rich young ruler to have a sale and turn the proceeds over to the poor, Jesus fingered the idolatry in his life. He really hadn't kept those commandments after all.

"Christ gave this man a test. He called upon him to choose between the heavenly treasure and worldly greatness."[2] The choice was his. But like many who at first come running to Jesus, he walked away slowly when he found that he must surrender his selfishness. He was sad that he couldn't have it both ways.

---

[1] *The Desire of Ages*, p. 518.
[2] *Ibid.*, p. 519.

MARY'S CHOICE

Mary hath chosen that good part, which shall not be taken away from her. Luke 10:42.

On the eastern slope of the Mount of Olives about a mile and a half (2.4 kilometers) from Jerusalem, lies the little village of Bethany.[1] Here was the home of Lazarus and his two sisters, Mary and Martha. If there was any place where Jesus could relax, it was in this home. Here He could chat without using parables.

One day Jesus and His disciples climbed the hot, toilsome road from Jericho and dropped in unexpectedly on this family. Martha was all astir trying to get a meal ready, while Mary sat listening in the living room.

Even though she chose to fuss and fume, it is easy to understand Martha's part. There is a time for everything, and listening right then didn't seem to be in harmony with dinner preparations. Yet Jesus understood why Mary had shifted her priorities.

Mary's choice was based on an experience. The closer she came to Jesus, the more she desired a fuller knowledge of His love. From the bits and fragments of inspired information, it is possible to piece together a composite picture of this Mary, who was also known as Mary Magdalene.

Simon the Pharisee had led her into sin.[2] If as a result of her shameful life Mary had left Bethany and moved north to Magdala, her story would still be in complete harmony with the Gospel record.[3]

At this juncture her life went from bad to worse. Not only was her body used and abused but her mind came under the control of demons. Then one day during His early Galilean tour Jesus went through this town on the western shore of the lake. Here He met Mary of Magdala and freed her from demon possession.

When Mary returned happily to Bethany she was transformed. So when Jesus stopped by that day, is it any wonder that she sat drinking in every word! She wasn't interested in food preparation. Just being with her Saviour was enough!

---

[1] *SDA Bible Dictionary,* p. 139.
[2] *The Desire of Ages,* p. 566.
[3] *The SDA Bible Commentary,* vol. 5, p. 765.

WHEN JESUS SEEMED TO NEGLECT

Then said Jesus unto them plainly, Lazarus is dead. And I am glad for your sakes that I was not there, to the intent ye may believe. John 11:14, 15.

Lazarus was one of His best friends, yet Jesus deliberately chose to neglect him during his serious illness. The disciples were puzzled, and Mary and Martha were nearly frantic, yet Jesus remained away while Lazarus grew steadily worse. The sisters sent word, " 'Lord, the one you love is sick,' " [1] and thought Jesus would respond immediately. They waited and prayed. In those agonizing hours they wondered what happened. They leaned over the dying form of their dear brother and whispered that Jesus would soon arrive, but finally Lazarus breathed his last. It was a bitter, wrenching experience.

Meanwhile the disciples could not fathom why Jesus seemed to receive the message so coolly. It was such a strange mystery, especially since Lazarus and his sisters were so tenderly tied to Him. For two whole days Jesus never even mentioned His friend Lazarus, and that seemed even more baffling.

But while the disciples were still wondering, Jesus suddenly announced that they would leave for Judea. He hadn't really forgotten His friend Lazarus after all. At first He told His disciples that Lazarus was asleep, then plainly explained that he had died. Furthermore, He was glad that He had not been there. He had been suffering all along with the sisters and with Lazarus, but He had more than the family to think of. He needed to establish firmly in the minds of His disciples the crowning proof of His divinity. If He had been there in the sickroom, Lazarus would never have passed away. Now a dramatic resurrection could take place. [2]

Whenever Jesus chooses to remain silent He has in mind a plan for greater good. "To all who are reaching out to feel the guiding hand of God, the moment of greatest discouragement is the time when divine help is nearest." [3]

---

[1] John 11:3, N.I.V.
[2] *The Desire of Ages,* pp. 526-528.
[3] *Ibid.,* p. 528.

MARTHA'S SELF-ASSERTION

Jesus saith unto her, Said I not unto thee, that, if thou wouldest believe, thou shouldest see the glory of God? John 11:40.

When Jesus finally set foot in Bethany, Martha hurried to meet Him, her lips quivering with conflicting emotions. Her faith in Jesus remained unshaken, but she could not comprehend why He had delayed so long.[1] " 'Lord, . . . if you had been here, my brother would not have died,' " she cried.[2]

Over and over again she and her sister had repeated that line, until now it tumbled out to Jesus, with all the anguish of those long hours of waiting behind it.

" 'But I know that even now God will give you whatever you ask,' " she added.

Jesus looked at her tear-stained face and tried to encourage her faith by directing her mind beyond the present to the reality of that glad, great resurrection day of the righteous. " 'Your brother will rise again,' " He assured her.

" 'I know he will rise again in the resurrection at the last day,' " she answered.

She had her theology correct, but Jesus wanted to direct her faith even further. " 'I am the resurrection and the life,' " He said.

Martha believed. Her confidence in Jesus was firm, yet when they came to the grave and Jesus ordered the large circular stone to be rolled away, her strong, determined practical nature rebelled against the thought. The very idea of exposing her brother's four-day-old decomposing body was too much. She decided to stop the proceedings. It was a choice prompted by Satan, who always intrudes whenever Jesus sets about to work.[3]

Today's text records Jesus' reproof to Martha. She should not have doubted for a moment His power or His requirements. "You have My word. If you will believe, you shall see the glory of God. Natural impossibilities cannot prevent the work of the Omnipotent One."[4]

[1] *The Desire of Ages,* p. 529.
[2] John 11:21ff., N.I.V.
[3] *Ibid.,* p. 535.
[4] *Ibid.*

THE EXPEDIENT CHOICE

It is expedient for us, that one man should die for the people. John 11:50.

Back in A.D. 18, while Jesus still worked in the carpenter's shop in Nazareth, the Romans appointed Joseph Caiaphas to serve as high priest.[1] During this tragic time, high priests frequently obtained their office by bribery and fraud.[2] The whole system reeked with dishonesty. Caiaphas could wear the expensive and richly ornate robes, but he was not a high priest ordained of God. He belonged to the wealthy, aristocratic secular wing of Judaism, the class who considered God some sort of absentee landlord.

The key word in Caiaphas' life was expediency. That is why he could sit there with a straight face that day and tell the Sanhedrin that it was expedient for Jesus to die. The resurrection of Lazarus had shattered the Sadducees' neat little doctrine that there wasn't any such thing. Now things had become a bit untidy, and something had to be done. So Caiaphas slipped into his natural habit of choosing expediency. It was expedient that they move ahead to rub out anyone who got in their way. It was expedient to bribe when it meant personal advantage. Steal, cheat, force— forge ahead always with number one in mind. It was expedient to hold the Sadducees' doctrine of no heaven, hell, angels, or resurrection. It was far more comfortable that way. And right at that moment it was expedient for them to get together—Pharisees and Sadducees—to discuss how to do away with Jesus.

Caiaphas had regarded Jesus with envy for a long time. He who left the crowds awestruck by his rich robes and retinue saw the populace turning to this young Galilean, and he grew extremely jealous. So when he announced the ultimate solution to the dilemma concerning this Man, he blindly acknowledged Jesus' very mission. But what a distortion! "One man should die," he declared! "On the lips of Caiaphas this most precious truth was turned into a lie. The policy he advocated was based on a principle borrowed from heathenism." [3] His policy was the sure result of the expedient choice.

---

[1] *SDA Bible Dictionary,* p. 171.
[2] *The SDA Bible Commentary,* Ellen G. White Comments, on Matt. 26:3, pp. 1100, 1101.
[3] *The Desire of Ages,* p. 540.

ONE CHOSE GRATITUDE

And one of them, when he saw that he was healed, turned back, and with a loud voice glorified God. Luke 17:15.

Jesus was making His final circuit that would bring Him back to Jerusalem. As He came to a village on the border between Galilee and Samaria, ten lepers accosted Him.[1] Undoubtedly from the rude little hut that they shared in the open field, they had spotted Jesus coming.[2] These ten lepers were far more careful than the leper who had rushed toward Jesus during the early part of His ministry. They stood at a safe distance, in keeping with the law.

"Master, have mercy on us!" they shouted.

And Jesus called back, "Go, show yourselves unto the priests."

It was enough. They had heard so many stories of how Jesus could heal that they knew He didn't actually have to touch them. Without looking back they hurried toward Jerusalem. It was while they had their backs to Jesus that the disease disappeared. We do not know who among them first discovered that the rough skin had become normal, but one by one they examined themselves. The miracle had transpired while they were on the move.

Nine kept right on going, but one, a Samaritan, was so touched by the miracle that he stopped short and turned back toward Jesus. He decided that before ever seeing any priest, he should thank Jesus for the wonderful miracle of healing. And he didn't just whisper his sense of gratitude. He glorified God "with a loud voice."

The choice to thank Jesus became a blessing to him. It would keep fresh the memory of the miracle.

Mournfully Jesus asked, "Were there not ten cleansed? but where are the nine?"[3]

The others had forgotten who had made them whole. Far too many today live like the nine ex-lepers in their tight circle of ingratitude. They never sense God's constant care for them. But it is our privilege to choose to be thankful. And like the grateful Samaritan, we should go back to Jesus after He answers our prayers and tell Him how much we appreciate His love.

---

[1] *The SDA Bible Commentary*, vol. 5, p. 838.
[2] *Ibid.*, p. 839.
[3] Luke 17:17.

THE SELFISH REQUEST

Whosoever will be great among you, let him be your minister; and whosoever will be chief among you, let him be your servant. Matt. 20:26, 27.

On His last trip to Jerusalem, Jesus privately told His disciples for the third time the details of forthcoming events. He would be betrayed to the chief priests and condemned to death. Then for the first time He told them specifically that the Jews would deliver Him to the Gentiles. He would be mocked and flogged and spit upon, then finally He would die a horrible death by crucifixion.[1] But on the third day He would rise again.

He included the explicit details, but the disciples were totally locked into the glory and grandeur of a kingdom in which they would sit on thrones and rule with power. Whatever Jesus told them about persecution or death seemed too vague and mysterious to sink into their minds.

In the request made by the mother of James and John immediately following Jesus' announcement of His upcoming trial, we catch the sharp contrast of Jesus' conception of His kingdom and that held by the disciples. With her boys by her side, she asked that James and John should sit one on the right hand and the other on the left in His new kingdom.

" 'You don't know what you are asking,' Jesus said to them. 'Can you drink the cup I am going to drink?'

" 'We can,' they answered.

"Jesus said to them, 'You will indeed drink from my cup, but to sit at my right or left is not for me to grant. These places belong to those for whom they have been prepared by my Father.' "[2]

It was a selfish request, an ambitious choice to be number one. As a result of this self-aggrandizing force, the other disciples became miffed when they heard about the request.

Jesus gave those words of our text for today in response to their irritation, because in His kingdom there are no favorites. Neither is there any way to earn credit or merit. Position is based solely on character.[3]

---

[1] *The SDA Bible Commentary,* vol. 5, pp. 464, 465.
[2] Matt. 20:22, 23, N.I.V.
[3] *The Desire of Ages,* p. 549.

THE LITTLE SWINDLER'S CHOICE
This day is salvation come to this house. Luke 19:9.

Living down in Jericho was a local publican who had hit the big time. Zacchaeus had become the chief superintendent of taxes, a commissioner who had grown wealthy from kickbacks, extortion, and injustice. He was a little man in stature, but a big-time operator with the full backing of the Romans. Yet his hardened, worldly-wise ways were really a veneer.

When the news that a publican like Levi-Matthew had been converted began to spread, this little swindler in Jericho began to stir.[1] He tried to retrace his steps, but even this brought only suspicion and distrust.

No wonder Zacchaeus wanted desperately to see Jesus. When he heard that the Saviour was coming to town he was ecstatic. But he couldn't see above or through the crowds no matter how hard he craned his neck. So running on ahead, he scrambled up a sycamore-fig tree. He just couldn't let the parade pass by without seeing Jesus. This rich tax collector made quite a sight sitting in all his finery on a limb, but from his leafy grandstand he hoped that he could get at least one peek.

But he enjoyed more than just a peek. Jesus stopped right under the tree and looked up. Imagine the thrill when he, Zacchaeus, heard that Jesus wanted to come to his house that day! This is the only record of Jesus' inviting Himself home for dinner![2] Zacchaeus slid down that tree and buoyantly escorted Jesus to his house.

The crowd's reaction was the same as it would undoubtedly be today. Jesus actually planned on dining in the home of a known crook!

But Zacchaeus didn't care. All he knew was that Jesus was there, and the unselfish choice he made that day confirmed his conversion. He would restore fourfold. The little swindler's choice was based on a love for Jesus that surmounts all obstacles and gives proof of true repentance.[3]

[1] *The Desire of Ages*, p. 553.
[2] *The SDA Bible Commentary*, vol. 5, p. 852.
[3] *The Desire of Ages*, p. 555.

MARY'S MEMORIAL

Verily I say unto you, Wheresoever this gospel shall be preached throughout the whole world, this also that she hath done shall be spoken of for a memorial of her. Mark 14:9.

Mary's decision to offer that expensive perfume to Jesus remains fragrant with love to this day!

It happened on a Saturday night in the spring of A.D. 31, six days before the Passover.[1] Simon the Pharisee, whom Jesus had healed of leprosy, had invited Jesus to a supper in His honor. Undoubtedly Simon had selected the best caterer in town, so Martha was there.

And Mary came too. She may have gotten somewhat in the way and she may not have been specifically invited, but she couldn't stay away when Jesus was near. Her heart overflowed with gratitude.

Sometime during the feast, the conversation swung around to the possibilities of Jesus' being crowned king. Mary was so eager to be first to honor Him that she made a quick, loving decision. Rushing home, she picked up something that she had been saving for a long time—an alabaster box made of soft light-gray translucent limestone. She had specifically bought an ointment of pure spikenard, a powerful perfume extracted from a Himalayan plant.[2] It represented almost a year's wages for an average person.

Rushing back to the banquet with her treasure, Mary broke open the box of ointment and poured the contents on Jesus' head and feet. Then kneeling, she wiped His feet with her beautiful long hair.

Nostrils dilated, and the party stopped. It was too much for Judas. His own selfishness simply could not tolerate such an act, and he triggered the murmuring against her, until Jesus halted the embarrassment for Mary. "Let her alone!" He demanded.

Then in His own lovely way He explained the profound meaning of her simple act. She was anointing His body for burial. He closed with an eloquent prophecy, predicting that Mary would walk down through the centuries with Him. Wherever His story would be told, hers would be also.

---

[1] *The Desire of Ages*, p. 557.
[2] *The SDA Bible Commentary*, vol. 5, p. 762.

SIMON'S CONVERSION

Wherefore I say unto thee, Her sins, which are many, are forgiven; for she loved much: but to whom little is forgiven, the same loveth little. Luke 7:47.

When Mary's perfume hung heavy in the room and she kept kissing Jesus' feet, Simon the host was totally exasperated. He sensed that his guests were wondering with distrust and displeasure why Jesus permitted this woman to behave in such a fashion.[1] The old pharisaical thinking pattern ran true to form.

If Jesus were really a prophet, he thought, he would know what kind of woman is touching Him, for she is a sinner.

Simon ought to know. He had seduced Mary into sin in the first place. But his proud heart only condemned Mary, and he felt that Jesus ought to repulse her on the spot.

Jesus knew Simon was a long way from understanding the love of God, so He related a little parable about two debtors. One owed ten times as much as the other, but when neither could pay, the lender canceled both debts.

" 'Which of them will love him more?' " Jesus asked.

" 'I suppose the one who had the bigger debt canceled,' " replied Simon.

" 'You have judged correctly,' Jesus said."[2]

Then He reminded Simon that since He had arrived at the banquet Mary had shown far more appreciation for what He had done for her than His host had. Simon, whose sins were much greater, had done little by comparison.

Suddenly Simon saw himself as he really was—a sinner who needed salvation. He felt grateful that Jesus had not exposed him, and for the first time he chose to accept Jesus as his Saviour. Before, he had accepted Jesus only as a miracle worker who had healed him of leprosy. Now he saw Him as more than just a prophet. He saw Him as one who could read his motives and yet extend forgiveness to him. "He saw the magnitude of the debt which he owed his Lord. His pride was humbled, he repented, and the proud Pharisee became a lowly, self-sacrificing disciple."[3]

---

[1] *The Desire of Ages*, p. 566.
[2] Luke 7:42, 43, N.I.V.
[3] *Ibid.*, p. 568.

THE REVENGEFUL DECISION

And Judas Iscariot, one of the twelve, went unto the chief priests, to betray him unto them. Mark 14:10.

The murmuring against Mary for spilling the precious perfume over Jesus started with Judas.[1] His nostrils dilated in disgust. Simon the host picked up on the criticism, along with the rest of the guests, and even the disciples whispered their disapproval of the extravagance.

"Why this waste?" Judas asked craftily. Then he suggested that Mary's expensive gift could have been sold and the proceeds given to the poor.

But all the fuss was merely a smoke screen to cover his own avarice. If the perfume had been sold, his own hand would have been in the bag pilfering the money. "Because," as John wrote later, "he was a thief, and had the bag."[2]

Mary's loving deed angered Judas. It made him, as treasurer, look bad personally. That Jesus should receive a gift suitable for a ruling monarch jarred loose all his jealous feelings.[3]

When Jesus glanced over at Judas, he knew that the Master read his perverted heart like an open book. That cut. Jesus openly ordered the whole group to leave her alone, explaining that her act was intended to anoint His body for the burial.[4] They would always have the poor with them, but they would not always have Him. Such words stung Judas to the quick.

The rebuke rankled Judas so much that he decided right there and then that when the party ended he would go see the authorities and strike up a bargain for betrayal.

There was more than money involved in this deal. He would betray Jesus for far less than Mary's expensive perfume had cost. Judas, like all those activated by Satan, could not accept any thought of real love or courtesy. And the startling fact remains that this dangerous attitude could still lurk among those who profess to be Christ's disciples.

---

[1] *The Desire of Ages*, p. 559.
[2] John 12:6.
[3] *Ibid.*, p. 564.
[4] *Ibid.*, p. 563.

WEEPING OVER JERUSALEM

And when he was come near, he beheld the city, and wept over it. Luke 19:41.

Jesus had less than two miles (three kilometers) to ride the colt for His royal entry into Jerusalem, but with all the palm-branch pageantry and the masses eager to proclaim Him the rightful King of Israel, the going was very slow.[1] By the time the procession reached the brow of the Mount of Olives it was late afternoon. Three hundred feet (ninety-one meters) below shone the pride of Jerusalem—the Temple. The sun was striking the gleaming white marble walls, and the gold-overlaid pillars illuminated the setting with a magnificence that could not help making the hearts of all those in that vast crowd swell with pride.[2] Their city! Their Temple! And to think they now had a King riding forth to set up His throne!

Looking to Jesus with expectancy, they hoped to hear from Him some wonderful words of admiration similar to what they felt. But the crowd was shocked when they heard Jesus wail aloud. Swaying back and forth on the donkey, Jesus wept with supreme agony.

The very sight of Jerusalem stabbed His heart with a piercing pain. He knew something that nobody else in that procession knew. Jerusalem was making her final choice! How Jesus longed to win this city! He had performed such great miracles within its walls and had given so many evidences that He had come to call it to repentance. Yet a stubborn pharisaical pride and hypocrisy blotted out every true picture of the loving heavenly Father whom He had tried to present. Jesus cried because He had exhausted every resource at His command to turn the hardhearted populace to Himself. And yet this city, the very one that should have been a light to the whole world, was fast closing its doors to God's mercy. Soon it would reap the whirlwind of disaster, because of its adamant choice. So Jesus wept.

But the sad fact remains that He still weeps. Not for the ancient city of Jerusalem, but for all His professed people who, like the Jews then, refuse Him access to their heart.

[1] *The SDA Bible Commentary,* vol. 5, p. 468.
[2] *Ibid.,* p. 469; *The Desire of Ages,* p. 575.

THE WITHERING CURSE

And when he saw a fig tree in the way, he came to it, and found nothing thereon, but leaves only, and said unto it, Let no fruit grow on thee henceforward for ever. And presently the fig tree withered away. Matt. 21:19.

Our text does not sound like a twenty-four-hour time span, but Jesus cursed the fig tree on Monday, and on Tuesday it was dead.[1] What the verse does reveal is the only miracle of Jesus that brought injury.

After spending a whole night in prayer at Bethany, Jesus and His disciples headed for the Temple.[2] As they passed a fig orchard they noticed one tree that looked remarkably advanced. This was late March or early April, and the time of the early crop of ripe figs was June.[3] Yet this one tree with its rich foliage gave evidence of an abundant crop. The greenery was most impressive, but when Jesus examined it He could not find one fig. And that was the moment He uttered His withering curse. No amount of watering, no generous supply of fertilizer, and no careful pruning would do a whit of good. The tree was doomed to die.

And it did. Peter remarked about it the next day. "Master, the tree You cursed is dead!"

The disciples crowded around in astonishment. The formerly lush-looking tree was dead from the roots up. It seemed such a strange act for Jesus, who always had been known to heal and restore. Why had He chosen to curse the tree?

"Jesus had come to the fig tree hungry, to find food. So He had come to Israel, hungering to find in them the fruits of righteousness."[4] Jesus chose to give this acted parable in order that His disciples could see the full results of the hypocrisy of the Jewish nation. And there was a warning for all professed Christians to the end of time. The curse against the fig tree still stands as a reminder of how hateful to God are promises without production.

---

[1] *The SDA Bible Commentary*, vol. 5, p. 644.
[2] *The Desire of Ages*, p. 581.
[3] *The SDA Bible Commentary*, vol. 5, p. 644.
[4] *The Desire of Ages*, p. 583.

RUNNING RULERS AND REJOICING

And Jesus saith unto them, Yea; have ye never read, Out of the mouth of babes and sucklings thou hast perfected praise? Matt. 21:16.

In the spring of A.D. 28, Jesus had announced His mission as Messiah by cleansing the Temple of its illicit traffic.[1] Three springs later He returned to the same spot and found the greedy money changers and cattle traders still in business within the Temple court. There was a painful silence as Jesus stood there with dignity and glory, His piercing eyes sweeping the whole irreverent scene. Then, in a voice that sounded like a trumpet blast, He ordered the whole business to stop.

At that precise moment the Temple rulers had to decide. Either they had to challenge His authority by ignoring the command, and stay and listen to Him preach, or flee. They quickly chose the latter. And it wasn't the pitter-patter of sandaled feet heard leaving, but men and beasts stampeding for the nearest exit.

They had so much to hide, yet they were the ones who had claimed that it would never happen again. Ashamed of their first hasty retreat, they were sure there would not be a recycling of such an event. But it was even worse this time. They were even more frightened of His penetrating gaze than before.

But not all the people fled. Those who needed Jesus' help pressed their way against the tide, seeking Him who was their only hope.[2] And the children came too. Soon the sounds ringing through the Temple court were those of rejoicing.

When the rulers finally got up enough nerve to return, the happy sounds of children crowding around Jesus and the voices of others shouting His praise met their ears. It was too much for these bigots, and they told Jesus to order the commotion stopped immediately. Today's text gives Jesus' answer. If the children had ceased their glad sounds, the very pillars of the Temple would have cried out.

---

[1] *The SDA Bible Commentary*, vol. 5, pp. 471, 923.
[2] *The Desire of Ages*, p. 592.

HYPOCRITES PROFESSING IGNORANCE

And Jesus answered and said unto them, I will also ask of you one question, and answer me, and I will tell you by what authority I do these things. The baptism of John, was it from heaven, or of men? answer me. Mark 11:29, 30.

The Sanhedrin had all the evidence that Jesus was the Messiah, yet they refused to accept Him.[1] The morning after Jesus had cleansed the Temple for the second time, the high priest and his retinue came to Him, hoping that He would say something they could twist to His condemnation. "By what authority do You do these things?" they asked.

Using the accepted rabbinical practice of answering a question by propounding another, Jesus again revealed His divinity.[2] His question was too quick and too well thought out. The baptism of John, was it of Heaven or of men? If they said from Heaven, He would surely ask why they had not accepted Him, because John had pointed to Jesus as the true Messiah. If they answered that John's baptism was of men, the people would stone them on the spot, because the populace believed that John was a true prophet.

Suddenly things weren't turning out as they had planned in committee. They huddled in a quick ad hoc meeting and whispered their concern. It didn't take much low, agitated mumbling to realize that Jesus had them backed into a corner. Sweat formed on their brows. It was so embarrassing, because the gathering crowd was on tiptoe, waiting expectantly for their answer. And Jesus waited too. They had to decide.

Gulping, they gave their answer: "We cannot tell."[3]

What a hypocritical decision! What did they mean, they couldn't tell? Publicly they had professed to accept the ministry of John, and now they waffled.

"By their cowardice and indecision they had in a great measure forfeited the respect of the people, who now stood by, amused to see these proud, self-righteous men defeated."[4] When people avoid facing the issues of God, they invariably make fools of themselves.

---

[1] *The Desire of Ages,* p. 593.
[2] *The SDA Bible Commentary,* vol. 5, p. 473.
[3] Mark 11:33.
[4] *The Desire of Ages,* p. 594.

ERROR OF THE SADDUCEES

Jesus answered and said unto them, Ye do err, not knowing the scriptures, nor the power of God. For in the resurrection they neither marry, nor are given in marriage, but are as the angels of God in heaven. Matt. 22:29, 30.

The Sadducees had made God in their own image, and that image had shaped their character. While they believed that God was the Creator, they thought He showed little interest in His creation. Thus it was no great secret why they had little regard for one another. They could not accept the idea that the Holy Spirit worked on human lives, because this would interfere with their freedom to control events. That Jesus spoke of God's power to transform lives and of a future life ran counter to their philosophy.

Since the Sadducees considered themselves to be the real intellectuals who could easily discredit the straitlaced Pharisees, it seemed to them an easy matter to bring Jesus into disrepute.[1] They brought out one of their old stock questions on the resurrection, which had stumped the Pharisees so many times. It seemed logical to them that a resurrected body would have to be composed of the same matter as before, and thus that life would go on the same.

Jesus swept this all aside, showing them that their whole premise was false. He did not charge them with hypocrisy as He had the Pharisees, but simply told them that they were off base in their belief.[2] They had forgotten the power of God. Choosing a lesser god who would fit neatly into the scheme of their thinking, they went astray in their religion.

The Sadducees among us are still making a similar choice. Because they cannot understand the mysteries of God, they cling tenaciously to their materialistic ideas and unbelief. "They cannot explain the wonderful exhibition of divine power in His providences, therefore they reject the evidences of such power, attributing them to natural agencies which they can comprehend still less."[3] Their only safety is in accepting God's power.

---

[1] *The SDA Bible Commentary*, vol. 5, p. 482.
[2] *The Desire of Ages*, p. 605.
[3] *Ibid.*, p. 606.

THE HONEST SCRIBE

Jesus said unto him, Thou shalt love the Lord thy God with all thy heart, and with all thy soul, and with all thy mind. This is the first and great commandment. And the second is like unto it, Thou shalt love thy neighbour as thyself. Matt. 22:37-39.

We are never told his name, only his trade. He was a lawyer, or scribe—one versed in the Law of Moses and the traditional law of the various rabbinical schools.[1] The Pharisees had sent him to question Jesus, with the hope that He would commit Himself on which of the Ten Commandments had the greatest importance.

Without hesitation Jesus gave our scripture for today, and concluded His forceful summary by saying, "On these two commandments hang all the law and the prophets."[2] Jesus made it clear that only as we love God with all our heart is it possible to love our neighbors as ourselves.[3]

Instantly the scribe recognized that Jesus had spoken the truth. He saw that Jesus had a full understanding of the law and grasped the depths of its meaning. He felt convicted to acknowledge that fact and decided that such profound and thorough knowledge of the Scriptures should be publicly recognized. "Well, master, you have said the truth," the scribe declared.

Jesus was deeply touched by the scribe's readiness to speak his deep convictions despite the scowls and frowns from his colleagues. " 'You are not far from the kingdom of God,' "[4] Jesus said.

This scribe had recognized that doing righteous deeds was more acceptable than burnt offerings and sacrifices, but he had one more step to take, and that was to recognize Jesus as the divine Son of God, who could give him the power to keep those commandments.[5] Jesus knew that this honest scribe had almost reached that point. If he could choose to ignore the anger of his peers he could go the rest of the way and accept the Saviour. How often is someone so close to accepting Jesus but still needs that full commitment!

---

[1] *SDA Bible Dictionary*, pp. 662, 989.
[2] Matt. 22:40.
[3] *The Desire of Ages*, p. 607.
[4] Mark 12:34, N.I.V.
[5] *Ibid.*, p. 608.

THE WIDOW'S CHOICE

Verily I say unto you, That this poor widow hath cast more in, than all they which have cast into the treasury. Mark 12:43.

It was late Tuesday afternoon of the Passion Week.[1] Jesus had just finished a long and bitter confrontation with the religious leaders. He was about to leave the Temple courts forever when His face lighted up with joy. It wasn't that He had just emerged victorious over the rulers, but that He had seen an act that sharply contrasted with the ostentatious behavior of the wealthy.

A poor widow had hesitantly approached the collection box in the Temple court and had dropped in two mites, the smallest Jewish copper coins in circulation. The richly robed upper class had swept by with superfluous fanfare, announcing some great clanking contribution that had not deprived them of any comfort or even luxury. Their donations made a dull thud to the Saviour, but He knew that the widow's two mites made all heaven ring. Jesus had to commend her publicly because she had given all she had. Tears welled up in her eyes as she heard His words, for she realized that Someone understood and appreciated.[2]

This widow had chosen to give all that she had, not for any reward but out of her love to God. Her decision to give, in spite of the priests who grew fat on a system that entrenched them in greed, still sparkles. She gave to the cause she loved because she believed in her heavenly Father. Whatever the corrupt practices of the priests, she let the Lord take care of that, because she had determined to give her gift to God alone. Those two mites would undoubtedly get lost in the shuffle when the great coins were counted, but her motive was so superior that Heaven never even weighed the rest.

Jesus had just condemned the practice of those who would "devour widows' houses,"[3] and this widow's deed shone like a beacon. He had to give His commendation of a lasting memorial. "It is the motive that gives character to our acts, stamping them with ignominy or with high moral worth."[4]

---

[1] *The SDA Bible Commentary*, vol. 5, p. 648.
[2] *The Desire of Ages*, p. 615.
[3] Mark 12:40.
[4] *Ibid.*

THE GREEK REQUEST

And there were certain Greeks among them that came up to worship at the feast: the same came therefore to Philip, . . . saying, Sir, we would see Jesus. John 12:20, 21.

It was obvious to the disciples that, even though Jesus had won a dramatic victory over the religious rulers, the fact still remained that these same rulers were never going to accept Him as the Messiah.[1] It seemed to be such a devastating defeat.

But before Jesus left the Temple for the last time, the disciples were to catch a glimpse into the future concerning the truth about the gospel to the Gentiles. Some visiting Greeks from the West, like the Magi from the East at the time of Jesus' birth, requested to see Jesus. Somewhere out there in the court of the Gentiles they found Philip, who had a Greek name, and through him sent their request for a personal interview.[2] Philip couldn't make a decision without consulting his friend Andrew, and the two finally told Jesus.

These Greeks, after hearing the report of Jesus' triumphal entry and His cleansing of the Temple, decided that they must see Him and learn more about His mission. Their choice of a personal interview was granted, and when Jesus saw them He gave a short parable about the grain of wheat that dies in the soil so that a whole harvest is multiplied.

But after He gave this account His humanity recoiled from the forthcoming death on the cross. His heart was troubled, and He prayed while the Greeks listened, ''Father, save me from this hour: but for this cause came I unto this hour. Father, glorify thy name.''[3]

Like the rolling thunder, back came a voice from heaven: ''I have both glorified it, and will glorify it again.''[4]

Some thought it thundered, while others believed that an angel had spoken. But the Greeks heard the message and comprehended its meaning. Those who choose to seek Jesus with their whole heart will ever be alert to Heaven's communication.[5]

---

[1] *The Desire of Ages*, p. 621.
[2] *The SDA Bible Commentary*, vol. 5, p. 1022.
[3] John 12:27, 28.
[4] Verse 28.
[5] *The Desire of Ages*, p. 625.

DECISION OF DISCORD

And there was also a strife among them, which of them should be accounted the greatest. Luke 22:24.

All the other Passover suppers had been very special for the disciples.[1] They had enjoyed the calm, quiet joy of being with Jesus during the annual feast. But on Thursday night of Passion Week they turned this ceremonial meal into a bitter internal battle of who would be the top person in the new kingdom.[2]

In spite of Christ's constant counsel regarding the nature of His kingdom, they carried on this running feud behind His back. Their combative spirit, swept along with their misconception of the whole kingdom, created this continual strife. And on the night of the Last Supper, the discordant undercurrent broke out right in front of Jesus. Their body language and the ugly glances they shot at each other across the room signaled the sad results of their discord. They chose to keep alive the hope that each one of them personally would be the greatest. Each thought his talents needed to be appreciated and used to the fullest extent as a VIP.

To add to the dissension was the fact that no servant was present to do the customary foot washing. Not one disciple budged. The task would be considered too menial and demeaning, and whoever performed it would serve notice that he had accepted a lower position.

Jesus waited patiently to see what His disciples would do. The silence was painful. Each man sat there grim, square-jawed, and determined to remain frozen in place.

Finally Jesus rose. Taking off His outer garment, and wrapping the towel around His waist, He began washing the disciples' feet. "This action opened the eyes of the disciples. Bitter shame and humiliation filled their hearts. They understood the unspoken rebuke, and saw themselves in altogether a new light."[3]

When we see Jesus as the servant of servants, we will respond as did those early disciples. The sad choice of arguing over who is to get the credit will vanish when Jesus' love is kept alive.

---

[1] *The Desire of Ages*, p. 642.
[2] *The SDA Bible Commentary*, vol. 5, p. 1027.
[3] *The Desire of Ages*, p. 644.

WILLING TO BE CHANGED

Now there was leaning on Jesus' bosom one of his disciples, whom Jesus loved. John 13:23.

John classifies himself as "the disciple whom Jesus loved." [1] He was the youngest of the twelve and by far the most affectionate. He loved to be as close to Jesus as possible. But with John it was more than mere human friendship. He saw Jesus as his Saviour and could not restrain his feelings. And he was the one disciple who most reflected the life of Christ.

But when John first met Jesus he owned some very serious defects. The lovely characteristics we behold later didn't come naturally. His early profile had an accumulated list on the minus side. He was proud, peevish, self-assertive, ambitious for recognition, impetuous, combative with a short fuse, and to top the list, he carried with him the spirit of criticism. He and his brother James may have legally been the sons of Zebedee, but their explosive characters earned them the nickname "sons of thunder." [2]

Jesus looks at each of us on the basis of our tremendous potential if our humanity is linked with His divinity. Beneath the hotheaded, blustering ill temper, Jesus saw something in John. He "discerned the ardent, sincere, loving heart." [3]

Often we feel like giving up. The old "I can't make it, so why try?" syndrome settles in, and we slump lower on the scale. We need to remember that everything depends on the right action of the will.

"John and Judas are representatives of those who profess to be Christ's followers. Both these disciples had the same opportunities to study and follow the divine Pattern. Both were closely associated with Jesus and were privileged to listen to His teaching. Each possessed serious defects of character; and each had access to the divine grace that transforms character." [4] But John's affectionate choice kept him from resisting the molding influence of the Holy Spirit. He chose to accept correction again and again. The transformation in his life came about because he was willing for it to happen.

---

[1] John 21:20.
[2] Mark 3:17.
[3] *The Acts of the Apostles*, p. 540.
[4] *Ibid.*, p. 558.

THE CHOICE OF NIGHT

And when he had dipped the sop, he gave it to Judas Iscariot, the son of Simon. And after the sop Satan entered into him. . . . He then having received the sop went immediately out: and it was night. John 13:26-30.

The case of Judas needs careful study because upon closer examination we just might discover the potential of evil within ourselves. "Judas was constantly planning to benefit self. In this he represents a large class of professed Christians of today." [1]

Yet of all the disciples, Judas was the one most likely to succeed. He had a commanding personality and polish. He was the only one not from Galilee.[2] It was like having an Ivy League man on the team. If you were going to select someone to build a public-relations image for Jesus, you would probably choose Judas. He could say the right things to the right people and pull a few strings to get results. Undoubtedly he had a way with people, a distinct brand of friendliness. The disciples held a high opinion of him and right up to the last moment never suspected him.

But the problem was that Judas never quite came to the point of total commitment to Christ. He had too high an opinion of his own qualifications for that. He would use the methods borrowed from the world even if they countered Christ's ways.

In the upper room when Jesus washed his feet, Judas almost repented; but he didn't.[3] The old feelings of worldly honor returned, and he shook off the notion of confession. Jesus could not be the king of Israel if He would stoop to this level.

When Jesus handed him the sop as evidence that He knew that Judas was the one who would betray Him, he made a grim choice. The record tells us that he went out, "and it was night." The curtain dropped for Judas. The one who had all that accumulated talent, the one who had participated with the others in miracles, healings, and exorcisms, who knew the power of Christ, ended up as a suicide case, because he simply would not allow the miracle of Christ's transforming power to work in his own heart.[4]

---

[1] *Testimonies*, vol. 6, p. 264.
[2] *SDA Bible Dictionary*, p. 629.
[3] *The Desire of Ages*, p. 645.
[4] *Ibid.*, p. 717.

SLEEPING IN GETHSEMANE

And he came and found them asleep again: for their eyes were heavy. Matt. 26:43.

Jesus and His disciples often used Gethsemane as a quiet retreat for prayer and rest. But on the night of Jesus' great decision and betrayal it became far more than a garden of prayer. It was a battleground—a place where the whole world's destiny hung in the balance.

The disciples sensed that something was wrong. They had never seen Jesus behave in such a sad and silent fashion. It wasn't like Him at all. It was an effort for Jesus to take even one step. Twice He staggered and nearly fell.[1]

Leaving all but Peter, James, and John at the entrance, Jesus slowly made His way into the quiet recesses of the garden. He especially wanted these three to be near Him. And they, of all people, should have caught Jesus' human longing for sympathy in suffering. He made such a simple request: "Watch with me."[2]

The three did watch for a while, but a head-nodding drowsiness overtook them. And at this point they each had to make a decision. They either would yield to the heavy-eyelid feeling or would resist it by God's power and pray with Jesus during this crisis. Jesus had warned them to watch and pray lest they enter into temptation. The temptation was to fall asleep at the moment of Jesus' greatest need. They would have stayed awake had they realized the need, yet they could have realized it. The problem was self-sufficiency. The stupor would have left them if they had really tried to shake it off. And they could have been such a support to Jesus. "But the disciples trusted to themselves. They did not look to the mighty Helper as Christ had counseled them to do. Thus when the Saviour was most in need of their sympathy and prayers, they were found asleep."[3]

It was a tragic choice, yet professed disciples are often spiritually lethargic because they trust to their own efforts.

---

[1] *The Desire of Ages,* p. 686.
[2] Matt. 26:38.
[3] *Ibid.,* pp. 688, 689.

PETER'S SWORD-SWINGING DECISION

Then said Jesus unto him, Put up again thy sword into his place: for all they that take the sword shall perish with the sword. Matt. 26:52.

Earlier in the evening Peter had vowed his allegiance to Jesus. "I will lay down my life for thy sake"! he had exclaimed.[1]

No one for a moment doubted Peter's sincerity. But Peter had a habit of spewing off exclamations without much thought. He didn't really know himself. He, along with the other disciples, fell asleep when Jesus needed him most. He even went back to sleep after the angel had come down to strengthen Jesus. Not even the brilliant light of heaven and the form of the angel holding Jesus was enough to rouse him thoroughly.[2]

But suddenly Peter and the others were wide awake. The mob was upon them, surrounding Jesus with swords and staves as if they were out night-hunting some wild beast. Action! There was plenty of it on hand right then. No sleepy time now. At that moment Peter made one of his rash choices. He would show the garden intruders who was boss. Whipping out his trusty sword, he fully intended to give the first comer a taste of his old fisherman's zeal. Since Malchus, the servant of the high priest, was closest, he caught the violence of Peter's wrath. He could well have been decapitated, but Peter's wild swing only lopped off an ear. One moment Malchus had an ear, and the next moment it was gone.

Even though Jesus was tightly bound, He pulled His hands loose and immediately healed the ear.[3] Then turning to Peter, He spoke the words of today's text. Put the sword up, Peter. This is not how it is done. Jesus reminded him that His heavenly Father could send whole armies of angels if need be. Peter's notion of using violence to further God's cause was based on worldly ideas. They who take up the sword will die by the sword. God's kingdom operates entirely on the principle of peace.

---

[1] John 13:37.
[2] *The Desire of Ages*, p. 694.
[3] *Ibid.*, p. 696.

CAIAPHAS UNDER CONVICTION

Nevertheless I say unto you, Hereafter shall ye see the Son of man sitting on the right hand of power, and coming in the clouds of heaven. Matt. 26:64.

They had faced off earlier in the week in the Temple. But now the scene had shifted. Caiaphas was seated on his throne. His silver hair and beard, highlighted by the flickering torchlights, added to his commanding appearance.[1] Before him stood Jesus, bound like some common criminal. Caiaphas needed a condemnation. And despite the fact that the night session of the Sanhedrin was illegal, he was determined to get it.[2]

But trotting out false witnesses who couldn't agree with their own testimony didn't start things right. Finally in desperation two witnesses were called who mistook Christ's words about raising up the Temple in three days. But the rulers knew that even this wasn't enough evidence for the Romans to issue a death warrant.

Things were going from bad to worse. Caiaphas was in an angry sweat. Something had to be done, and done quickly. Raising his right hand, he turned to Jesus. " 'I charge you under oath by the living God: Tell us if you are the Christ, the Son of God.' "[3]

Now it was time for Jesus to speak. "Weighted with such great results, it was to Christ one of the most wonderful moments of His life."[4] Publicly He declared Himself one with God, and then He quickly reminded Caiaphas that the next time they met He would be coming in the clouds of heaven. The very thought of a resurrection and judgment sent shock waves quivering through the high priest.

When Caiaphas regained his composure he chose to go through the motions of mock horror.[5] Taking a firm grip on his rich robe, he tore it as a public display against blasphemy. The decision to rend his robe, however, should have cost him his life, because according to the Levitical law, no high priest was ever to do this.[6] But when anyone rebels under such deep conviction, his anger thrusts him headlong into rash acts.

---

[1] *The Desire of Ages,* p. 594.
[2] *The SDA Bible Commentary,* vol. 5, p. 538.
[3] Matt. 26:63, N.I.V.
[4] *Ibid.,* Ellen G. White Comments, on Matt. 26:63, 64, p. 1104.
[5] *The Desire of Ages,* p. 708.
[6] *The SDA Bible Commentary,* vol. 5, p. 531.

PETER'S CHOICES

And Peter called to mind the word that Jesus said unto him, Before the cock crow twice, thou shalt deny me thrice. And when he thought thereon, he wept. Mark 14:72.

Peter had set himself up for temptation. If he had chosen to watch and pray in the garden he would not have fallen into sin in the judgment hall courtyard.[1]

When Peter entered the judgment hall he was pretending. It was a faulty choice, because now in his assumed role of careless bystander he invited Satan to tempt him. Suddenly as he huddled over the fire, the woman who kept the gate spotted him. She could not suppress her curiosity. "Aren't you one of this man's disciples?" she asked.

Peter's head jerked up. The sudden query startled and confused him. At first he acted as though he didn't understand, but the woman persisted.

Angrily Peter answered, " 'Woman, I don't know him.' "[2] And immediately the rooster crowed for the first time.

By associating with those who didn't love Jesus and picking up their rude jesting, he had hoped to conceal his real identity. He signaled Satan to be on hand. Again someone suggested that Peter was one of Jesus' disciples, and again Peter denied it.[3] Finally one of Malchus' relatives, whose ear Peter had lopped off, squinted. "Didn't I see you in the garden?" he asked. "Surely you are one of them, for you have that Galilean speech."

And with that Peter made an immediate choice. He reverted to his old fisherman's language and swore to cover his identity. Again the rooster crowed.

At that precise moment Jesus turned from those angry judges and faced His disciple. When their eyes met, something happened to Peter. He could not bear to face those sad, pitying eyes of Jesus, and his decision was made. With tears streaming down his face he stumbled back to Gethsemane and prayed earnestly. If he had done this first he would not have sinned.[4]

[1] *The Desire of Ages*, pp. 713, 714.
[2] Luke 22:57, N.I.V.
[3] *Ibid.*, p. 712.
[4] *Ibid.*, p. 713.

THE SUICIDE DECISION

And he cast down the pieces of silver in the temple, and departed, and went and hanged himself. Matt. 27:5.

Toward the last part of the Sanhedrin's day trial of Christ there was a sudden interruption that caused terrifying panic for the priests.[1] A hoarse voice shouted from the rear as the only witness to testify for Jesus' innocence. "He is innocent; spare Him, O Caiaphas!"[2]

It took no guesswork to realize whose voice it was. Judas, who stood head and shoulders above the rest, pressed his anxious way from the rear of the judgment hall and strode right to the throne. Taking the thirty pieces of silver, he threw them down with a vengeance in front of Caiaphas. Then grabbing the high priest's robe, he begged that Jesus be released immediately. It all happened so quickly! Suddenly Caiaphas and his colleagues found themselves in a very sticky situation. Obviously they had broken the law of Moses by bribing Judas.[3]

" 'I have sinned,' " Judas cried, " 'in betraying innocent blood.' "[4]

Caiaphas flushed and gulped. His mandibles moved, but nothing came out. How frightfully embarrassing. Finally gaining his self-possession, he jerked loose from Judas. "What is that to us?" Caiaphas asked with a sneer. "That's your business!"

Judas whirled around and rushed from the judgment hall. Yes, he knew he had one more piece of business to attend to. He had made his last choice—suicide. That terrible decision to take his own life came because he had reached the outer limits of endurance of a guilty conscience. Yet he did not repent in the sense of being sorry for his great sin. His confession was wrenched from a heart terrified by the awful sense of guilt and forthcoming judgment.[5] Nothing about Judas had changed. His mangled body, which had fallen for the wild dogs to devour, gave mute but horrible warning to those who would tenaciously cling to their selfishness.

---

[1] *The SDA Bible Commentary,* vol. 5, p. 543.
[2] *The Desire of Ages,* p. 721.
[3] *The SDA Bible Commentary,* vol. 5, p. 543.
[4] Matt. 27:4, R.S.V.
[5] *The Desire of Ages,* p. 722.

THE VACILLATING GOVERNOR

And so Pilate, willing to content the people, released Barabbas unto them, and delivered Jesus, when he had scourged him, to be crucified. Mark 15:15.

The text reveals Pilate's basic weakness. He was willing to placate the people rather than to make a firm decision for right. He longed to deliver Jesus, but he chose to sacrifice his integrity and honesty in the vain hope that he could retain his high position with the Roman government.

From the moment the Jews brought Jesus to Pilate for ratification of the death sentence, the governor had tried his best to avoid handling the case. At first he urged the Jewish leaders to take care of Jesus themselves, but he soon saw that they thirsted for blood.[1] Next he tried passing the case off to Herod, but this didn't work either. The long-standing animosity between him and Herod was healed, but Jesus was brought back to his jurisdiction. He tried to release Jesus as the pardoned Passover prisoner, but the Jews clamored for Barabbas instead. Finally Pilate had Jesus scourged, hoping this would placate the mob. But in answer to this came the cry "Crucify Him!"

In desperation Pilate had a basin of water brought so that he could symbolically wash his hands as evidence of his innocence in the case. But it didn't work. His guilt remained. Pilate had made his choice. He had ignored his wife's desperate warning to avoid condemning Jesus and had repeatedly shown his flawed character to the Jews. They knew that if they kept pressing, Pilate would at last yield. The vacillating governor would rather sacrifice an innocent life than lose what was so dear to him. And in the end he lost everything. "His honors were stripped from him, he was cast down from his high office, and, stung by remorse and wounded pride, not long after the crucifixion he ended his own life. So all who compromise with sin will gain only sorrow and ruin."[2]

[1] *The SDA Bible Commentary,* pp. 545, 546.
[2] *The Desire of Ages,* p. 738.

CHOOSING SATAN AS LEADER

Will ye therefore that I release unto you the King of the Jews? Then cried they all again, saying, Not this man, but Barabbas. Now Barabbas was a robber. John 18:39, 40.

It was a choice that would haunt the Jewish leaders to their dying day. They were so determined to see Christ crucified that they willingly accepted Barabbas, the criminal, rather than Him. "In making this choice they accepted him who from the beginning was a liar and a murderer. Satan was their leader. As a nation they would act out his dictation. His works they would do. His rule they must endure." [1]

Knowing that Pilate was already under suspicion by the Roman government and could be recalled at any time, the Jews used a hypocritical appeal to the rule of Caesar to tap onto the governor's weak point. [2] "Whosoever maketh himself a king speaketh against Caesar," they cried. [3]

"Shall I crucify your King?" Pilate asked. [4]

Compounding their first decision for Barabbas, they little thought what they were shouting. But back came the blasphemous answer from the chief priests, "We have no king but Caesar"!

They really were not ready to give up their hope of a Messiah, but they hated Jesus so much that they were willing to reject God as their king. Now they had no deliverer. Caiaphas and his whole council had brought the nation to this terrible sin and to this dark ruin. [5]

Finally on that Friday morning they cried, "His blood be on us, and on our children." [6]

Heaven recorded that request and allowed it to be granted. From the days of the destruction of Jerusalem down through the long centuries, the Jews have suffered. [7]

[1] *The Desire of Ages*, p. 739.
[2] *Ibid.*, p. 737.
[3] John 19:12.
[4] Verse 15.
[5] *Ibid.*, p. 738.
[6] Matt. 27:25.
[7] *Ibid.*, p. 739.

December 2

THE ELEVENTH-HOUR DECISION

And he said unto Jesus, Lord, remember me when thou comest into thy kingdom. Luke 23:42.

At first both of the thieves who were crucified with Christ hurled insults at Him. One of the hardened criminals seemed to sum up their attitude when he sneered, " 'Aren't you the Christ? Save yourself and us!' " [1]

But as the excruciating minutes ticked away and time dragged painfully forward, the other thief began to piece things together. He was not the desperate and defiant criminal that his companion was. In fact, he had actually seen and heard Jesus teaching, and he had felt the tug to become a disciple.[2] He would have, too, except for the priests and rulers. But his conscience kept bothering him. And like so many with a bad case of guilt, he went over the brink into worse sins until finally, carried along in crime, he was arrested and sentenced to die. But now things began to fall into place. The judgment hall scene, the attempt by Pilate to release Jesus, the words of those along the agonizing way to Golgotha—it all fit into a pattern.

He and his companion in crime were about to close their careers for good. There was nothing more to fear from any human. With the wrenching pain bearing down on him and the sense that it soon would all be over, he rebuked the other thief.

" 'Don't you fear God,' he said, 'since you are under the same sentence? We are punished justly, for we are getting what our deeds deserve. But this man has done nothing wrong.' " [3]

Now was the moment to decide. Even with the wrenching pain, he turned to Jesus and called Him Lord. He knew he needed the Saviour. And in those pathetic and touching tones he said, "Remember me."

Jesus sensed that the dying thief had made his choice for time and eternity. He might not understand all there was to know about His kingdom, but Jesus promised him a place in paradise at the resurrection.[4]

[1] Luke 23:39, N.I.V.
[2] *The Desire of Ages*, p. 749.
[3] Verses 40, 41, N.I.V.
[4] *The SDA Bible Commentary*, vol. 5, pp. 877, 878.

DECISION OF TWO INFLUENTIAL MEN

Joseph of Arimathaea, being a disciple of Jesus, but secretly for fear of the Jews, besought Pilate that he might take away the body of Jesus. . . . And there came also Nicodemus, which at the first came to Jesus by night. John 19:38, 39.

Both Joseph of Arimathea and Nicodemus were members of the Sanhedrin, and they had successfully thwarted earlier plans to kill Christ.[1] They had not accepted Him openly, fearing that they would be excluded from the council. But when the final moment arrived, the slippery priests who had schemed the execution made sure these two members of the Sanhedrin were absent.[2]

But on that Friday afternoon, these two influential men stepped forward to take their stand as disciples of Jesus. While the rest of the disciples were cowering like frightened sheep, these wealthy and powerful leaders openly declared their decision to become full-fledged followers of the Saviour.

We catch the impact of their decision when Joseph appeared boldly before Pilate and requested the body of Jesus. Ordinarily a traitor to Rome would be given a dishonorable burial in some field reserved for the worst criminals. But Joseph didn't care whether Rome had stamped its approval on the execution of Jesus, or that the highest Jewish council had branded Him a blasphemer.[3] He wanted the Master to have a decent burial and he was willing to provide his own tomb. He approached Pilate while his colleague Nicodemus went into the city to purchase, at considerable cost, about seventy-two pounds (thirty-three kilograms) of spices for burial.[4]

The other disciples could not conceive what to do next. But what had shattered them only confirmed these wealthy and cultured men. "The very event that destroyed the hopes of the disciples convinced Joseph and Nicodemus of the divinity of Jesus. Their fears were overcome by the courage of a firm and unwavering faith."[5]

[1] *The Desire of Ages,* p. 539.
[2] *Ibid.,* p. 773.
[3] *The SDA Bible Commentary,* vol. 5, p. 551.
[4] *Ibid.,* p. 1064.
[5] *The Desire of Ages,* pp. 775, 776.

ACCEPTING THE BIG BRIBE

And when they were assembled with the elders, and had taken counsel, they gave large money unto the soldiers, saying, Say ye, His disciples came by night, and stole him away while we slept. Matt. 28:12, 13.

Under the blinding brilliance of God's angel who appeared to call Jesus as the glorified Christ from the tomb, the Roman guards around the sepulchre collapsed as if dead. But once they regained their senses they staggered back to Jerusalem with the greatest single news report ever uttered by humans. Pointing back toward the empty tomb, they babbled their story to everyone they met. The soldiers intended to tell Pilate, but the chief priests and rulers called for them first.[1] Flushed with the exciting news, they told just what had happened. They didn't delete or alter a single line.

The hastily assembled members of the Sanhedrin suddenly looked as ashen as if they needed embalming. Caiaphas finally found his voice as the soldiers were leaving. "Wait, wait"! he croaked. "Tell no one the things you have seen."[2]

The Jewish rulers fumbled for money. No need of any special session of the bribery committee. The main point was to get the soldiers back out on the streets with the concocted story that the disciples had stolen the body.

The soldiers could not believe what they were hearing. If they had been asleep on duty, how would they have known that the disciples had stolen the body? And if it really were the disciples who had done the grave robbing, the priests would be the loudest to scream and report the incident to Pilate.[3] But the rulers assured the sentinels that they would bribe the governor, too. So right there the soldiers had to make a decision. In the end the flash of cash had too much of a magnetic pull, and they chose to leave with a lying report. All accepted bribes carry with them a built-in uneasiness, and this one would haunt the Romans to their grave.

---

[1] *The Desire of Ages*, p. 781.
[2] *Ibid.*, p. 781.
[3] *Ibid.*, p. 782.

WHEN SO MUCH HINGED ON HOSPITALITY

And he made as though he would have gone further. But they constrained him, saying, Abide with us: for it is toward evening, and the day is far spent. Luke 24:28, 29.

Cleopas and his companion hadn't even noticed when the Stranger joined them en route to Emmaus. They were so absorbed in their own gloom over the events of the weekend that He slipped up on them. Jesus, whom they had hoped would deliver Israel, had been crucified!

Jesus could have dried their tears immediately by revealing Himself, but first He wanted to impress on their minds the great prophecies that pointed to Himself. The best place, of course, to begin was with the writings of Moses, and then work right through the Old Testament. As they walked those eight miles (thirteen kilometers) from Jerusalem their sadness gradually gave way to hope as this Stranger opened to them the Scriptures.[1] Sometimes as they looked intently at Him they couldn't help thinking how His words sounded so much like the ones Jesus would have used. But it never occurred to them that He was walking right beside them.[2]

By the time they arrived home the sun had set. And there in the twilight the precious moment had come. But when the Stranger appeared to head on down the road, they made their decision. Their choice to urge Him to stay with them that evening made all the difference. For when He spread His hands out to bless the simple meal, they recognized Him!

Jesus never actually ate the bread that evening, because He vanished from their sight. But He left them a lesson that none should ever forget. Had they chosen to wave goodbye and not press Him to stay, they would never have known that He was their risen Saviour.

"Christ never forces His company on anyone. He interests Himself in those who need Him. Gladly will He enter the humblest home, and cheer the lowliest heart. But if men are too indifferent to think of the heavenly Guest, or ask Him to abide with them, He passes on."[3]

---

[1] *The Desire of Ages*, pp. 795, 796.
[2] *Ibid.*, p. 796.
[3] *Ibid.*, p. 800.

THOMAS' DECISION TO DOUBT

Except I shall see in his hands the print of the nails, and put my finger into the print of the nails, and thrust my hand into his side, I will not believe. John 20:25.

Now that is a most unreasonable condition for faith! If all chose to make this their criterion of acceptance, only a few hundred disciples who had seen Jesus would ever have existed.[1]

But there were reasons why Thomas chose to doubt. Whenever we hear such unbelief expressed, it is good to probe deeper for the real reasons.

In the case of Thomas, he happened to have been absent when Jesus appeared to the other disciples in the upper room. When he heard the exciting report that Jesus had risen from the grave, it was too much for him. It wrecked his theory of a literal kingdom.[2] If Jesus had been resurrected there was no hope of ever having a place in power.

And second to this pride-filled thought came the vain notion elbowing its way forward, Why hadn't Jesus appeared to him, anyway? If He came to Mary, then to Simon Peter, then to Cleopas and his companion, and then to all the rest in the upper room, why had he been left out? It got to him. So he sulked. And in his sullen mood he gathered all the dark doubts that he could wrap around his wounded pride. It was a tragic decision, because he refused to look through the eyes of his colleagues or to listen to reason. For a whole week he made himself miserable. All the excitement of the grand resurrection event only confirmed him in his resistance to believing.

When Jesus finally appeared again, He singled out Thomas, urging that he reach his hand out and feel for himself. "And be not faithless, but believing," He said.[3] Thomas needed this gentle rebuke, but he also needed the kind consideration that the Saviour supplied in place of argument. And all who see Him in His love will exclaim as did Thomas, "My Lord and my God"![4]

---

[1] *The SDA Bible Commentary*, vol. 5, p. 1067.
[2] *The Desire of Ages*, pp. 806, 807.
[3] John 20:27.
[4] Verse 28.

DOUBTING EVEN WITH JESUS PRESENT

And when they saw him, they worshipped him: but some doubted. Matt. 28:17.

Even before His death Jesus had arranged to meet with the disciples on a mountain in Galilee after His resurrection. But the experience of seeing Jesus die on the cross obliterated the thought of any resurrection. And so the angel at the tomb had to tell the women to remind the disciples of the special appointment.[1]

The word spread quickly among the disciples, and soon about five hundred began making their circuitous way to that mountain. They did not travel by caravan, but came from various directions, for fear of exciting the jealousy of the Jews. After they all finally arrived, the mountainside was dotted with groups chatting about the thrilling account of the resurrection. The eleven made their way from group to group, telling their personal story of having seen Jesus.[2] Thomas, of course, added his special account, which was most convincing.

Suddenly Jesus appeared among them, and those small knots of people quickly gathered around the Saviour. Many of the folk had not even seen Jesus before, but they certainly noticed His scarred hands and feet. The thrill of just being there must have been overwhelming as Jesus gave the Great Commission to go into all the world with the good news.

But still some chose to doubt. Now, of all times and in all places, this is difficult to fathom. But there will always be doubters. Among the disciples of Jesus, even with Him right before their eyes, there were those who had a hard time believing. Why is it that some choose to take their stand on the doubting side? "Disguise it as they may, the real cause of doubt and skepticism, in most cases, is the love of sin."[3] A personal examination of the deep motives of the heart is essential for a foundation of faith.

---

[1] *The Desire of Ages*, p. 818; Mark 16:7.
[2] *Ibid.*, p. 819.
[3] *Steps to Christ*, p. 111.

THE BROTHERS CONVERTED AT LAST

These all continued with one accord in prayer and supplication, with the women, and Mary the mother of Jesus, and with his brethren. Acts 1:14.

After Jesus ascended to heaven the disciples made their way back to the now-familiar upper room. It was a time for rejoicing, because they had personally heard the angels tell them that Jesus would return just as they had seen Him go to heaven. It was time to prepare for fulfilling the Great Commission to tell the world the good news of His life, death, resurrection, and return.

So we see that little nucleus of about 120 believers choosing now to put away all differences, along with clamoring over who would be the greatest, and doing their best to find a closer fellowship with God. And in drawing near to Him, they found the love for one another that Jesus so anxiously prayed for while He was with them.

Our text for today indicates that not only was Mary the mother of Jesus in that group but His brothers too. Something had happened along the way to change their hearts. They had lost so much by their unbelief while Jesus was with them, and even when He appeared after His resurrection. "They had been among the number who doubted when Jesus appeared in Galilee. But they now firmly believed that Jesus was the Son of God, the promised Messiah. Their faith was established." [1]

The Scriptures mention four brothers—James, Joses, Simon, and Judas. Up to this time they had been critical and had remained aloof from identifying with Jesus. The Gospels don't even mention them as being among those gathered around the cross. Yet now they took their stand with the believers. They had at last been converted and had chosen to become one with Jesus. We hear nothing more about Simon and Joses, but a strong case can be made for identifying James as a leader in the early church, and possibly as the author of the Epistle of James. And Judas may well be the Jude who wrote the little book that bears his name. [2]

---

[1] *The SDA Bible Commentary,* Ellen G. White Comments, on Acts 1:14, p. 1054.
[2] *The SDA Bible Commentary,* vol. 6, p. 127.

THE REBELLION OF THE SADDUCEES

And the Sadducees came upon them, being grieved that they taught the people, and preached through Jesus the resurrection from the dead. Acts 4:1, 2.

The day of Pentecost exploded into the reality of lives fired by the Holy Spirit. Now the timidity of the disciples was gone, and they preached boldly of the resurrection and of Jesus' power to save. All Jerusalem was astir, and later when Peter and John healed the lame beggar at the Temple gate, it agitated things even further. Peter used the leaping, jumping former lame man as an attention-getting step in preaching to the crowd that collected.

Just a few weeks had passed since the religious authorities had congratulated themselves that they had gotten rid of Jesus. Their circulation department had been busily scattering the false report of the nocturnal body snatching. Yet now a miracle had been done in the name of Jesus, right in broad daylight. And Peter not only had pronounced them murderers but had countered with the truth about the resurrection.

According to the Sadducees' so-called scientific reasoning, such a thing as a resurrection simply could not happen. And further, if such a notion was openly taught with the backing of a real miracle, their whole reputation would be ruined.

So the Sadducees, and others, instigated the arrest of Peter and John, and in so doing they entrenched themselves even further against Jesus. These would-be intellectuals refused to repent and be saved. Every day they chose to resist the Holy Spirit with some fresh points of malignity. Their rebellion was so thorough that there is not one record in the New Testament of a Sadducee ever accepting the gospel.[1] The calls to repentance only made them decide to resist even further as they recycled the sins of the past in defiance of all the light God had given them.

---

[1] *The SDA Bible Commentary*, vol. 6, p. 164.

THE VOICE OF THE NEW PETER

Be it known unto you all, and to all the people of Israel, that by the name of Jesus Christ of Nazareth, whom ye crucified, whom God raised from the dead, even by him doth this man stand here before you whole. Acts 4:10.

These ringing words filled the courtroom with a stunning power. Neither the old retired Annas, his son-in-law high priest Caiaphas, nor all the dignitaries assembled to try Peter and John could withstand those words.[1] The authorities had arrested these disciples in connection with the healing of the lame man and had flattered themselves that they could intimidate these unlearned men.

"By what power, or by what name, have ye done this?" the haughty leaders questioned.[2]

They asked for it, and Peter's answer rocked them. Without flinching, this burly ex-fisherman courageously replied that the healing had come through the power of Jesus. And that was not all. He followed through with a reminder that, while they may have turned Jesus over to Pilate for sentencing, it was they, the Jewish authorities, who were responsible for killing Him. And as if that wasn't enough, Peter touched on the resurrection, sweeping away all their concocted lies. For Caiaphas, the staunch Sadducee, this must have been especially galling. They had brought Peter and John back to the same judgment hall where they had condemned Christ. But these scowling faces did not intimidate the disciples.

The authorities had not counted on a converted Peter. The man who had denied knowing Jesus on the night of His trial had made a decision to turn with all his heart to the Saviour. He would redeem his cowardice with vigor. The formerly boastful, self-confident Peter was now modest and solely dependent on the Holy Spirit. His decision to die to self and wholly submit to Jesus made all the difference. Now all his ardor was channeled in the right direction, and God could use him with power.

---

[1] *SDA Bible Dictionary*, p. 171.
[2] Acts 4:7.

DEATH OF THE PRETENDERS

But a certain man named Ananias, with Sapphira his wife, sold a possession, and kept back part of the price, his wife also being privy to it, and brought a certain part, and laid it at the apostles' feet. Acts 5:1, 2.

Today this sort of copy would not be considered good publicity for the church. It would undoubtedly be deleted from any news releases. But the Holy Spirit directed Dr. Luke to write the story of Ananias and Sapphira without the slightest variation from the truth. There was no cover-up. Heaven saw that a warning needed to be released so that all might understand the dangers of covetousness and hypocrisy.

This couple were swept up in the deep movings of God's Spirit and felt the tug of generosity when others gave their possessions to the infant church. The apostles did not stipulate the amount. Nobody gave any directive on the exact figure. Ananias and Sapphira openheartedly responded in accordance with the tremendous need.

But when they got home a problem arose. As they discussed their pledge, covetousness crowded into their thinking. And the more they talked about the promise, the more they thought their decision might have been a bit hasty. They realized how highly esteemed the givers were among the early believers, and they liked that part. It was just that the cash amount was a bit high. Ashamed to tell the church that they had reneged on their pledge, they decided to hold back a large part while pretending to give the whole. It seemed so smart. That way they could get the smiling approval of their church members, cash in on the common supplies, and keep a large chunk of cash for themselves.[1] Covetousness always seems so slick and neat!

But Heaven flashed their corrupt decision along to Peter, who had their bodies carried out for burial.

One wonders how many bodies would require burial today if God should visit His church as He did in days of old.

---

[1] *The Acts of the Apostles*, p. 72.

TMTD-12

NO FEAR OF DEATH

And they stoned Stephen, calling upon God, and saying, Lord Jesus, receive my spirit. Acts 7:59.

With trumped-up charges of seeking to destroy the Temple and the Law of Moses, Stephen was hailed before the Sanhedrin. The false witnesses were quick to finger the deacon. After all, if anyone believed his preaching of Jesus, the whole system of sacrifices would end. But Stephen, like his Master, was pointed in his arguments, showing forcefully how Jesus had come to amplify the law. And as the scripture says, "They were not able to resist the wisdom and the spirit by which he spake." [1] And because Stephen could not be answered, the Jewish authorities turned to the only measures they knew would work.

When he faced his antagonists that day, Stephen related a sweeping history of the Israelites. The judges sat spellbound as he unraveled the whole course of events in God's leading of His chosen people. But suddenly Stephen stopped short. In the faces and actions of those angry men he could read that he had touched on a sore point. [2] He had connected Jesus with the prophecies and had shown that their excessive veneration of the Temple did not harmonize with true worship. [3]

But his fear of death had long gone. He had decided that he might as well come to the point. And in some of the sharpest language recorded in Scripture, Stephen laid bare the truth about their resistance to the Holy Spirit. He classed them with the Gentiles and murderers. He could not have formulated a greater insult, and like wild beasts they charged at Stephen, dragging him outside so they could stone him without further hearing.

Stephen was unafraid because he knew Jesus. He could afford to remain calm, in the face of those infuriated men, because he knew that the Lord would raise him on the resurrection day. His decision to give the Sanhedrin the unvarnished truth came with the quiet assurance of this very fact.

---

[1] Acts 6:10.
[2] *The Acts of the Apostles*, p. 100.
[3] *The SDA Bible Commentary*, vol. 6, p. 204.

PHILIP'S OBEDIENT CHOICES

And the angel of the Lord spake unto Philip, saying, Arise, and go toward the south unto the way that goeth down from Jerusalem unto Gaza, which is desert. And he arose and went. Acts 8:26.

With the martyrdom of Stephen, the full fury of persecution exploded on the early church.[1] But this was the very means of scattering the believers and spreading the gospel. Philip headed for the safety of Samaria. His ministry as one of the seven deacons involved far more than simply picking up the offering on Sabbath morning. He also preached Jesus.

But at the height of his evangelistic campaign, the angel of the Lord directed him to start hiking south toward the desert. Today's verse shows an interesting decision on Philip's part. He could have argued that with all the success there in Samaria, it would be foolish to leave for some strange desert enterprise. He did not report the angel's signal to some ministerial committee that might suggest that the numerical growth pattern would be hindered if he should drop his work for an unknown project. He did not hesitate for a moment. He obeyed. And that decision opened one of the most exciting chapters in early church history. For out there on that desert road south of Jerusalem, he saw a chariot coming with one of Ethiopia's high-ranking officials.

Again God directed in a very explicit way. "The Spirit told Philip, 'Go to that chariot and stay near it.' "[2]

Out of Philip's prompt decisions comes the story of a Bible study in a swaying chariot and a stopover for a baptism that would spread the gospel even farther, because of the candidate's high position in government.

"This Ethiopian represented a large class who need to be taught by such missionaries as Philip—men who will hear the voice of God and go where He sends them."[3] The key to successful ministry depends on being sensitive to the Spirit's movings. And we must obey promptly when they come, whether or not they seem beneficial at the time.

---

[1] *The Acts of the Apostles*, p. 103.
[2] Acts 8:29, N.I.V.
[3] *Ibid.*, p. 109.

SAUL'S CONVERSION

And he fell to the earth, and heard a voice saying unto him, Saul, Saul, why persecutest thou me? And he said, Who art thou, Lord? And the Lord said, I am Jesus whom thou persecutest. Acts 9:4, 5.

When we read of Saul's conversion there doesn't seem to be any decision-making on the persecutor's part. En route to hunt down the disciples of Jesus and bring them to Jerusalem for trial and death, he was suddenly slammed to the ground by the brilliance of the presence of Jesus. The bright light and thunderous voice were certainly enough to arrest the attention of even this stubborn Pharisee. Yet we cannot say that God used force to make him yield to the Holy Spirit.

In order to understand the reason for God's brilliant attention-getting device, we must go back in Saul's life and see him struggling under tremendous conviction. He had witnessed Stephen's calm surrender to the awful death by stoning, and he had seen other disciples cheerfully yield up their lives for Jesus. It was more than hard to shake the feeling that these people knew something he didn't. "At such times he had struggled for entire nights against the conviction, and always he had ended the matter by avowing his belief that Jesus was not the Messiah, and that His followers were deluded fanatics." [1]

It was while Paul was in this state of mind that Jesus appeared to him on the Damascus road. And it was during the next three days, while sitting in total darkness, that he yielded himself fully to the Lord. [2] In those long, trying hours of seeming abandonment, Saul saw clearly the mistakes of his zealous pharisaical life and his need of a Saviour. His choice was made, and from that hour we find Saul being shaped as the "chosen vessel" to preach not only to the Gentiles but to kings and the children of Israel. His decision to yield to God's Spirit rather than to resist provided Heaven a means of preaching the gospel far and wide, and gave opportunity for him to write letters to the young churches, letters that remain with us even today.

---

[1] *The Acts of the Apostles,* pp. 116, 117.
[2] *Ibid.,* p. 119.

BARNABAS, THE CONNECTING LINK

And when Saul was come to Jerusalem, he assayed to join himself to the disciples: but they were all afraid of him, and believed not that he was a disciple. But Barnabas took him, and brought him to the apostles. Acts 9:26, 27.

The early church in Jerusalem had a right to fear Saul. The last they had seen of him was when he had stormed out of the city on one of his hot pursuits against believers. The reports must surely have filtered back to headquarters that Saul had been converted on the way to Damascus and had escaped into the Arabian Desert. And now, three years later, he suddenly showed up again. What would any honest church member believe? Saul's track record had been filled with an intensity that did not make for quiet Sabbath reading. For all they knew, he might be up to some clever trick to worm his way into the church and obtain a membership list. It certainly looked suspicious.

But then came Barnabas, the man who had liberally contributed his cash for the cause of relieving the poor. He had known Saul personally when Saul was in direct opposition to the believers.[1] And when he heard that Saul had arrived back in town he renewed his acquaintance and listened intently to his miraculous story. Right then and there Barnabas believed. He chose to believe because there was a ring of truth in Saul's account and because his own character responded quickly to those in desperate need.

Taking Saul by the hand, he led him to Peter and James, the only apostles in Jerusalem at the time.[2] Barnabas related the story he had just heard of how Jesus had personally met Saul and had actually talked with him, and how Saul had recovered his sight after the visit from Ananias. But perhaps most convincing of all was Saul's hard-hitting preaching of Christ in Damascus that eventually caused him to flee for his life. Peter and James could not hesitate now, and they gave this former persecutor the right hand of fellowship—all because of Barnabas' warm choice in becoming the connecting link.

---

[1] *The Story of Redemption,* p. 277.
[2] *Ibid.,* p. 278.

BREAKING PETER'S PREJUDICE

And he said unto them, Ye know how that it is an unlawful thing for a man that is a Jew to keep company, or come unto one of another nation; but God hath shewed me that I should not call any man common or unclean. Acts 10:28.

The events that led up to Peter's presence in the home of Cornelius, the Roman centurion, were timed perfectly by Heaven. Cornelius, who had never taken out membership in the Jewish church, had learned enough about God from the Jews to bring Him into his daily life. He had even erected an altar at home.[1] Throughout the whole region where he lived Cornelius was known for his generosity, yet the Jews considered him to be heathen and unclean. But God had spotted his sincere devotion and sent an angel to guide him.

Meanwhile, back at Joppa, about thirty miles (forty-eight kilometers) south of Caesarea, where Cornelius lived, Peter received a stomach-turning vision.[2] Right at mealtime, when he was very hungry, Peter saw a sheet with a menagerie of unclean, creeping, crawling, and flapping creatures. A voice said, "Rise, Peter; kill, and eat."[3] But Peter balked. This wasn't exactly the kind of food found in a Jewish cookbook. Three times he saw this ugly-looking sight that was supposed to pass for a meal. But the voice from heaven declared, "What God hath cleansed, that call not thou common."[4]

While Peter puzzled over the meaning of the vision, Cornelius' men arrived downstairs at the gate. The angel had given them Peter's exact address.

The next day Peter had to make a decision. If he was to go into the house of this Roman officer, the church folk would severely criticize him. But the longer Peter thought about how all the pieces fell into place with such precision, the more he realized God's guiding hand. Despite his own prejudice and the certainty of rankling the Jewish Christians, he chose to step inside and tell Cornelius and his people the truth about Jesus. Prejudice should always give way to the unquestionable providence of God.

---

[1] *The Acts of the Apostles*, p. 133.
[2] *The SDA Bible Commentary*, vol. 6, pp. 248, 249.
[3] Acts 10:13.
[4] Verse 15.

HEROD'S FATAL CHOICE

**And immediately the angel of the Lord smote him, because
he gave not God the glory: and he was eaten of worms, and
gave up the ghost. Acts 12:23.**

The capital city of Caesarea was alive with pleasure lovers
from every quarter of Palestine.[1] Herod Agrippa I, the grandson of
Herod the Great, had arrived for a gala celebration in his own
honor.[2] With plenty of food and wine, the festival was bound to be
a political success.

The king had prepared and rehearsed an eloquent speech just
for the occasion. And his tailor had created a special robe that
glittered in the sunlight with silver and gold. All the pomp and
ceremony he could command accompanied his grand appearance.
The shouts of adulation and the standing ovation swelled his ego to
the bursting point. Some of the same people who had cried "Away
with Jesus! Crucify Him, crucify Him!" were now worshiping this
arrogant Roman ruler.[3]

And at this point Herod decided to accept such veneration. He
knew very well that he didn't deserve any of it, but he accepted
their idolatrous claims on him as a deity. "It is the voice of a god,
and not of a man"! the people shouted.[4]

Herod nodded and smiled, but suddenly the same angel who
had miraculously released Peter from prison struck him, and
Herod's smile turned into an agonizing grimace. "The angel
smote Peter to arouse him from slumber; it was with a different
stroke that he smote the wicked king, laying low his pride and
bringing upon him the punishment of the Almighty. Herod died in
great agony of mind and body, under the retributive judgment of
God."[5]

Writhing in pain, Herod was carried away. His mind raced
with remorse. He remembered how he had mercilessly cut down
the apostle James just to please the Jews. Now he knew, as all who
choose to follow their own pride and passion will ultimately know,
that he was in the hands of the Ruler of the universe.

[1] *The Acts of the Apostles*, p. 150.
[2] *SDA Bible Dictionary*, p. 482.
[3] *The Acts of the Apostles*, p. 150.
[4] Acts 12:22.
[5] *Ibid.*, p. 152.

THE CONFIDENCE OF BARNABAS

And Barnabas determined to take with them John, whose surname was Mark. But Paul thought not good to take him with them, who departed from them from Pamphylia, and went not with them to the work. Acts 15:37, 38.

The excitement of taking a boat ride to Cyprus and making the first missionary tour across the island and back to the mainland faded for John Mark. Once they reached Asia Minor things got a bit rough. John Mark faced hardships he hadn't counted on, and the dangers lurking along the road made him shudder. The whole missionary trip turned into a weary, discouraging, perilous ordeal.

John Mark thought about his mother and the good home she had in Jerusalem, and the more he thought about it, the more he felt sure that the best thing for him to do was to buy a ticket and sail for home.[1]

Paul found this sort of behavior very disgusting. He was tough and could take it, and anyone who couldn't was not worth taking on his next trip. But Barnabas wanted his cousin along on the second missionary tour. He saw something in John Mark that would prove useful when the young man was rightly trained. He could excuse John Mark on the basis of inexperience and he decided that he wanted him by his side.

"He felt anxious that Mark should not abandon the ministry, for he saw in him qualifications that would fit him to be a useful worker for Christ. In after years his solicitude in Mark's behalf was richly rewarded, for the young man gave himself unreservedly to the Lord and to the work of proclaiming the gospel message in difficult fields."[2]

We know now that Barnabas made a wise choice. John Mark did become a valuable worker, in spite of Paul's writing him off. Barnabas was the type of person who could visualize the latent luster in another person. There will always be room for people who, like Barnabas, can choose to go ahead with confidence in someone even when others see no worthwhile possibilities.

---

[1] *SDA Bible Dictionary*, p. 606.
[2] *The Acts of the Apostles*, p. 170.

TIMOTHY'S LASTING CHOICE

Paul, an apostle of Jesus Christ by the will of God, according to the promise of life which is in Christ Jesus, to Timothy, my dearly beloved son. 2 Tim. 1:1, 2.

The aged apostle wrote this touching greeting to Timothy, his "dearly beloved son," from a Roman dungeon when Paul knew his end was near.[1]

The relationship between Paul and Timothy was bonded by a deep affection and firm ties of loyalty and love that nothing could sever. Timothy's natural father, of Greek descent, never came close to fulfilling this special relationship of father and son.[2] Paul and Timothy were father and son far closer than any blood ties.[3]

But the starting point of this relationship began when this young man was in his late teens. Timothy had been converted to Jesus by the preaching of Paul on the first missionary tour, which brought the apostle to Lystra.[4] During that time the Jews had stirred up the whole city against Paul. When the surging, volatile crowd stoned Paul and then dragged his bruised and battered body outside the city, everyone, including the weeping Christian converts, assumed that he was dead.

Timothy had been an eyewitness to all this, and he, along with the other believers, took his stand beside Paul's poor bleeding body. When Paul miraculously arose after the unmerciful stoning, Timothy chose to remain by his side. His decision was not some one-time thing, but a lifelong love for the gospel and for the man who had brought it to him.

In his subsequent association with the great preacher, Timothy always sought Paul's advice and counsel. He learned to work for Jesus just as Paul did. He was the type of young person who was willing to tap onto years of experience. He never took a know-it-all attitude. His close connection with Paul fitted him for real leadership in the churches, and all his years of service hinged entirely on his early and lasting choice.

---

[1] *SDA Bible Dictionary,* p. 1123.
[2] *Ibid.,* p. 1122.
[3] *The SDA Bible Commentary,* vol. 6, p. 323.
[4] *The Acts of the Apostles,* p. 184.

PETER'S UNWISE CHOICE

I said unto Peter before them all, If thou, being a Jew, livest after the manner of Gentiles, and not as do the Jews, why compellest thou the Gentiles to live as do the Jews? Gal. 2:14.

Of all the early church leaders who should have understood God's purpose in carrying the gospel to the Gentiles, Peter should have. Heaven's miraculous leading to bring him to Cornelius should have afforded convincing proof that the Gentiles were to be included in the Christian faith.[1]

Peter himself had eloquently addressed the Jerusalem Council and had convinced the assembly that they ought to listen patiently to Paul and Barnabas concerning their work with the Gentiles.[2] Through that council the Holy Spirit led the apostles to accept the fact that the Gentiles should not be forced to adhere to the Jewish ceremonial law. Peter was there and Peter had approved.

But when Peter went to Antioch he suddenly switched roles. He came with the openness he knew to be right. He was willing to put aside his natural prejudice and to eat with the Gentile converts. But when the firm-jawed Jewish Christians from Jerusalem arrived and insisted that Jewish practice should be imposed on all believers, Peter decided to avoid the Gentiles. It was a most injudicious choice. His pretending to side with the Judaizers could well have caused a rift in the church. But Paul arose to square off publicly with Peter, and, as he says, "withstood him to the face, because he was to be blamed."[3] Paul's hard-hitting question in today's text was directed right at Peter, who had nothing to say for his obvious inconsistency.

"God, who knows the end from the beginning, permitted Peter to reveal this weakness of character in order that the tried apostle might see that there was nothing in himself whereof he might boast. Even the best of men, if left to themselves, will err in judgment."[4]

---

[1] *The SDA Bible Commentary,* vol. 6, pp. 948, 949.
[2] *The Acts of the Apostles,* p. 194.
[3] Gal. 2:11.
[4] *Ibid.,* p. 198.

NEW LIFE FOR THE JAILER

Sirs, what must I do to be saved? And they said, Believe on the Lord Jesus Christ, and thou shalt be saved, and thy house. Acts 16:30, 31.

When he went to work that morning, the Philippian jailer expected only the usual routine prison duties. He had no hint that before the next dawn he and his entire family would be baptized members of the new Christian faith.

As local jailer, he was more than just a turnkey. He was the official prisonkeeper, responsible for all criminals. His salary may not have been very high, but if anyone escaped it would cost his life, so he watched with tiger-bright eyes.[1]

Paul and Silas had been severely beaten by the excitable Philippian mob. The city authorities sanctioned this ill treatment because the two out-of-town missionaries had cast out a demon from a local female fortuneteller, an act that threatened to put her merchant masters out of business.[2] New doctrine was one thing, but financial ruin was quite another. So they ordered the jailer to attend to these new prisoners' security. The jailer immediately placed Paul and Silas in stocks and slammed the door to the inner prison, leaving these two cellmates in an excruciating position.

The jailer was amazed at the sounds he heard coming from the dark dungeon. Instead of moans and groans and bitter curses, he heard songs of praise and prayer.[3] And he was even more amazed when an earthquake jarred all the prison doors wide open. The jailer would have committed suicide had not Paul let him know that everyone was still safely inside.

That is when the jailer made his choice. He wanted desperately to know about this new way of life. Made tender by the Holy Spirit, he responded quickly. Paul and Silas gave him and his family a fast-paced Bible study and baptized them all. The jailer's decision that memorable night has always been a source of encouragement.

[1] *The SDA Bible Commentary*, p. 333.
[2] *The Acts of the Apostles*, p. 213.
[3] *Ibid.*, p. 215.

ATHENIAN PRIDE

For all the Athenians and strangers which were there spent their time in nothing else, but either to tell, or to hear some new thing. Acts 17:21.

Today's verse is a parenthetical remark inserted by Dr. Luke regarding the Athenian attitude toward life. The Athenians spent their time in a restless, inquisitive state, never really coming to a knowledge of the truth. When the apostle Paul came to town he naturally drew an audience. Some in the crowd who first heard him, however, considered this stranger far beneath them socially and intellectually.[1]

"Some of them asked, 'What is this babbler trying to say?' Others remarked, 'He seems to be advocating foreign gods.' They said this because Paul was preaching the good news about Jesus and the resurrection."[2]

Before long these intellectuals discovered that Paul could go head to head with any of them. His sound logic and eloquence matched the best they had, so they escorted him to Mars' Hill to hear him out.

Paul knew the difficulty in meeting these sophisticated minds. They were not bound by the grosser heathenism he had seen in Asia Minor, but they lived in the rarified air of philosophy and learning. Surrounded by every cultural and artistic expression, these Athenians glossed over the fact that they were still steeped in paganism—with gods galore. Luke condenses Paul's speech into ten verses, but obviously Paul spoke at some length to convince them to turn to the true God.[3]

Only a few responded. Dionysius, one of the high-ranking citizens, a woman by the name of Damaris, and a few others chose to accept Jesus, but no great multitude of believers resulted. Most of his listeners, even though they might have been under conviction, chose to remain locked into their own pride of intellect. The Athenian attitude of thinking highly of personal wisdom remains with us to this day.

---

[1] *The Acts of the Apostles*, p. 235.
[2] Acts 17:18, N.I.V.
[3] *The SDA Bible Commentary*, vol. 6, p. 350.

DANGERS OF THE PARTY SPIRIT

Therefore let no man glory in men. For all things are your's; whether Paul, or Apollos, or Cephas, or the world, or life, or death, or things present, or things to come; all are your's; and ye are Christ's; and Christ is God's. 1 Cor. 3:21-23.

For a year and a half Paul preached in the wicked and highly immoral city of Corinth.[1] Because he stayed consistently with the basics of the gospel message, presenting it in its simplest form, he was able to organize a church even among these people steeped in gross paganism.

Later Apollos, a Jew from Alexandria, arrived with a fresh style that captivated crowds. He had an eloquent tongue and was able both publicly and privately to present Jesus in a very convincing way.

Soon the enemy saw his opportunity to create division, and he began working the old competition line among the believers. Because Apollos was so successful, some chose to contrast him with the apostle Paul.

Paul could have used a more eloquent style, but the Corinthians were not ready at that time for anything more than the "milk," as he put it.[2] He reminded them that even right then they were not able to taste the "meat" of the Word, because they were so slow in advancing spiritually. "I have planted, Apollos watered; but God gave the increase," he wrote.[3]

Then there rose another segment who refused to recognize either Paul or Apollos. They chose Peter as their leader.[4] These folk decided that Peter had been so close to Jesus that he should have preference. Paul had previously persecuted the church, so he should not be exalted. And so it went, until there was evidence that the very party spirit which began with Lucifer in heaven was about to divide the early church. Paul's words in today's verse fix the believer's attention on the Lord and not on man.

---

[1] *The Acts of the Apostles*, p. 270.
[2] *Ibid.*, p. 271; 1 Cor. 3:2.
[3] Verse 6
[4] *Ibid.*, p. 279.

GOD'S ANSWER TO PAUL'S ARREST

The Lord stood by him, and said, Be of good cheer, Paul: for as thou hast testified of me in Jerusalem, so must thou bear witness also at Rome. Acts 23:11.

These words, spoken by Jesus Himself, came at a time when Paul was incarcerated in the Tower of Antonia in Jerusalem.[1] A fear crept over Paul that maybe he had not followed the Lord by traveling to Jerusalem in the first place. Perhaps he had made a mistake in trying so hard to work in harmony with the Jewish leaders in the Christian faith. The whole arrest and sudden change of events made him wonder about his choice in trying to please.

And seeking to please was the problem. Paul need not have made the concession he did with the leading brethren.[2] It was a faulty choice, yet an honest one. He wanted so much to live in harmony, and knew all along that the prejudice against him for preaching to the Gentiles was strong.

These leaders had already said that the Gentile converts should not be subject to the Jewish rituals, yet they clung to their concept that the sacrifices and circumcision were important. Neither was true, and their demand that Paul placate the Jews by making a ritual vow with four other men was cowardly.[3] It was an inconsistent decision that would deprive the Christian community of a great preacher and missionary.

Decisions based on prejudice invariably go awry and hurt the gospel message. These leaders privately held it against Paul for working so freely with the Gentiles. The leaders were not listening to the Holy Spirit, who was far in advance of their narrow notions. So the apostle Paul made a mistake in yielding to their demand that he make a ritual vow, but they made the greater mistake in even suggesting such a thing. It didn't work anyway. The Jews became incensed that Paul should even appear in the Temple. Yet out of this whole ordeal and double-faulty decision we see the kind hand of Providence guiding so that others might hear the gospel.

---

[1] *The SDA Bible Commentary,* vol. 6, p. 416.
[2] *The Acts of the Apostles,* p. 405.
[3] *Ibid.,* p. 404.

CONVENIENCE THAT CORRUPTS

And as he reasoned of righteousness, temperance, and judgment to come, Felix trembled, and answered, Go thy way for this time; when I have a convenient season, I will call for thee. Acts 24:25.

It was a strange sort of private gathering, a God-given opportunity, really. Paul, still under arrest but at liberty to receive friends and guests, was summoned to appear before Felix and his beautiful young second wife, Drusilla.[1]

"So violent and cruel had been the course of Felix that few had ever before dared even to intimate to him that his character and conduct were not faultless. But Paul had no fear of men. He plainly declared his faith in Christ, and the reasons for that faith."[2] With all the persuasion possible, Paul showed the true meaning of man's duty to live a clean, healthful life. He also pointed out that such a life was possible through accepting the great sacrifice of Jesus. His presentation led to the logical conclusion of a coming judgment. Paul was not using scare tactics, but simply warning of that moment in time and space when all must face the penetrating scrutiny of Heaven.

The carnal mind seeks to escape such uncomfortable reality. The convenient season is a typical expediency; it is a great stall. Felix never did find a convenient season. "He had slighted his last offer of mercy. Never was he to receive another call from God."[3] It is true that Felix visited Paul several times after that and listened attentively. He seemed friendly enough, but his real motive was to obtain a large sum of cash. But Paul was too noble to stoop to this. He had done no wrong and was not about to appeal to the sympathy or generosity of the church to gain his freedom. No committee on bribery ever met for him.

Felix was finally summoned to Rome for his gross wrongs against the Jews. His ways had caught up with him, and he was removed from office in disgrace.[4] Deprived of his ill-gotten wealth, he died in obscurity after marrying for the third time. It was a tragic end for a man who had made the expedient choice.

[1] *The SDA Bible Commentary*, vol. 6, p. 426.
[2] *The Acts of the Apostles*, p. 423.
[3] *Ibid.*, p. 427.
[4] *Ibid.*

ENDING IN HOT LAVA

For what is a man profited, if he shall gain the whole world, and lose his own soul? or what shall a man give in exchange for his soul? Matt. 16:26.

The day Paul stood before Felix and Drusilla, two choices had to be made. The Bible records only the words of Felix, but Drusilla's choice also ended in tragedy. What made it so terrible is that she would have had everything going for her if she had chosen Jesus Christ.

At 21 Drusilla married Felix, who was old enough to be her father. What charms of witchcraft and satanic devices he had upon her we can only guess, but we do know that Felix had to do some fast manipulating to get her.[1] "Through the deceptive arts of Simon Magus, a Cyprian sorcerer, Felix had induced this princess to leave her husband and to become his wife. Drusilla was young and beautiful, and moreover a Jewess, She was devotedly attached to her husband, who had made a great sacrifice to obtain her hand."[2] It certainly must have taken some evil scheming for her to go against her strongest prejudices and marry such a man as Felix.

Drusilla was the daughter of Herod Agrippa I, the tyrant who had put James to death. She was only 6 years old at the time of this tragic event. Perhaps she knew of Peter's miraculous escape from prison. Most certainly she knew of her father's unhappy death, when he was smitten by an angel of the Lord and was eaten of worms.

As Drusilla listened to Paul that day, she well understood the claims of the sacred law that she had openly transgressed. Her husband may not have heard it before, but she knew what Paul was talking about. Yet she steeled herself against the words of life. Undoubtedly she too never received another call from God. This was her last chance. Her prejudice against Jesus locked her into the prison of her own carnal desires. What tragic tales wove the tight meshes about her we are not told. Felix finally divorced her and remarried, but "Drusilla, the partner of his guilt, afterward perished, with their only son, in the eruption of Vesuvius."[3]

Down through the corridors of time echo the dangers of the prejudiced choice.

[1] *The SDA Bible Commentary*, vol. 6, pp. 426, 1066.
[2] *Ibid.*, Ellen G. White Comments, on Acts 24:2, 3, p. 1066.
[3] *Ibid.*

SO CLOSE TO CONVERSION

**Then Agrippa said unto Paul, Almost thou persuad,
to be a Christian. And Paul said, I would to God, that not
thou, but also all that hear me this day, were both almost, &
altogether such as I am, except for these bonds. Acts 26:28, 2.**

After two years of weary waiting, Paul finally appealed to the
new governor, Festus, for a trial in Rome. Paul well knew that
appealing to Caesar would be safer than being brought before the
bigoted Jews in the Sanhedrin.[1]

It was in this setting that King Agrippa appeared with his sister
Bernice. His Jewish background and pro-Roman leanings made
him a natural counselor for Festus. The visiting king had custody
of the Temple treasury, and carried the privilege of appointing the
high priest. So it was quite natural for Festus to turn to him for
advice in determining Paul's case.[2]

When Festus related Paul's story of how Felix had kept him
bound but could find no accusation against him, King Agrippa
became interested. He would like to hear the prisoner for himself.

Festus arranged for a hearing the next day, using the occasion
for all the pomp and pageantry possible. He pulled out all the stops
to make the hearing imposing, attended by high-ranking officials
and armed soldiers.

Before Agrippa, Paul stood chained to his guard, yet totally
unintimidated by all the court splendor.[3] He had been too close to
the King of the universe to be awed by this. When Agrippa gave
him permission to speak, Paul eloquently outlined his own
conversion story and the reasons for his faith.

Agrippa felt the tug of the Holy Spirit on his heart. For one
thing, he was living in an incestuous relationship with his sister
Bernice, which was a byword among both Romans and Jews.[4]
"Deeply affected, Agrippa for a moment lost sight of his
surroundings and the dignity of his position."[5] Involuntarily he
told Paul that he himself was almost persuaded. Like many others
he came so close, yet he missed his opportunity completely.

---

[1] *The Acts of the Apostles*, p. 430.
[2] *The SDA Bible Commentary*, vol. 6, pp. 432, 433.
[3] *The Acts of the Apostles*, pp. 434, 435.
[4] *The SDA Bible Commentary*, vol. 6, p. 433.
[5] *The Acts of the Apostles*, p. 438.

NERO'S FINAL OPPORTUNITY

It is a fearful thing to fall into the hands of the living God. Heb. 10:31.

Persistent rumors kept pressing forward that the emperor Nero had set fire to Rome.[1] The destruction of nearly half the city was not something that could be easily dismissed.

Nero was already an angry man. The converts to Christianity had become so numerous that their influence shook the high-ranking authorities of Rome itself. And when members of Nero's own household accepted the Christian faith, it was too much. Now he saw a pretext for venting his own brand of cruelty on the Christians. With the incessant rumors pointing toward him as the arsonist, he had to do something fast. In anger and desperation he fingered the Christians as responsible for the fire, and the accusation stuck. The aroused populace hunted down men, women, and children—and murdered them.

The unbelieving Jews who had hated and hunted Paul saw their chance and urged that the old apostle be arrested on the charge that he had instigated the burning of Rome.[2] Nero had released Paul before, but this second arrest would be final.

When Paul was brought before Nero this time, he stood totally unashamed and unafraid in that vast assembly hall. He knew, as did they all, that the charges against him were false. But Paul used the opportunity to speak of the upcoming judgment and the need for Jesus. Temporarily his ringing words touched even the emperor. It was decision time for Nero.

"For a moment, heaven was opened to the guilty and hardened Nero, and its peace and purity seemed desirable. That moment the invitation of mercy was extended even to him. But only for a moment was the thought of pardon welcomed. Then the command was issued that Paul be taken back to his dungeon; and as the door closed upon the messenger of God, the door of repentance closed forever against the emperor of Rome."[3]

---

[1] *The Acts of the Apostles*, p. 487.
[2] *Ibid.*, p. 489.
[3] *Ibid.*, p. 496.

TRIUMPH OF PAUL'S MARTYRDOM

I have fought a good fight, I have finished my course, I have kept the faith: henceforth there is laid up for me a crown of righteousness, which the Lord, the righteous judge, shall give me at that day: and not to me only, but unto all them also that love his appearing. 2 Tim. 4:7, 8.

Paul's impressive speech before Nero plunged the emperor temporarily into a state of indecision.[1] Neither did he condemn the old apostle to death nor did he release him. But the time finally came when Nero was so totally exasperated at his frustrated attempts to crush Christianity that he gave the execution order. Since Paul was a Roman citizen, there would be no torture. He would be decapitated swiftly and surely by a seasoned executioner.

According to tradition, Paul was kept in the dank, dark Mamertine Prison, with only a hole in the ceiling for light.[2] We can only imagine his last moments as he was led out into the brilliance of that summer day so many centuries ago. Somewhere along the Ostian Way the sword descended.[3] Nero had specified that the execution must be private. He well knew the power of one of Paul's speeches. But even those allowed to witness the execution were touched. Paul's cheerfulness and forgiveness toward the soldiers responsible for the ugly task revealed his total trust in Jesus. And even some of them turned to the Saviour and were willing martyrs because of Paul's unconscious influence.[4]

And what was it that kept Paul so cheerful at such a time? Certainly not many would go smiling to their own beheading. What was it that kept him so calm? The secret lies in a decision that Paul had made before this particular hour had rolled around. Paul could relax and be glad because he knew in whom he had believed. Faith was no guesswork with him. The quiet assurance of God's peace is always with one who makes such a commitment to God. Paul knew that he would surely rise at Christ's coming.

[1] *The Acts of the Apostles*, p. 509.
[2] *The SDA Bible Commentary*, vol. 7, plate opposite p. 352.
[3] *SDA Bible Dictionary*, p. 857.
[4] *The Acts of the Apostles*, p. 510.

PETER'S FINAL CHOICE

Beloved, think it not strange concerning the fiery trial which is to try you, as though some strange thing happened unto you: but rejoice, inasmuch as ye are partakers of Christ's sufferings; that, when his glory shall be revealed, ye may be glad also with exceeding joy. 1 Peter 4:12, 13.

Of all the apostles, Peter would be the most likely to write those words. Jesus had foretold Peter's martyrdom years before, and He had even prophesied that his persecutors would stretch his own hands on a cross.[1] It would truly be a fiery ordeal, yet Peter did not concentrate on the torture, but on the triumph when Jesus would return.

In God's providence Peter was destined to be in Rome about the time of Paul's last arrest. He too would feel the hatred of Nero and experience the long, dismal hours in a dark prison. Both he and Paul would be at the capital of the world for their final testimony of their devotion to Jesus.

But for Peter the execution would not be swift. As a Jew and foreigner, he would suffer the excruciating torture of both scourging and crucifixion, the ultimate punishment that Rome could administer.

As Peter lay in his cell and contemplated his final hour he could not help thinking of that moment years before when he had denied Jesus. He knew that Jesus had long ago forgiven him, yet he could not forgive himself for that shameful profanity and denial.[2]

So Peter made a final choice. He could not go to his fearful death just as Jesus had. He had one last favor to ask. Could he be crucified upside down? His executioners granted his request, but undoubtedly wondered why any man would choose this added torture. But this once boastful, self-assertive man now had a deep sense of his own unworthiness. Peter's choice should teach us of that kind of trust which transforms a person to share gladly in Jesus' sufferings.

---

[1] *The Acts of the Apostles*, p. 537.
[2] *Ibid.*, p. 538.

JOHN'S GLAD RESPONSE
Even so, come, Lord Jesus. Rev. 22:20.

The last of the original apostles was finally summoned to Rome to go on trial for his faith. The authorities trotted out all sorts of false witnesses for a quick condemnation, but John's straightforward and simple testimony shattered the whole prearranged proceedings.[1] The emperor Domitian could not answer John's ringing words of faith in Jesus. In anger he lashed out by ordering the apostle to be dropped into a cauldron of boiling oil.[2] John did not flinch. Willing to suffer for Jesus' sake, John went down into the hot oil.

But the agonizing death Rome had planned for John failed miserably. The authorities had not counted on Heaven's miraculous deliverance. It was unnerving to see John's head above the boiling, turbulent oil—a serene smile on his face. His persecutors were forced to lift him out.

Domitian had one recourse left. He signed an order to ship John to the penal colony on the island of Patmos on the Aegean Sea. There among the other criminals of Rome, far removed from society, the emperor hoped John would lapse into silence.

But that is where Domitian made a mistake. John not only shared his faith with the others on that bleak, rocky outpost, but also gave the world one of the grandest and most glorious prophecies in the entire Word of God—the book of Revelation. Elevated by vision into the very throne room of God and seeing the future spread before him, John penned words that would influence people to the end of time.

John chose to look beyond the rocky reaches of Patmos. Instead of dwelling on the barrenness, he saw God's grandeur in nature. He did not succumb to discouragement, but he decided in favor of being captivated by the promise that Jesus would return. In a simple but eloquent plea, he closed the book of Revelation with his own personal response, "Even so, come, Lord Jesus."

---

[1] *The Acts of the Apostles,* p. 569.
[2] *Ibid.,* pp. 569, 570.

SCRIPTURE INDEX